BEAUTY
AND · THE
BEAST
›OF‹
PARADISE
›LOST‹

Synopsis

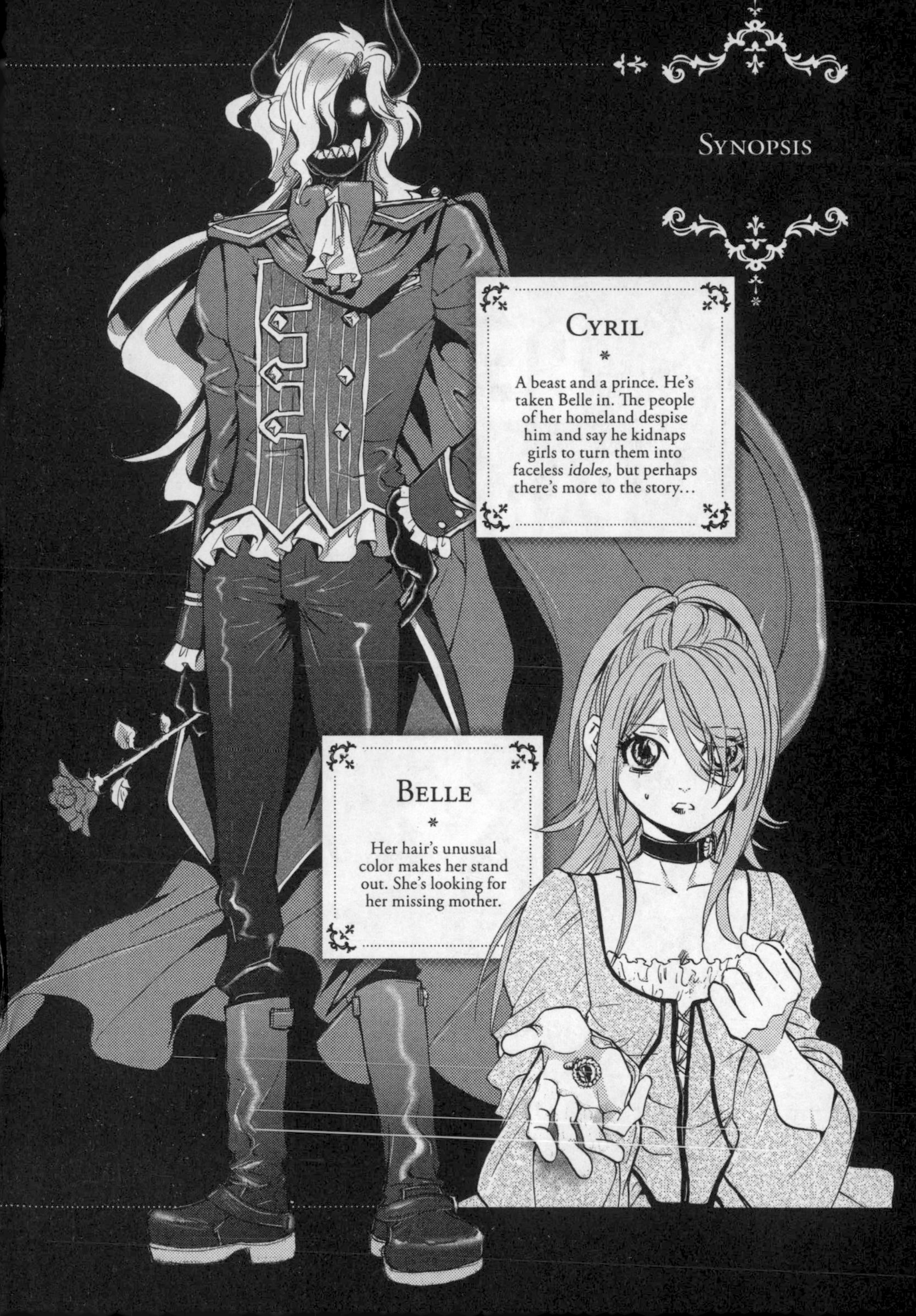

Cyril

A beast and a prince. He's taken Belle in. The people of her homeland despise him and say he kidnaps girls to turn them into faceless *idoles,* but perhaps there's more to the story...

Belle

Her hair's unusual color makes her stand out. She's looking for her missing mother.

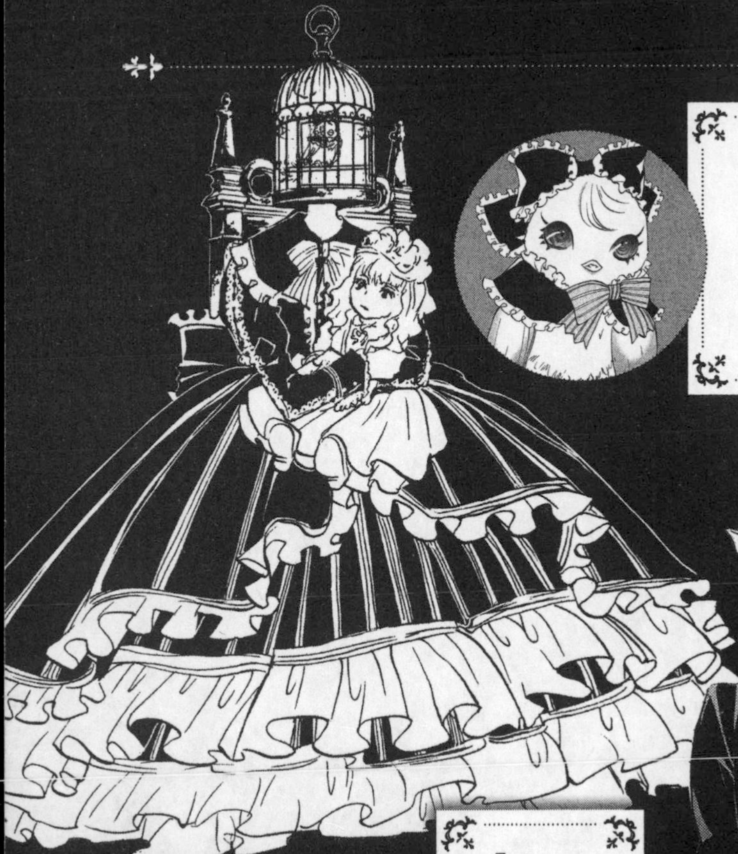

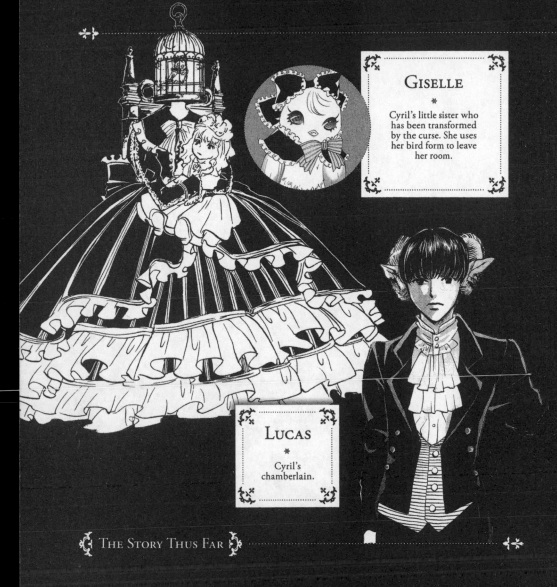

Giselle

*

Cyril's little sister who has been transformed by the curse. She uses her bird form to leave her room.

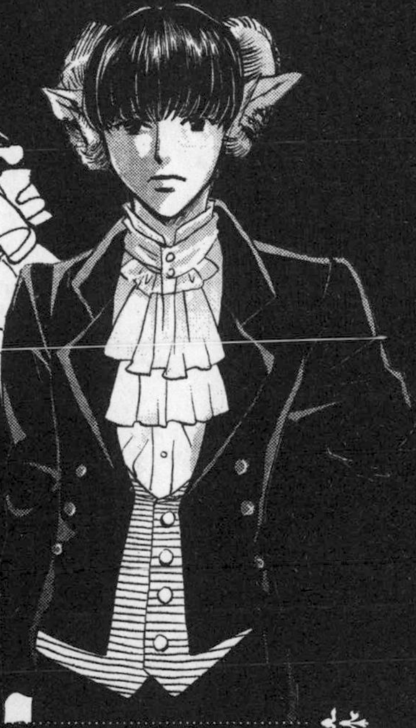

Lucas

*

Cyril's chamberlain.

The Story Thus Far

When Belle was just a little girl, a Beast known to spirit away beautiful women kidnapped her mother. Years later, she finds him and tries to kill him, only to almost end up with her face stolen. Cyril, however, rescues her. Later, after learning that the man who raised her wasn't her true father, she resolves to live in Cyril's castle as a seamstress in order to find her mother and discover the truth of who she is.

La belle et la bête
du paradis perdu

Table des matières

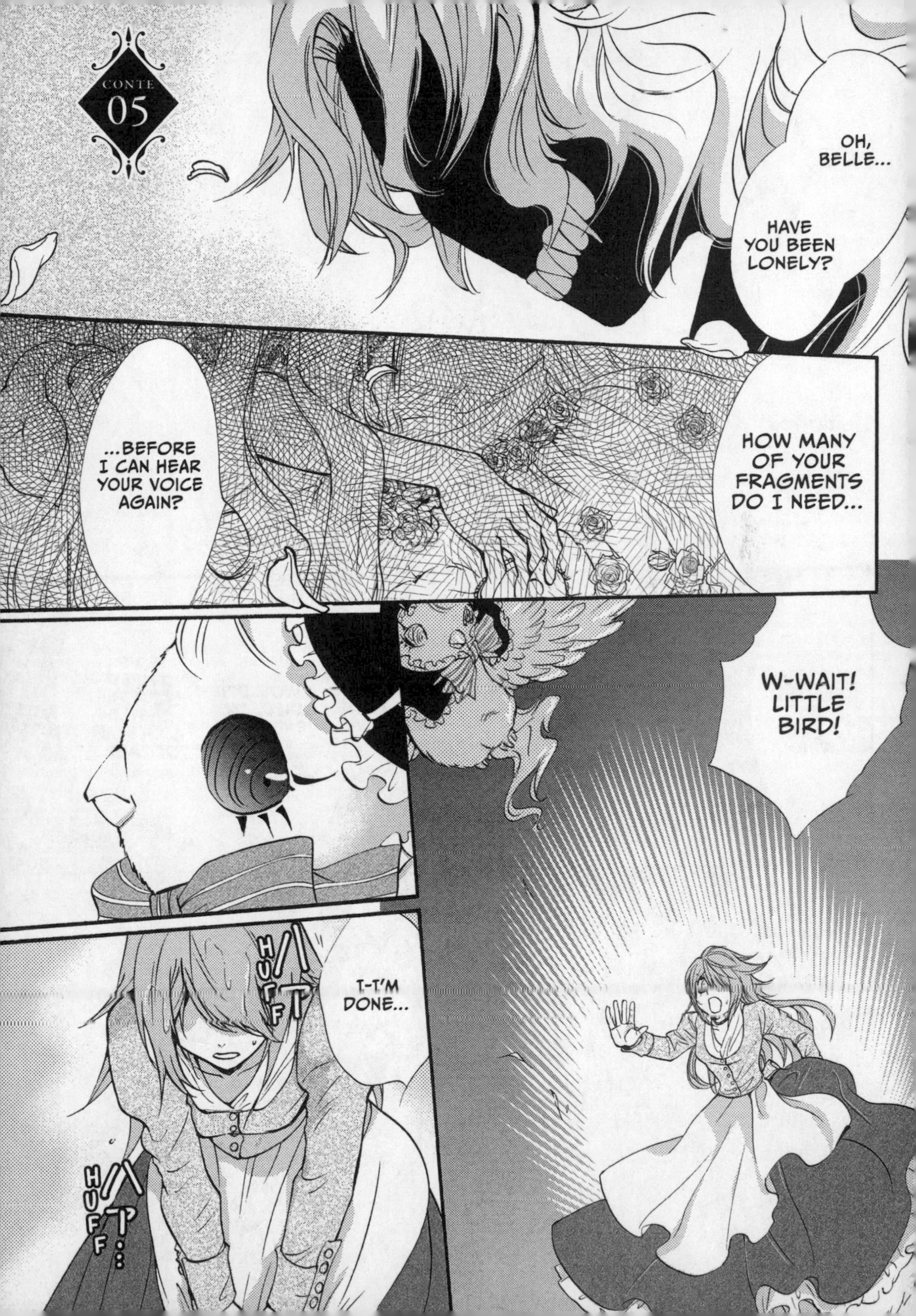
CONTE
05
OH, BELLE...
HAVE YOU BEEN LONELY?
HOW MANY OF YOUR FRAGMENTS DO I NEED...
...BEFORE I CAN HEAR YOUR VOICE AGAIN?
W-WAIT! LITTLE BIRD!
HUFF
T-I'M DONE...
HUFF

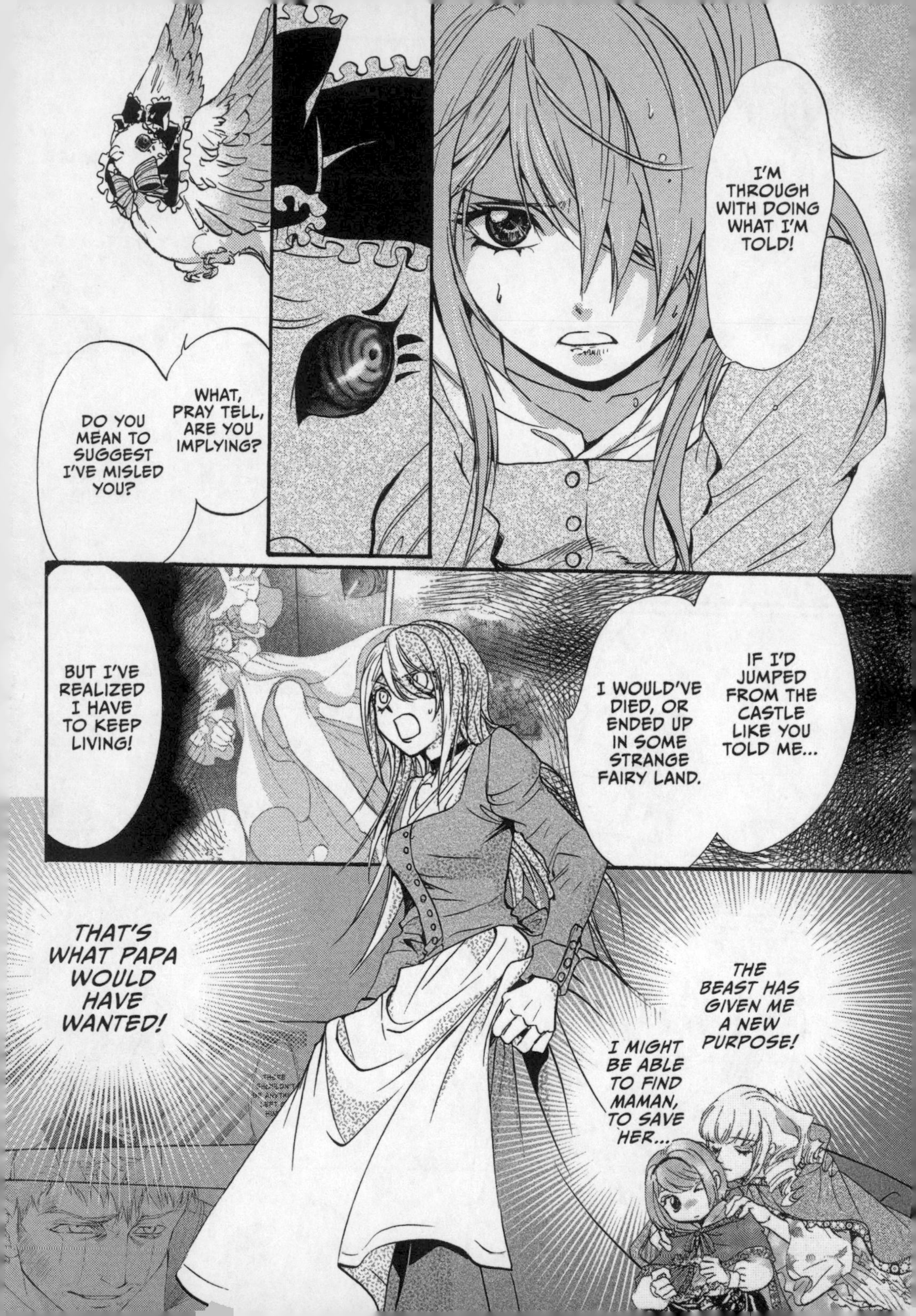
I'M THROUGH WITH DOING WHAT I'M TOLD!
WHAT, PRAY TELL, ARE YOU IMPLYING?
DO YOU MEAN TO SUGGEST I'VE MISLED YOU?
IF I'D JUMPED FROM THE CASTLE LIKE YOU TOLD ME...
I WOULD'VE DIED, OR ENDED UP IN SOME STRANGE FAIRY LAND.
BUT I'VE REALIZED I HAVE TO KEEP LIVING!
THE BEAST HAS GIVEN ME A NEW PURPOSE!
I MIGHT BE ABLE TO FIND MAMAN, TO SAVE HER...
THAT'S WHAT PAPA WOULD HAVE WANTED!

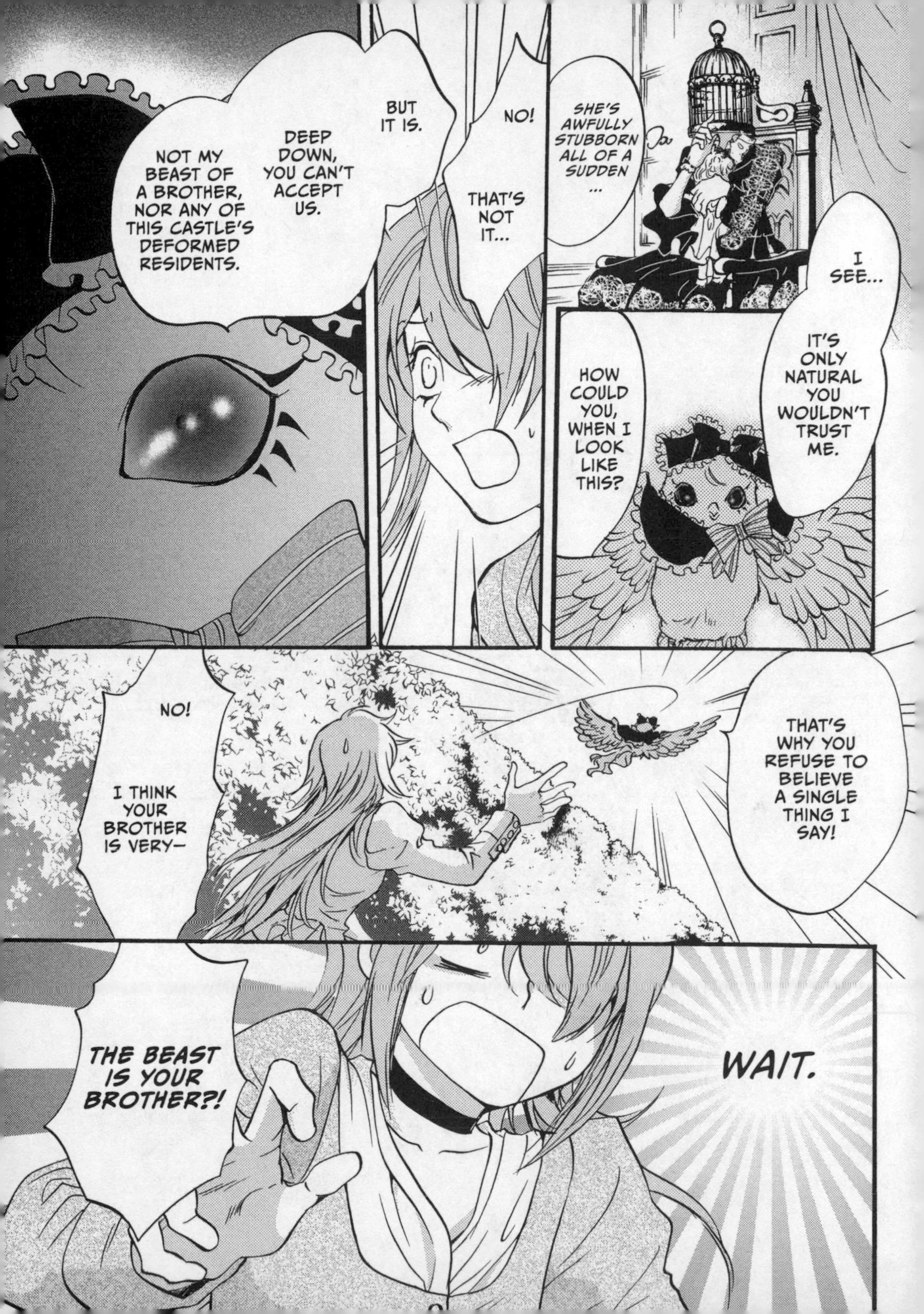
SHE'S AWFULLY STUBBORN ALL OF A SUDDEN ...
I SEE...
IT'S ONLY NATURAL YOU WOULDN'T TRUST ME.
HOW COULD YOU, WHEN I LOOK LIKE THIS?
NO!
THAT'S NOT IT...
BUT IT IS.
DEEP DOWN, YOU CAN'T ACCEPT US.
NOT MY BEAST OF A BROTHER, NOR ANY OF THIS CASTLE'S DEFORMED RESIDENTS.
THAT'S WHY YOU REFUSE TO BELIEVE A SINGLE THING I SAY!
NO!
I THINK YOUR BROTHER IS VERY—
WAIT.
THE BEAST IS YOUR BROTHER?!

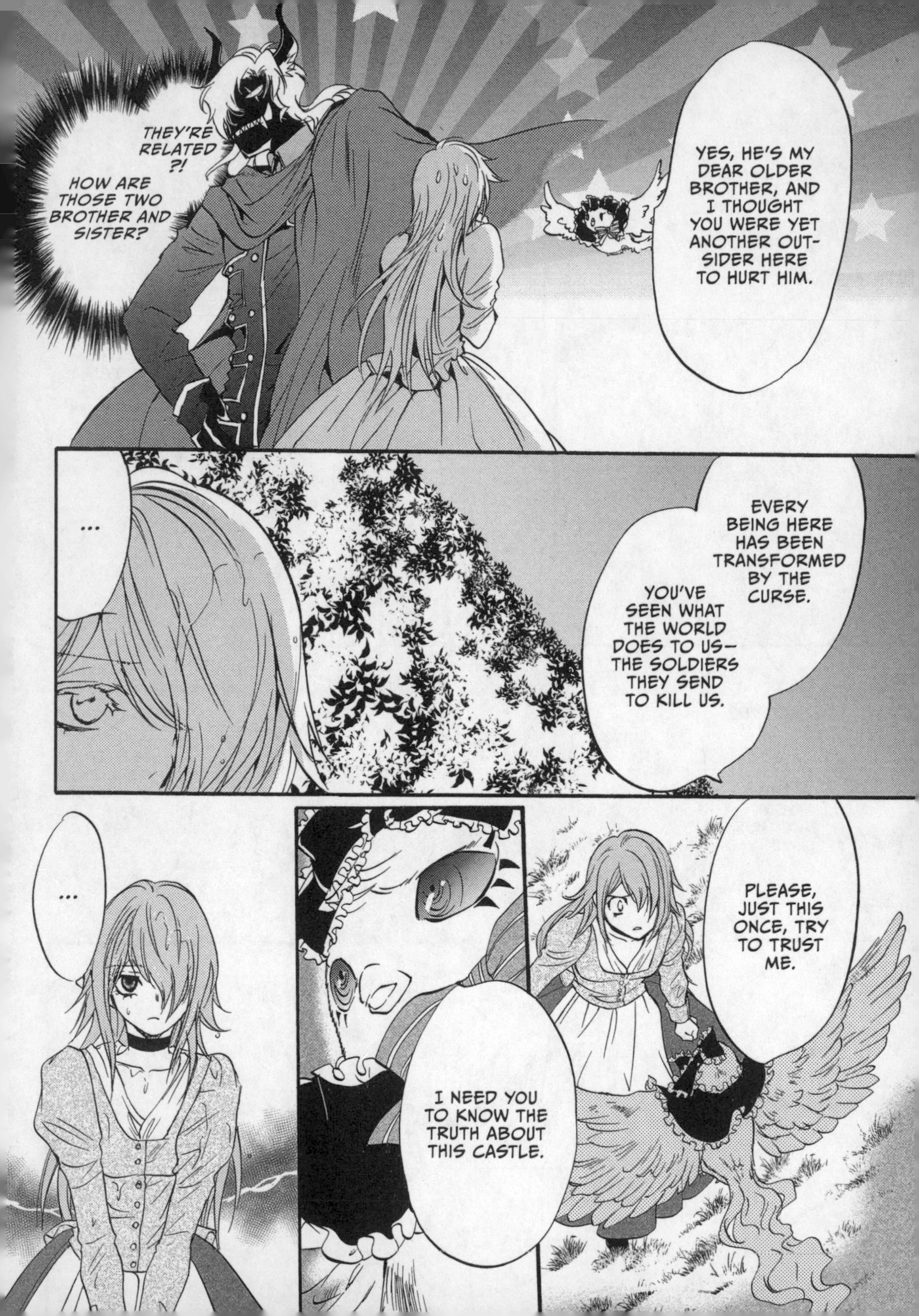
YES, HE'S MY DEAR OLDER BROTHER, AND I THOUGHT YOU WERE YET ANOTHER OUT-SIDER HERE TO HURT HIM.
THEY'RE RELATED ?!
HOW ARE THOSE TWO BROTHER AND SISTER?
EVERY BEING HERE HAS BEEN TRANSFORMED BY THE CURSE.
YOU'VE SEEN WHAT THE WORLD DOES TO US— THE SOLDIERS THEY SEND TO KILL US.
...
PLEASE, JUST THIS ONCE, TRY TO TRUST ME.
I NEED YOU TO KNOW THE TRUTH ABOUT THIS CASTLE.
...

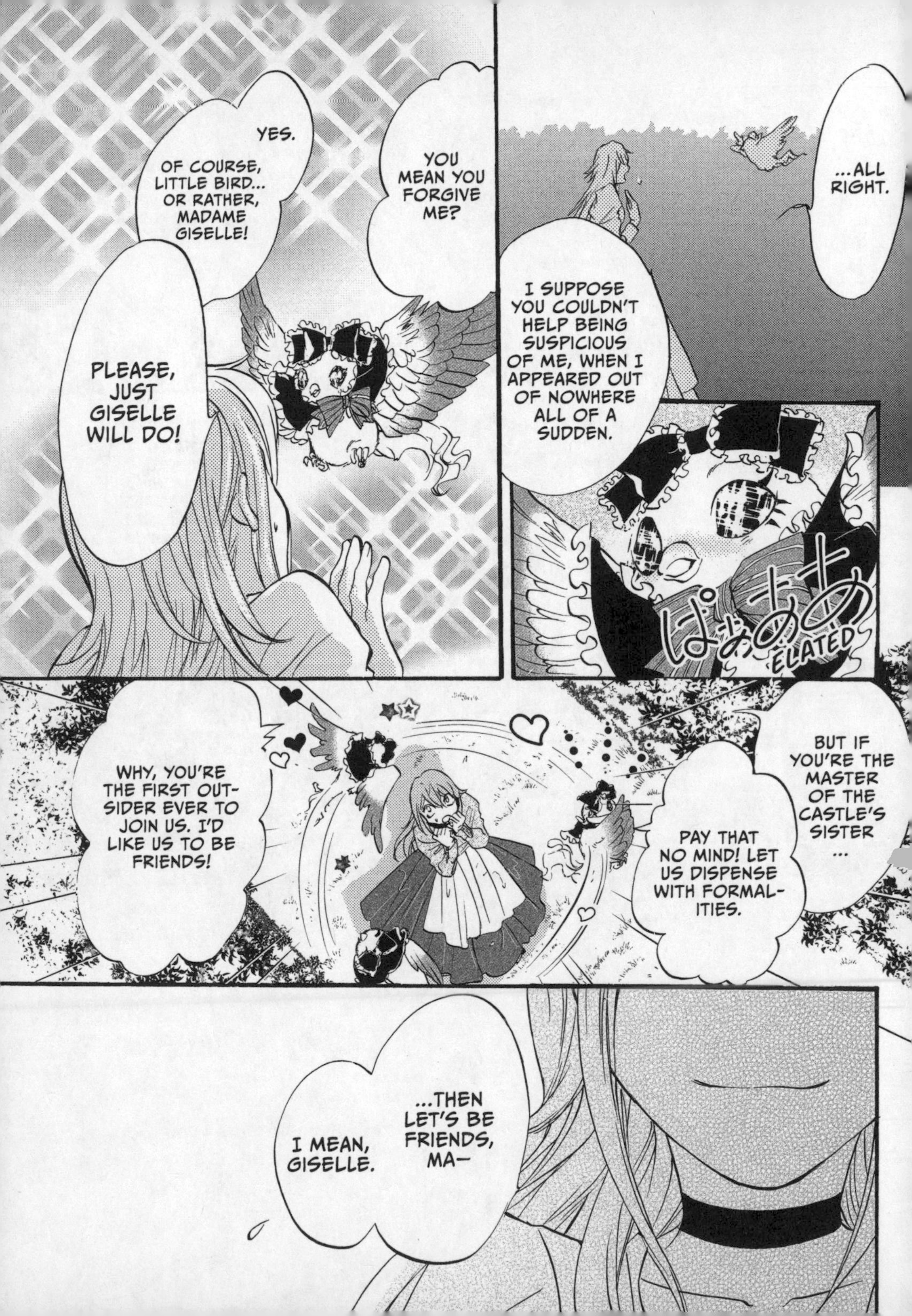
...ALL RIGHT.
I SUPPOSE YOU COULDN'T HELP BEING SUSPICIOUS OF ME, WHEN I APPEARED OUT OF NOWHERE ALL OF A SUDDEN.
ぱぁああ
ELATED
YOU MEAN YOU FORGIVE ME?
YES.
OF COURSE, LITTLE BIRD... OR RATHER, MADAME GISELLE!
PLEASE, JUST GISELLE WILL DO!
BUT IF YOU'RE THE MASTER OF THE CASTLE'S SISTER ...
PAY THAT NO MIND! LET US DISPENSE WITH FORMALITIES.
WHY, YOU'RE THE FIRST OUTSIDER EVER TO JOIN US. I'D LIKE US TO BE FRIENDS!
...THEN LET'S BE FRIENDS, MA—
I MEAN, GISELLE.

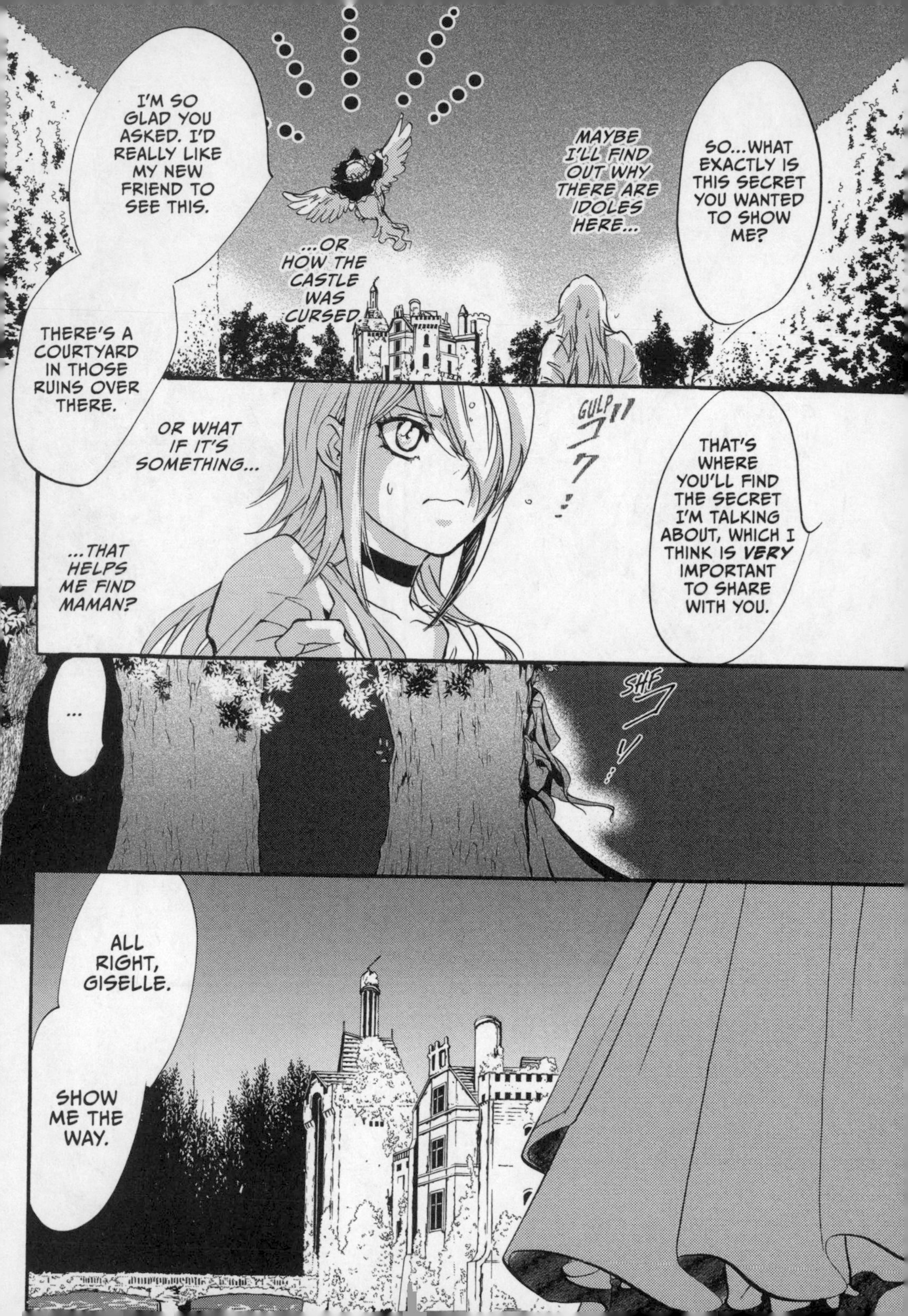

SO...WHAT EXACTLY IS THIS SECRET YOU WANTED TO SHOW ME?
MAYBE I'LL FIND OUT WHY THERE ARE IDOLES HERE...
...OR HOW THE CASTLE WAS CURSED.
I'M SO GLAD YOU ASKED. I'D REALLY LIKE MY NEW FRIEND TO SEE THIS.
THERE'S A COURTYARD IN THOSE RUINS OVER THERE.
THAT'S WHERE YOU'LL FIND THE SECRET I'M TALKING ABOUT, WHICH I THINK IS **VERY** IMPORTANT TO SHARE WITH YOU.
GULP
OR WHAT IF IT'S SOMETHING...
...THAT HELPS ME FIND MAMAN?
SHF
...
ALL RIGHT, GISELLE.
SHOW ME THE WAY.

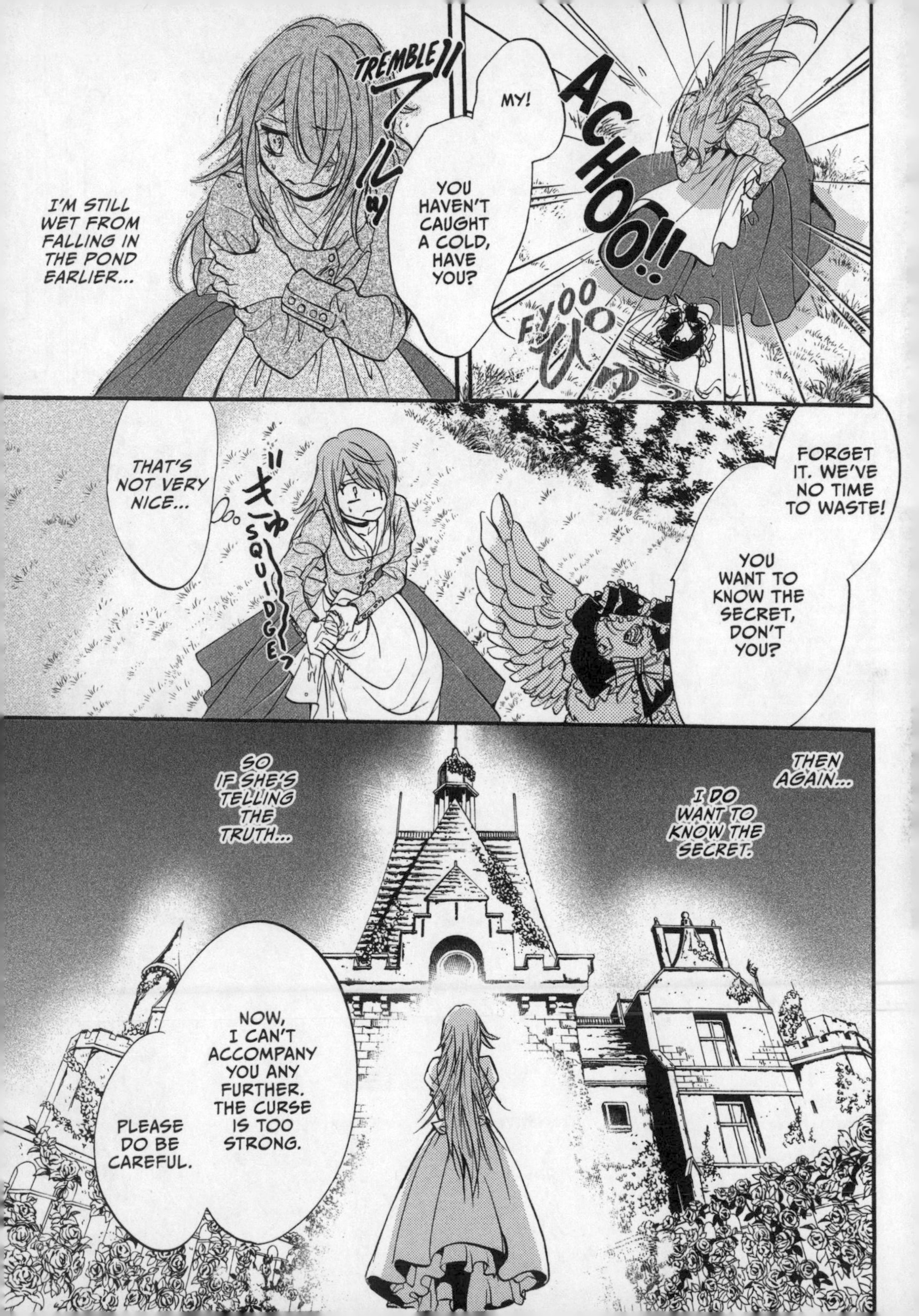

ACHOO!!
MY!
YOU HAVEN'T CAUGHT A COLD, HAVE YOU?
FYOO
TREMBLE
I'M STILL WET FROM FALLING IN THE POND EARLIER...
FORGET IT. WE'VE NO TIME TO WASTE!
YOU WANT TO KNOW THE SECRET, DON'T YOU?
SQUIDGE
THAT'S NOT VERY NICE...
THEN AGAIN...
I DO WANT TO KNOW THE SECRET.
SO IF SHE'S TELLING THE TRUTH...
NOW, I CAN'T ACCOMPANY YOU ANY FURTHER. THE CURSE IS TOO STRONG.
PLEASE DO BE CAREFUL.

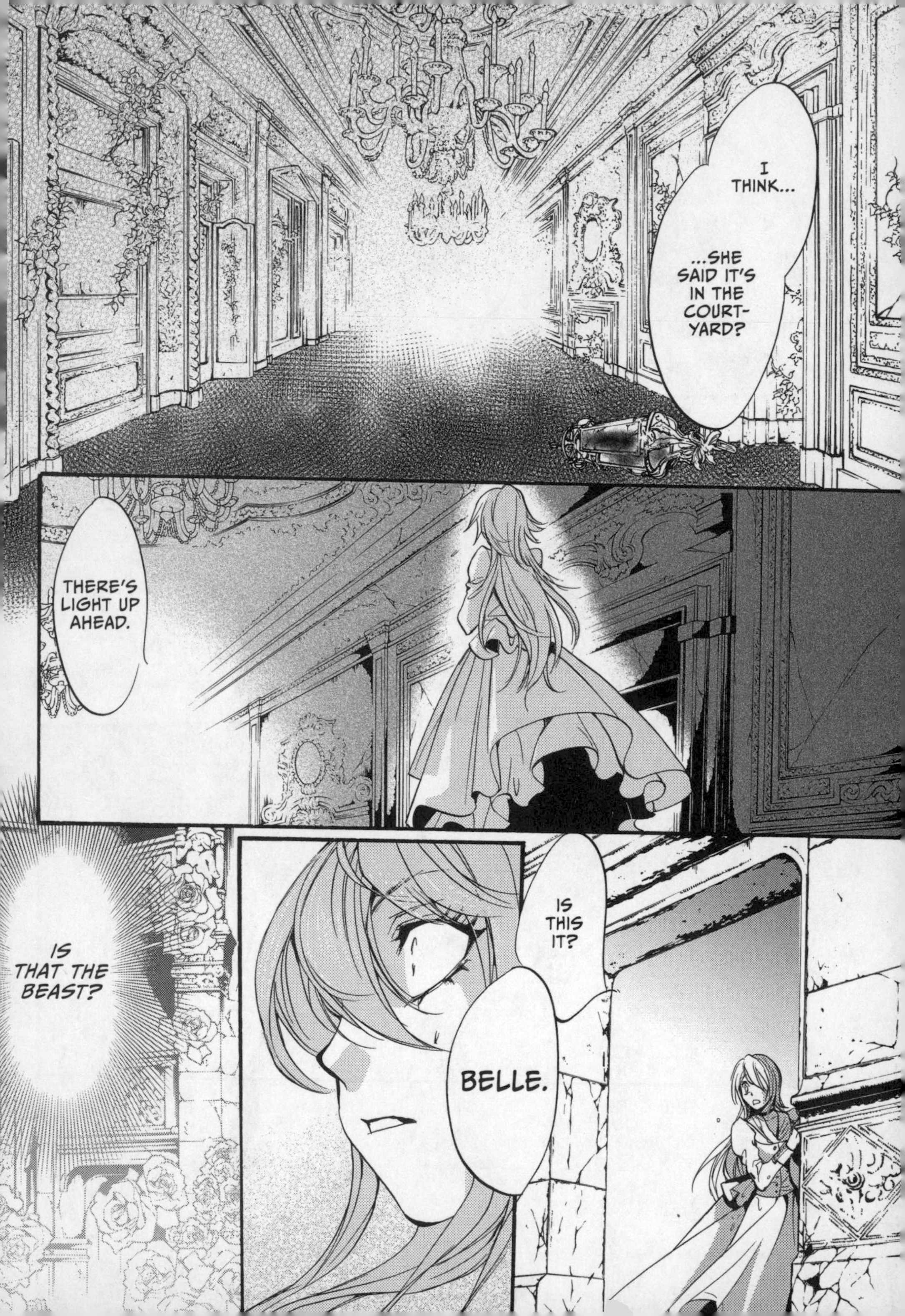
I THINK...
...SHE SAID IT'S IN THE COURT-YARD?
THERE'S LIGHT UP AHEAD.
IS THIS IT?
BELLE.
IS THAT THE BEAST?

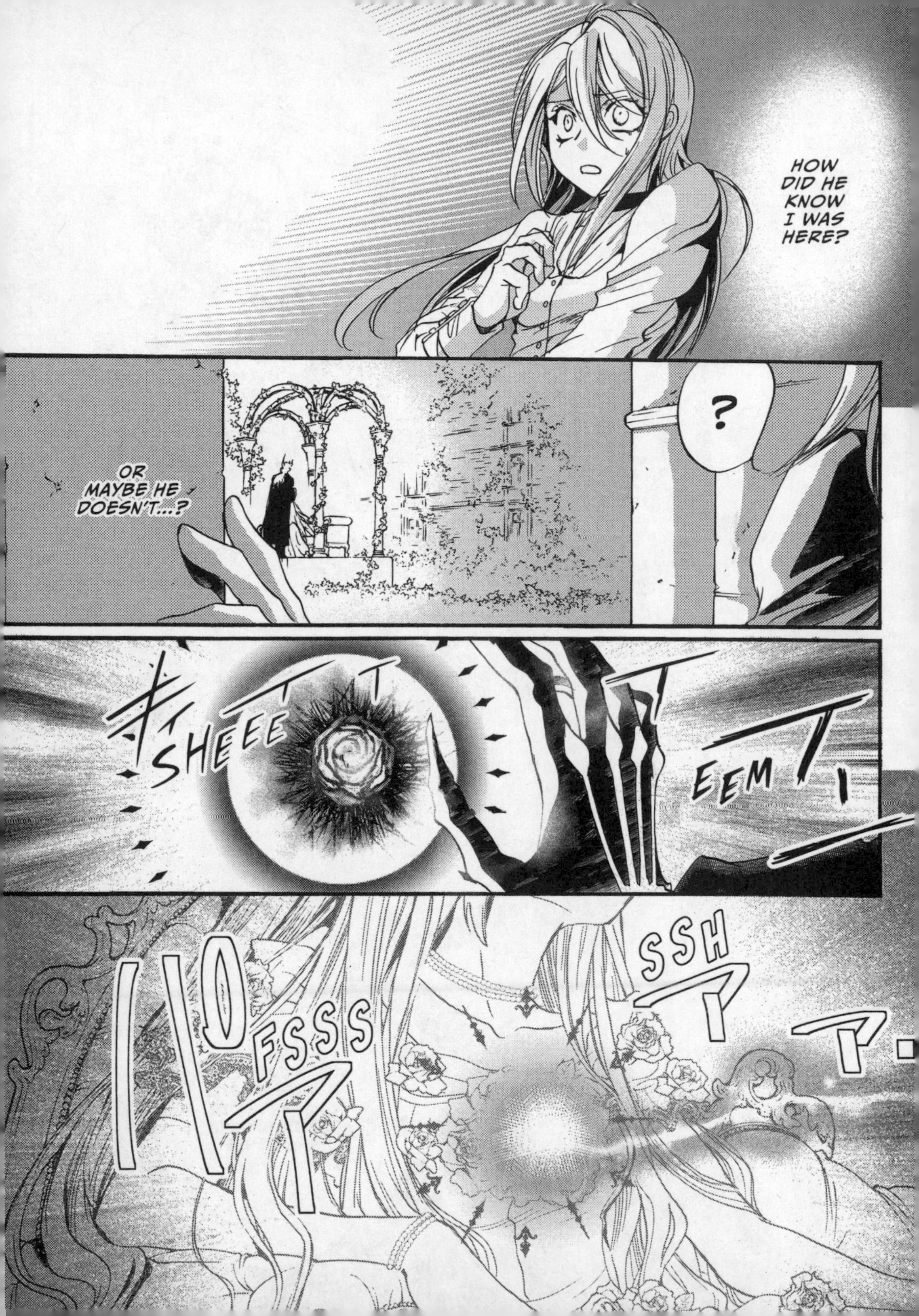
HOW DID HE KNOW I WAS HERE?
?
OR MAYBE HE DOESN'T...?
SHEEE
EEM
SSH
FSSS

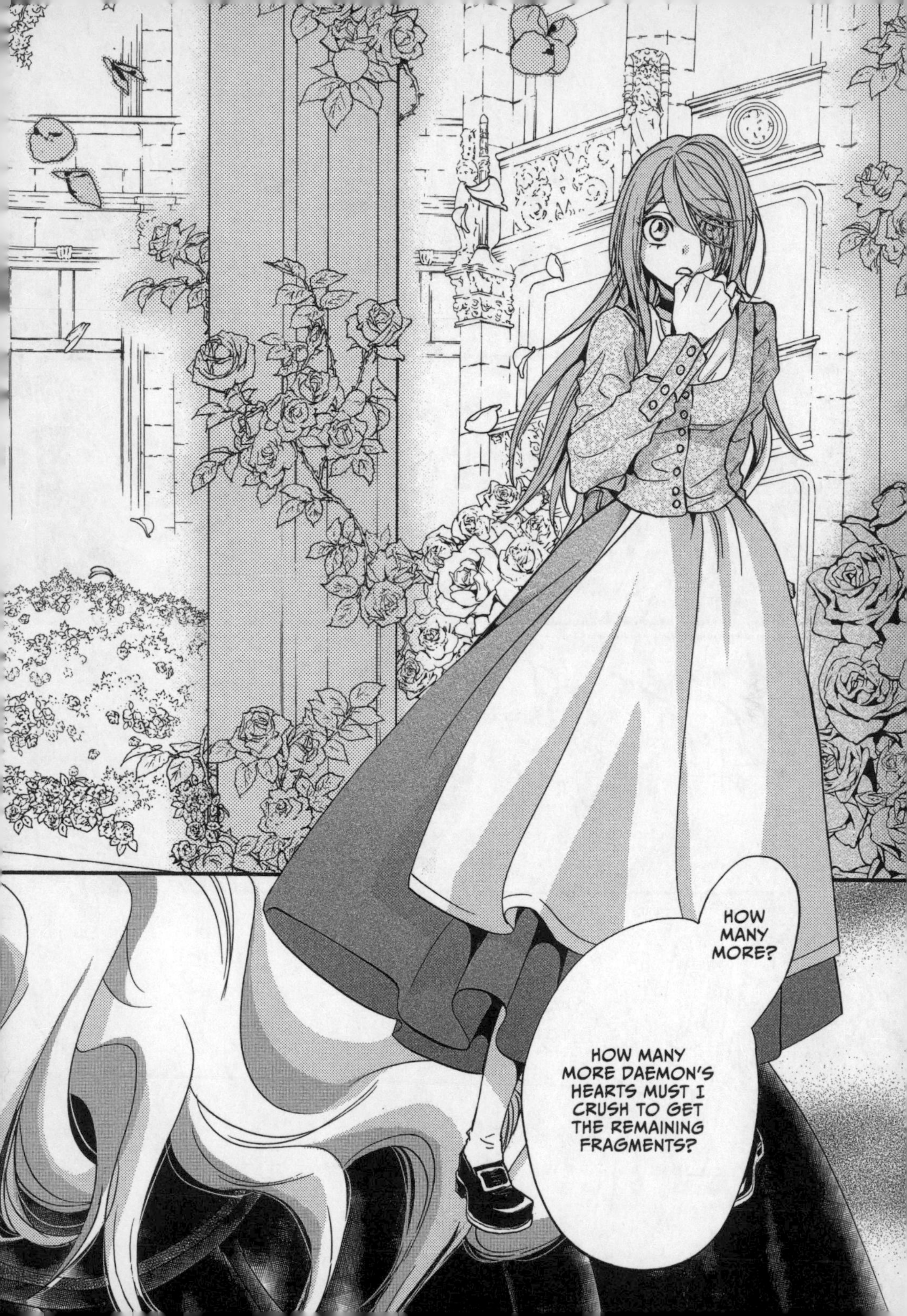
HOW MANY MORE?
HOW MANY MORE DAEMON'S HEARTS MUST I CRUSH TO GET THE REMAINING FRAGMENTS?

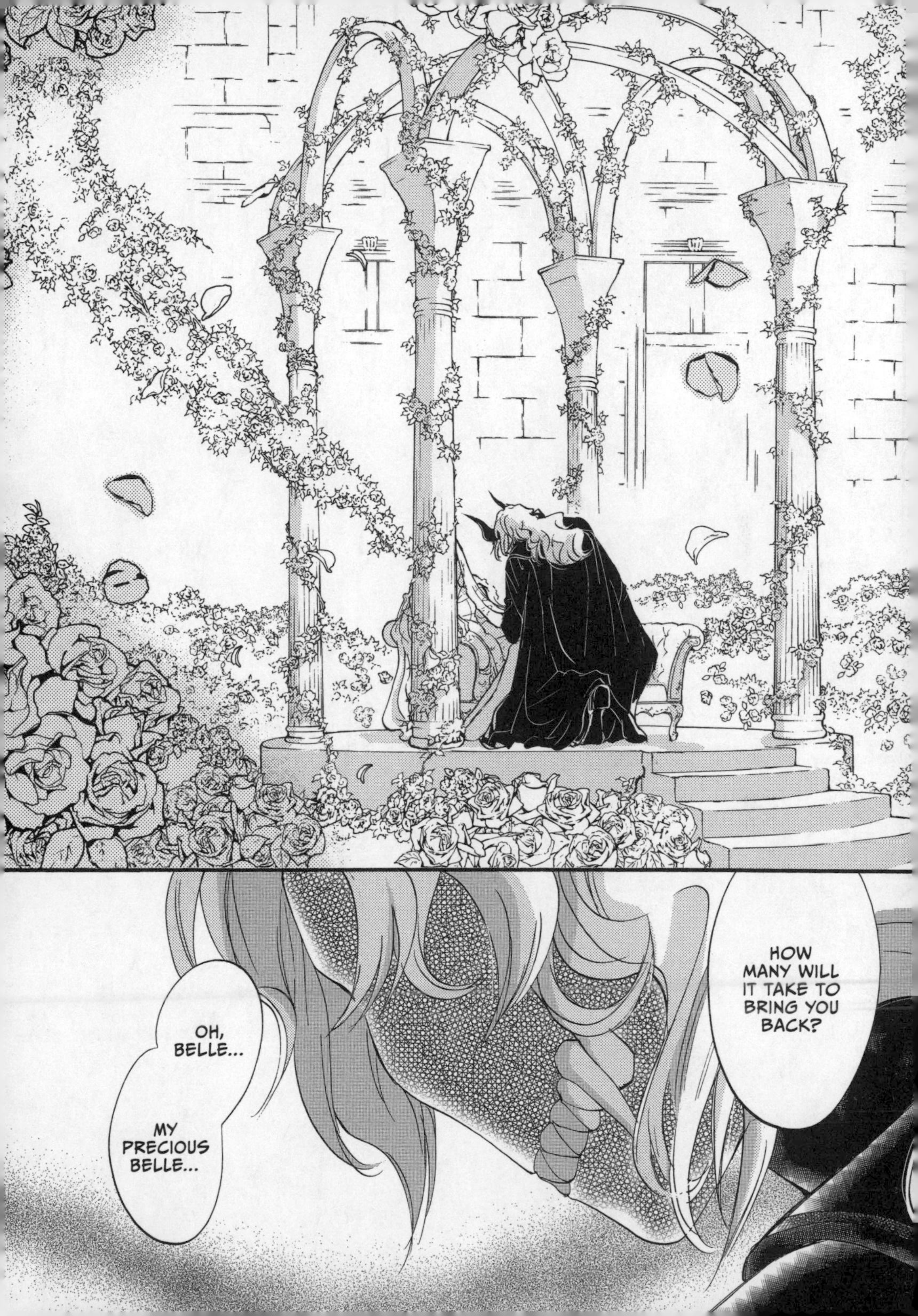
HOW MANY WILL IT TAKE TO BRING YOU BACK?
OH, BELLE...
MY PRECIOUS BELLE...

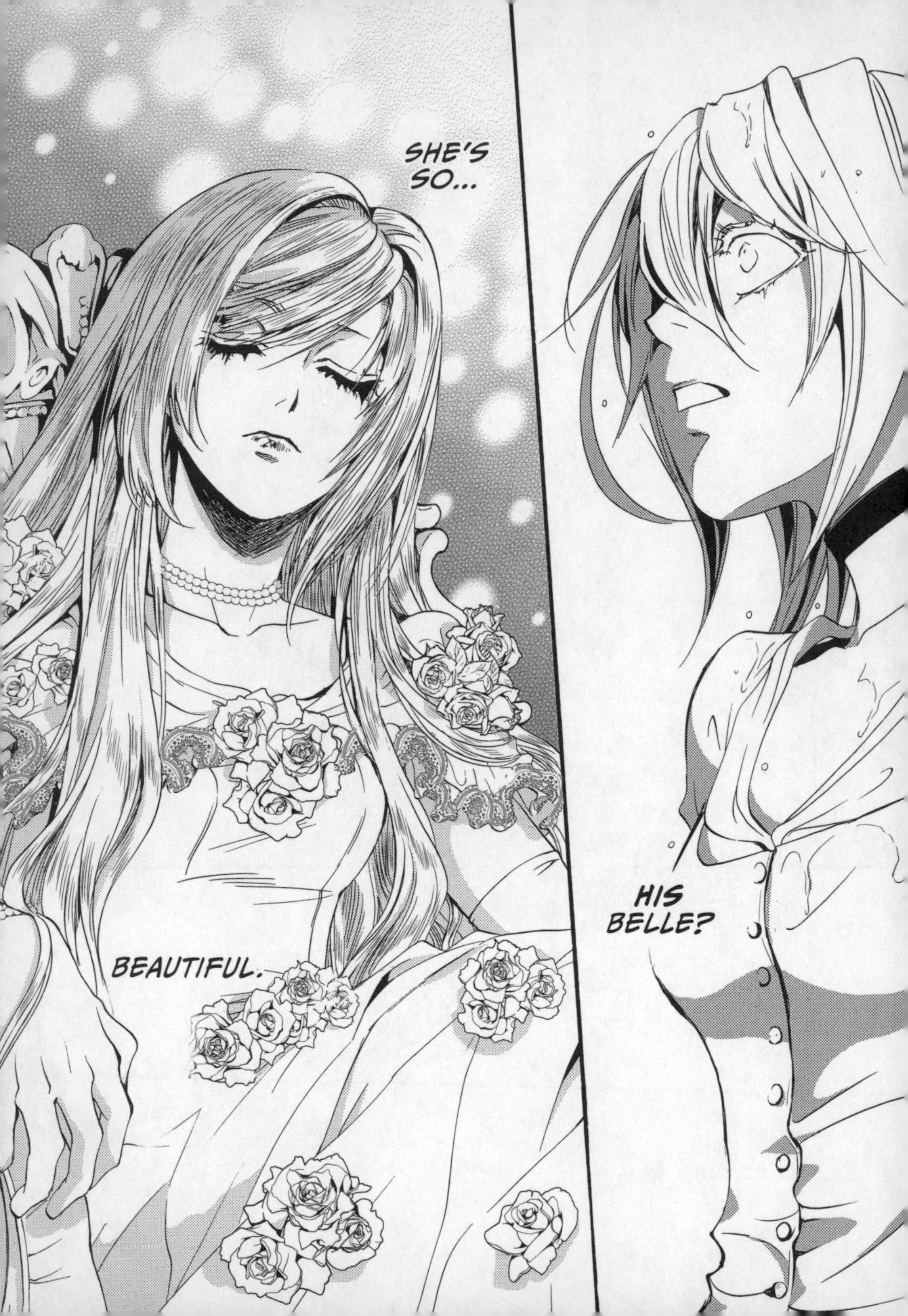
HIS BELLE?
SHE'S SO...
BEAUTIFUL.

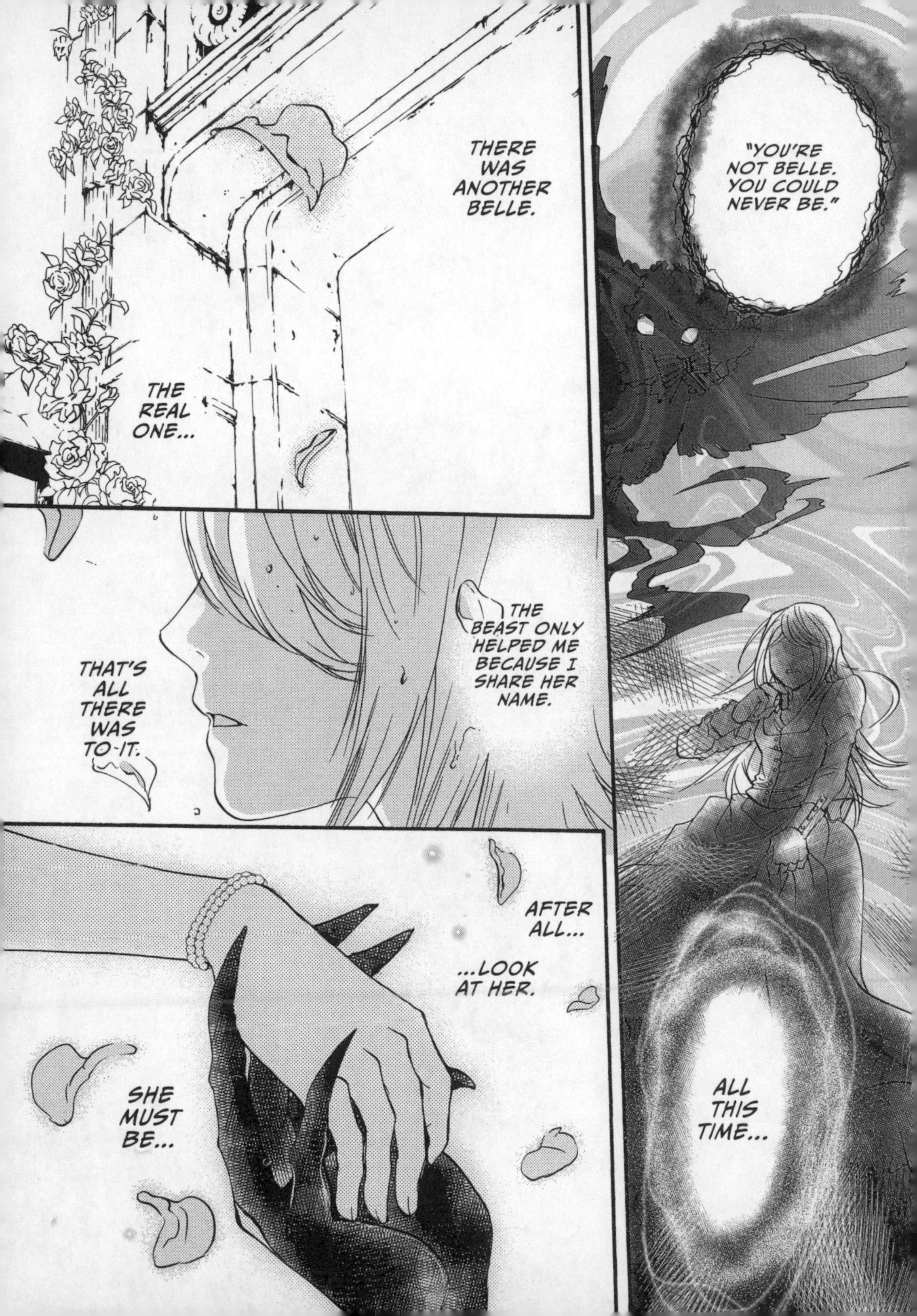
"YOU'RE NOT BELLE. YOU COULD NEVER BE."
ALL THIS TIME...
THERE WAS ANOTHER BELLE.
THE REAL ONE...
THE BEAST ONLY HELPED ME BECAUSE I SHARE HER NAME.
THAT'S ALL THERE WAS TO IT.
AFTER ALL...
...LOOK AT HER.
SHE MUST BE...

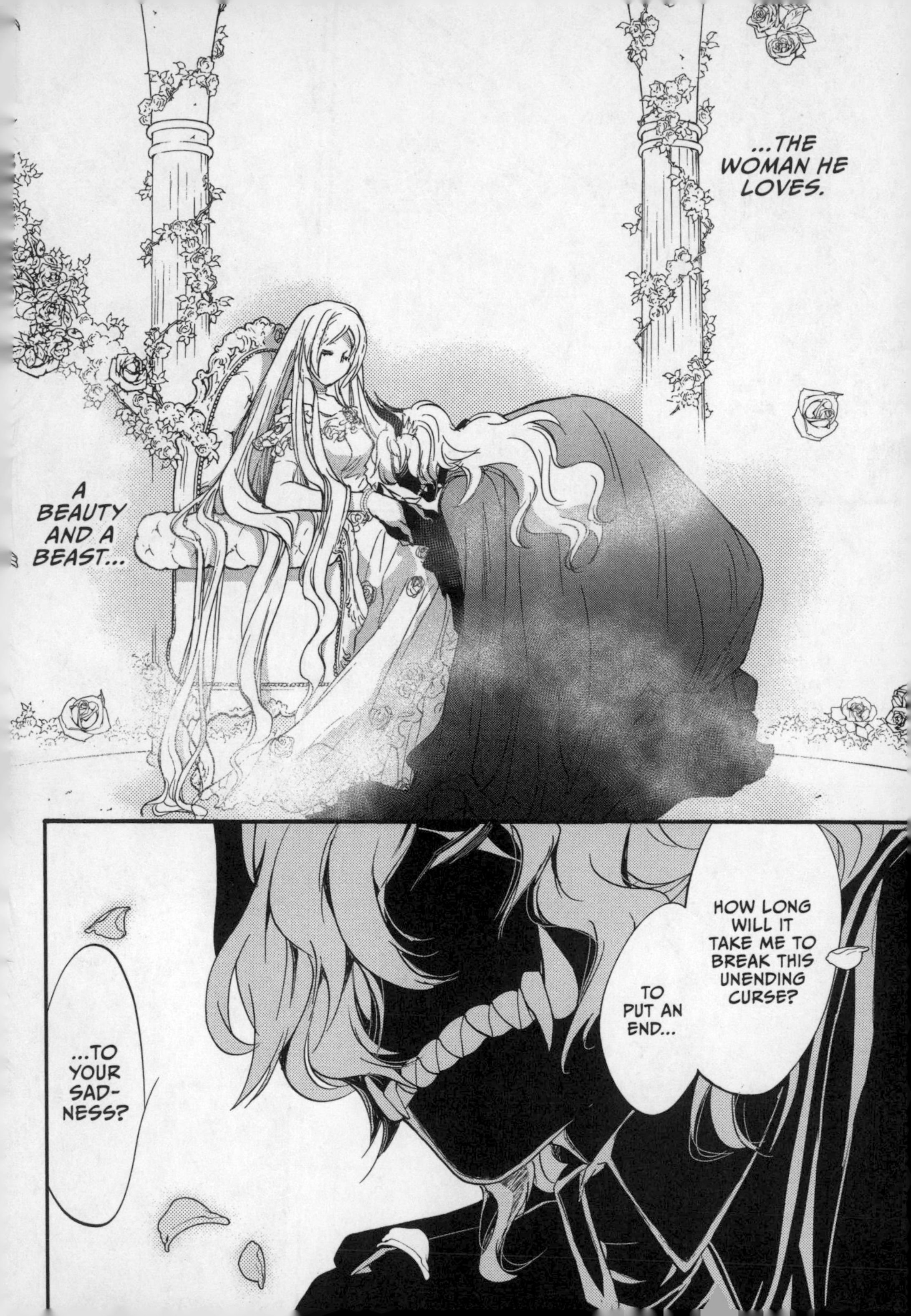
...THE WOMAN HE LOVES.
A BEAUTY AND A BEAST...
HOW LONG WILL IT TAKE ME TO BREAK THIS UNENDING CURSE?
TO PUT AN END...
...TO YOUR SADNESS?

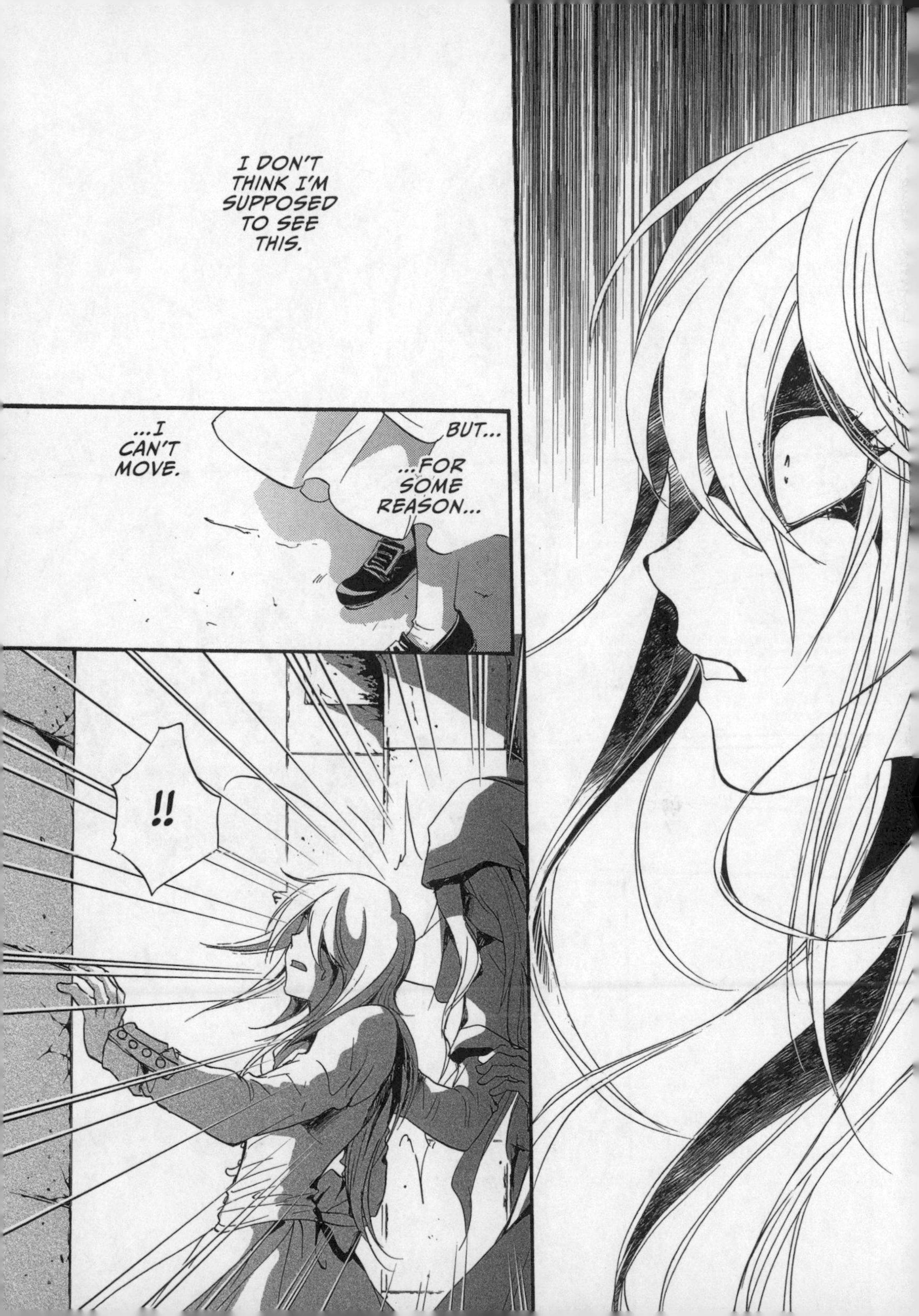
I DON'T THINK I'M SUPPOSED TO SEE THIS.
BUT...
...FOR SOME REASON...
...I CAN'T MOVE.
!!

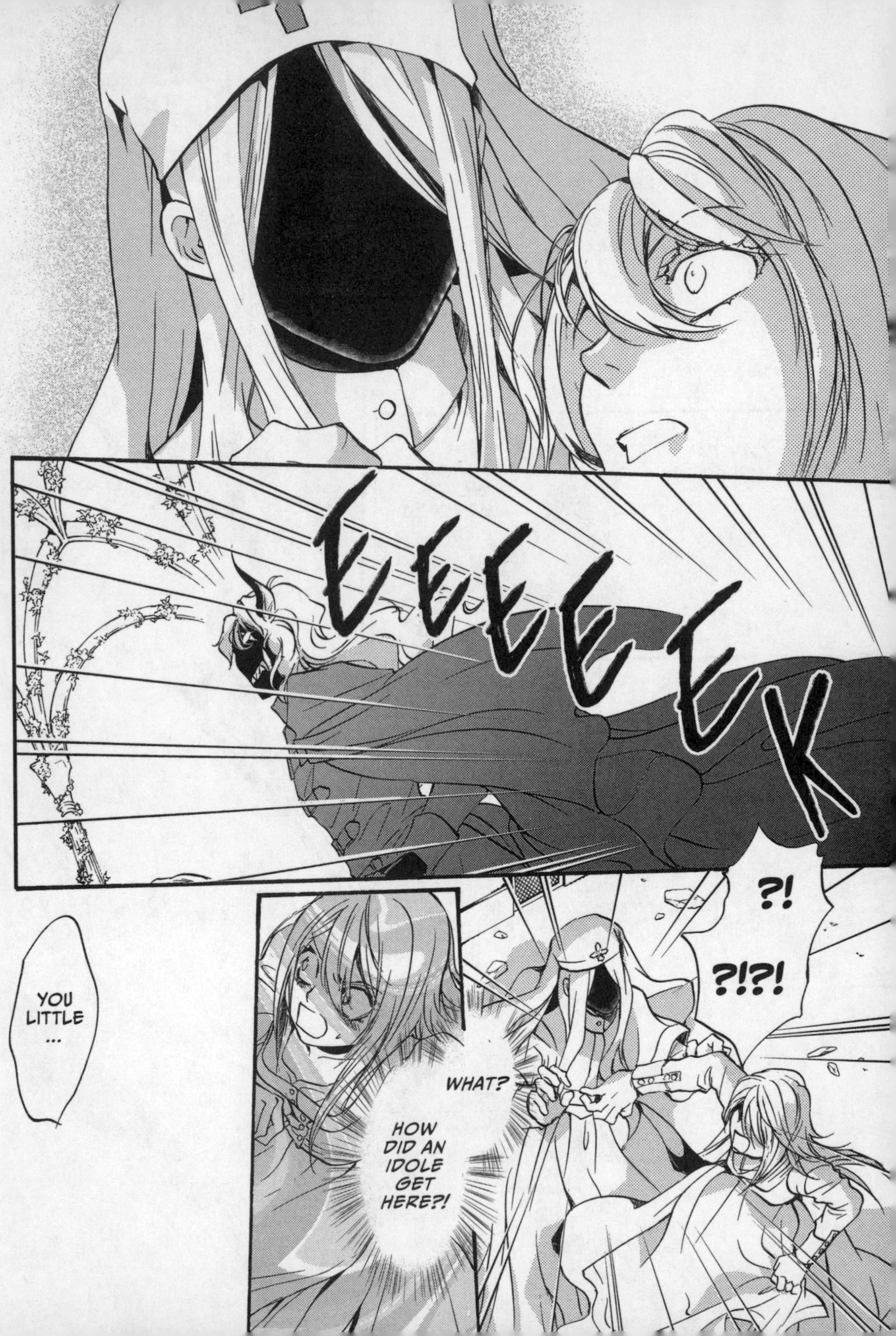
EEEEEEK
?!
?!?!
WHAT?
HOW DID AN IDOLE GET HERE?!
YOU LITTLE ...

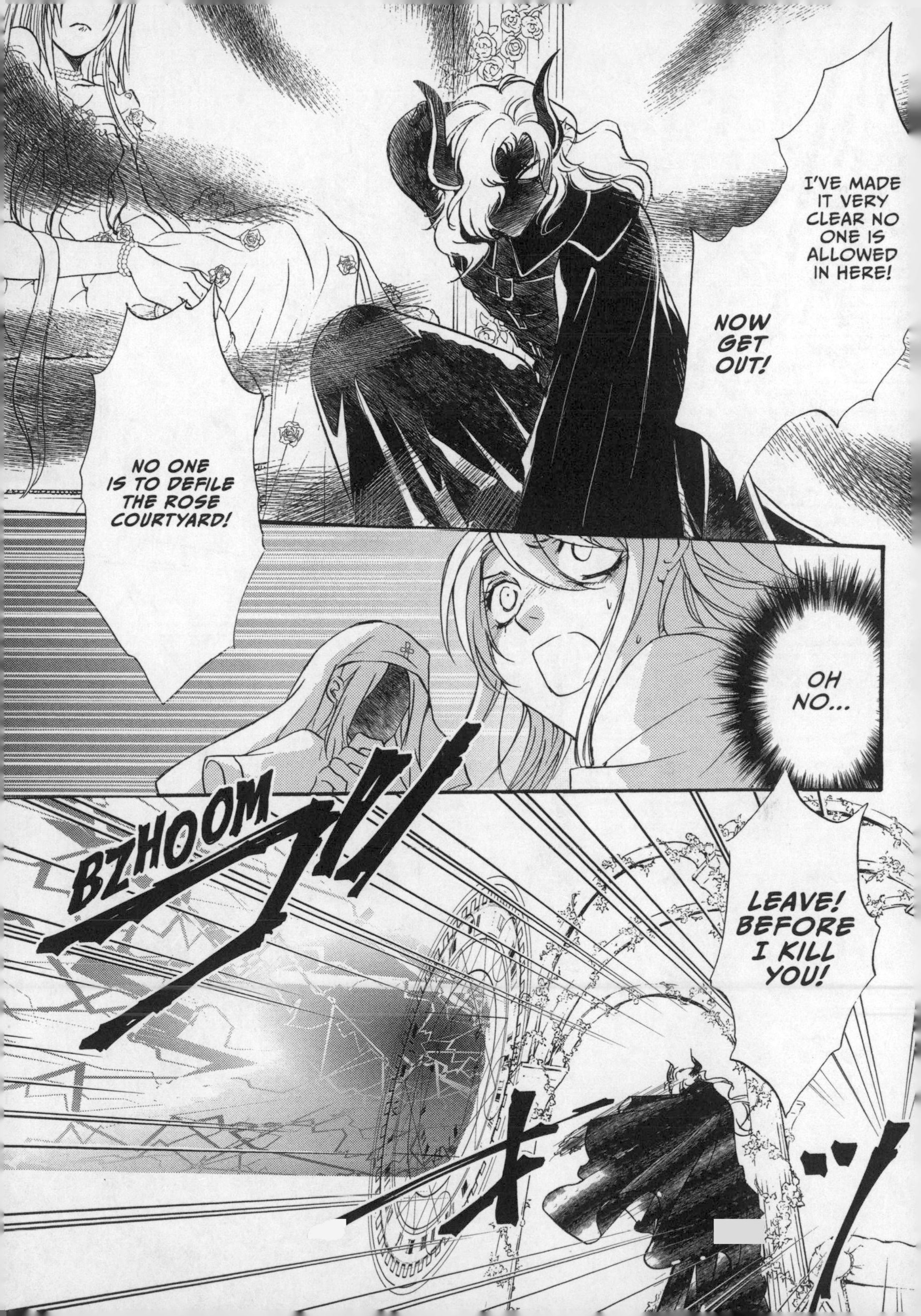
I'VE MADE IT VERY CLEAR NO ONE IS ALLOWED IN HERE!
NOW GET OUT!
NO ONE IS TO DEFILE THE ROSE COURTYARD!
OH NO...
LEAVE! BEFORE I KILL YOU!
BZHOOM

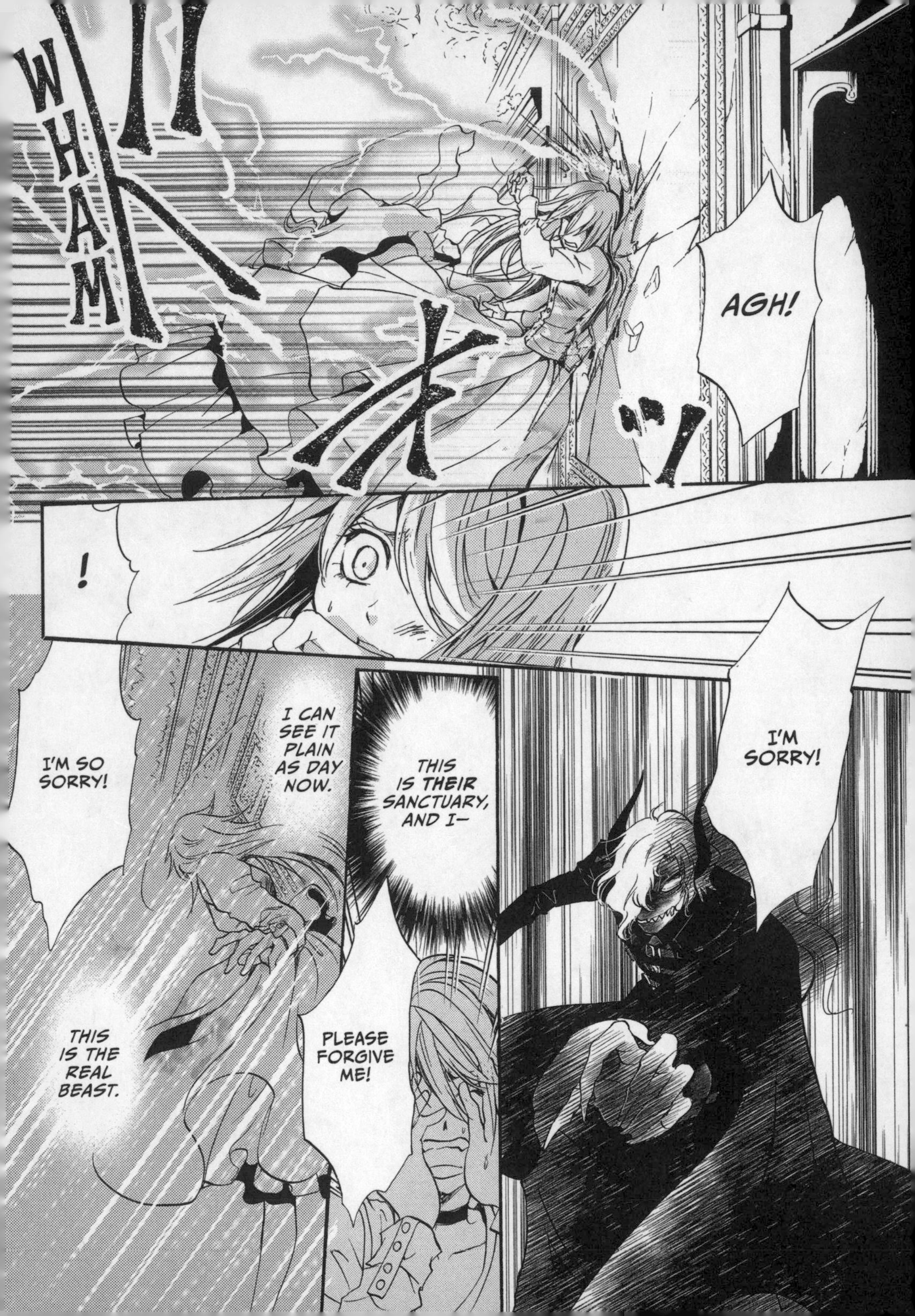
AGH!
WHAM
!
I'M SORRY!
THIS IS THEIR SANCTUARY, AND I—
I CAN SEE IT PLAIN AS DAY NOW.
PLEASE FORGIVE ME!
I'M SO SORRY!
THIS IS THE REAL BEAST.

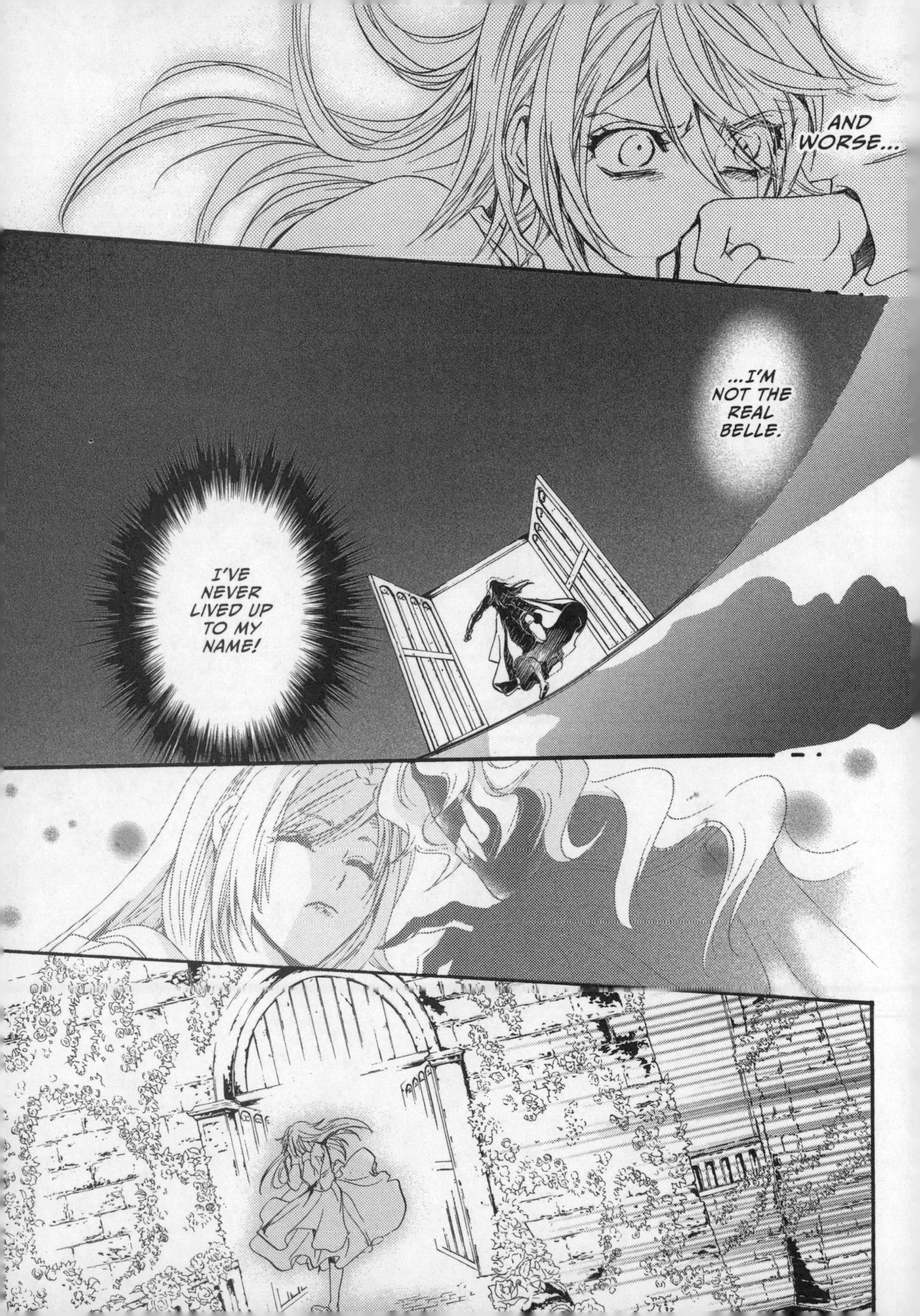
AND WORSE...
...I'M NOT THE REAL BELLE.
I'VE NEVER LIVED UP TO MY NAME!

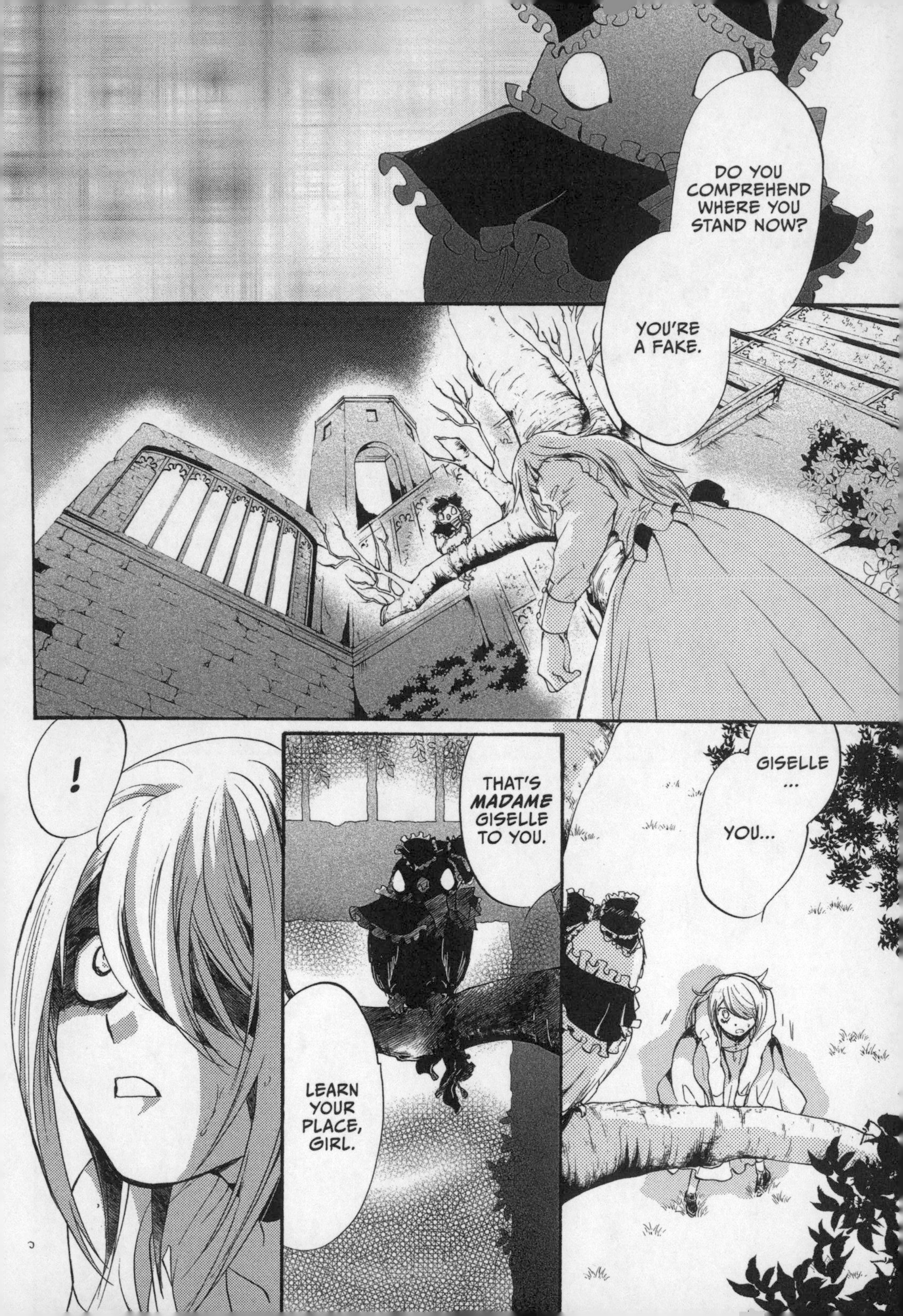
DO YOU COMPREHEND WHERE YOU STAND NOW?
YOU'RE A FAKE.
GISELLE ...
YOU...
THAT'S *MADAME* GISELLE TO YOU.
LEARN YOUR PLACE, GIRL.
!

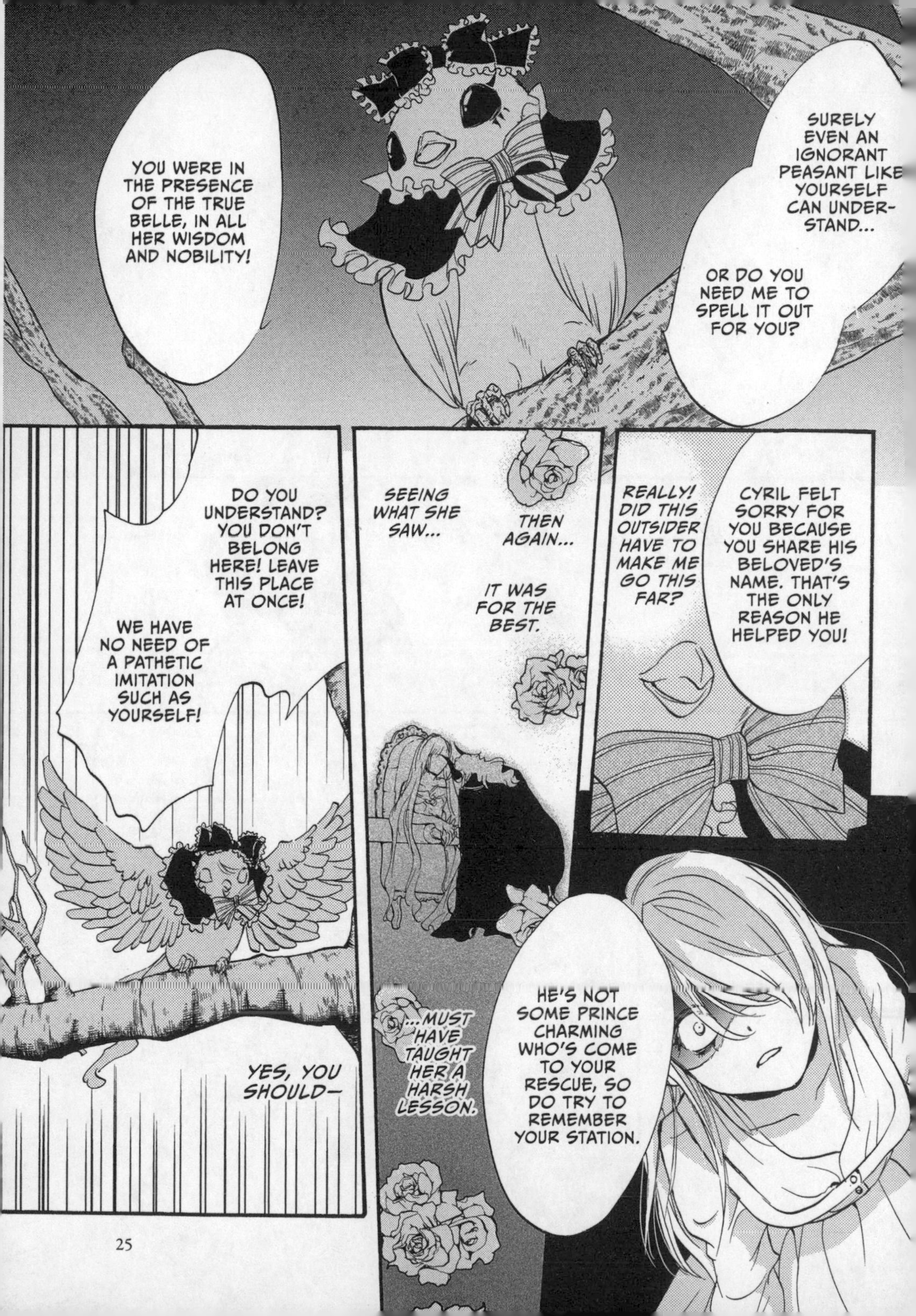

SURELY EVEN AN IGNORANT PEASANT LIKE YOURSELF CAN UNDERSTAND...
OR DO YOU NEED ME TO SPELL IT OUT FOR YOU?
YOU WERE IN THE PRESENCE OF THE TRUE BELLE, IN ALL HER WISDOM AND NOBILITY!
CYRIL FELT SORRY FOR YOU BECAUSE YOU SHARE HIS BELOVED'S NAME. THAT'S THE ONLY REASON HE HELPED YOU!
REALLY! DID THIS OUTSIDER HAVE TO MAKE ME GO THIS FAR?
HE'S NOT SOME PRINCE CHARMING WHO'S COME TO YOUR RESCUE, SO DO TRY TO REMEMBER YOUR STATION.
THEN AGAIN...
SEEING WHAT SHE SAW...
IT WAS FOR THE BEST.
...MUST HAVE TAUGHT HER A HARSH LESSON.
DO YOU UNDERSTAND? YOU DON'T BELONG HERE! LEAVE THIS PLACE AT ONCE!
WE HAVE NO NEED OF A PATHETIC IMITATION SUCH AS YOURSELF!
YES, YOU SHOULD—

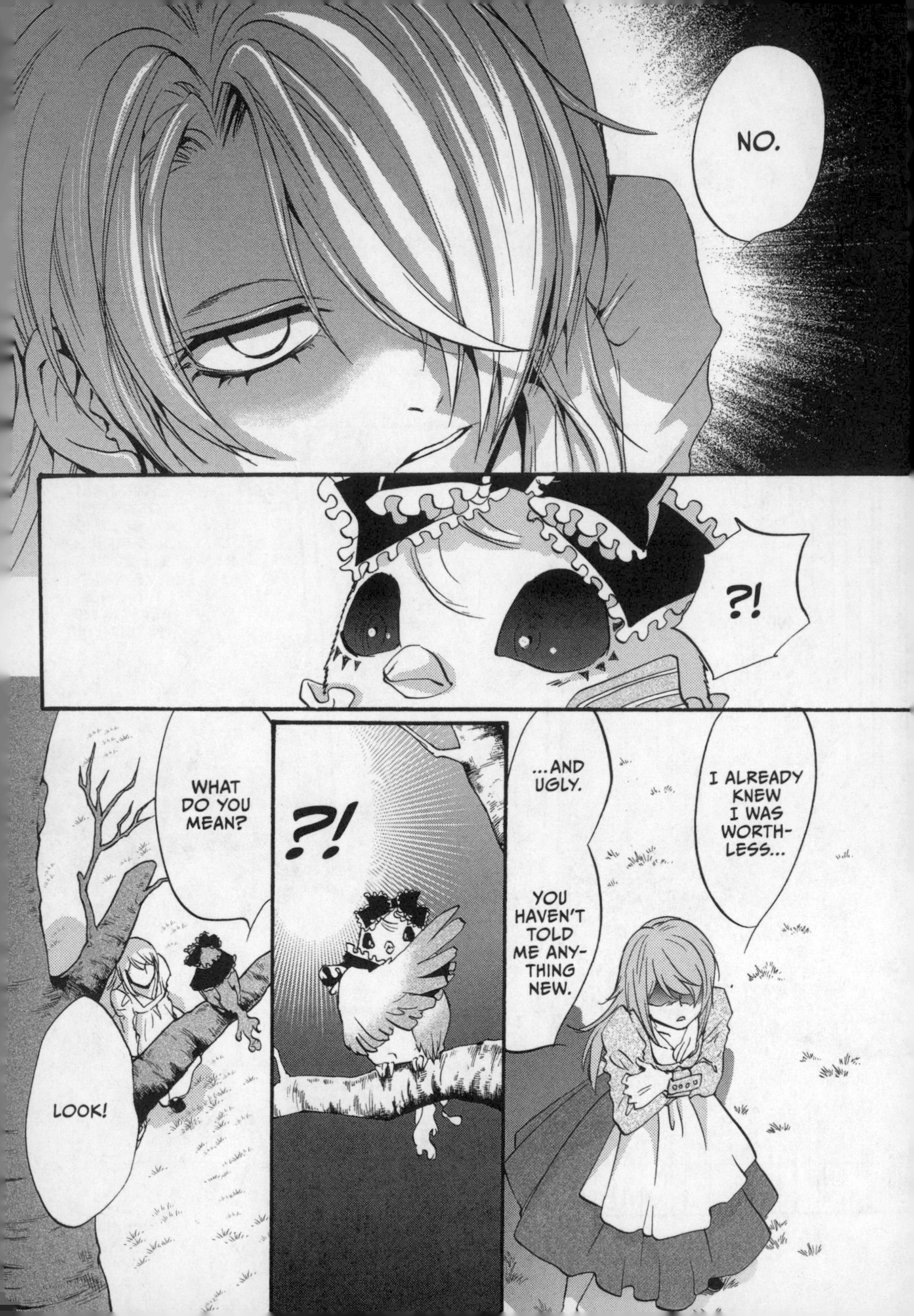
NO.
?!
I ALREADY KNEW I WAS WORTHLESS...
...AND UGLY.
YOU HAVEN'T TOLD ME ANYTHING NEW.
?!
WHAT DO YOU MEAN?
LOOK!

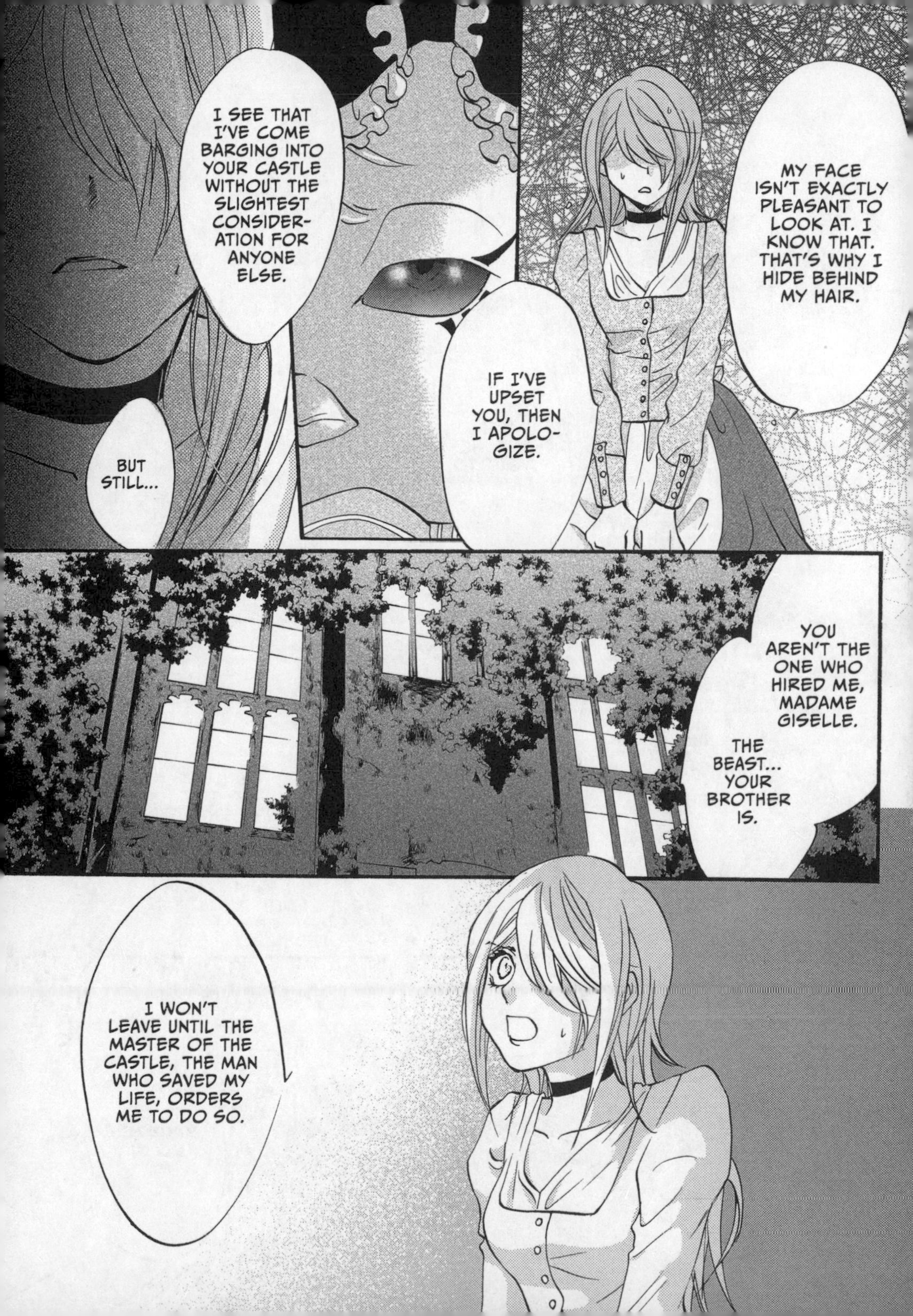
MY FACE ISN'T EXACTLY PLEASANT TO LOOK AT. I KNOW THAT. THAT'S WHY I HIDE BEHIND MY HAIR.
I SEE THAT I'VE COME BARGING INTO YOUR CASTLE WITHOUT THE SLIGHTEST CONSIDER-ATION FOR ANYONE ELSE.
IF I'VE UPSET YOU, THEN I APOLO-GIZE.
BUT STILL...
YOU AREN'T THE ONE WHO HIRED ME, MADAME GISELLE.
THE BEAST... YOUR BROTHER IS.
I WON'T LEAVE UNTIL THE MASTER OF THE CASTLE, THE MAN WHO SAVED MY LIFE, ORDERS ME TO DO SO.

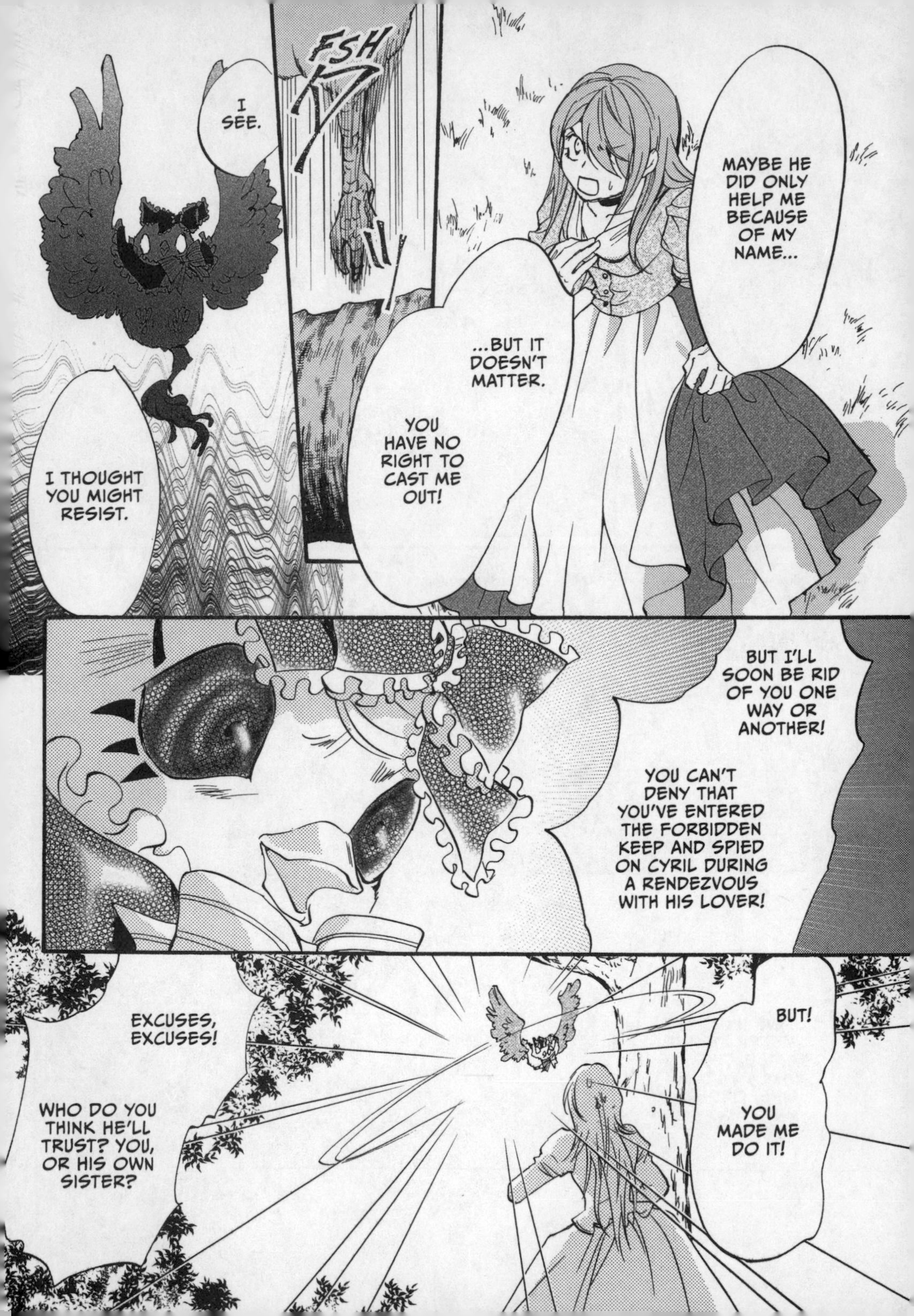
MAYBE HE DID ONLY HELP ME BECAUSE OF MY NAME...
...BUT IT DOESN'T MATTER.
YOU HAVE NO RIGHT TO CAST ME OUT!
FSH
I SEE.
I THOUGHT YOU MIGHT RESIST.
BUT I'LL SOON BE RID OF YOU ONE WAY OR ANOTHER!
YOU CAN'T DENY THAT YOU'VE ENTERED THE FORBIDDEN KEEP AND SPIED ON CYRIL DURING A RENDEZVOUS WITH HIS LOVER!
BUT!
YOU MADE ME DO IT!
EXCUSES, EXCUSES!
WHO DO YOU THINK HE'LL TRUST? YOU, OR HIS OWN SISTER?

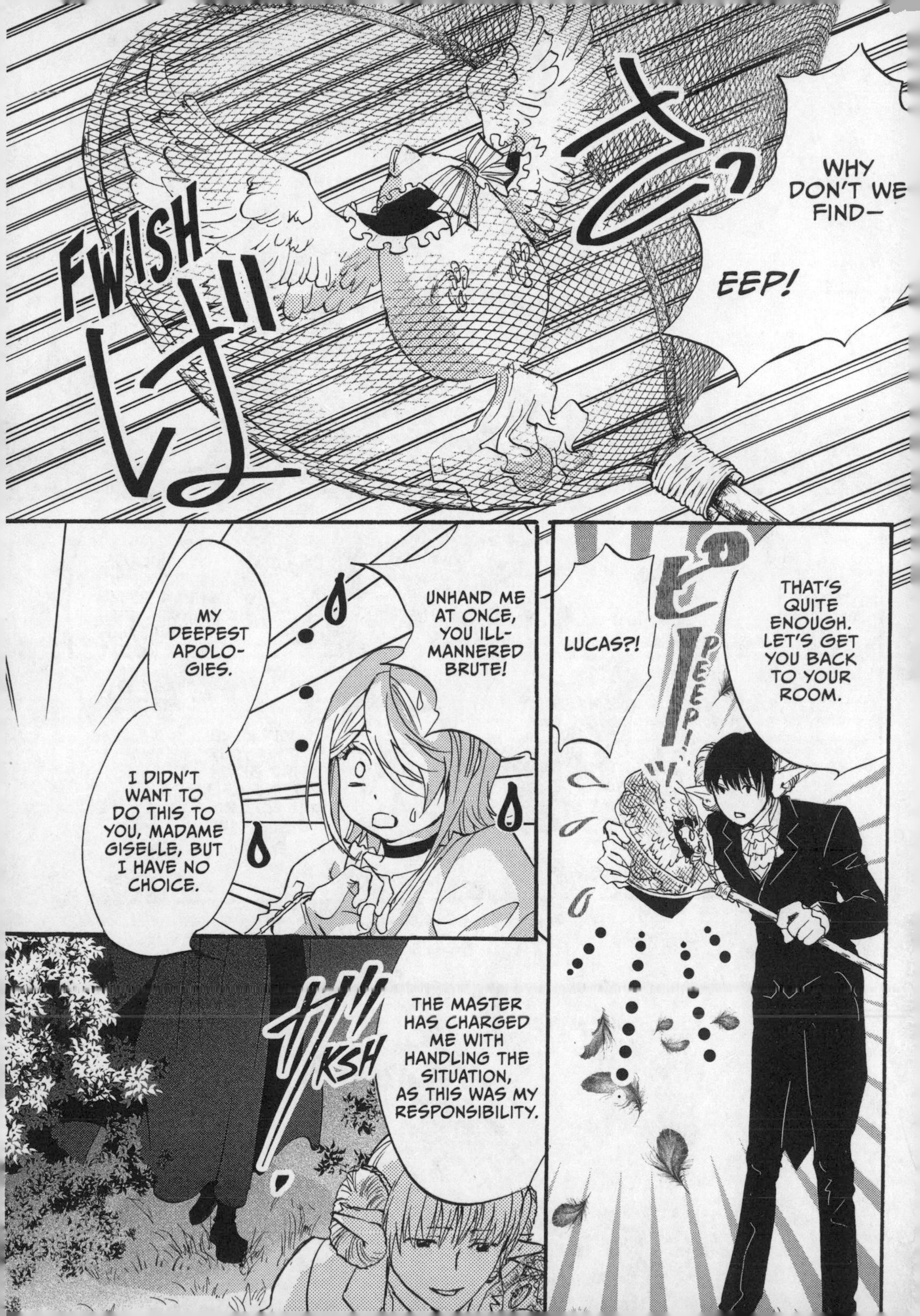
WHY DON'T WE FIND—
EEP!
FWISH
THAT'S QUITE ENOUGH. LET'S GET YOU BACK TO YOUR ROOM.
PEEEP!!
LUCAS?!
UNHAND ME AT ONCE, YOU ILL-MANNERED BRUTE!
MY DEEPEST APOLOGIES.
I DIDN'T WANT TO DO THIS TO YOU, MADAME GISELLE, BUT I HAVE NO CHOICE.
THE MASTER HAS CHARGED ME WITH HANDLING THE SITUATION, AS THIS WAS MY RESPONSIBILITY.
KSH

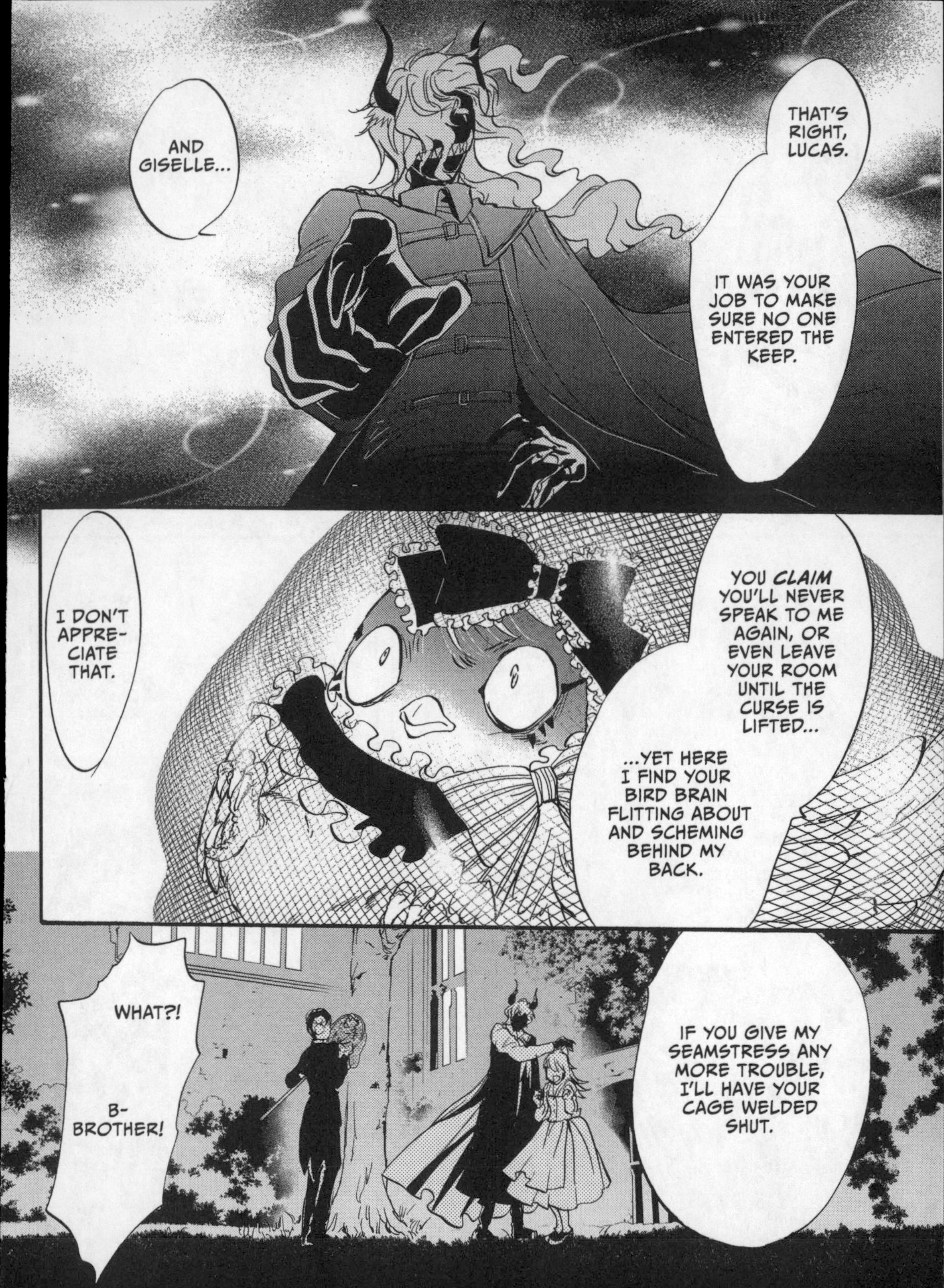
THAT'S RIGHT, LUCAS.
IT WAS YOUR JOB TO MAKE SURE NO ONE ENTERED THE KEEP.
AND GISELLE...
YOU *CLAIM* YOU'LL NEVER SPEAK TO ME AGAIN, OR EVEN LEAVE YOUR ROOM UNTIL THE CURSE IS LIFTED...
...YET HERE I FIND YOUR BIRD BRAIN FLITTING ABOUT AND SCHEMING BEHIND MY BACK.
I DON'T APPRECIATE THAT.
IF YOU GIVE MY SEAMSTRESS ANY MORE TROUBLE, I'LL HAVE YOUR CAGE WELDED SHUT.
WHAT?!
B-BROTHER!

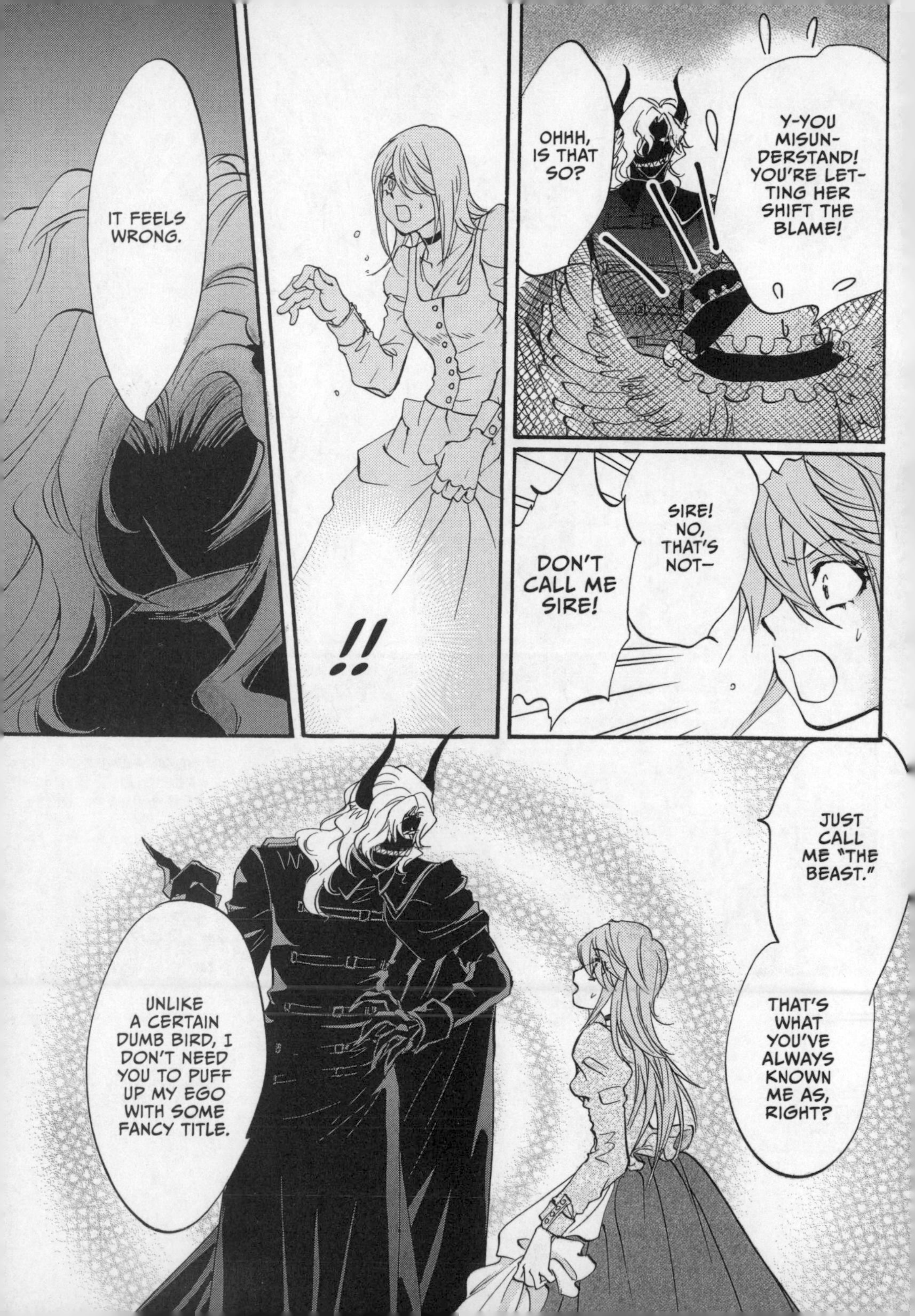
Y-YOU MISUNDERSTAND! YOU'RE LETTING HER SHIFT THE BLAME!
OHHH, IS THAT SO?
SIRE! NO, THAT'S NOT—
DON'T CALL ME SIRE!
!!
IT FEELS WRONG.
JUST CALL ME "THE BEAST."
THAT'S WHAT YOU'VE ALWAYS KNOWN ME AS, RIGHT?
UNLIKE A CERTAIN DUMB BIRD, I DON'T NEED YOU TO PUFF UP MY EGO WITH SOME FANCY TITLE.

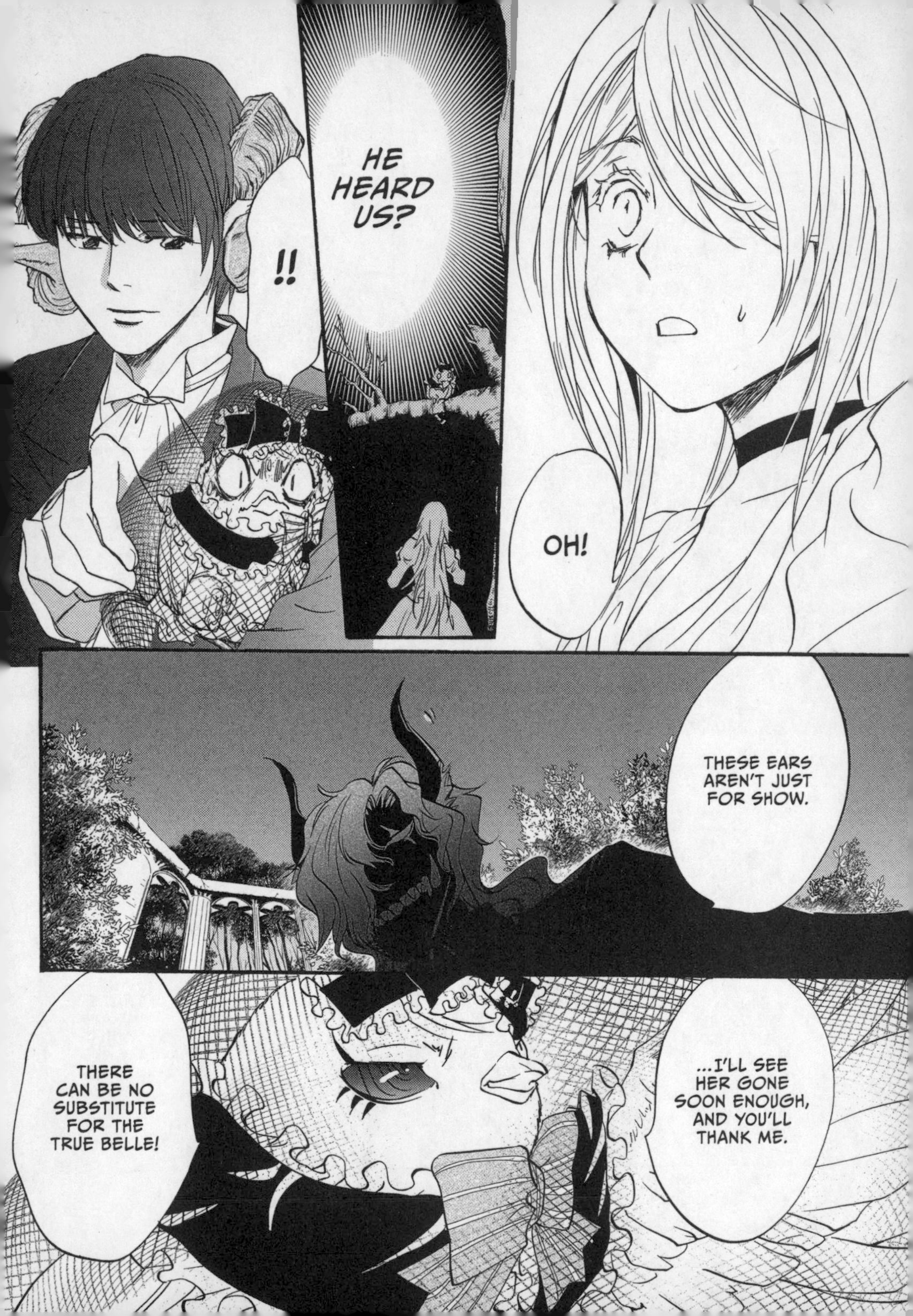
OH!
HE HEARD US?
!!
THESE EARS AREN'T JUST FOR SHOW.
...I'LL SEE HER GONE SOON ENOUGH, AND YOU'LL THANK ME.
THERE CAN BE NO SUBSTITUTE FOR THE TRUE BELLE!

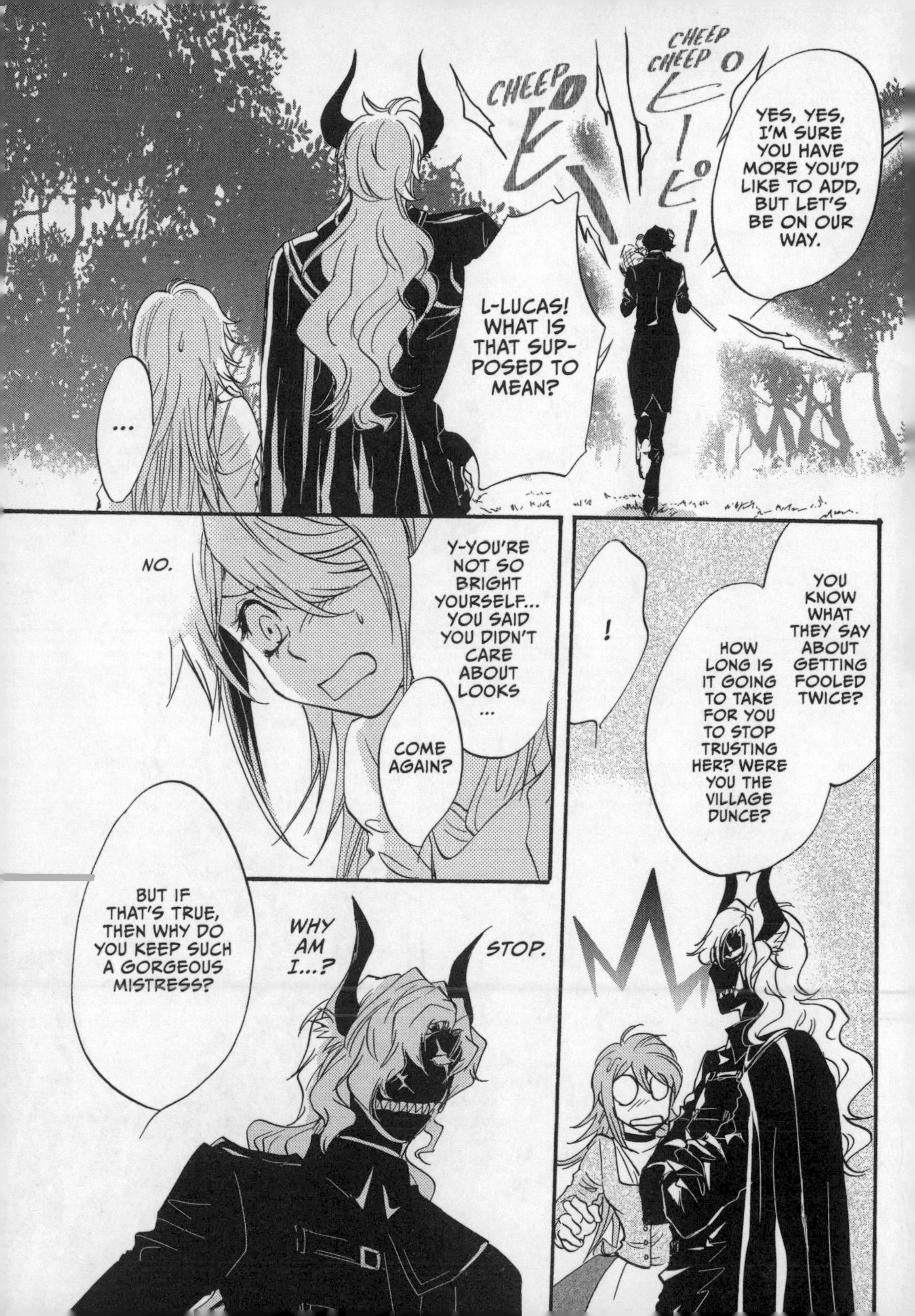
CHEEP CHEEP
CHEEP
YES, YES, I'M SURE YOU HAVE MORE YOU'D LIKE TO ADD, BUT LET'S BE ON OUR WAY.
L-LUCAS! WHAT IS THAT SUP-POSED TO MEAN?
...
YOU KNOW WHAT THEY SAY ABOUT GETTING FOOLED TWICE?
HOW LONG IS IT GOING TO TAKE FOR YOU TO STOP TRUSTING HER? WERE YOU THE VILLAGE DUNCE?
!
Y-YOU'RE NOT SO BRIGHT YOURSELF... YOU SAID YOU DIDN'T CARE ABOUT LOOKS ...
NO.
COME AGAIN?
BUT IF THAT'S TRUE, THEN WHY DO YOU KEEP SUCH A GORGEOUS MISTRESS?
WHY AM I...?
STOP.

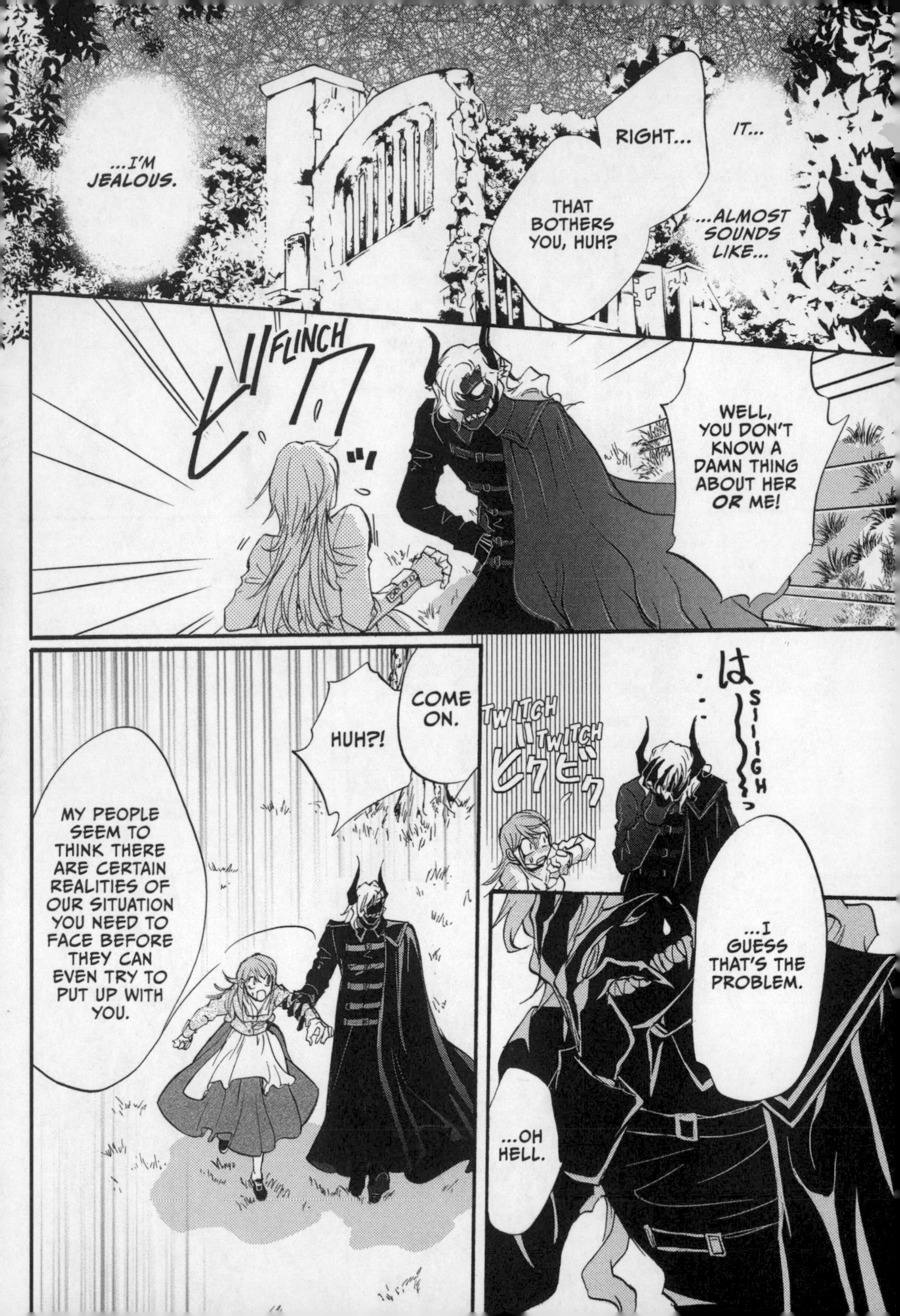
IT...
...ALMOST SOUNDS LIKE...
RIGHT... THAT BOTHERS YOU, HUH?
...I'M JEALOUS.
WELL, YOU DON'T KNOW A DAMN THING ABOUT HER OR ME!
FLINCH
SIIIGH
TWITCH TWITCH
...I GUESS THAT'S THE PROBLEM.
...OH HELL.
COME ON.
HUH?!
MY PEOPLE SEEM TO THINK THERE ARE CERTAIN REALITIES OF OUR SITUATION YOU NEED TO FACE BEFORE THEY CAN EVEN TRY TO PUT UP WITH YOU.

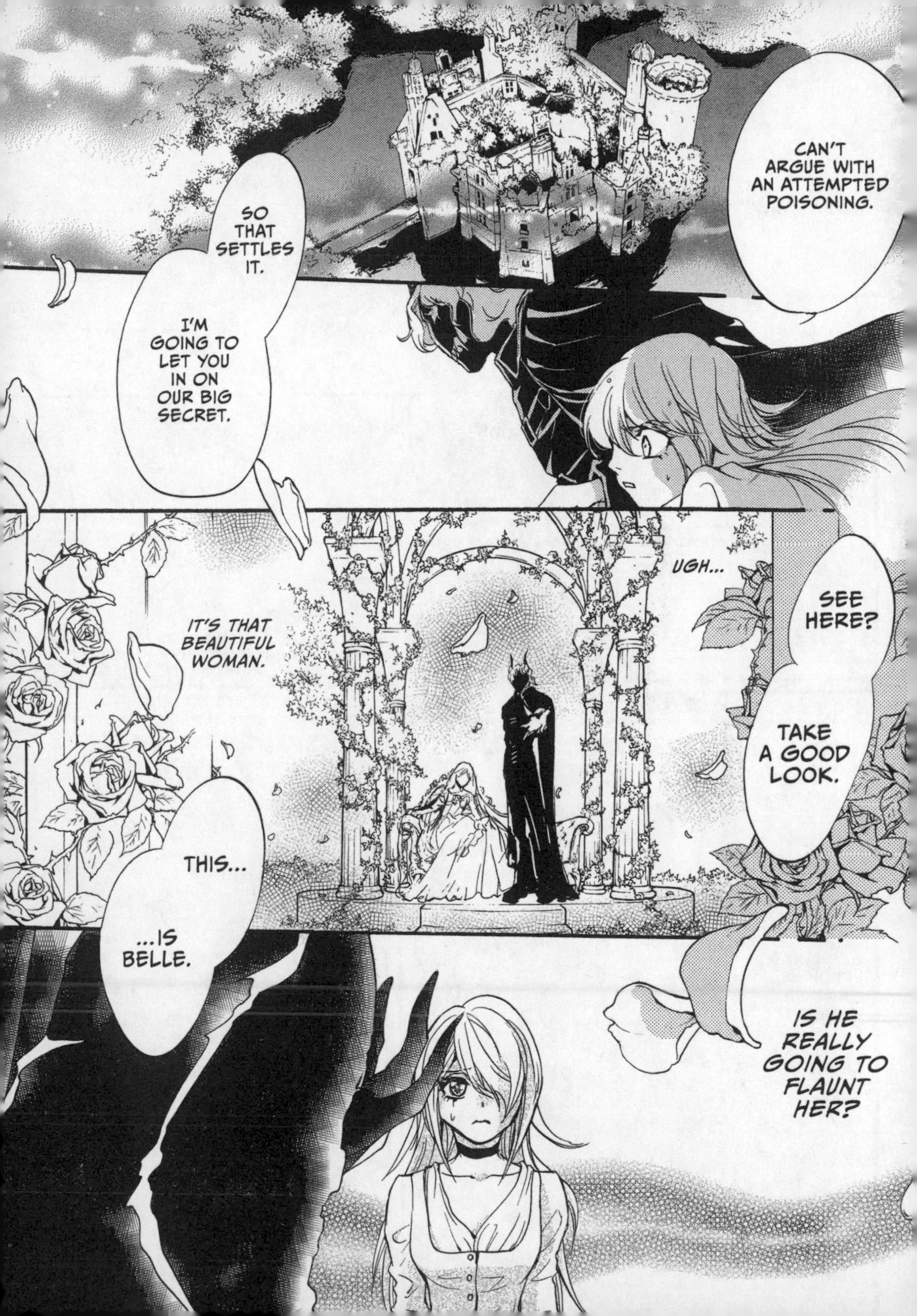
CAN'T ARGUE WITH AN ATTEMPTED POISONING.
SO THAT SETTLES IT.
I'M GOING TO LET YOU IN ON OUR BIG SECRET.
SEE HERE?
TAKE A GOOD LOOK.
UGH...
IT'S THAT BEAUTIFUL WOMAN.
THIS...
...IS BELLE.
IS HE REALLY GOING TO FLAUNT HER?

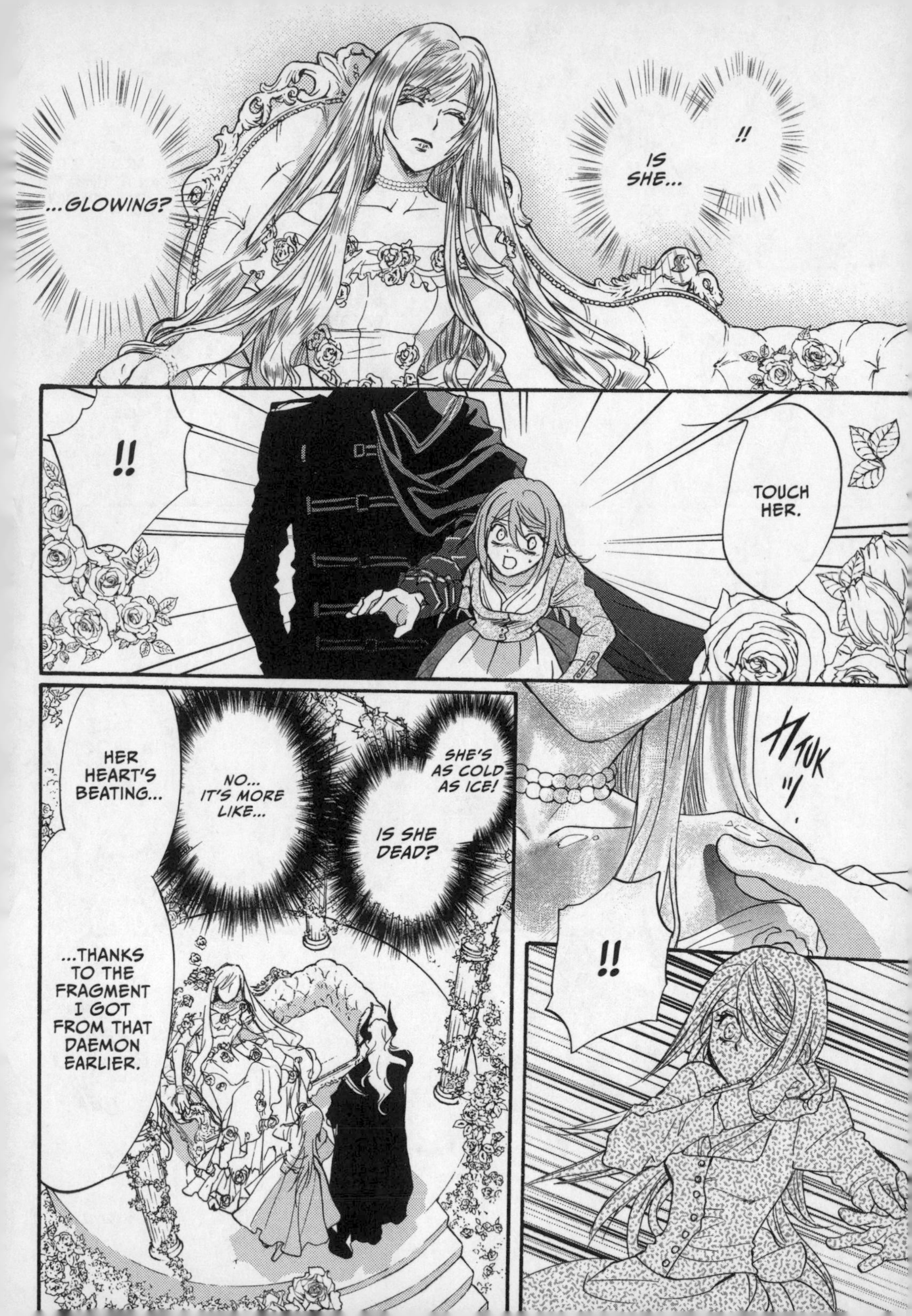
!!
IS SHE...
...GLOWING?
TOUCH HER.
!!
TUK
!!
SHE'S AS COLD AS ICE!
IS SHE DEAD?
NO... IT'S MORE LIKE...
HER HEART'S BEATING...
...THANKS TO THE FRAGMENT I GOT FROM THAT DAEMON EARLIER.

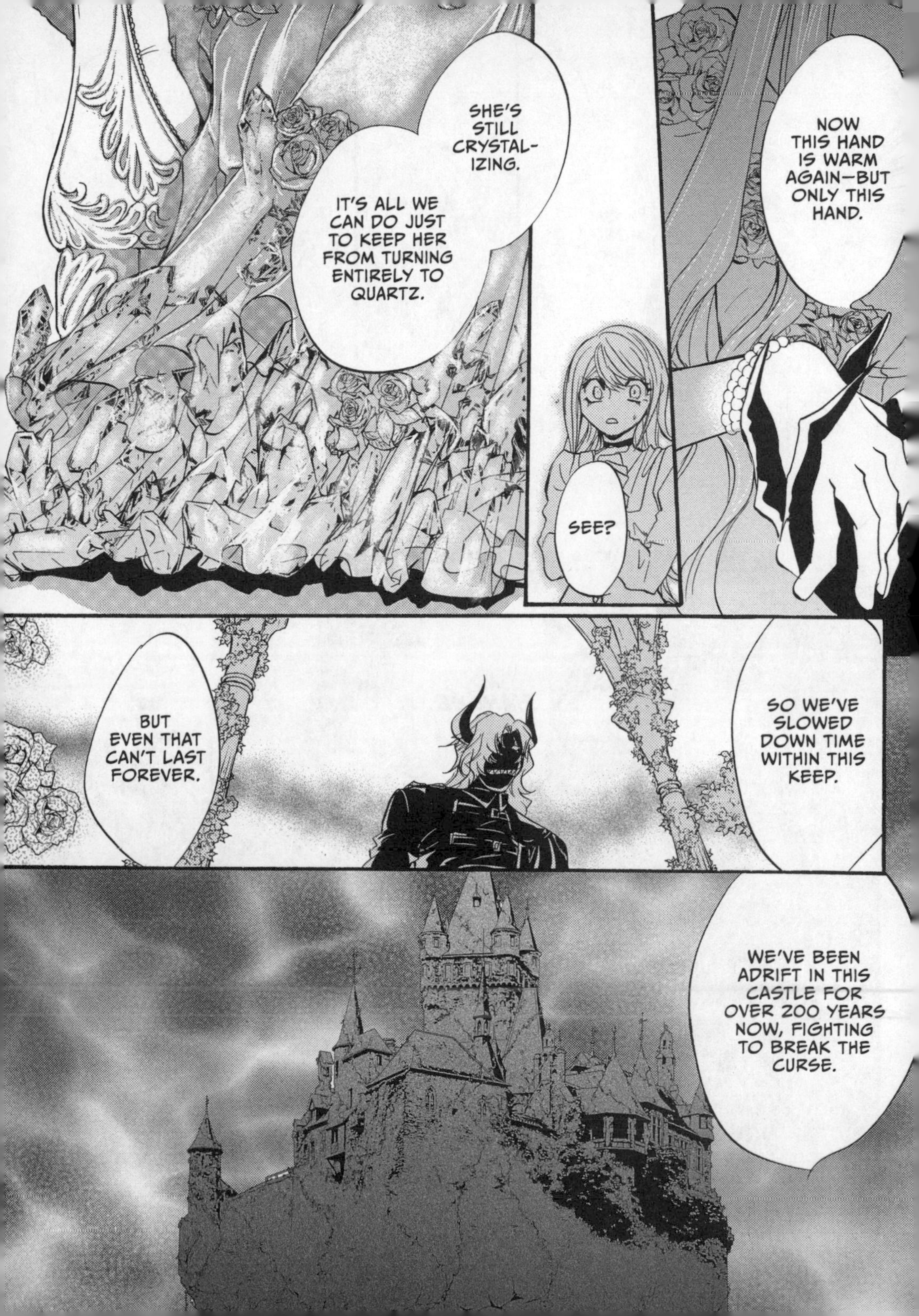
NOW THIS HAND IS WARM AGAIN—BUT ONLY THIS HAND.
SEE?
SHE'S STILL CRYSTAL-IZING.
IT'S ALL WE CAN DO JUST TO KEEP HER FROM TURNING ENTIRELY TO QUARTZ.
SO WE'VE SLOWED DOWN TIME WITHIN THIS KEEP.
BUT EVEN THAT CAN'T LAST FOREVER.
WE'VE BEEN ADRIFT IN THIS CASTLE FOR OVER 200 YEARS NOW, FIGHTING TO BREAK THE CURSE.

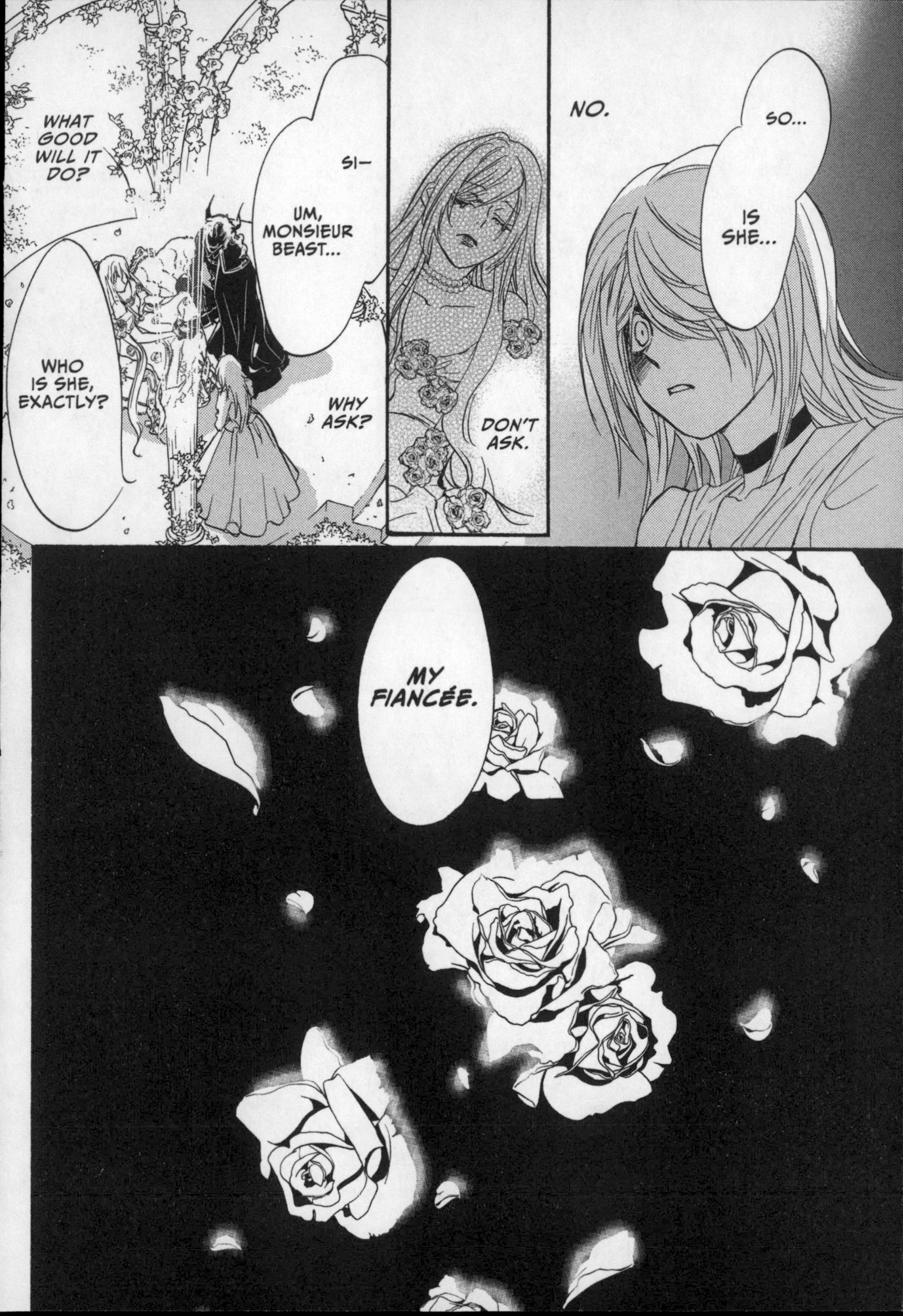
SO...
IS SHE...
NO.
DON'T ASK.
SI—
UM, MONSIEUR BEAST...
WHO IS SHE, EXACTLY?
WHY ASK?
WHAT GOOD WILL IT DO?
MY FIANCÉE.

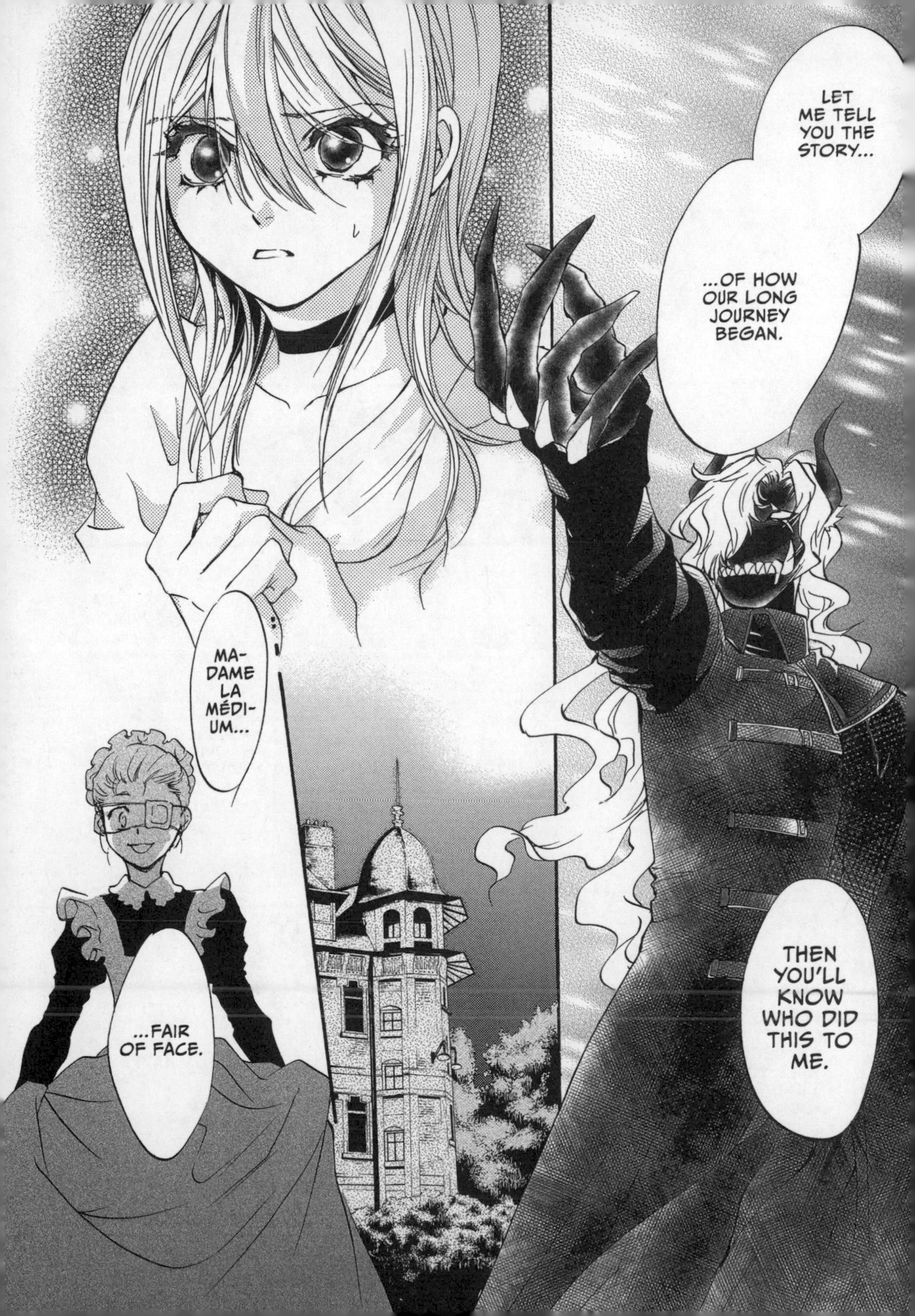
LET ME TELL YOU THE STORY...
...OF HOW OUR LONG JOURNEY BEGAN.
THEN YOU'LL KNOW WHO DID THIS TO ME.
MA-DAME LA MÉDI-UM...
...FAIR OF FACE.

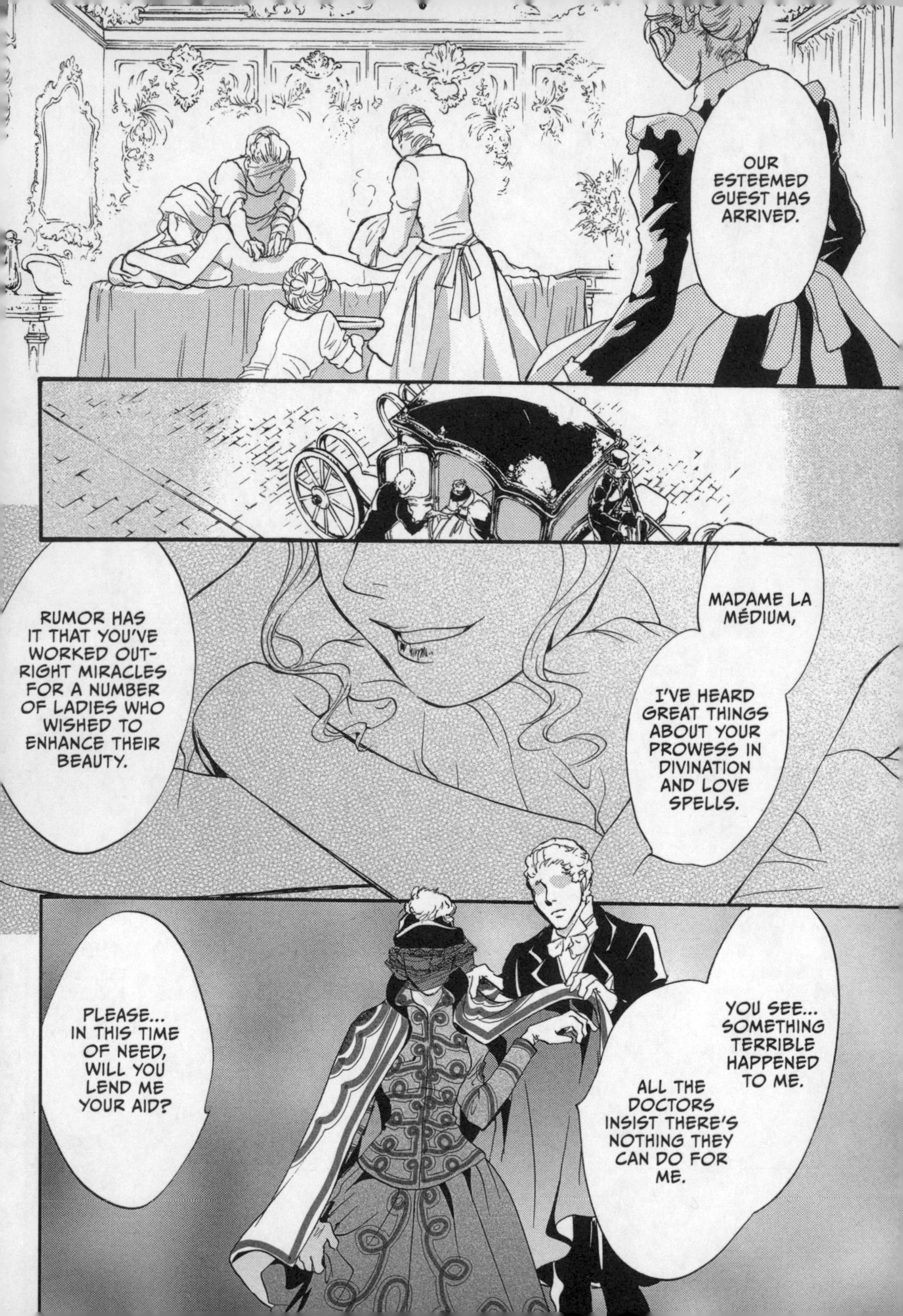
OUR ESTEEMED GUEST HAS ARRIVED.
MADAME LA MÉDIUM,
I'VE HEARD GREAT THINGS ABOUT YOUR PROWESS IN DIVINATION AND LOVE SPELLS.
RUMOR HAS IT THAT YOU'VE WORKED OUT-RIGHT MIRACLES FOR A NUMBER OF LADIES WHO WISHED TO ENHANCE THEIR BEAUTY.
YOU SEE... SOMETHING TERRIBLE HAPPENED TO ME.
ALL THE DOCTORS INSIST THERE'S NOTHING THEY CAN DO FOR ME.
PLEASE... IN THIS TIME OF NEED, WILL YOU LEND ME YOUR AID?

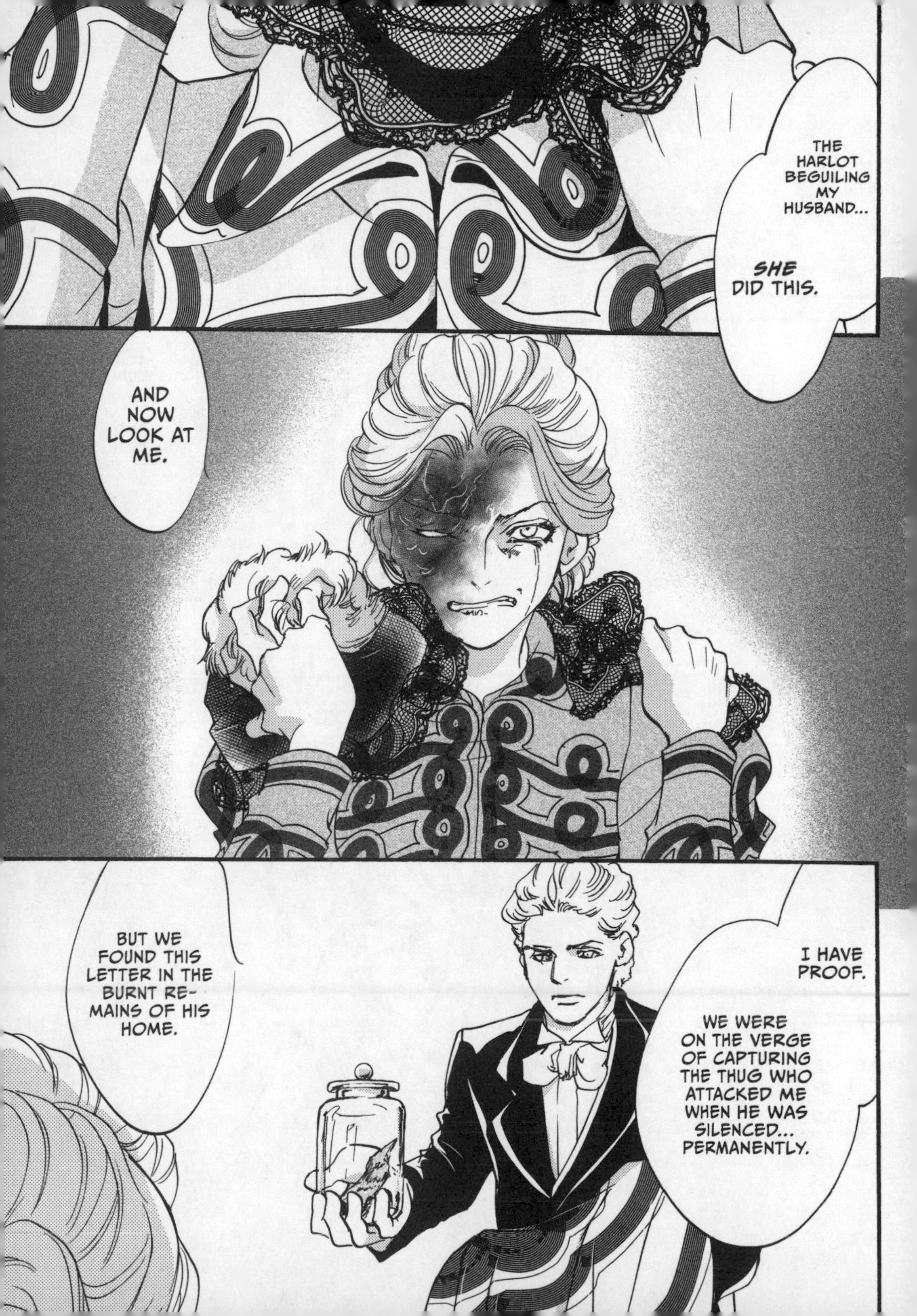
THE HARLOT BEGUILING MY HUSBAND...
SHE DID THIS.
AND NOW LOOK AT ME.
I HAVE PROOF.
WE WERE ON THE VERGE OF CAPTURING THE THUG WHO ATTACKED ME WHEN HE WAS SILENCED... PERMANENTLY.
BUT WE FOUND THIS LETTER IN THE BURNT RE-MAINS OF HIS HOME.

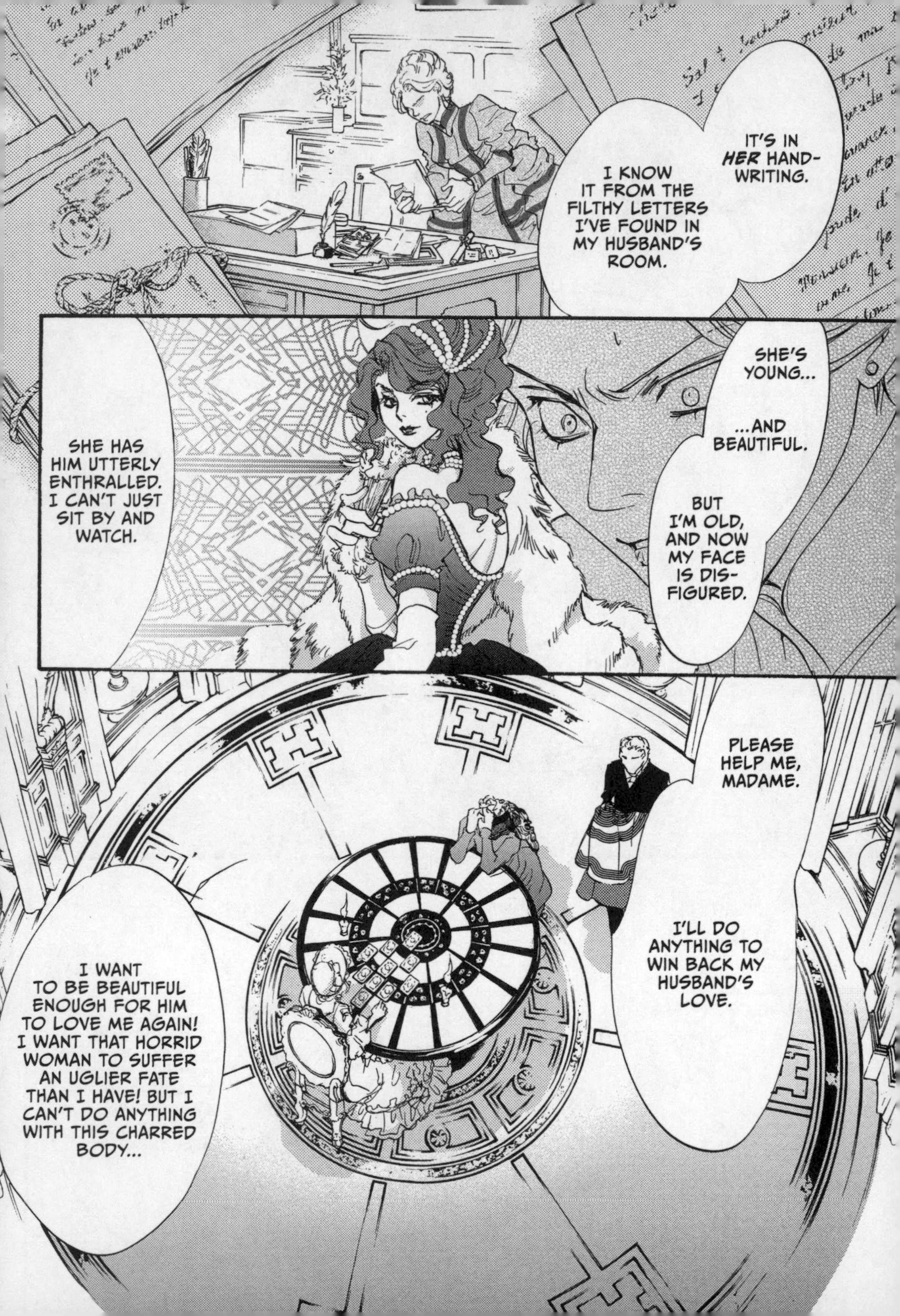
IT'S IN HER HAND-WRITING.
I KNOW IT FROM THE FILTHY LETTERS I'VE FOUND IN MY HUSBAND'S ROOM.
SHE'S YOUNG...
...AND BEAUTIFUL.
BUT I'M OLD, AND NOW MY FACE IS DIS-FIGURED.
SHE HAS HIM UTTERLY ENTHRALLED. I CAN'T JUST SIT BY AND WATCH.
PLEASE HELP ME, MADAME.
I'LL DO ANYTHING TO WIN BACK MY HUSBAND'S LOVE.
I WANT TO BE BEAUTIFUL ENOUGH FOR HIM TO LOVE ME AGAIN! I WANT THAT HORRID WOMAN TO SUFFER AN UGLIER FATE THAN I HAVE! BUT I CAN'T DO ANYTHING WITH THIS CHARRED BODY...

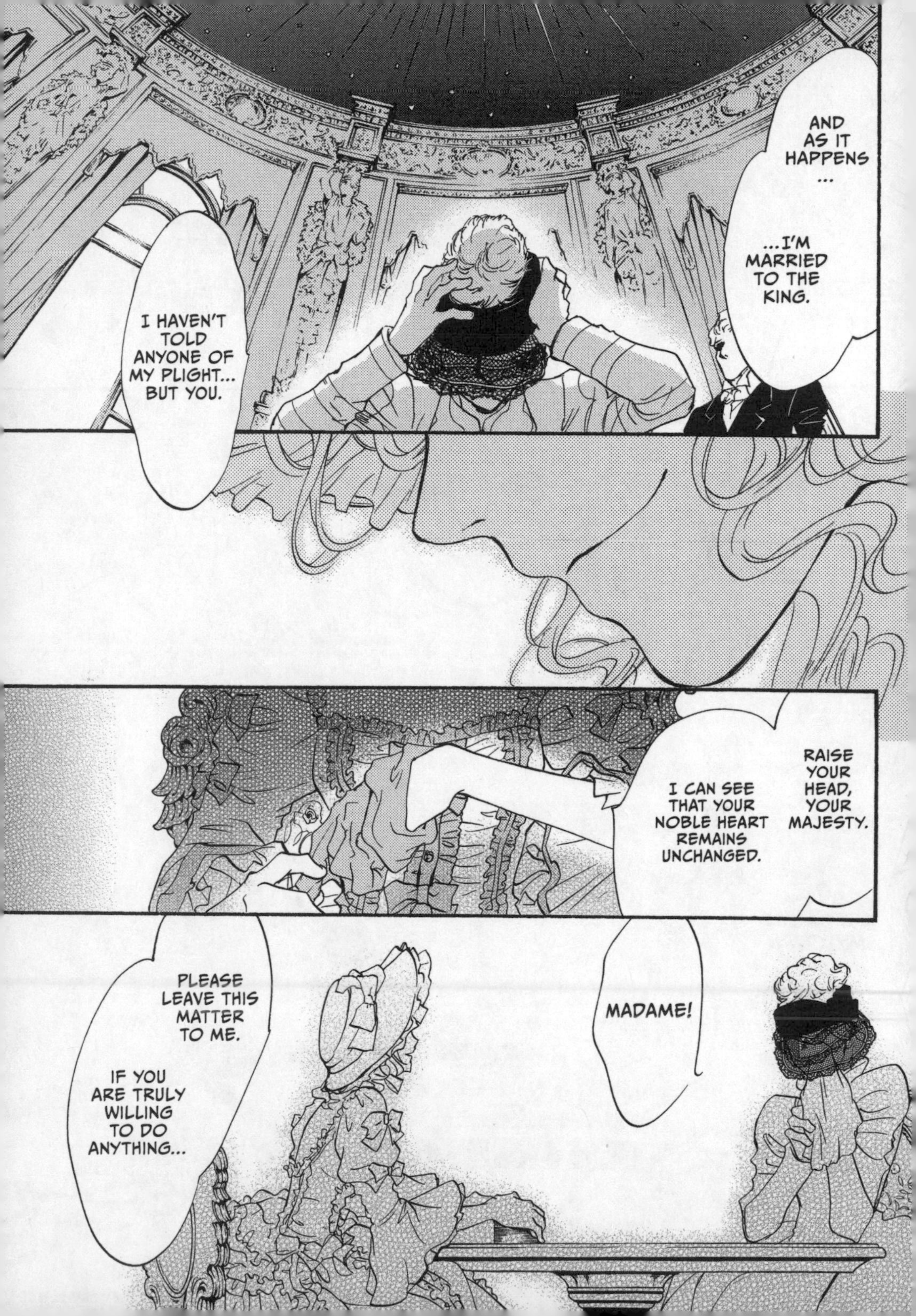
AND AS IT HAPPENS...
...I'M MARRIED TO THE KING.
I HAVEN'T TOLD ANYONE OF MY PLIGHT... BUT YOU.
RAISE YOUR HEAD, YOUR MAJESTY.
I CAN SEE THAT YOUR NOBLE HEART REMAINS UNCHANGED.
MADAME!
PLEASE LEAVE THIS MATTER TO ME.
IF YOU ARE TRULY WILLING TO DO ANYTHING...

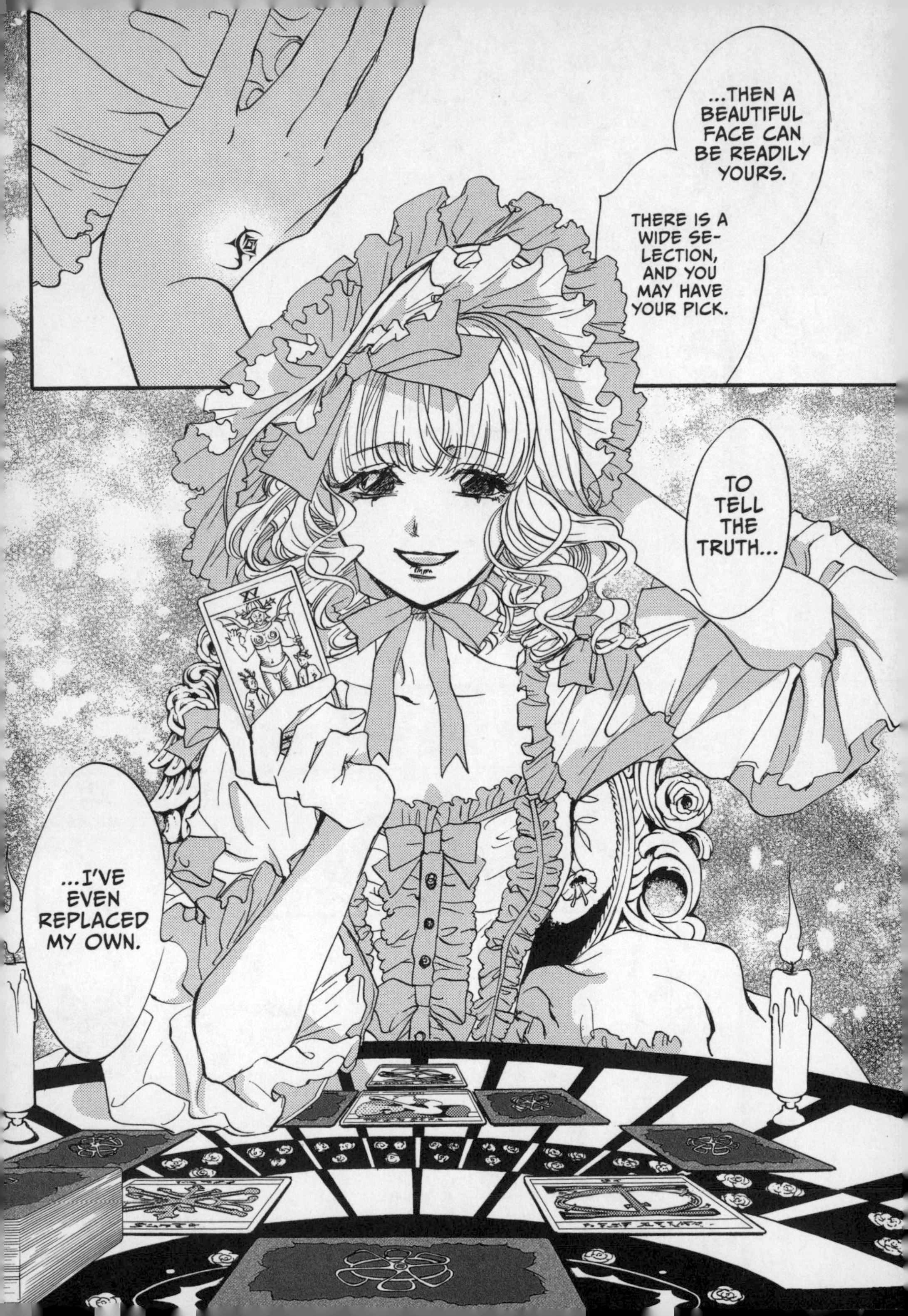
...THEN A BEAUTIFUL FACE CAN BE READILY YOURS.
THERE IS A WIDE SE-LECTION, AND YOU MAY HAVE YOUR PICK.
TO TELL THE TRUTH...
...I'VE EVEN REPLACED MY OWN.

LA BELLE ET LA BÊTE
DU PARADIS PERDU

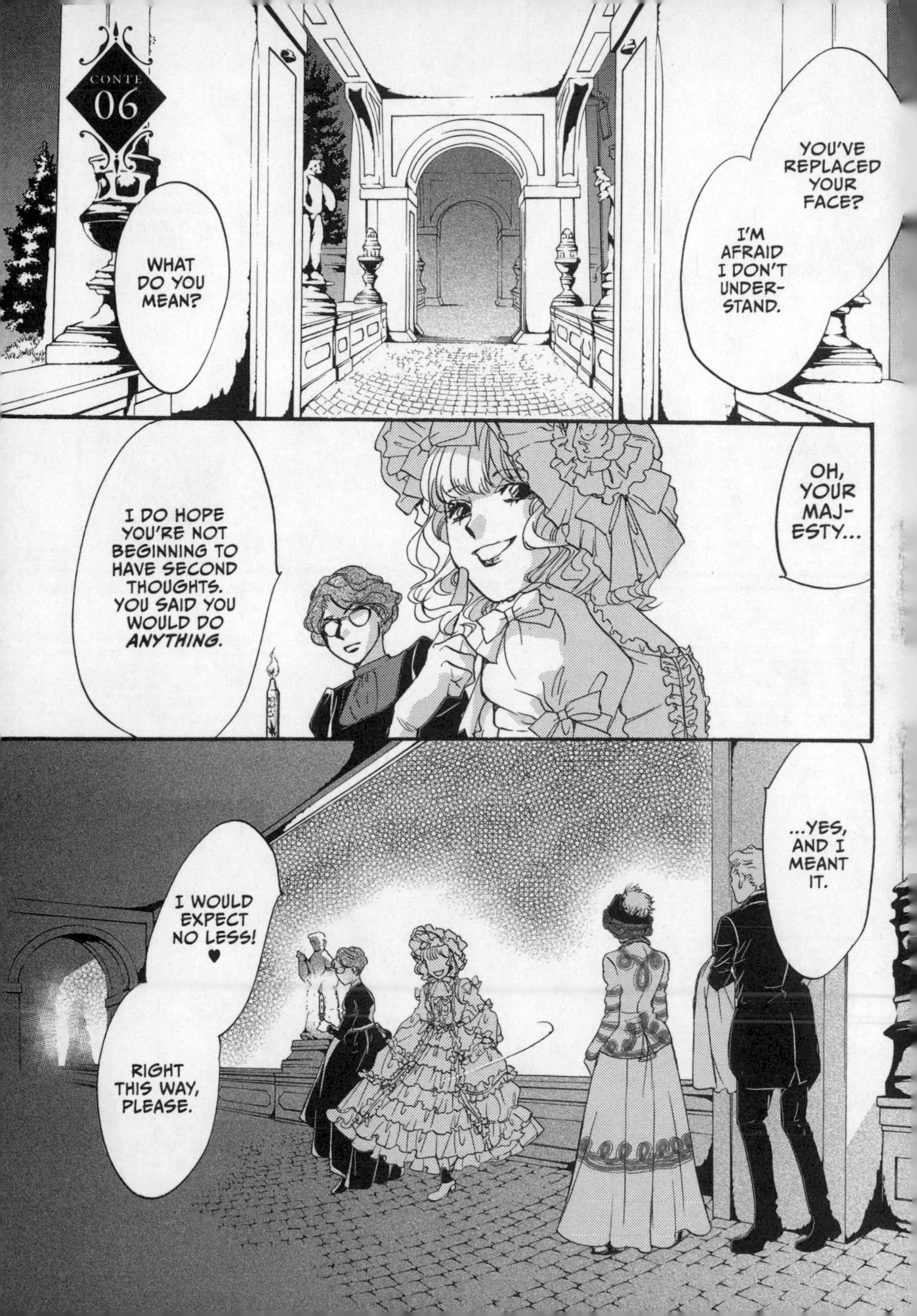
CONTE 06
YOU'VE REPLACED YOUR FACE?
I'M AFRAID I DON'T UNDER-STAND.
WHAT DO YOU MEAN?
OH, YOUR MAJ-ESTY...
I DO HOPE YOU'RE NOT BEGINNING TO HAVE SECOND THOUGHTS. YOU SAID YOU WOULD DO *ANYTHING*.
...YES, AND I MEANT IT.
I WOULD EXPECT NO LESS! ♥
RIGHT THIS WAY, PLEASE.

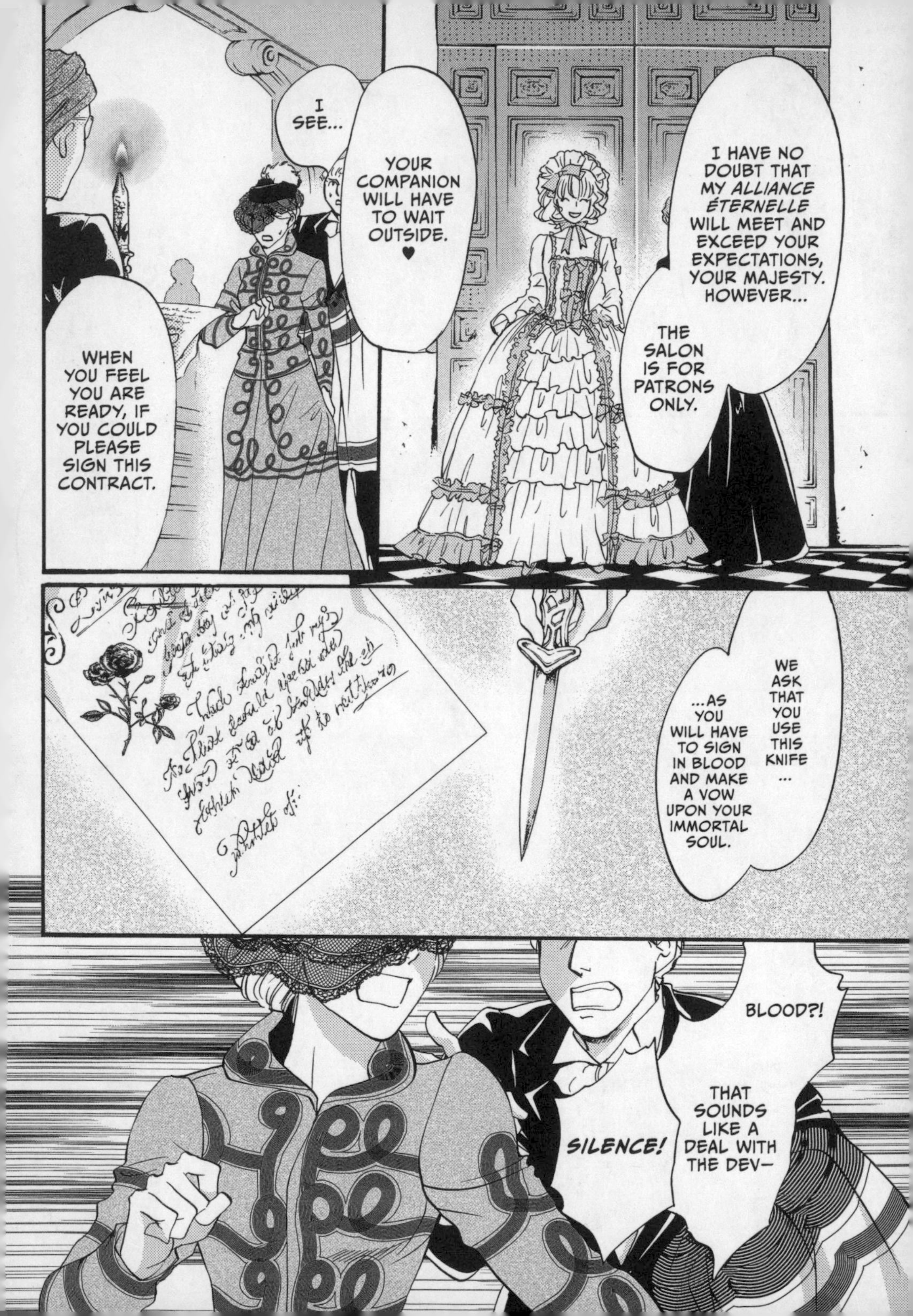
I HAVE NO DOUBT THAT MY *ALLIANCE ÉTERNELLE* WILL MEET AND EXCEED YOUR EXPECTATIONS, YOUR MAJESTY. HOWEVER...
THE SALON IS FOR PATRONS ONLY.
YOUR COMPANION WILL HAVE TO WAIT OUTSIDE. ♥
I SEE...
WHEN YOU FEEL YOU ARE READY, IF YOU COULD PLEASE SIGN THIS CONTRACT.
WE ASK THAT YOU USE THIS KNIFE ...
...AS YOU WILL HAVE TO SIGN IN BLOOD AND MAKE A VOW UPON YOUR IMMORTAL SOUL.
BLOOD?!
THAT SOUNDS LIKE A DEAL WITH THE DEV—
SILENCE!

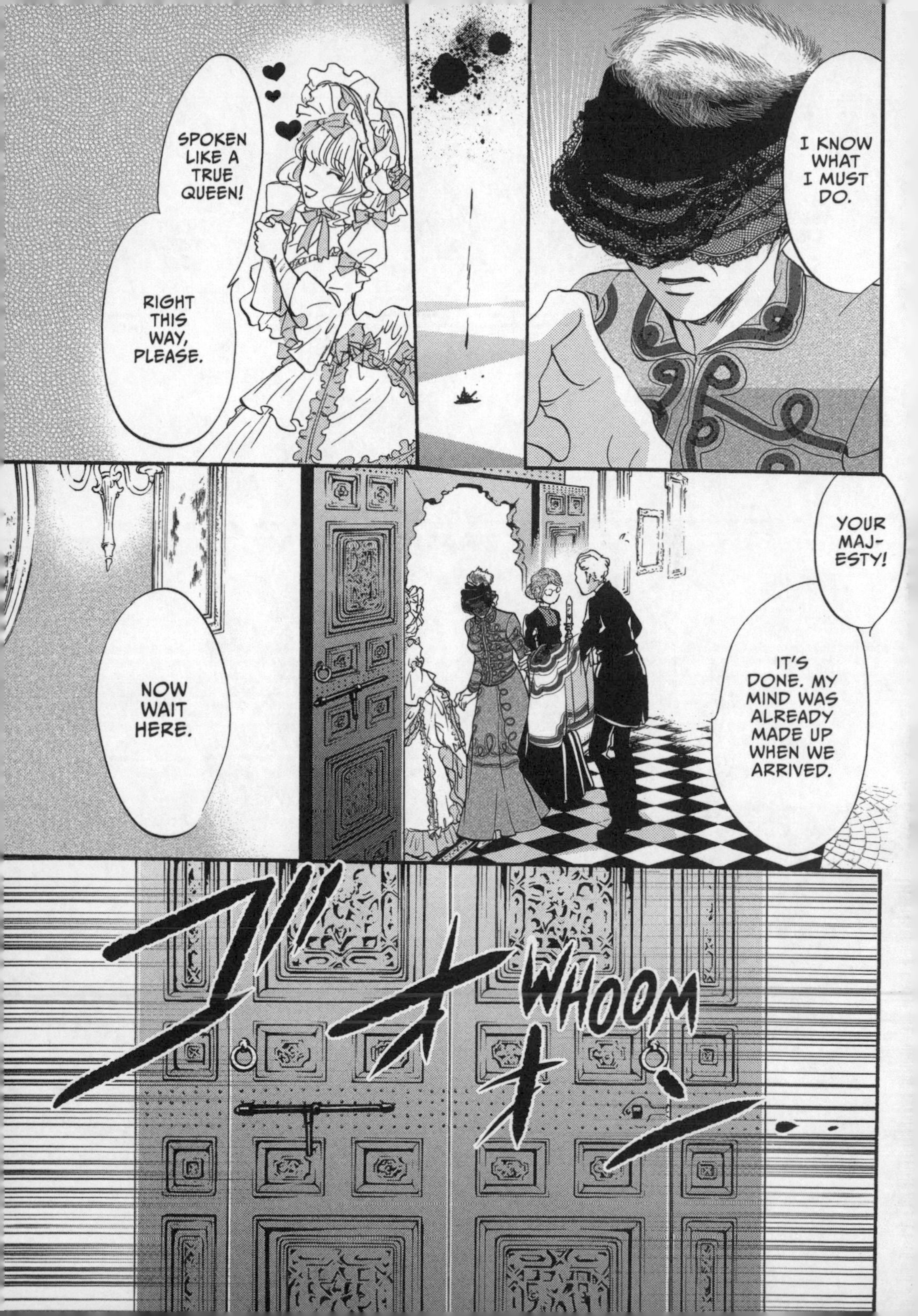
I KNOW WHAT I MUST DO.
SPOKEN LIKE A TRUE QUEEN!
RIGHT THIS WAY, PLEASE.
YOUR MAJ-ESTY!
IT'S DONE. MY MIND WAS ALREADY MADE UP WHEN WE ARRIVED.
NOW WAIT HERE.
WHOOM

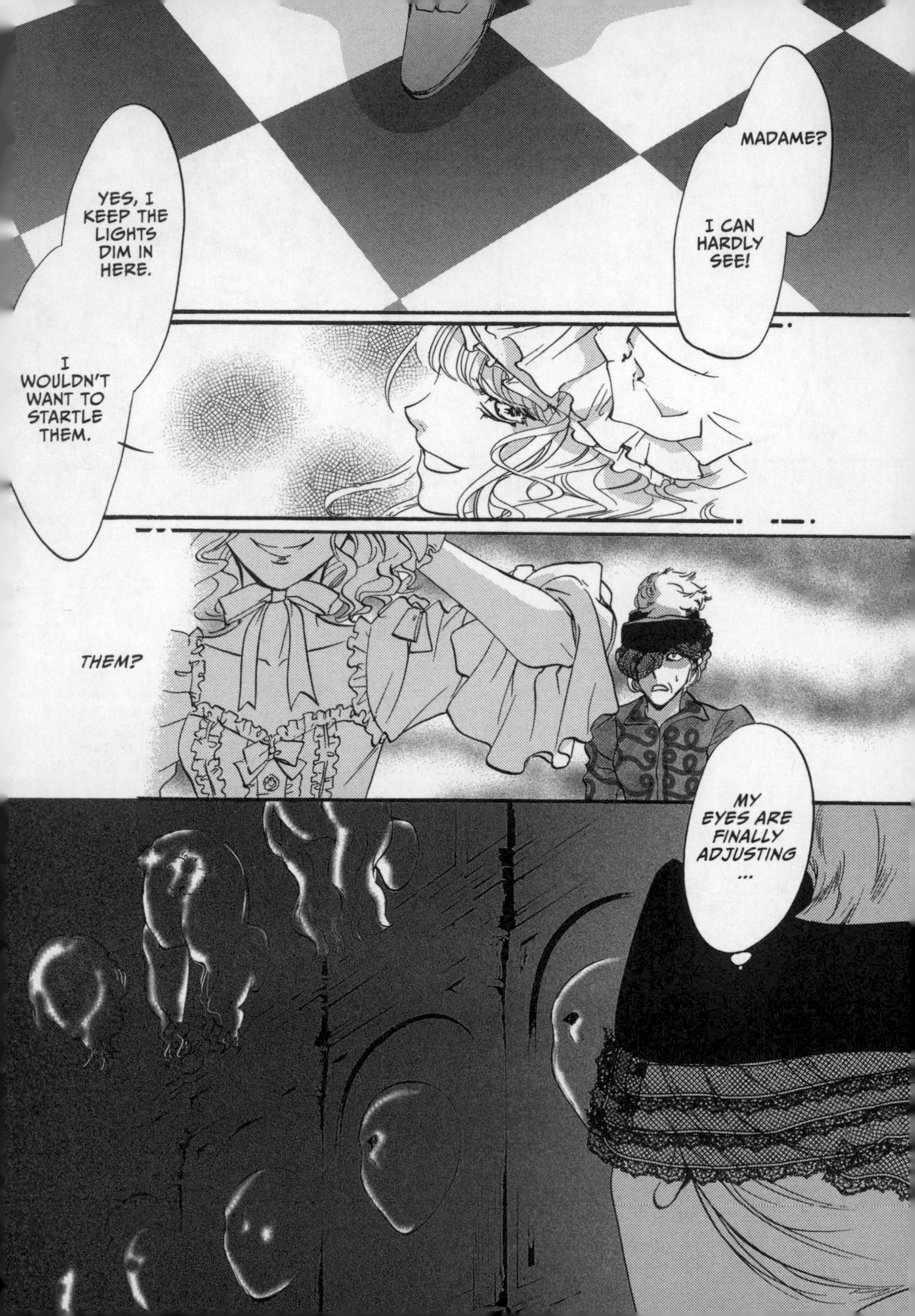
MADAME?
I CAN HARDLY SEE!
YES, I KEEP THE LIGHTS DIM IN HERE.
I WOULDN'T WANT TO STARTLE THEM.
THEM?
MY EYES ARE FINALLY ADJUSTING ...

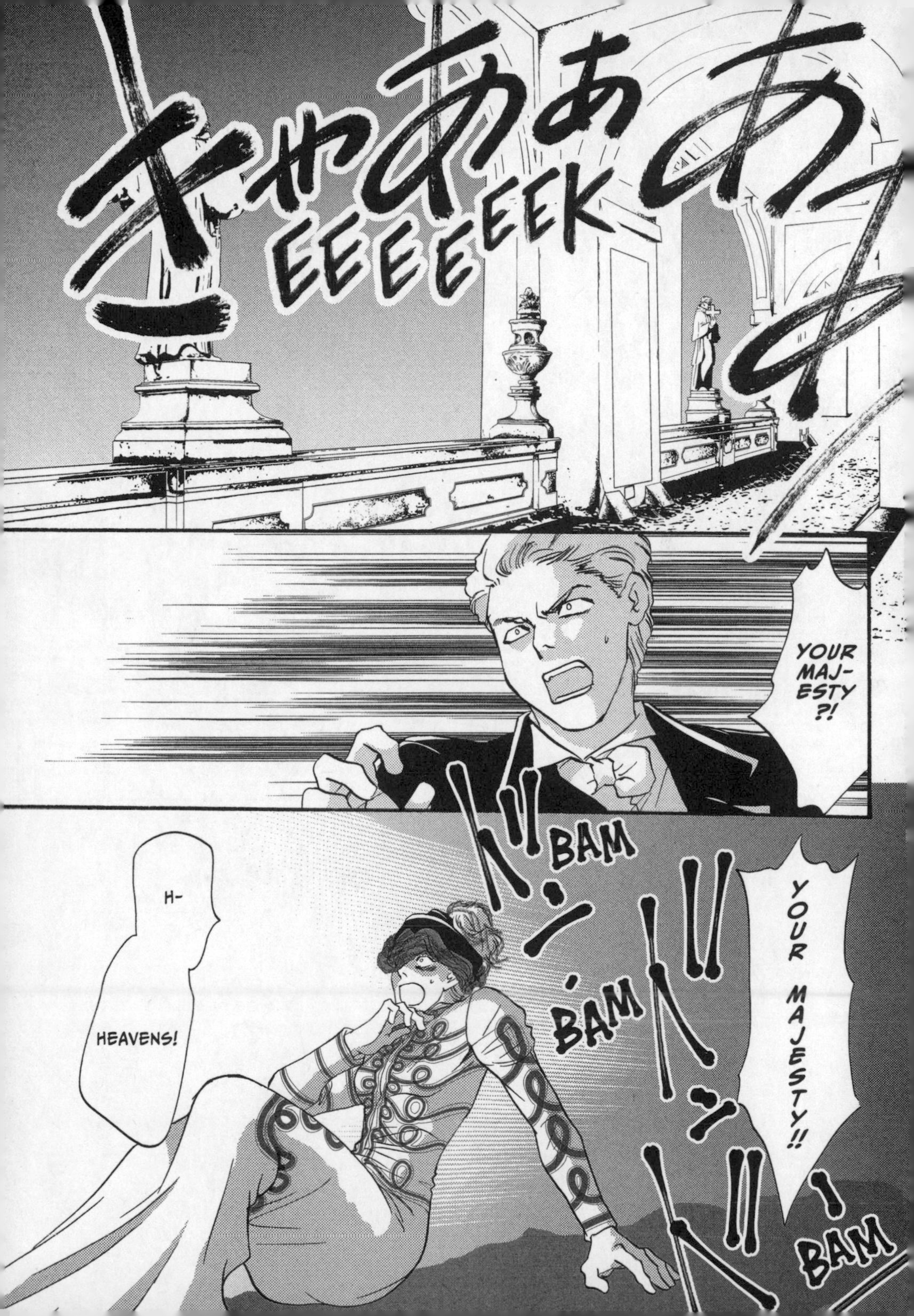

EEEEEEK
YOUR MAJ-ESTY?!
YOUR MAJESTY!!
BAM
BAM
BAM
H-
HEAVENS!

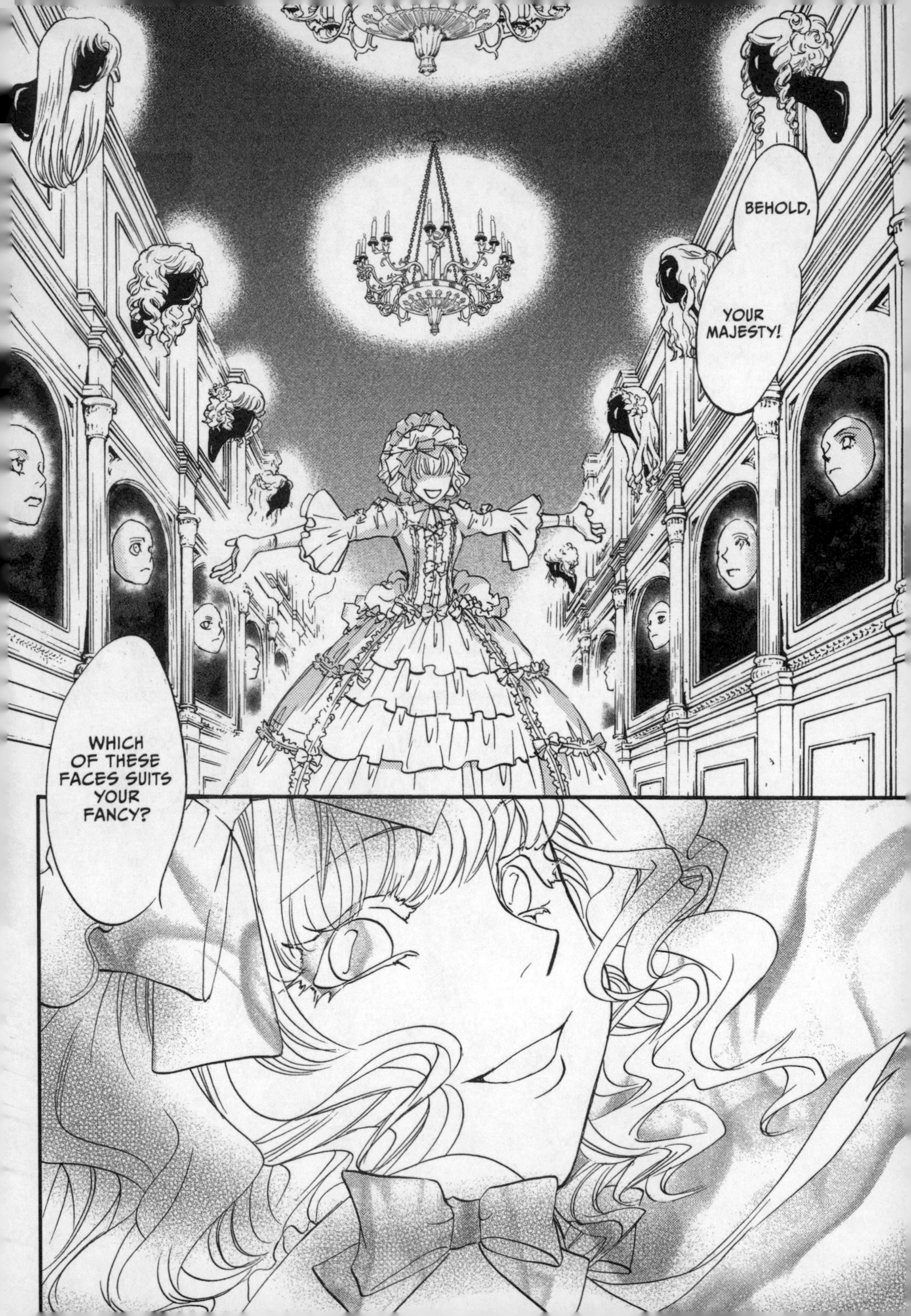
BEHOLD,
YOUR MAJESTY!
WHICH OF THESE FACES SUITS YOUR FANCY?

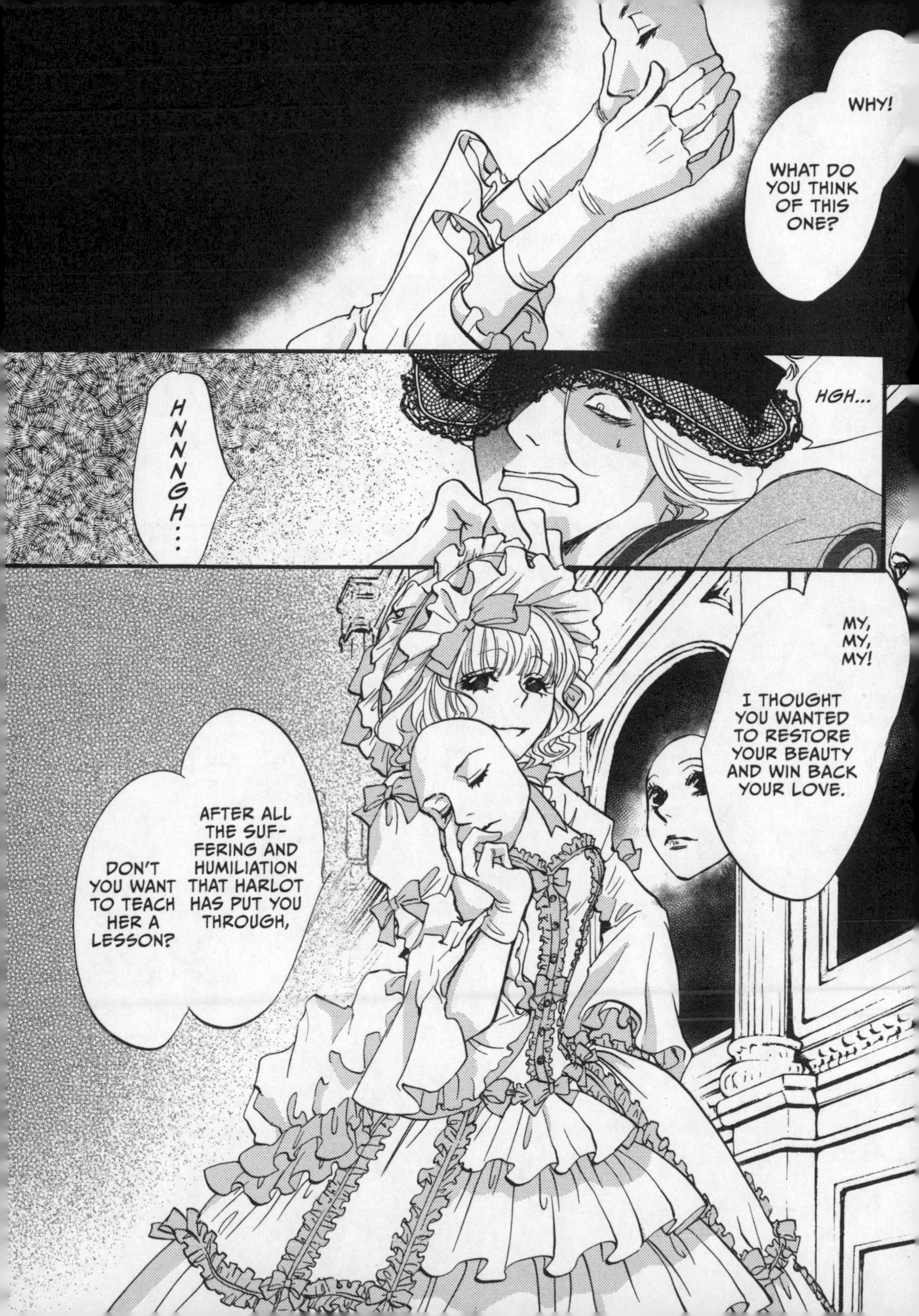
WHY!
WHAT DO YOU THINK OF THIS ONE?
HGH...
HNNNGH...
MY, MY, MY!
I THOUGHT YOU WANTED TO RESTORE YOUR BEAUTY AND WIN BACK YOUR LOVE.
AFTER ALL THE SUF-FERING AND HUMILIATION THAT HARLOT HAS PUT YOU THROUGH,
DON'T YOU WANT TO TEACH HER A LESSON?

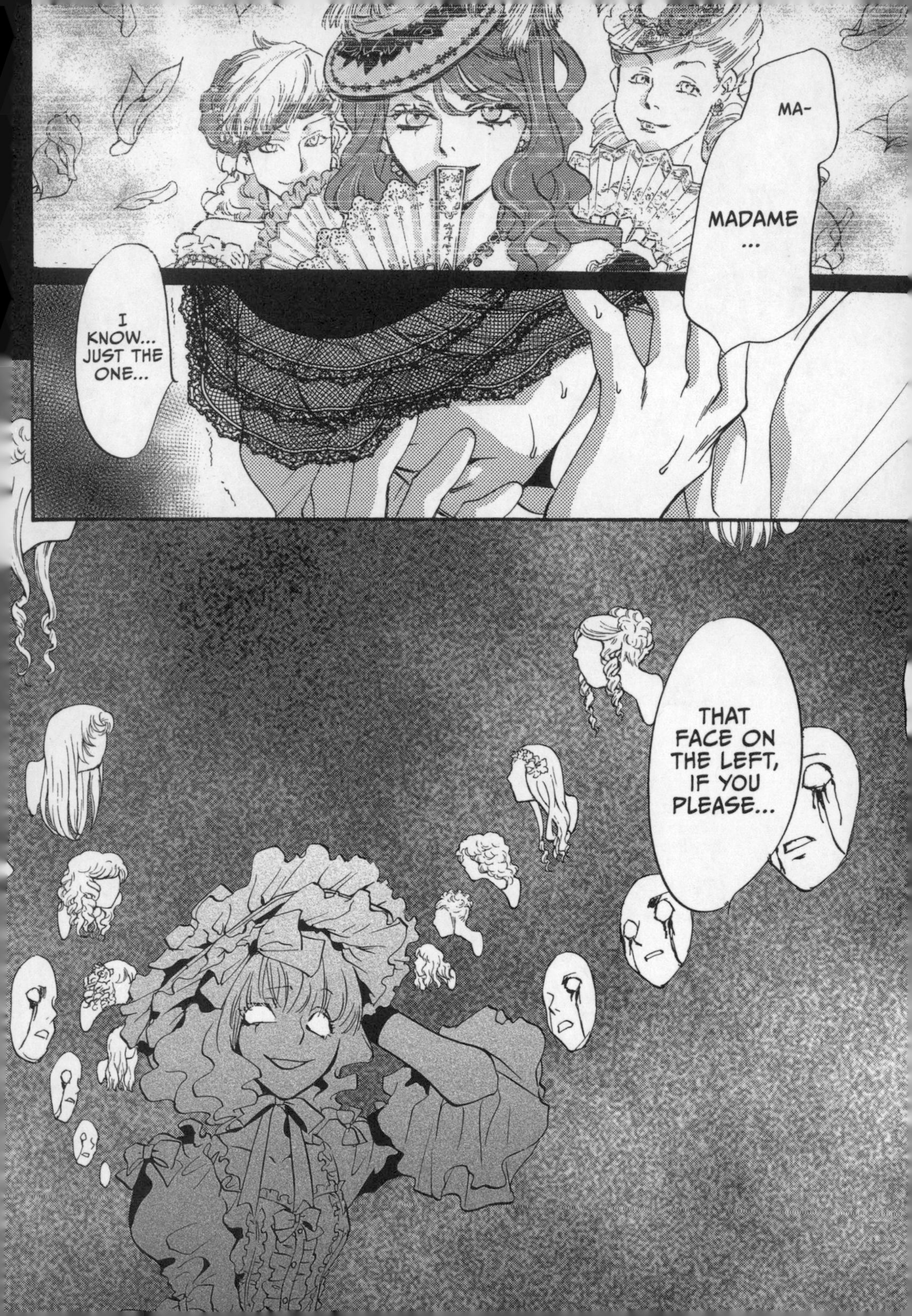
MA-
MADAME ...
I KNOW... JUST THE ONE...
THAT FACE ON THE LEFT, IF YOU PLEASE...

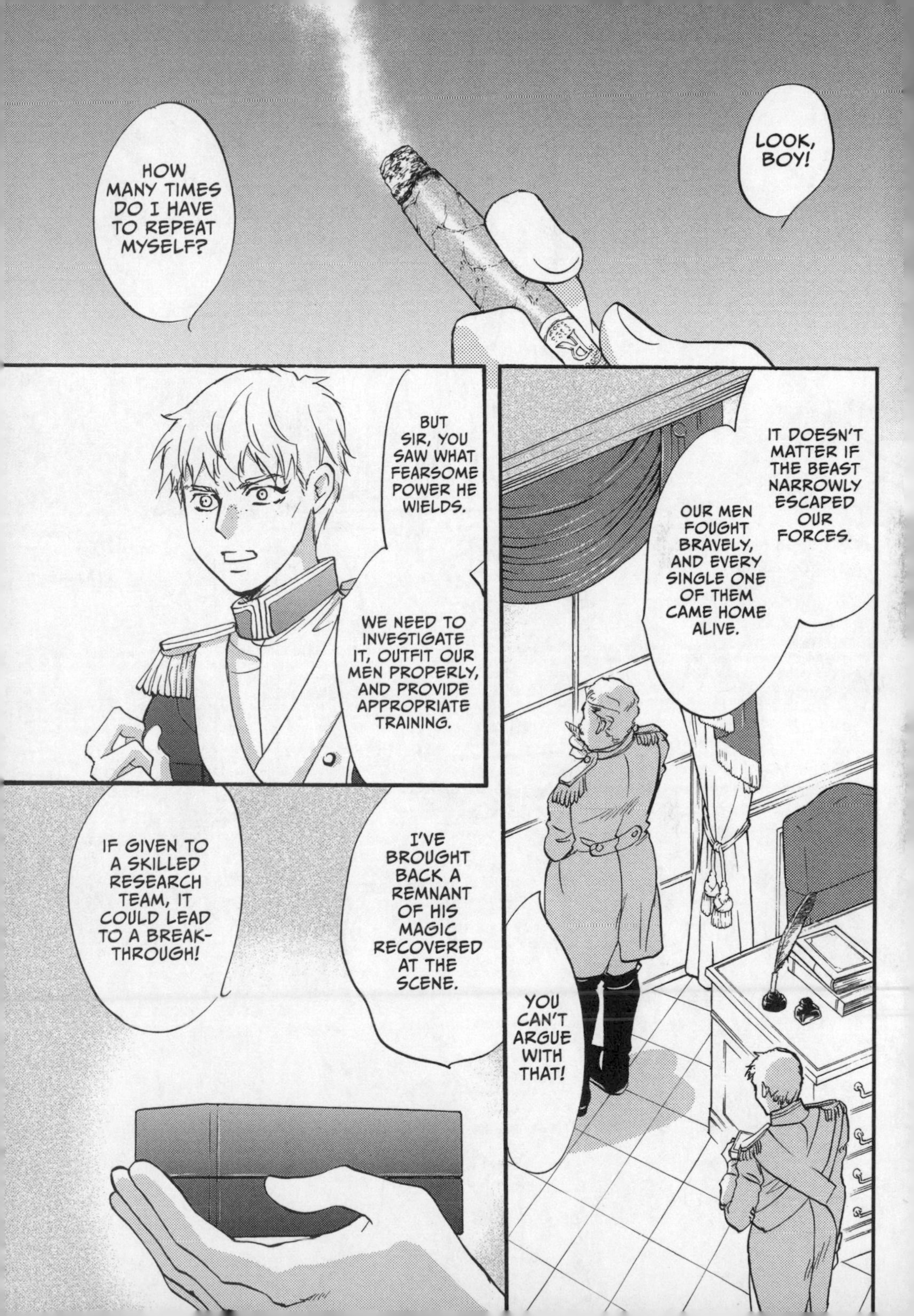
LOOK, BOY!
HOW MANY TIMES DO I HAVE TO REPEAT MYSELF?
IT DOESN'T MATTER IF THE BEAST NARROWLY ESCAPED OUR FORCES.
OUR MEN FOUGHT BRAVELY, AND EVERY SINGLE ONE OF THEM CAME HOME ALIVE.
YOU CAN'T ARGUE WITH THAT!
BUT SIR, YOU SAW WHAT FEARSOME POWER HE WIELDS.
WE NEED TO INVESTIGATE IT, OUTFIT OUR MEN PROPERLY, AND PROVIDE APPROPRIATE TRAINING.
I'VE BROUGHT BACK A REMNANT OF HIS MAGIC RECOVERED AT THE SCENE.
IF GIVEN TO A SKILLED RESEARCH TEAM, IT COULD LEAD TO A BREAK-THROUGH!

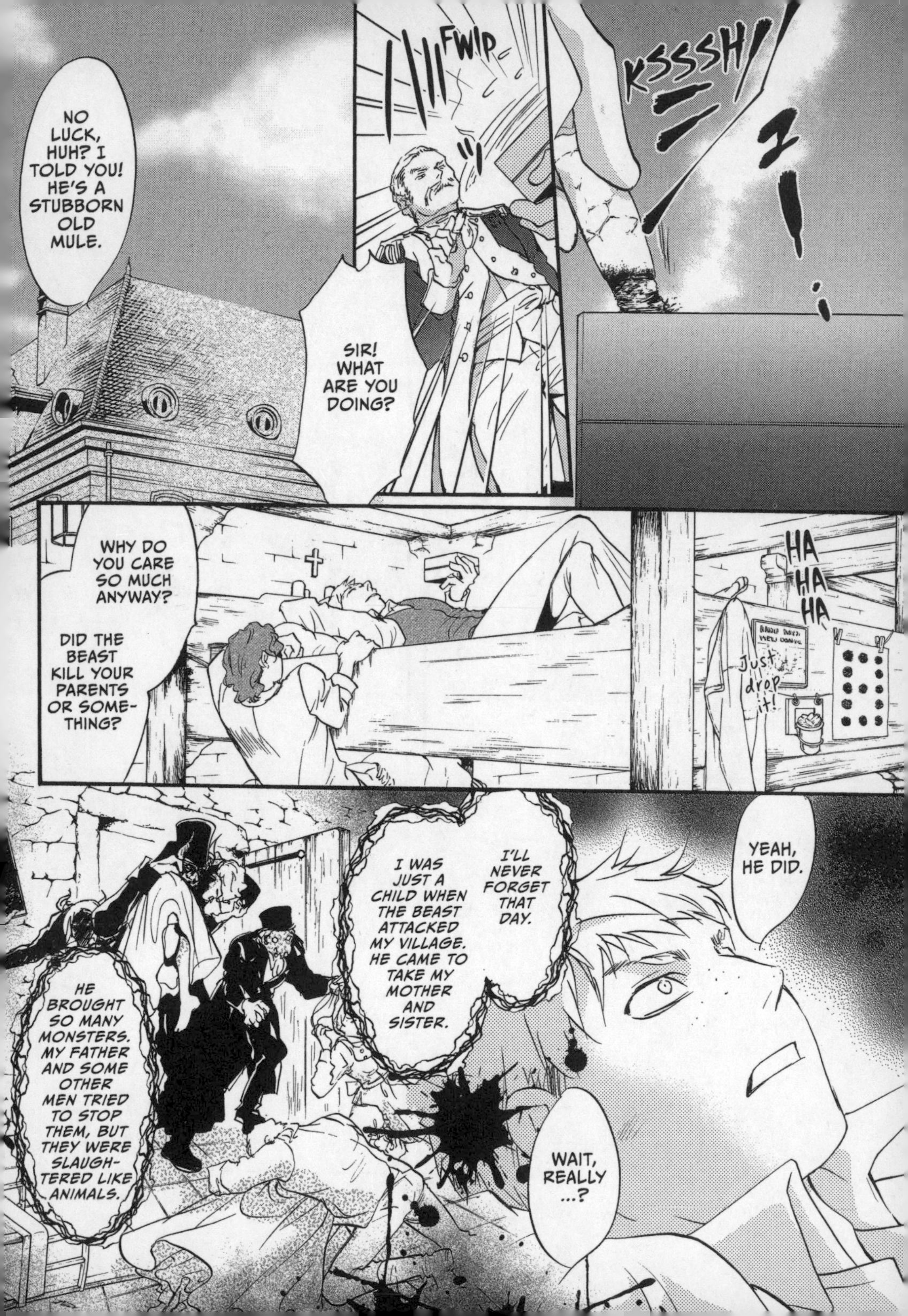
KSSSH
FWIP
SIR! WHAT ARE YOU DOING?
NO LUCK, HUH? I TOLD YOU! HE'S A STUBBORN OLD MULE.
HA HA HA
Just drop it!
WHY DO YOU CARE SO MUCH ANYWAY?
DID THE BEAST KILL YOUR PARENTS OR SOME-THING?
YEAH, HE DID.
WAIT, REALLY ...?
I'LL NEVER FORGET THAT DAY.
I WAS JUST A CHILD WHEN THE BEAST ATTACKED MY VILLAGE. HE CAME TO TAKE MY MOTHER AND SISTER.
HE BROUGHT SO MANY MONSTERS. MY FATHER AND SOME OTHER MEN TRIED TO STOP THEM, BUT THEY WERE SLAUGH-TERED LIKE ANIMALS.

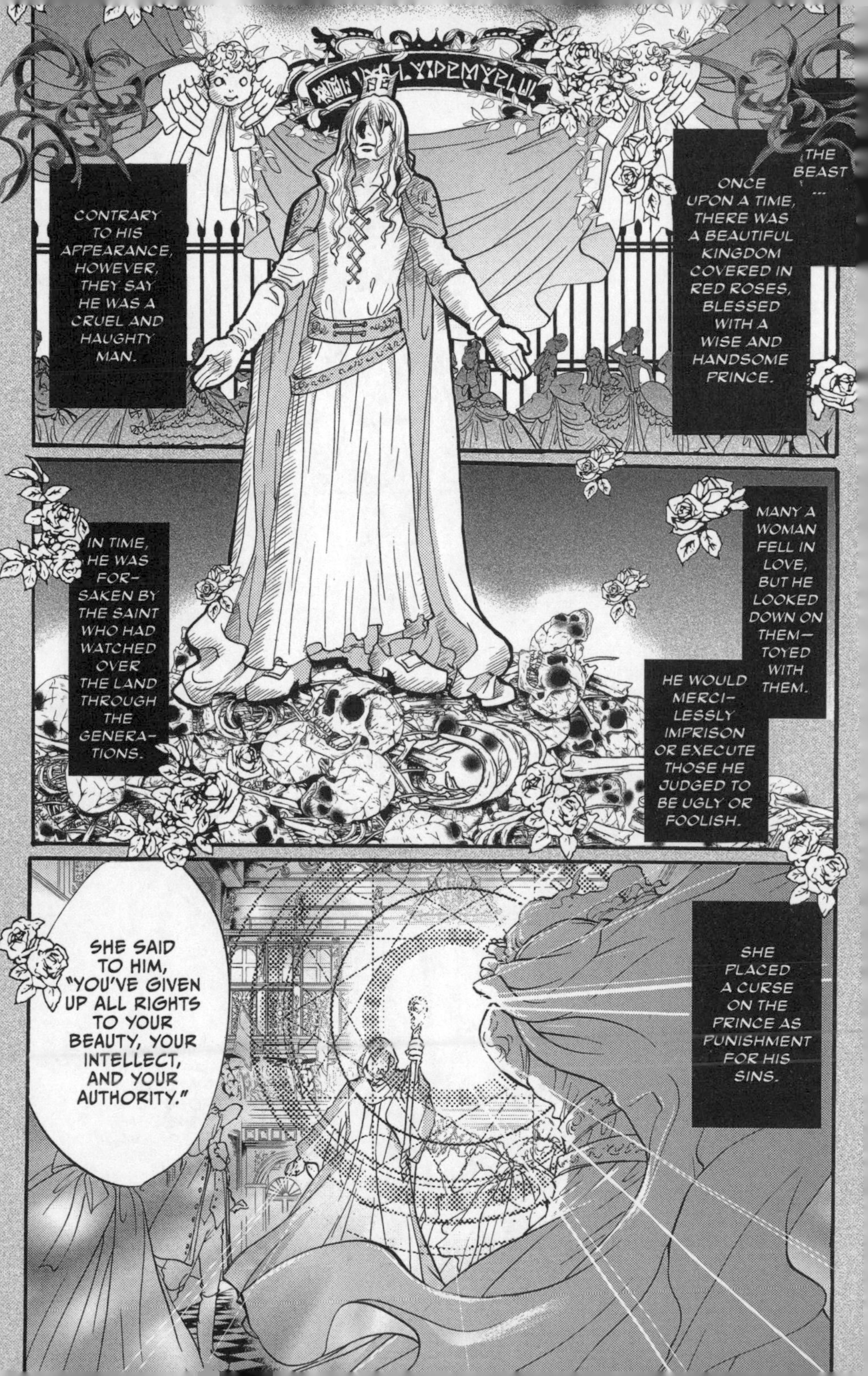
THE BEAST...
ONCE UPON A TIME, THERE WAS A BEAUTIFUL KINGDOM COVERED IN RED ROSES, BLESSED WITH A WISE AND HANDSOME PRINCE.
CONTRARY TO HIS APPEARANCE, HOWEVER, THEY SAY HE WAS A CRUEL AND HAUGHTY MAN.
MANY A WOMAN FELL IN LOVE, BUT HE LOOKED DOWN ON THEM—TOYED WITH THEM.
HE WOULD MERCILESSLY IMPRISON OR EXECUTE THOSE HE JUDGED TO BE UGLY OR FOOLISH.
IN TIME, HE WAS FORSAKEN BY THE SAINT WHO HAD WATCHED OVER THE LAND THROUGH THE GENERATIONS.
SHE PLACED A CURSE ON THE PRINCE AS PUNISHMENT FOR HIS SINS.
SHE SAID TO HIM, "YOU'VE GIVEN UP ALL RIGHTS TO YOUR BEAUTY, YOUR INTELLECT, AND YOUR AUTHORITY."

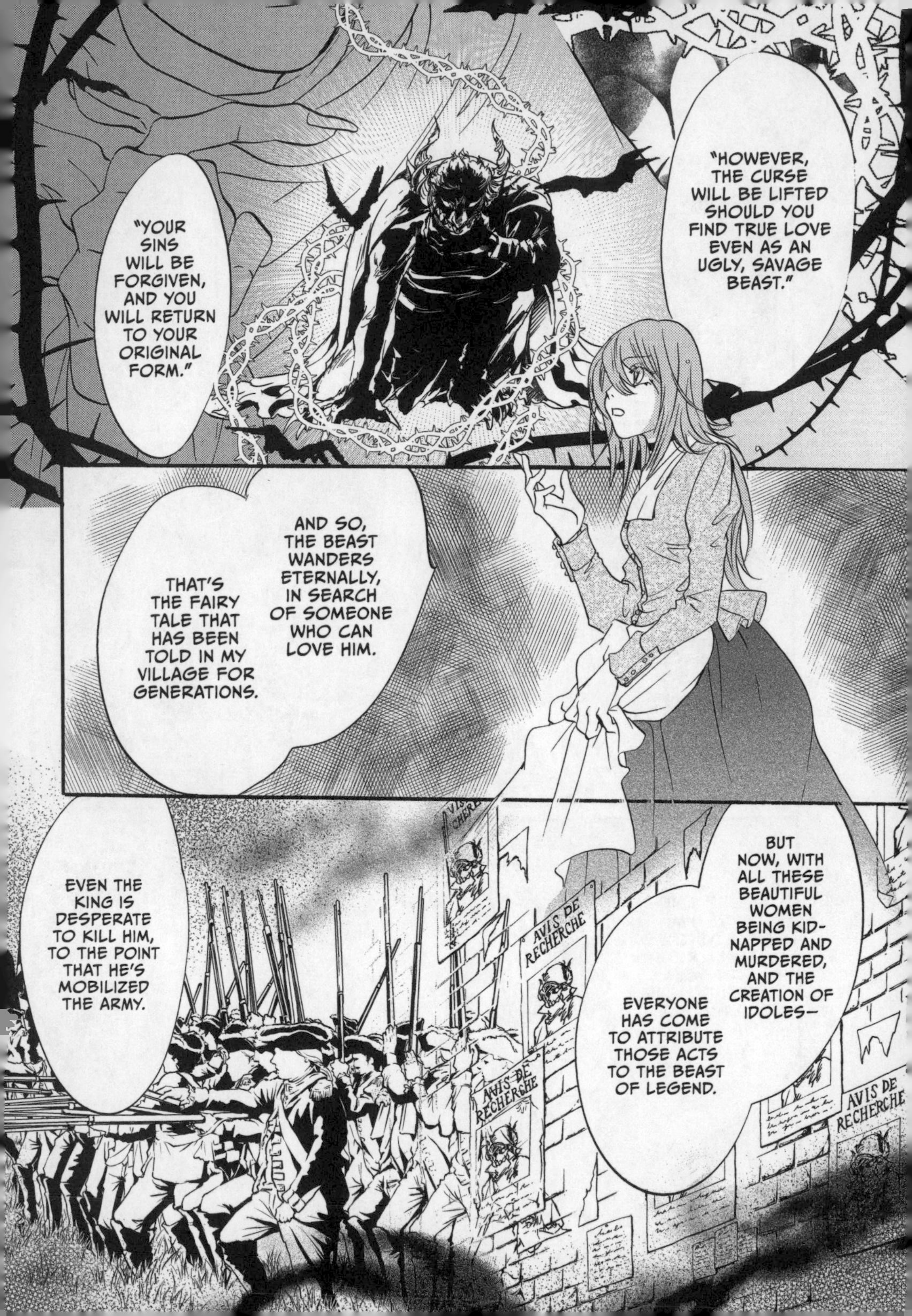
"HOWEVER, THE CURSE WILL BE LIFTED SHOULD YOU FIND TRUE LOVE EVEN AS AN UGLY, SAVAGE BEAST."
"YOUR SINS WILL BE FORGIVEN, AND YOU WILL RETURN TO YOUR ORIGINAL FORM."
AND SO, THE BEAST WANDERS ETERNALLY, IN SEARCH OF SOMEONE WHO CAN LOVE HIM.
THAT'S THE FAIRY TALE THAT HAS BEEN TOLD IN MY VILLAGE FOR GENERATIONS.
BUT NOW, WITH ALL THESE BEAUTIFUL WOMEN BEING KID-NAPPED AND MURDERED, AND THE CREATION OF IDOLES—
EVERYONE HAS COME TO ATTRIBUTE THOSE ACTS TO THE BEAST OF LEGEND.
AVIS DE RECHERCHE
AVIS DE RECHERCHE
AVIS DE RECHERCHE
EVEN THE KING IS DESPERATE TO KILL HIM, TO THE POINT THAT HE'S MOBILIZED THE ARMY.

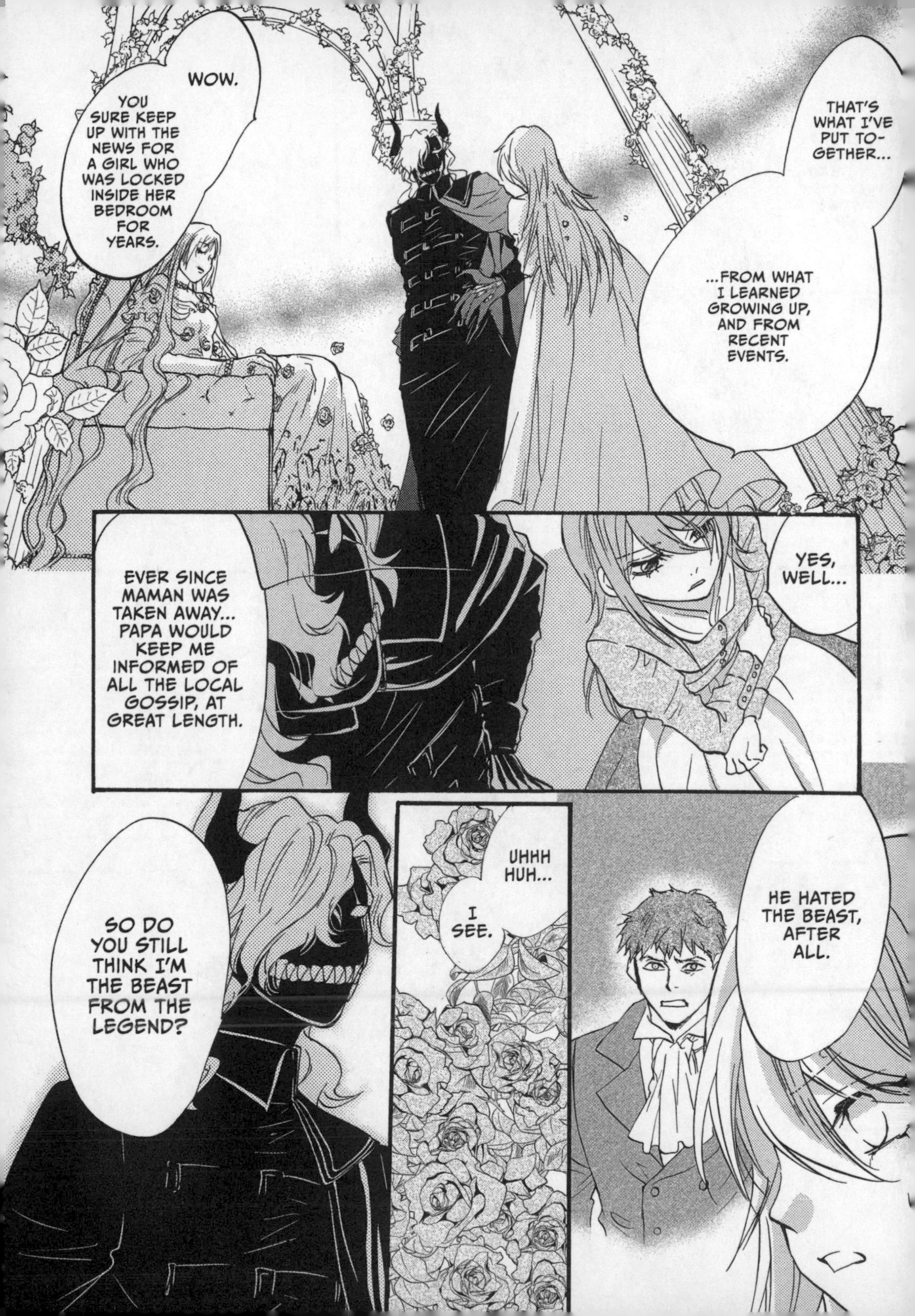
THAT'S WHAT I'VE PUT TO-GETHER...
...FROM WHAT I LEARNED GROWING UP, AND FROM RECENT EVENTS.
WOW.
YOU SURE KEEP UP WITH THE NEWS FOR A GIRL WHO WAS LOCKED INSIDE HER BEDROOM FOR YEARS.
YES, WELL...
EVER SINCE MAMAN WAS TAKEN AWAY... PAPA WOULD KEEP ME INFORMED OF ALL THE LOCAL GOSSIP, AT GREAT LENGTH.
HE HATED THE BEAST, AFTER ALL.
UHHH HUH...
I SEE.
SO DO YOU STILL THINK I'M THE BEAST FROM THE LEGEND?

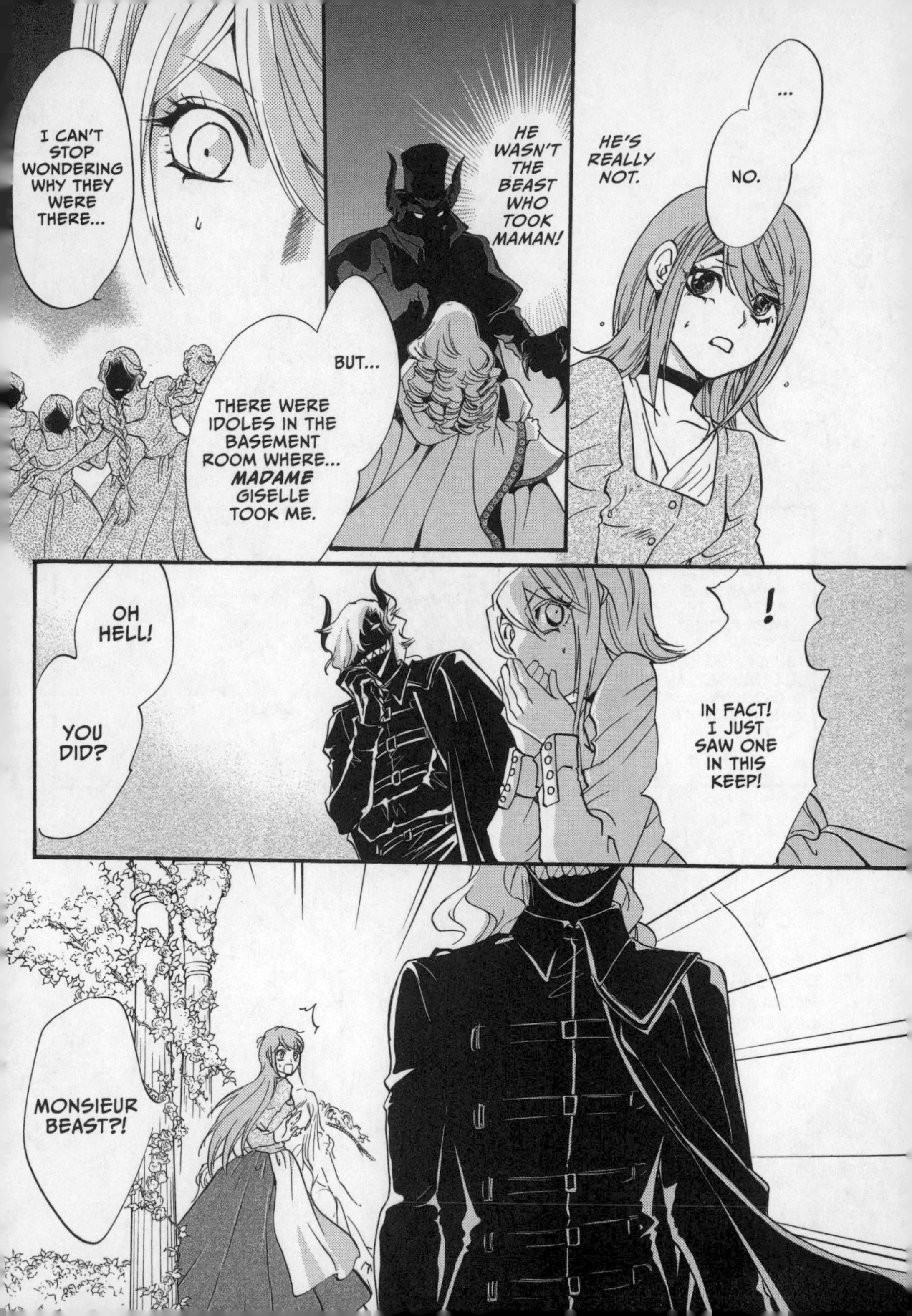
...
NO.
HE'S REALLY NOT.
HE WASN'T THE BEAST WHO TOOK MAMAN!
BUT...
THERE WERE IDOLES IN THE BASEMENT ROOM WHERE... *MADAME* GISELLE TOOK ME.
I CAN'T STOP WONDERING WHY THEY WERE THERE...
!
IN FACT! I JUST SAW ONE IN THIS KEEP!
OH HELL!
YOU DID?
MONSIEUR BEAST?!

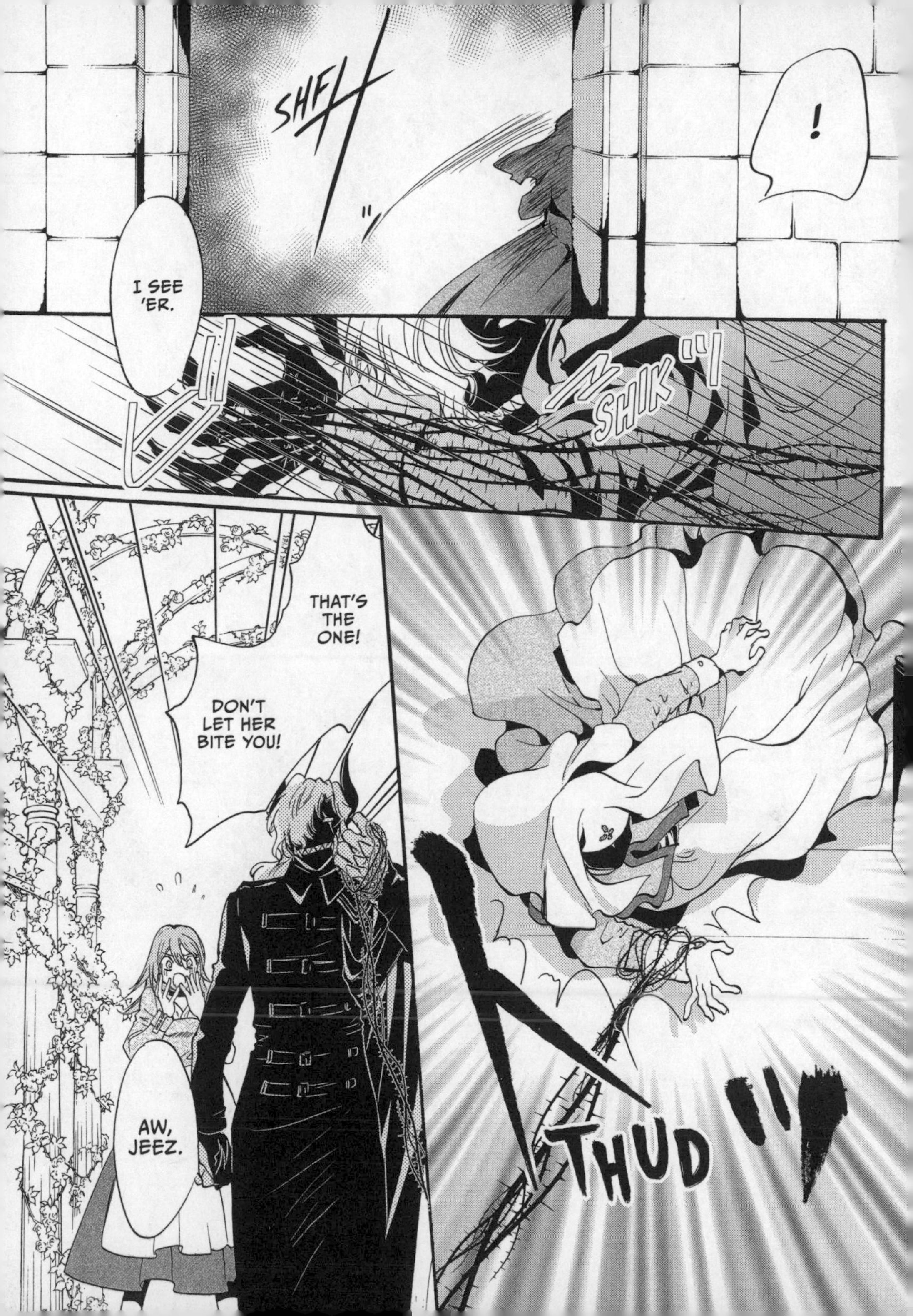

!
SHF
I SEE 'ER.
SHIK
THUD
THAT'S THE ONE!
DON'T LET HER BITE YOU!
AW, JEEZ.

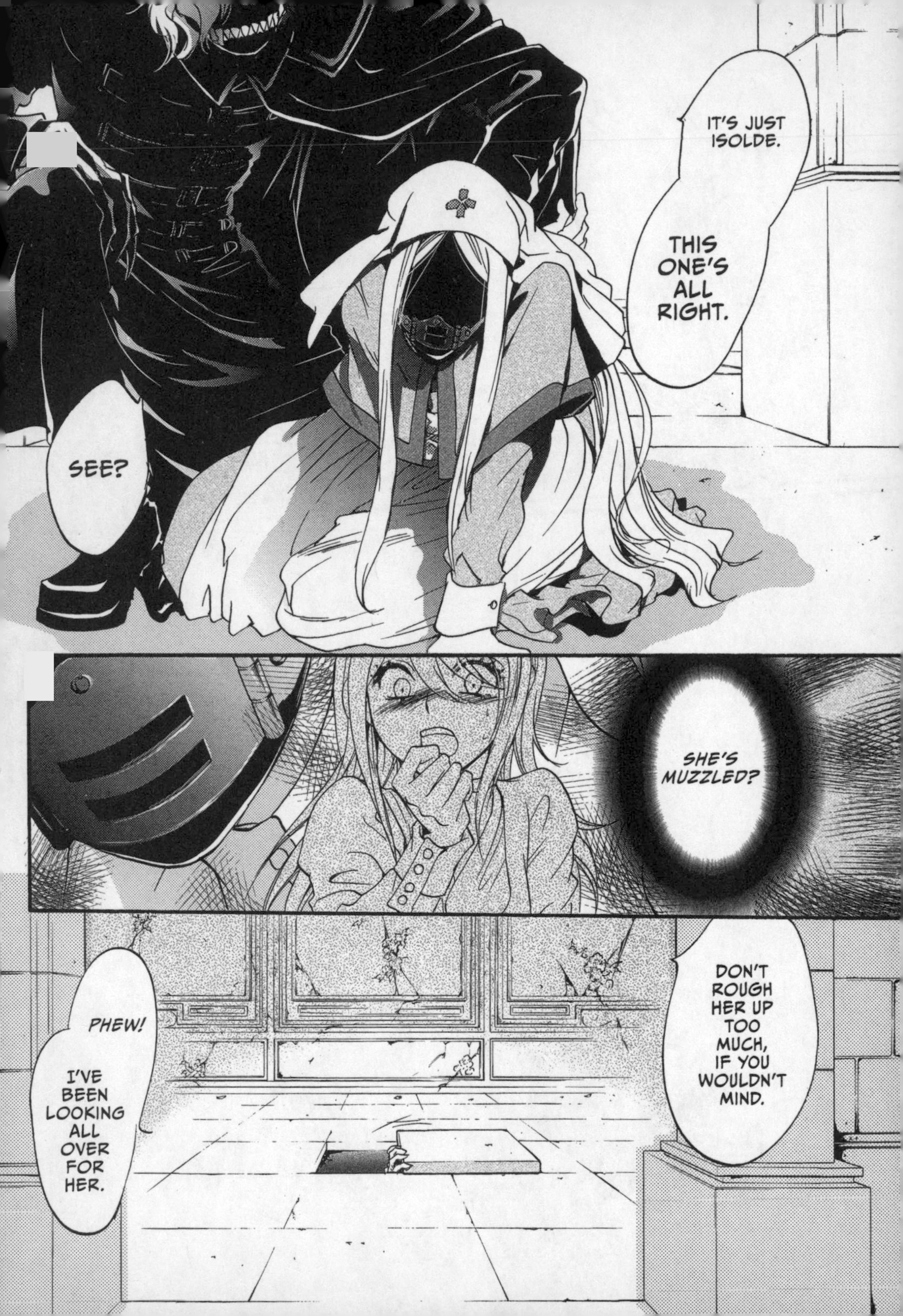
IT'S JUST ISOLDE.
THIS ONE'S ALL RIGHT.
SEE?
SHE'S MUZZLED?
DON'T ROUGH HER UP TOO MUCH, IF YOU WOULDN'T MIND.
PHEW!
I'VE BEEN LOOKING ALL OVER FOR HER.

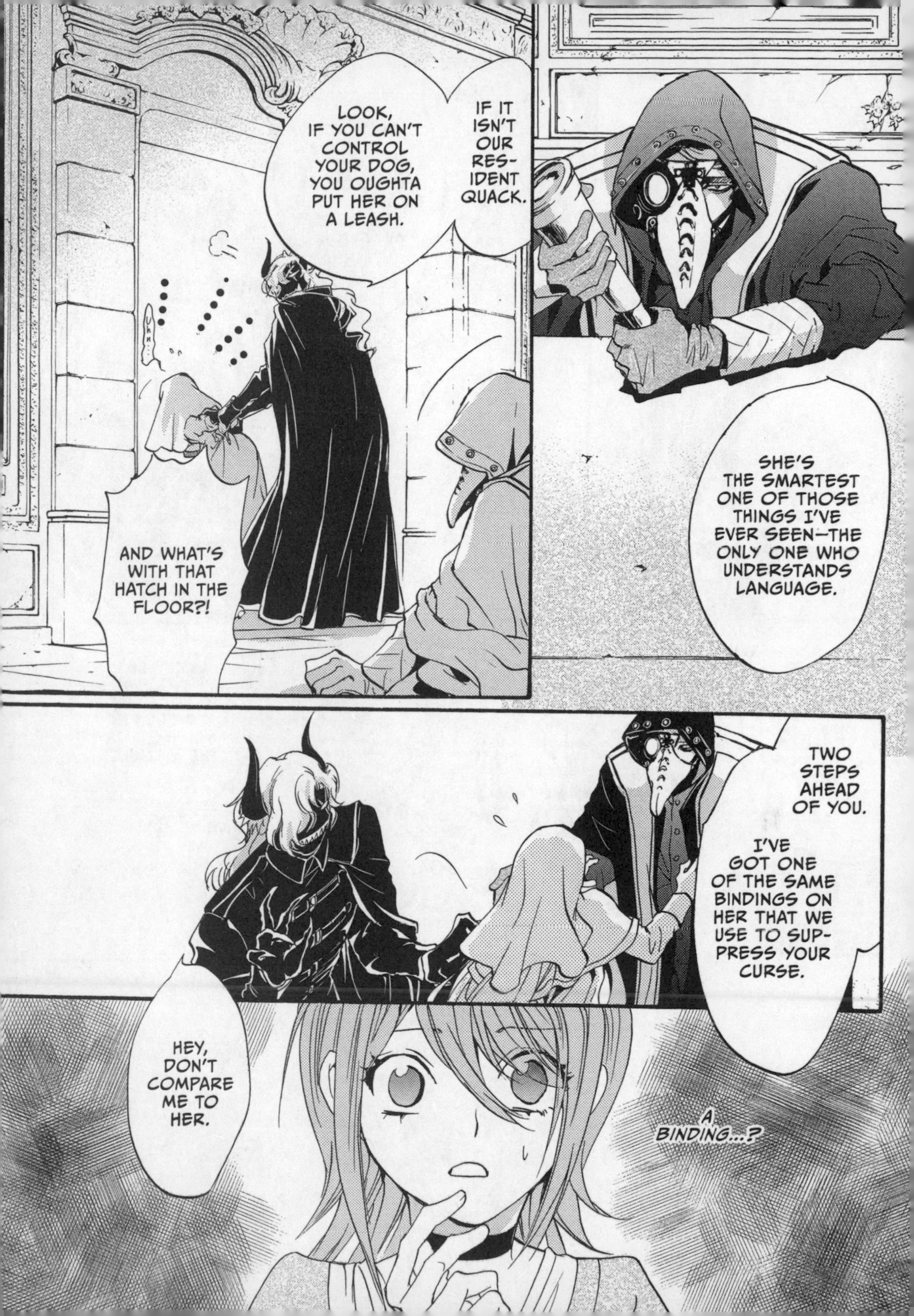
IF IT ISN'T OUR RESIDENT QUACK.
LOOK, IF YOU CAN'T CONTROL YOUR DOG, YOU OUGHTA PUT HER ON A LEASH.
Uhh...
AND WHAT'S WITH THAT HATCH IN THE FLOOR?!
SHE'S THE SMARTEST ONE OF THOSE THINGS I'VE EVER SEEN—THE ONLY ONE WHO UNDERSTANDS LANGUAGE.
TWO STEPS AHEAD OF YOU.
I'VE GOT ONE OF THE SAME BINDINGS ON HER THAT WE USE TO SUPPRESS YOUR CURSE.
HEY, DON'T COMPARE ME TO HER.
A BINDING...?

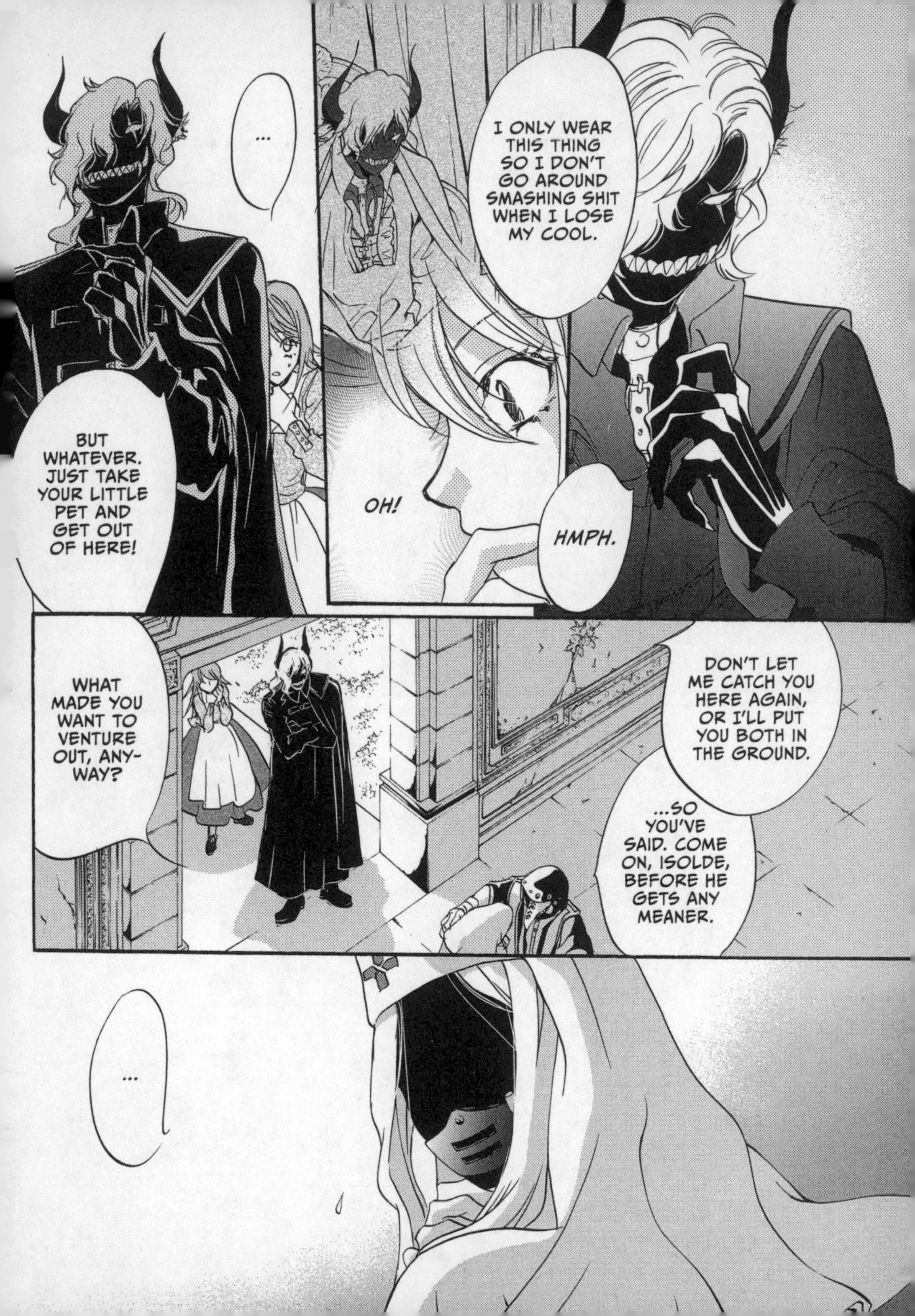
I ONLY WEAR THIS THING SO I DON'T GO AROUND SMASHING SHIT WHEN I LOSE MY COOL.
OH!
HMPH.
...
BUT WHATEVER. JUST TAKE YOUR LITTLE PET AND GET OUT OF HERE!
DON'T LET ME CATCH YOU HERE AGAIN, OR I'LL PUT YOU BOTH IN THE GROUND.
...SO YOU'VE SAID. COME ON, ISOLDE, BEFORE HE GETS ANY MEANER.
WHAT MADE YOU WANT TO VENTURE OUT, ANY-WAY?
...

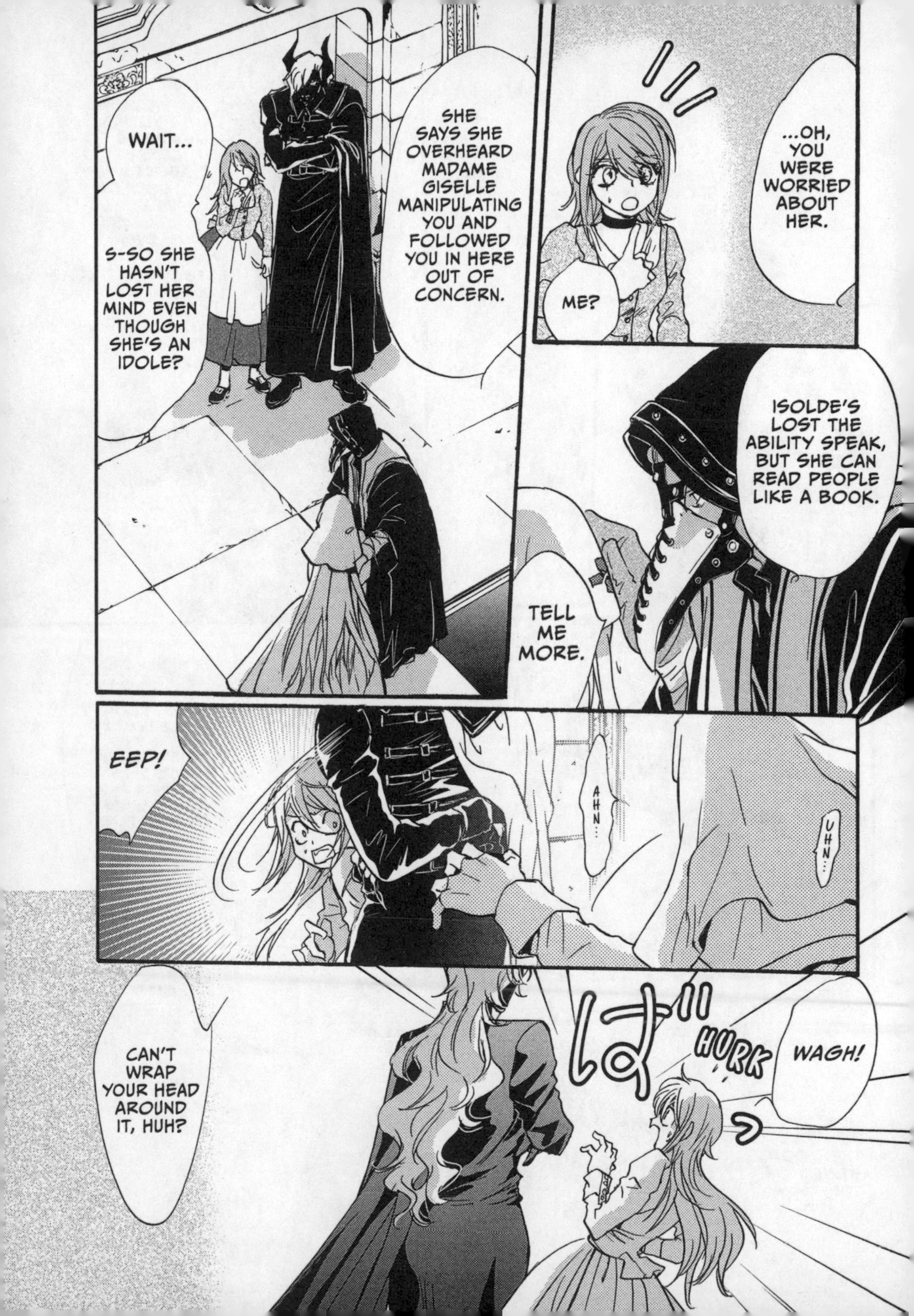
...OH, YOU WERE WORRIED ABOUT HER.
ME?
ISOLDE'S LOST THE ABILITY SPEAK, BUT SHE CAN READ PEOPLE LIKE A BOOK.
TELL ME MORE.
SHE SAYS SHE OVERHEARD MADAME GISELLE MANIPULATING YOU AND FOLLOWED YOU IN HERE OUT OF CONCERN.
WAIT...
S-SO SHE HASN'T LOST HER MIND EVEN THOUGH SHE'S AN IDOLE?
UHN...
AHN...
EEP!
WAGH!
ば
HURK
CAN'T WRAP YOUR HEAD AROUND IT, HUH?

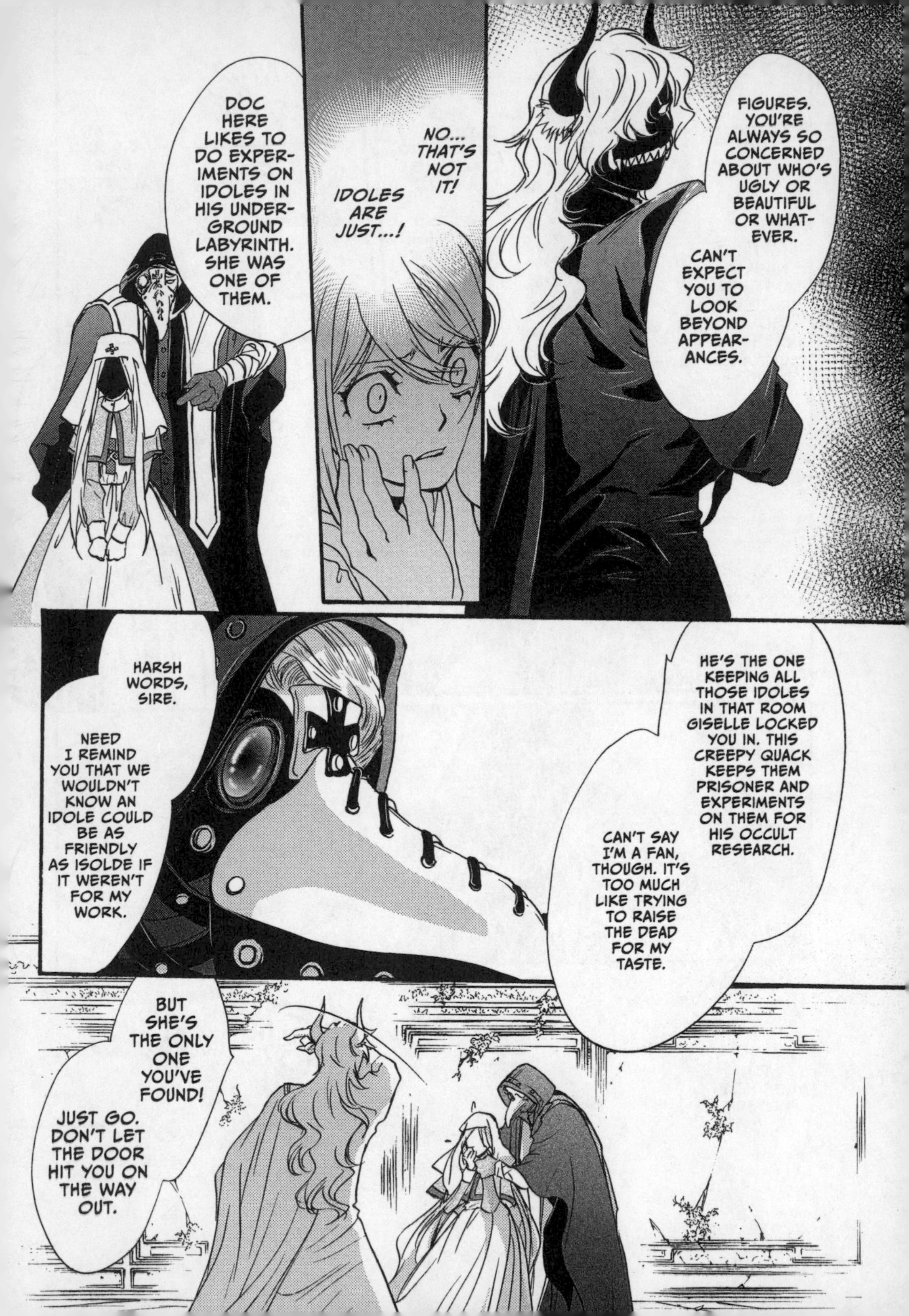
FIGURES. YOU'RE ALWAYS SO CONCERNED ABOUT WHO'S UGLY OR BEAUTIFUL OR WHATEVER.
CAN'T EXPECT YOU TO LOOK BEYOND APPEARANCES.
NO... THAT'S NOT IT!
IDOLES ARE JUST...!
DOC HERE LIKES TO DO EXPERIMENTS ON IDOLES IN HIS UNDERGROUND LABYRINTH. SHE WAS ONE OF THEM.
HE'S THE ONE KEEPING ALL THOSE IDOLES IN THAT ROOM GISELLE LOCKED YOU IN. THIS CREEPY QUACK KEEPS THEM PRISONER AND EXPERIMENTS ON THEM FOR HIS OCCULT RESEARCH.
CAN'T SAY I'M A FAN, THOUGH. IT'S TOO MUCH LIKE TRYING TO RAISE THE DEAD FOR MY TASTE.
HARSH WORDS, SIRE.
NEED I REMIND YOU THAT WE WOULDN'T KNOW AN IDOLE COULD BE AS FRIENDLY AS ISOLDE IF IT WEREN'T FOR MY WORK.
BUT SHE'S THE ONLY ONE YOU'VE FOUND!
JUST GO. DON'T LET THE DOOR HIT YOU ON THE WAY OUT.

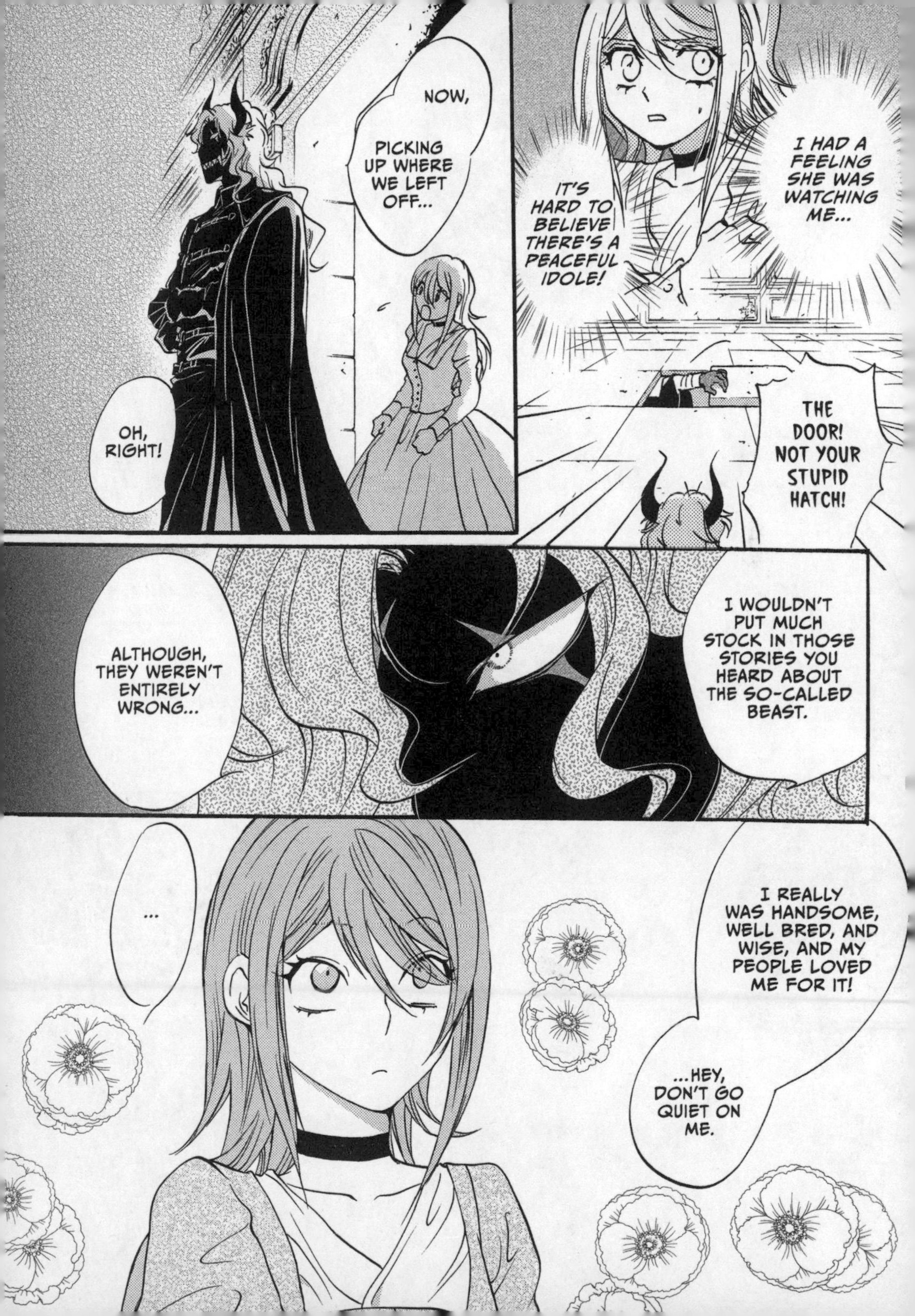

I HAD A FEELING SHE WAS WATCHING ME...
IT'S HARD TO BELIEVE THERE'S A PEACEFUL IDOLE!
THE DOOR! NOT YOUR STUPID HATCH!
NOW,
PICKING UP WHERE WE LEFT OFF...
OH, RIGHT!
I WOULDN'T PUT MUCH STOCK IN THOSE STORIES YOU HEARD ABOUT THE SO-CALLED BEAST.
ALTHOUGH, THEY WEREN'T ENTIRELY WRONG...
I REALLY WAS HANDSOME, WELL BRED, AND WISE, AND MY PEOPLE LOVED ME FOR IT!
...HEY, DON'T GO QUIET ON ME.
...

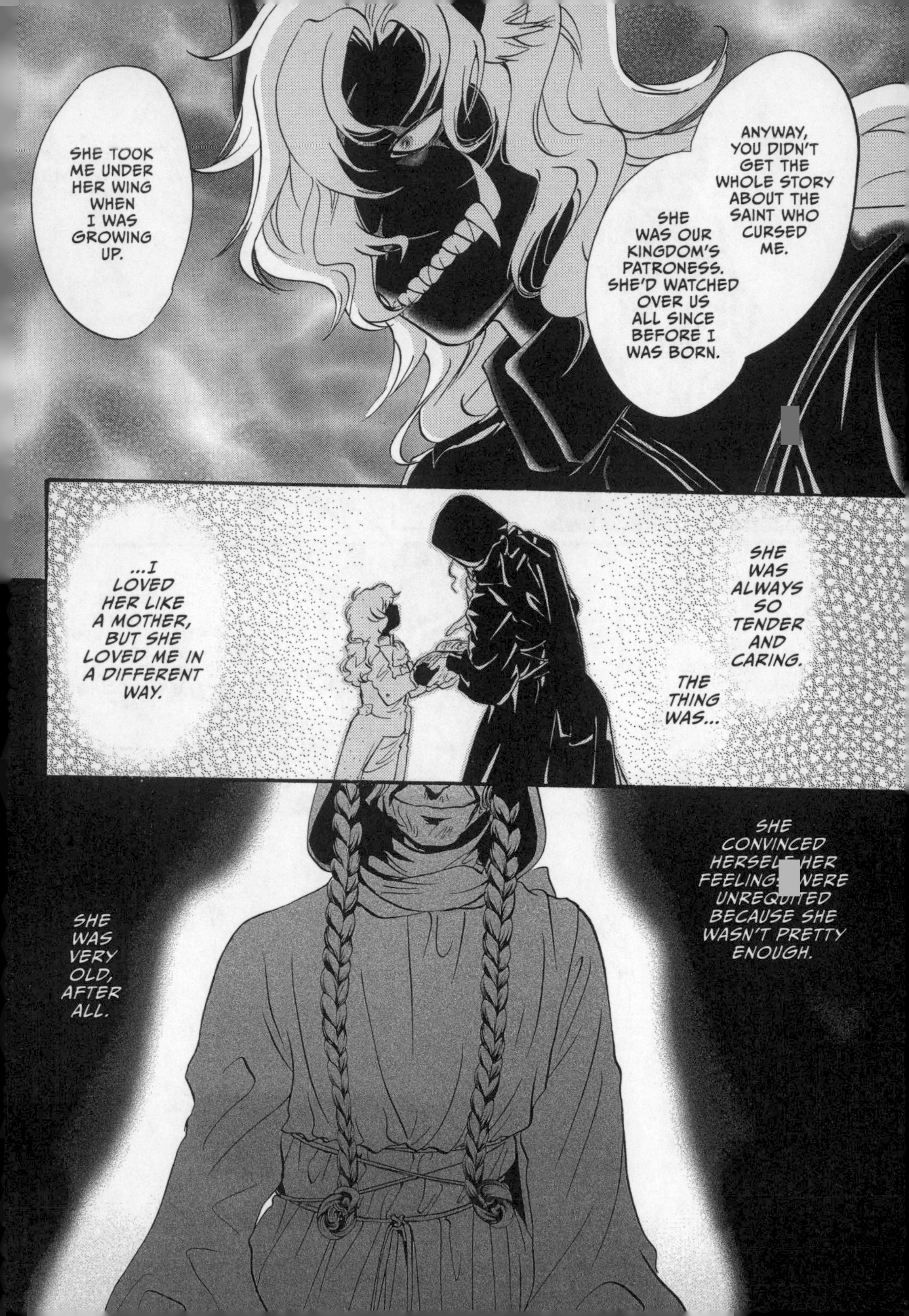
ANYWAY, YOU DIDN'T GET THE WHOLE STORY ABOUT THE SAINT WHO CURSED ME.
SHE WAS OUR KINGDOM'S PATRONESS. SHE'D WATCHED OVER US ALL SINCE BEFORE I WAS BORN.
SHE TOOK ME UNDER HER WING WHEN I WAS GROWING UP.
SHE WAS ALWAYS SO TENDER AND CARING.
THE THING WAS...
...I LOVED HER LIKE A MOTHER, BUT SHE LOVED ME IN A DIFFERENT WAY.
SHE CONVINCED HERSELF HER FEELINGS WERE UNREQUITED BECAUSE SHE WASN'T PRETTY ENOUGH.
SHE WAS VERY OLD, AFTER ALL.

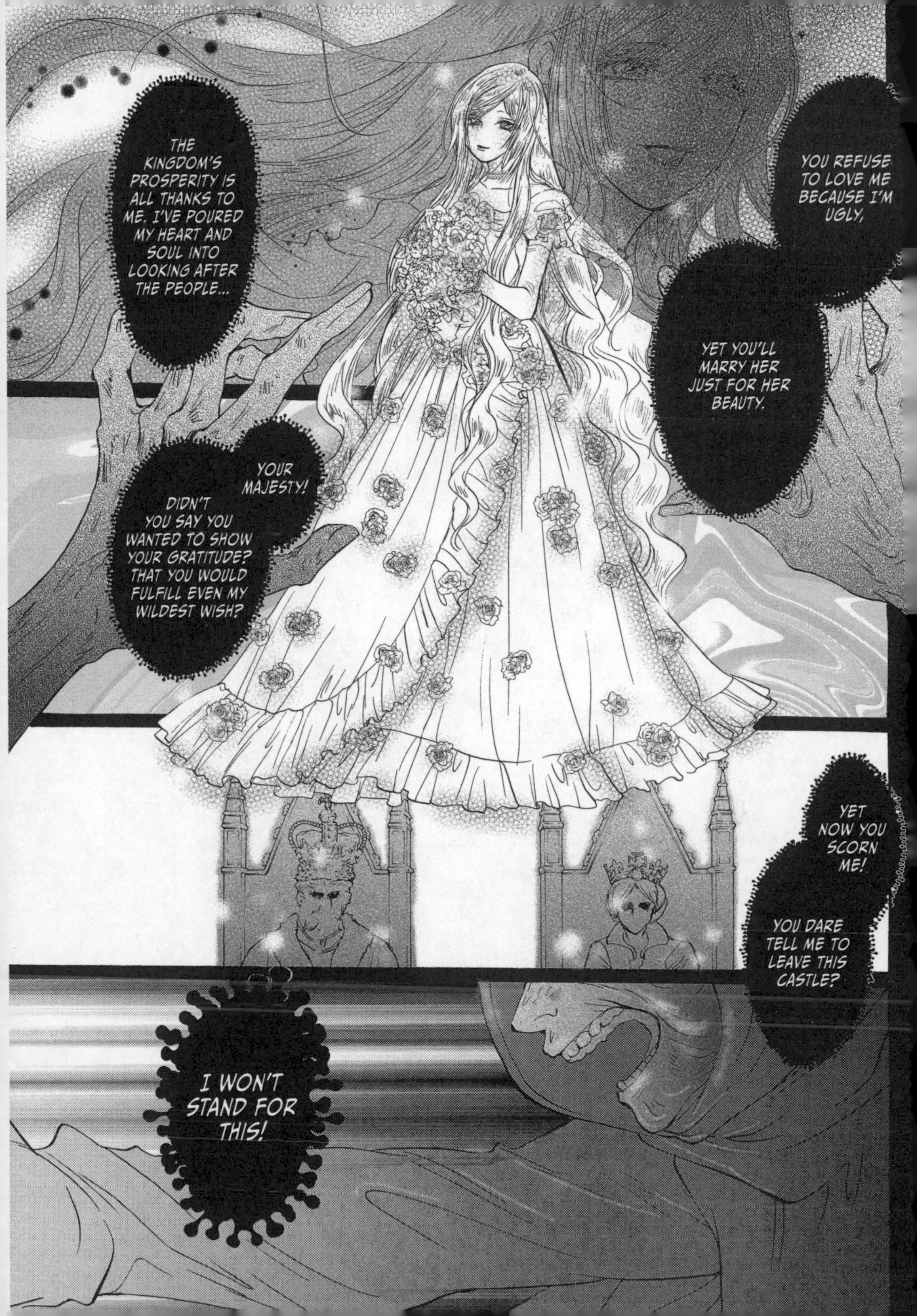
YOU REFUSE TO LOVE ME BECAUSE I'M UGLY,
YET YOU'LL MARRY HER JUST FOR HER BEAUTY.
THE KINGDOM'S PROSPERITY IS ALL THANKS TO ME. I'VE POURED MY HEART AND SOUL INTO LOOKING AFTER THE PEOPLE...
YOUR MAJESTY!
DIDN'T YOU SAY YOU WANTED TO SHOW YOUR GRATITUDE? THAT YOU WOULD FULFILL EVEN MY WILDEST WISH?
YET NOW YOU SCORN ME!
YOU DARE TELL ME TO LEAVE THIS CASTLE?
I WON'T STAND FOR THIS!

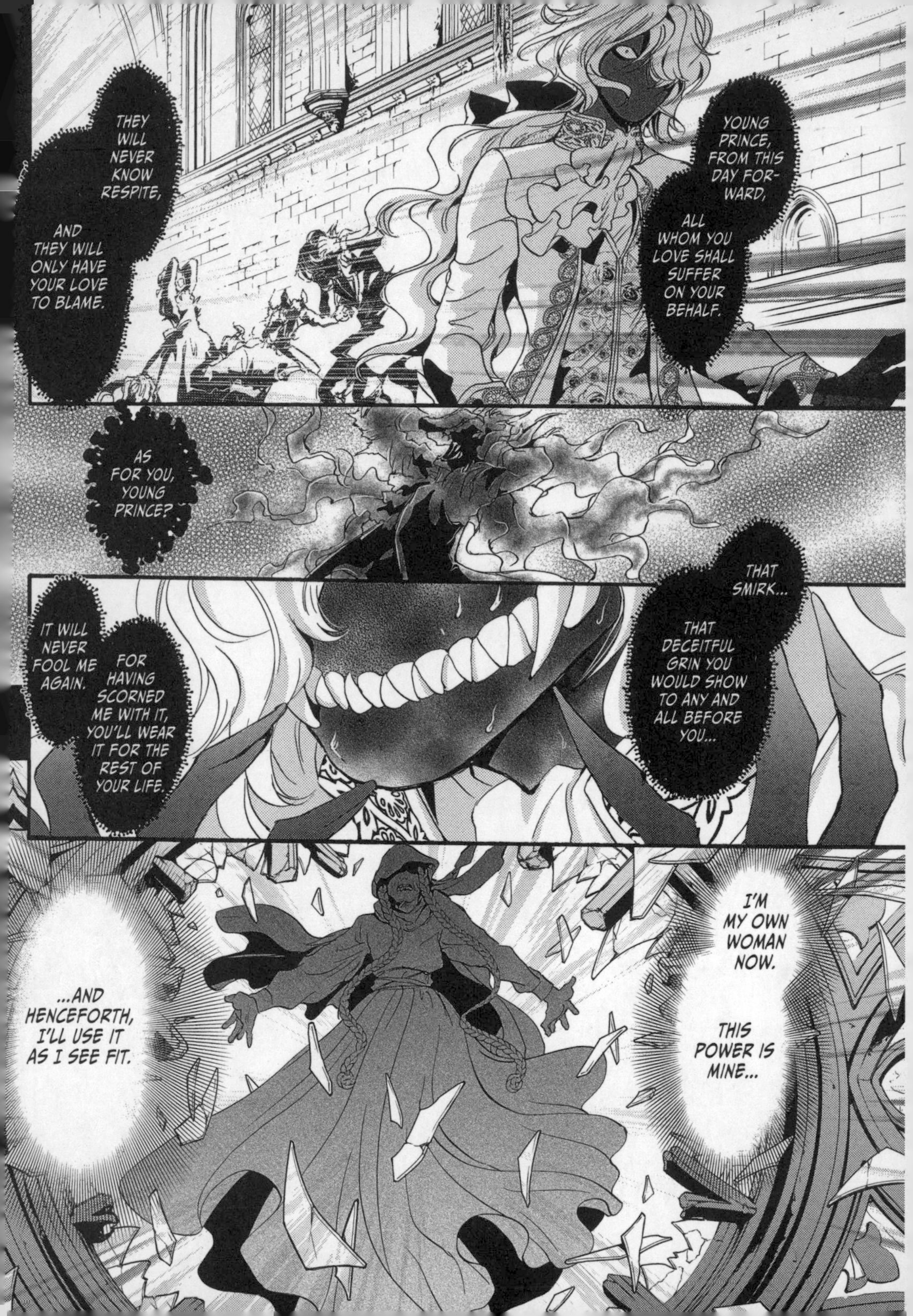
YOUNG PRINCE, FROM THIS DAY FOR-WARD,
ALL WHOM YOU LOVE SHALL SUFFER ON YOUR BEHALF.
THEY WILL NEVER KNOW RESPITE,
AND THEY WILL ONLY HAVE YOUR LOVE TO BLAME.
AS FOR YOU, YOUNG PRINCE?
THAT SMIRK...
THAT DECEITFUL GRIN YOU WOULD SHOW TO ANY AND ALL BEFORE YOU...
IT WILL NEVER FOOL ME AGAIN.
FOR HAVING SCORNED ME WITH IT, YOU'LL WEAR IT FOR THE REST OF YOUR LIFE.
I'M MY OWN WOMAN NOW.
THIS POWER IS MINE...
...AND HENCEFORTH, I'LL USE IT AS I SEE FIT.

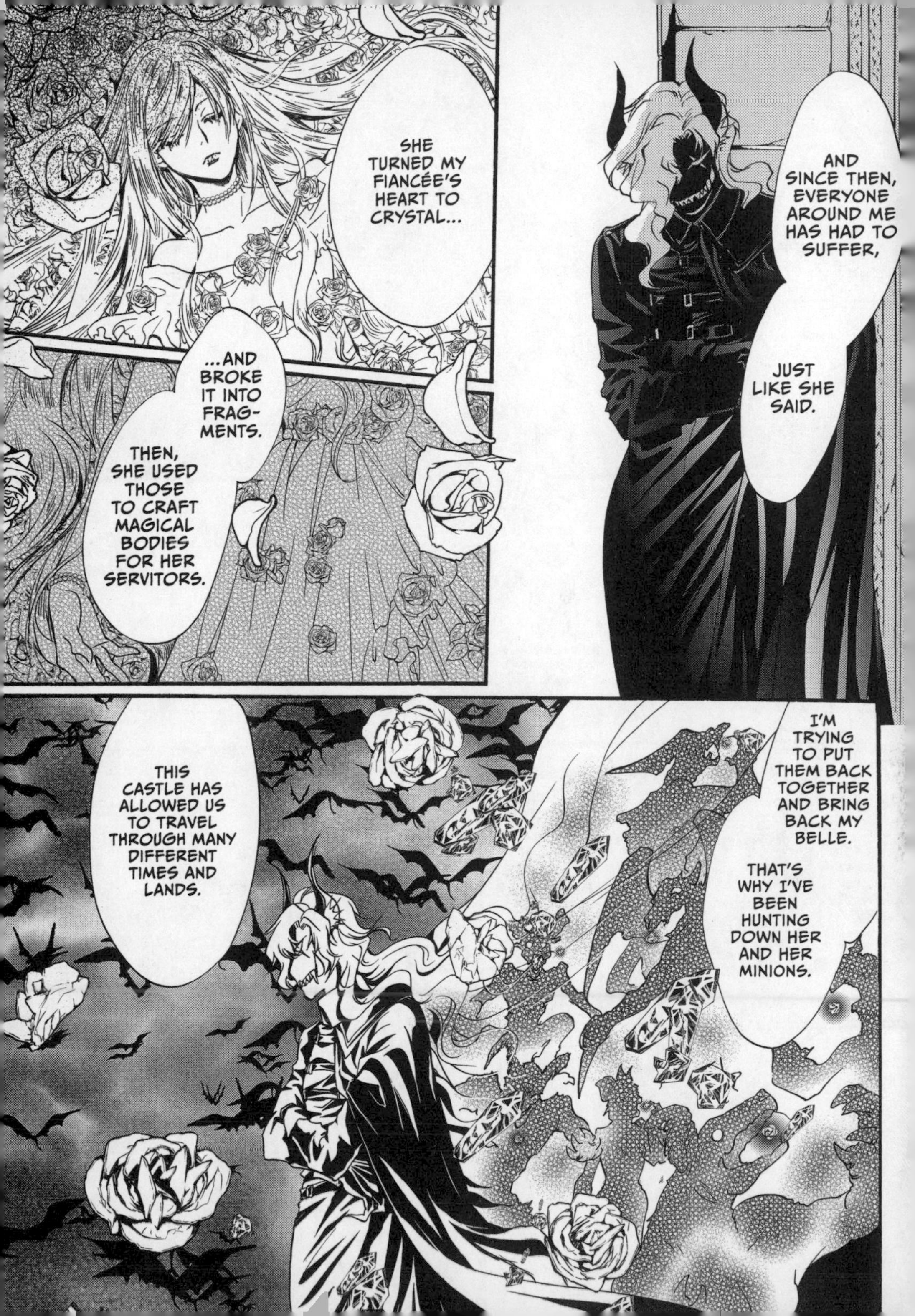

AND SINCE THEN, EVERYONE AROUND ME HAS HAD TO SUFFER,
JUST LIKE SHE SAID.
SHE TURNED MY FIANCÉE'S HEART TO CRYSTAL...
...AND BROKE IT INTO FRAG- MENTS.
THEN, SHE USED THOSE TO CRAFT MAGICAL BODIES FOR HER SERVITORS.
I'M TRYING TO PUT THEM BACK TOGETHER AND BRING BACK MY BELLE.
THAT'S WHY I'VE BEEN HUNTING DOWN HER AND HER MINIONS.
THIS CASTLE HAS ALLOWED US TO TRAVEL THROUGH MANY DIFFERENT TIMES AND LANDS.

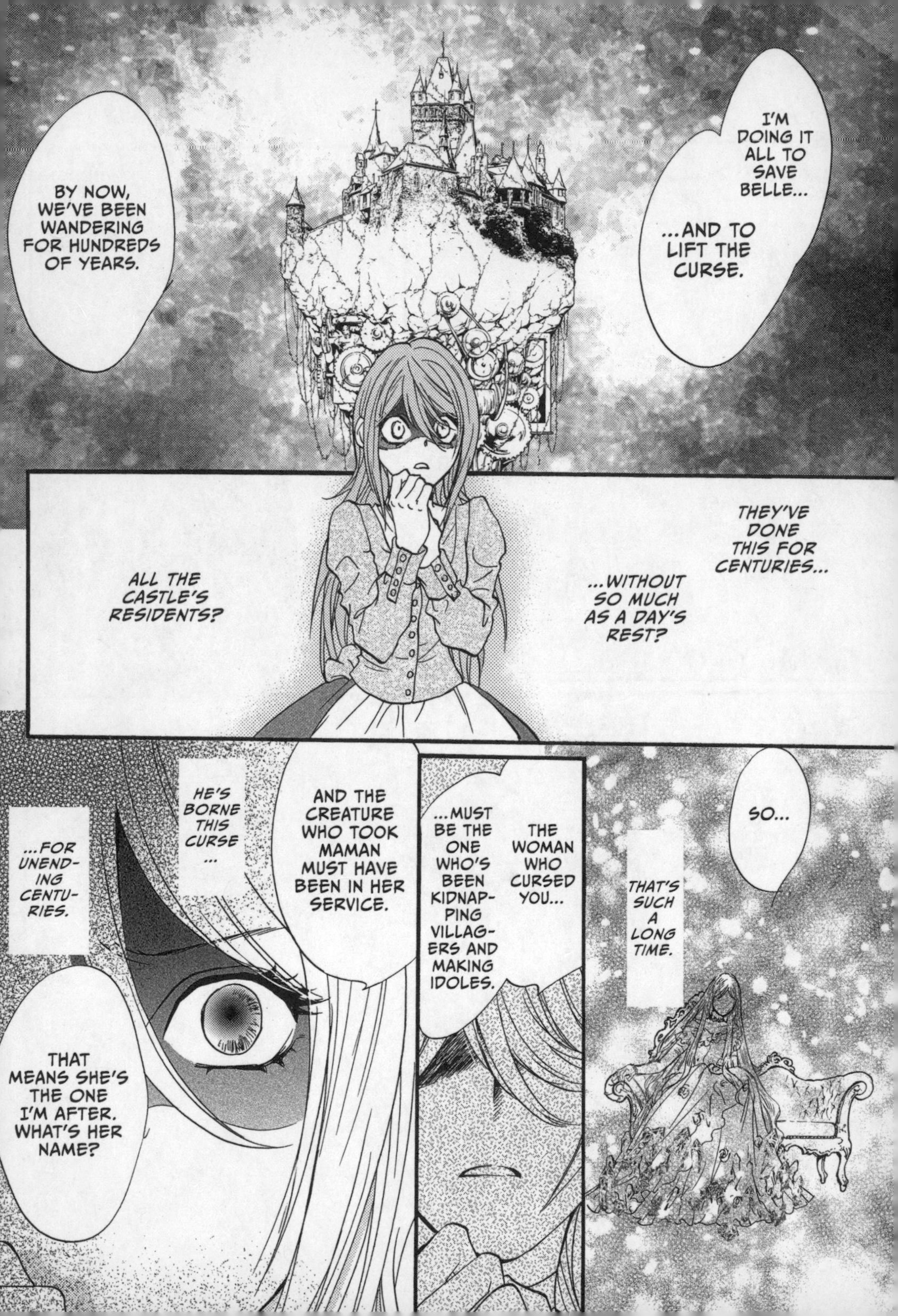
I'M DOING IT ALL TO SAVE BELLE...
...AND TO LIFT THE CURSE.
BY NOW, WE'VE BEEN WANDERING FOR HUNDREDS OF YEARS.
THEY'VE DONE THIS FOR CENTURIES...
...WITHOUT SO MUCH AS A DAY'S REST?
ALL THE CASTLE'S RESIDENTS?
SO...
THAT'S SUCH A LONG TIME.
THE WOMAN WHO CURSED YOU...
...MUST BE THE ONE WHO'S BEEN KIDNAPPING VILLAGERS AND MAKING IDOLES.
AND THE CREATURE WHO TOOK MAMAN MUST HAVE BEEN IN HER SERVICE.
HE'S BORNE THIS CURSE...
...FOR UNENDING CENTURIES.
THAT MEANS SHE'S THE ONE I'M AFTER. WHAT'S HER NAME?

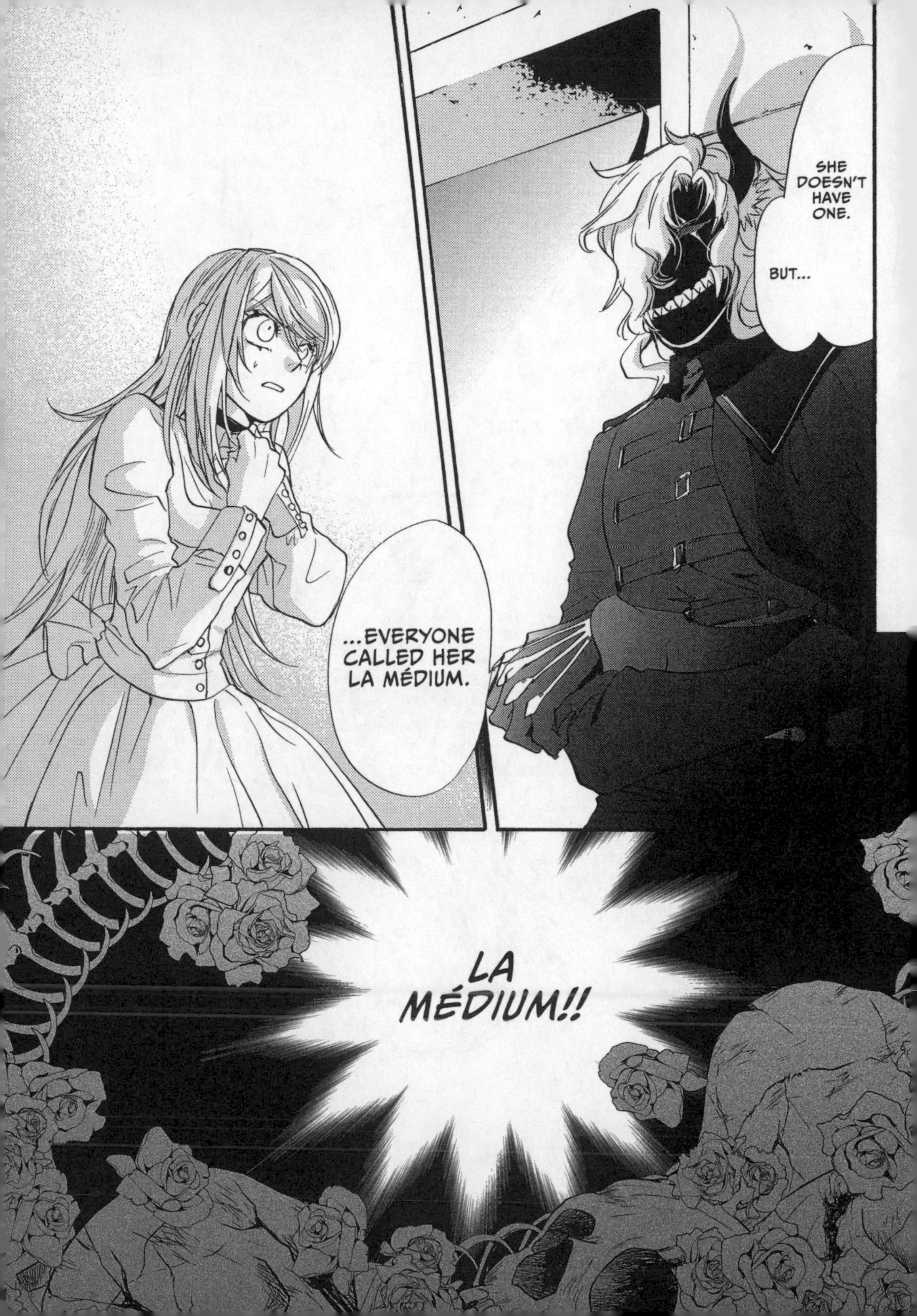
SHE DOESN'T HAVE ONE.
BUT...
...EVERYONE CALLED HER LA MÉDIUM.
LA MÉDIUM!!

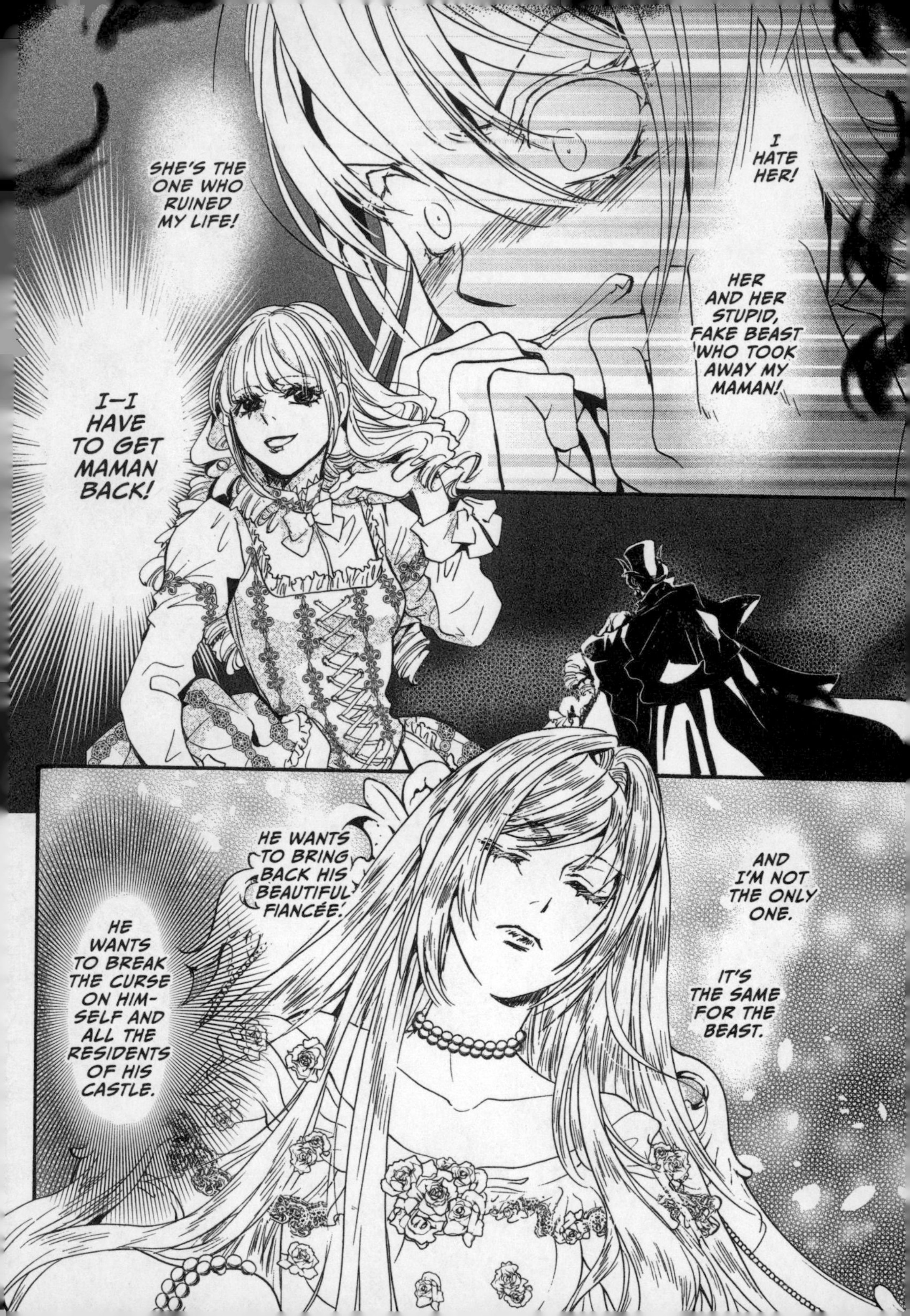
I HATE HER!
HER AND HER STUPID, FAKE BEAST WHO TOOK AWAY MY MAMAN!
SHE'S THE ONE WHO RUINED MY LIFE!
I—I HAVE TO GET MAMAN BACK!
AND I'M NOT THE ONLY ONE.
IT'S THE SAME FOR THE BEAST.
HE WANTS TO BRING BACK HIS BEAUTIFUL FIANCÉE.
HE WANTS TO BREAK THE CURSE ON HIM-SELF AND ALL THE RESIDENTS OF HIS CASTLE.

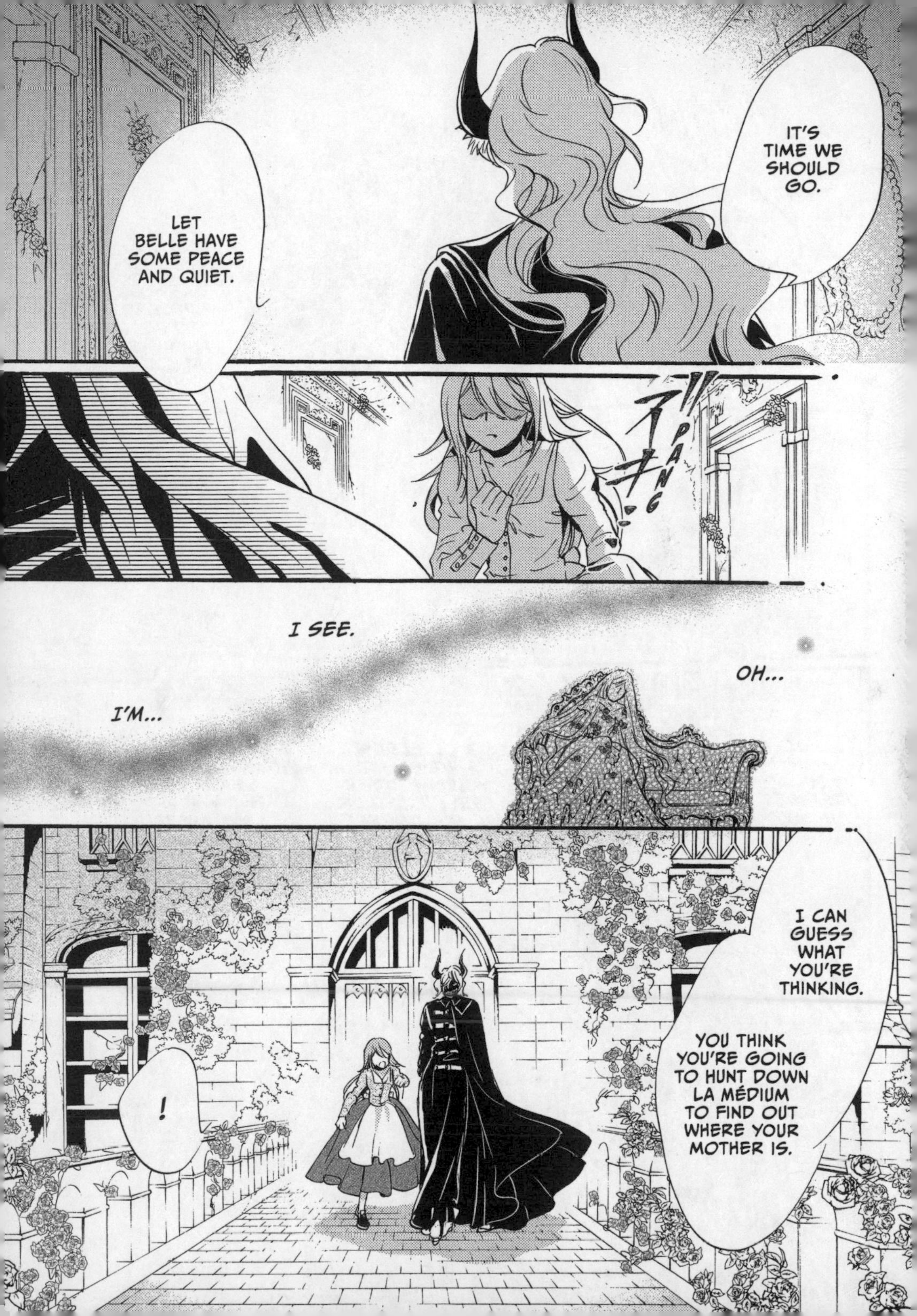
IT'S TIME WE SHOULD GO.
LET BELLE HAVE SOME PEACE AND QUIET.
PANG
OH...
I SEE.
I'M...
I CAN GUESS WHAT YOU'RE THINKING.
YOU THINK YOU'RE GOING TO HUNT DOWN LA MÉDIUM TO FIND OUT WHERE YOUR MOTHER IS.
!

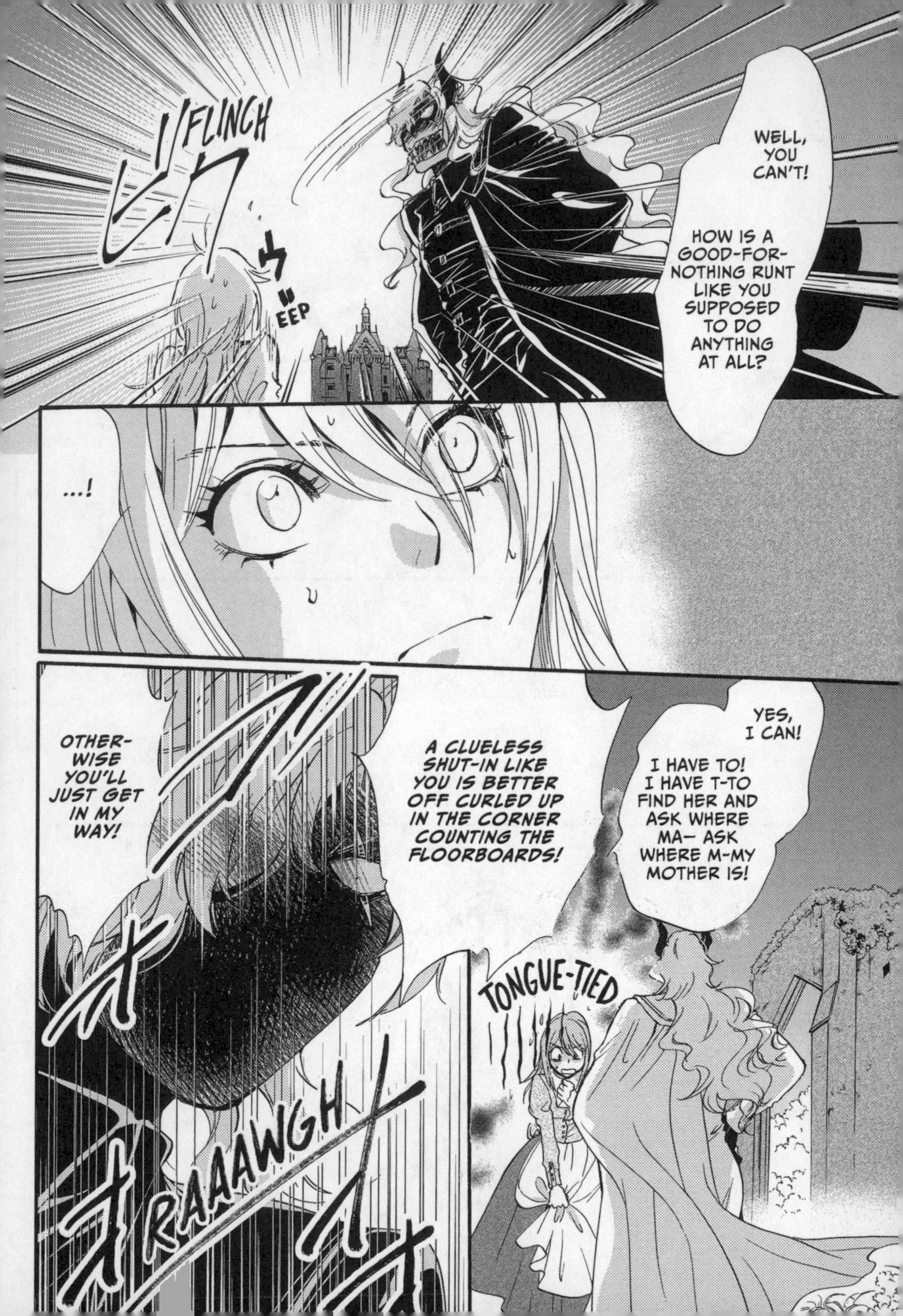
WELL, YOU CAN'T!
HOW IS A GOOD-FOR-NOTHING RUNT LIKE YOU SUPPOSED TO DO ANYTHING AT ALL?
FLINCH
EEP
...!
YES, I CAN!
I HAVE TO! I HAVE T-TO FIND HER AND ASK WHERE MA— ASK WHERE M-MY MOTHER IS!
TONGUE-TIED
A CLUELESS SHUT-IN LIKE YOU IS BETTER OFF CURLED UP IN THE CORNER COUNTING THE FLOORBOARDS!
OTHER-WISE YOU'LL JUST GET IN MY WAY!
RAAAAWGH

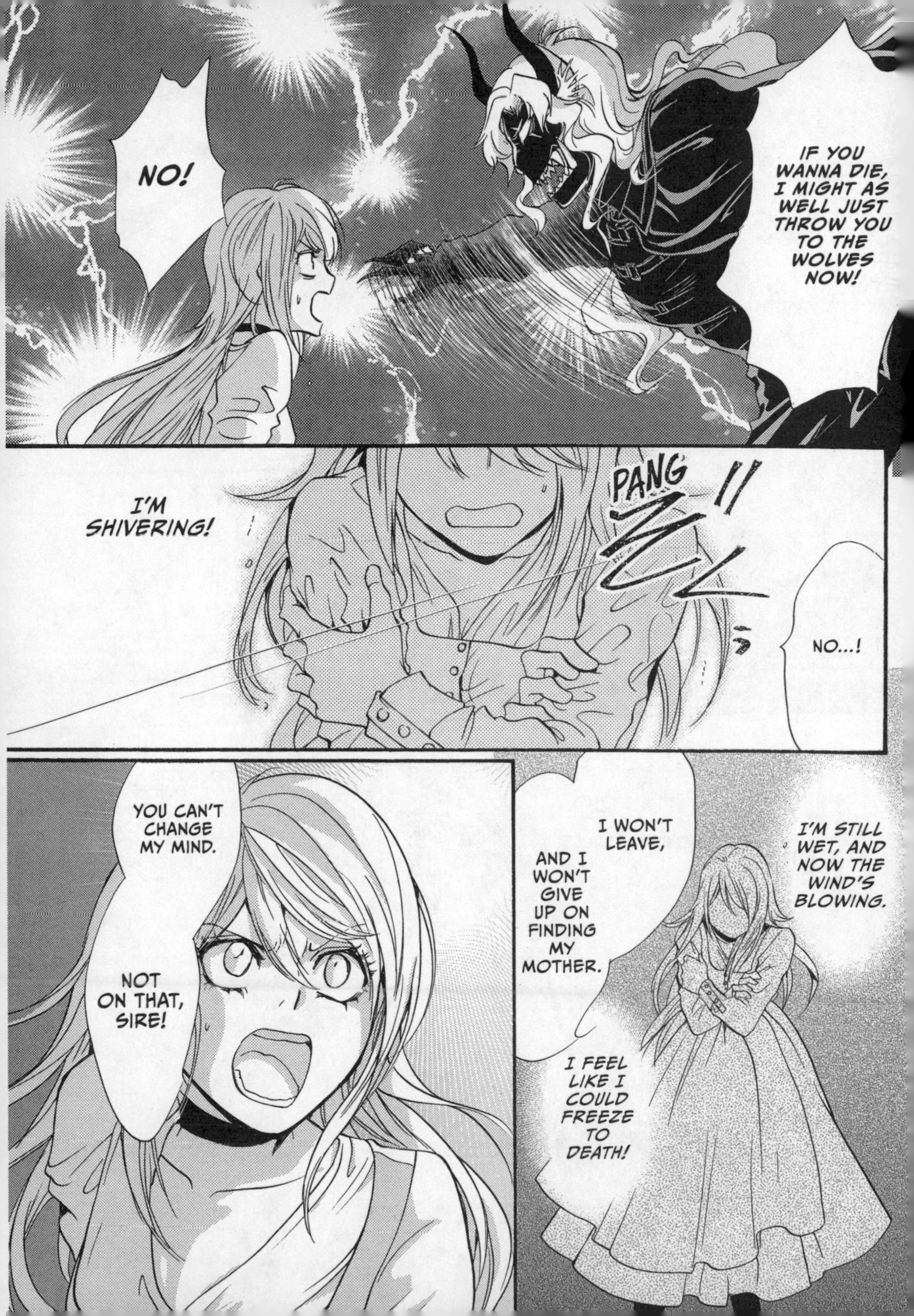
IF YOU WANNA DIE, I MIGHT AS WELL JUST THROW YOU TO THE WOLVES NOW!
NO!
PANG
NO...!
I'M SHIVERING!
I'M STILL WET, AND NOW THE WIND'S BLOWING.
I WON'T LEAVE,
AND I WON'T GIVE UP ON FINDING MY MOTHER.
I FEEL LIKE I COULD FREEZE TO DEATH!
YOU CAN'T CHANGE MY MIND.
NOT ON THAT, SIRE!

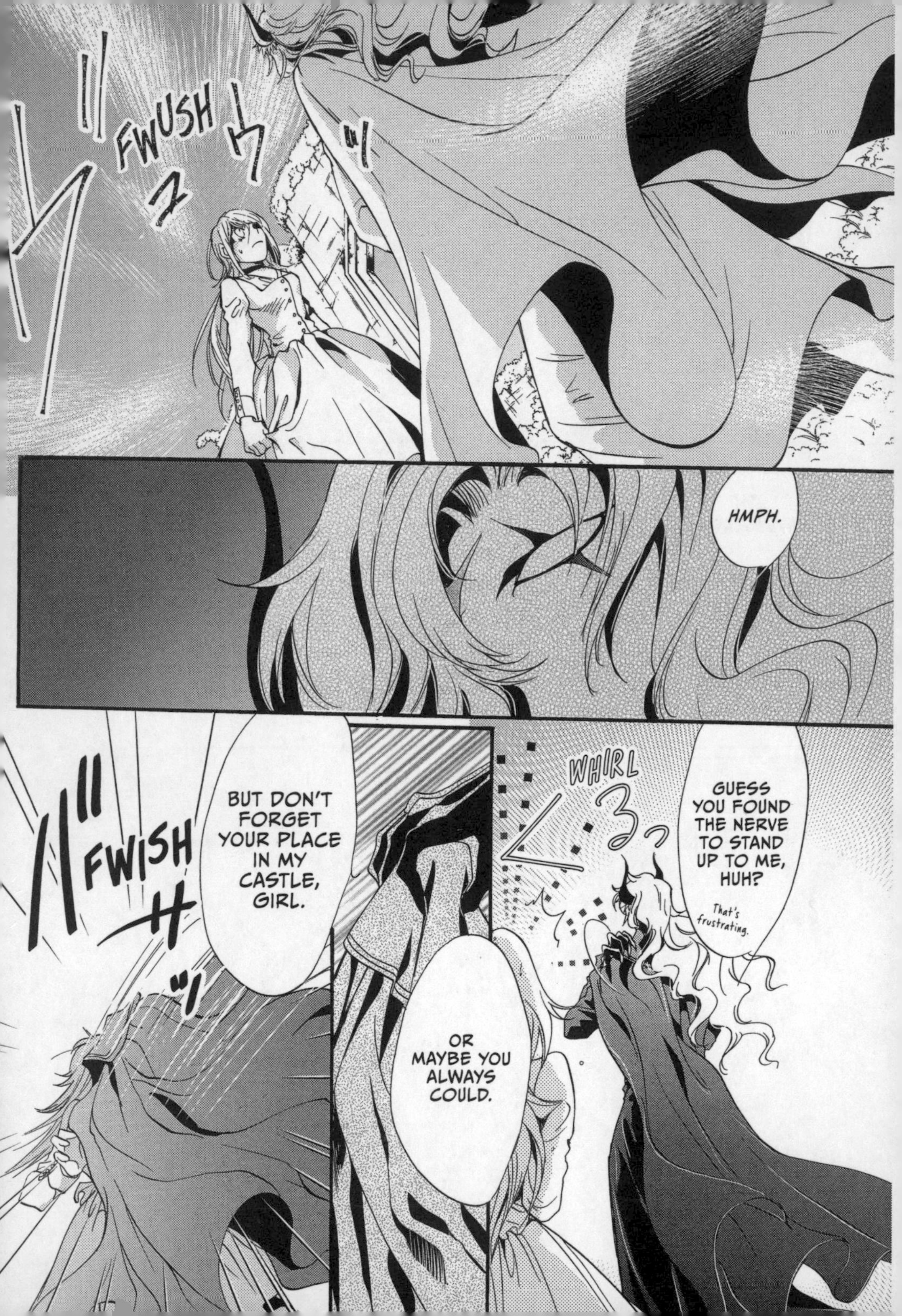
FWUSH
HMPH.
WHIRL
GUESS YOU FOUND THE NERVE TO STAND UP TO ME, HUH?
That's frustrating.
OR MAYBE YOU ALWAYS COULD.
FWISH
BUT DON'T FORGET YOUR PLACE IN MY CASTLE, GIRL.

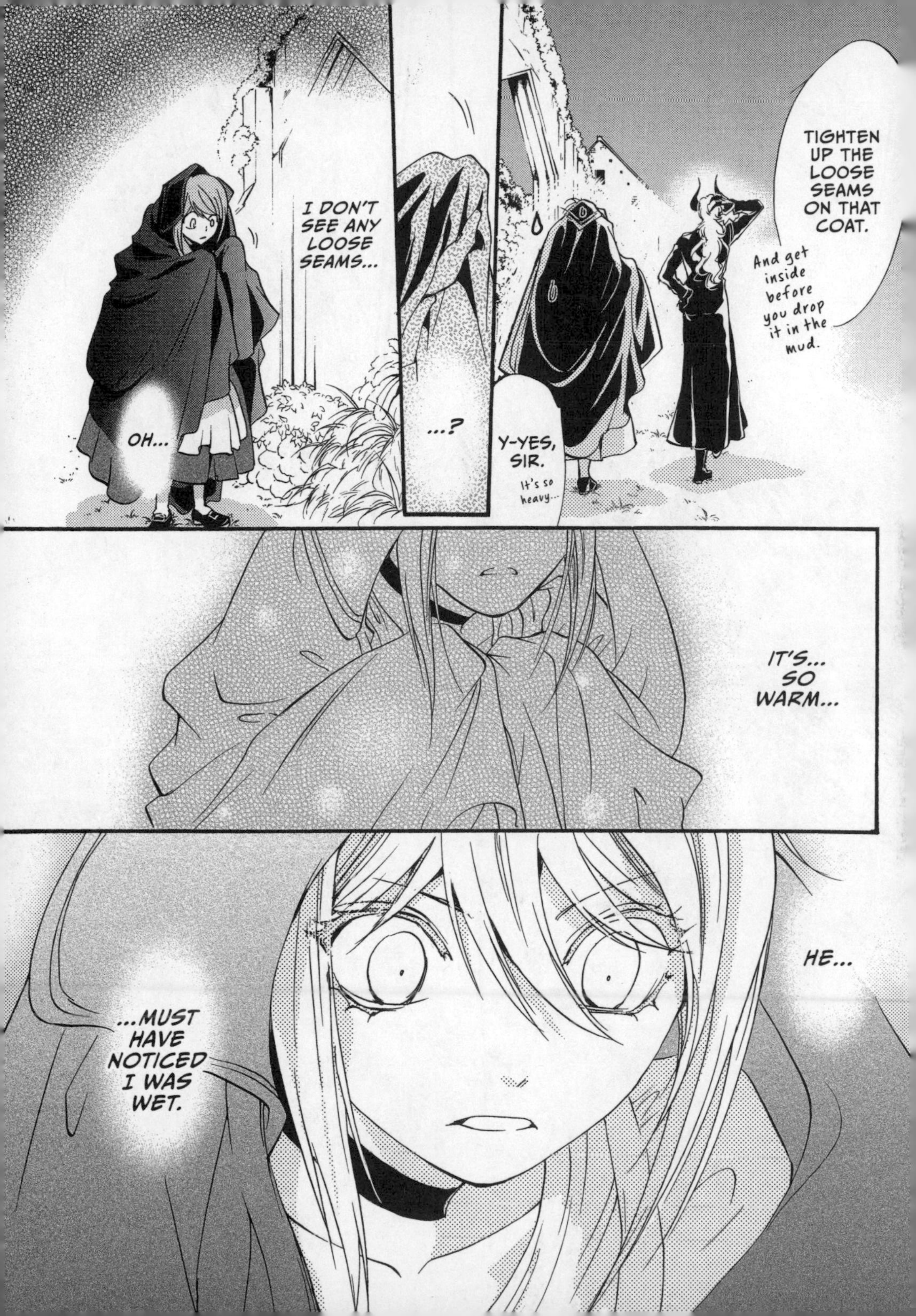

TIGHTEN UP THE LOOSE SEAMS ON THAT COAT.
And get inside before you drop it in the mud.
Y-YES, SIR.
It's so heavy...
...?
I DON'T SEE ANY LOOSE SEAMS...
OH...
IT'S... SO WARM...
HE...
...MUST HAVE NOTICED I WAS WET.

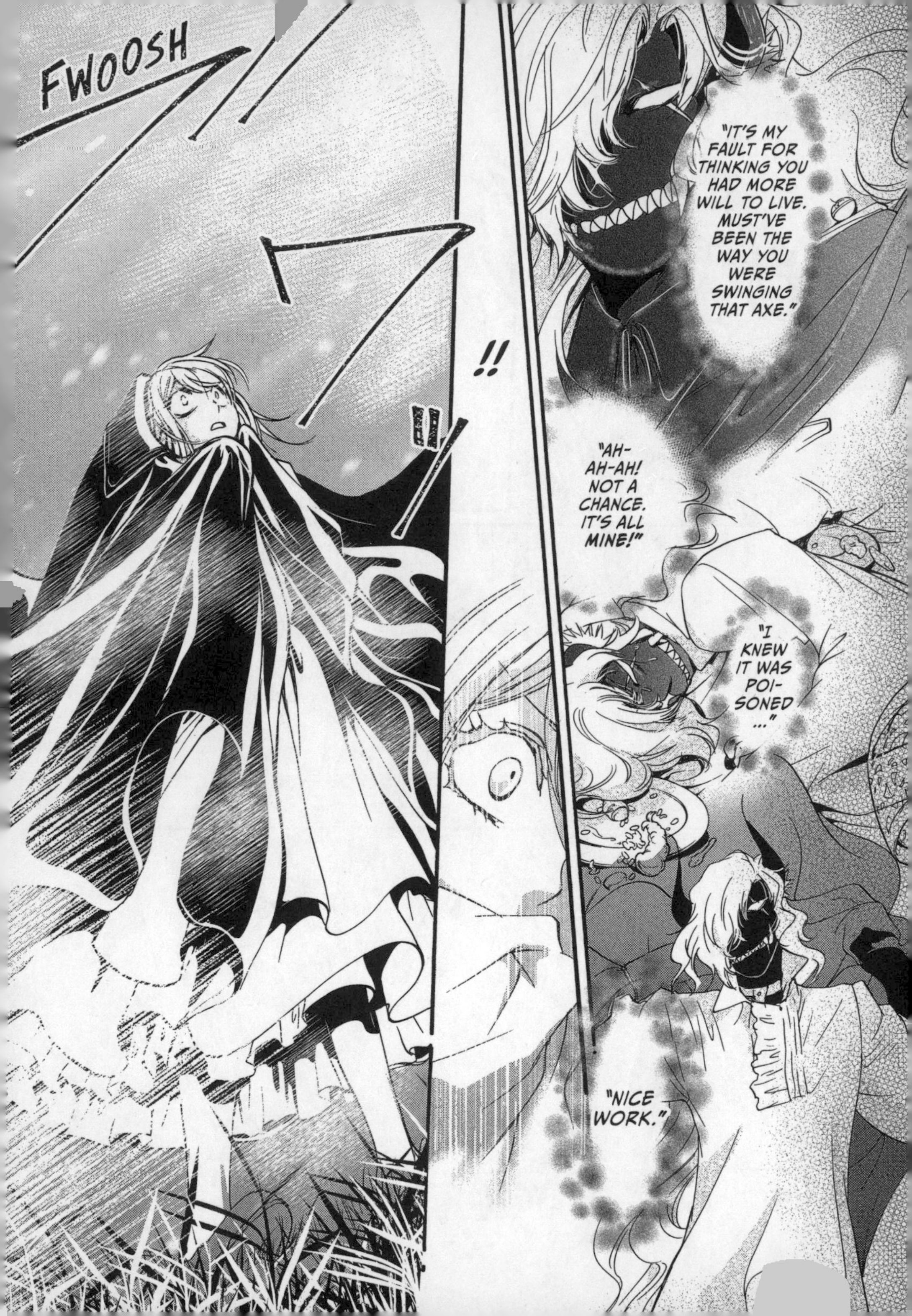
"IT'S MY FAULT FOR THINKING YOU HAD MORE WILL TO LIVE. MUST'VE BEEN THE WAY YOU WERE SWINGING THAT AXE."
"AH-AH-AH! NOT A CHANCE. IT'S ALL MINE!"
"I KNEW IT WAS POI-SONED ..."
"NICE WORK."
!!
FWOOSH

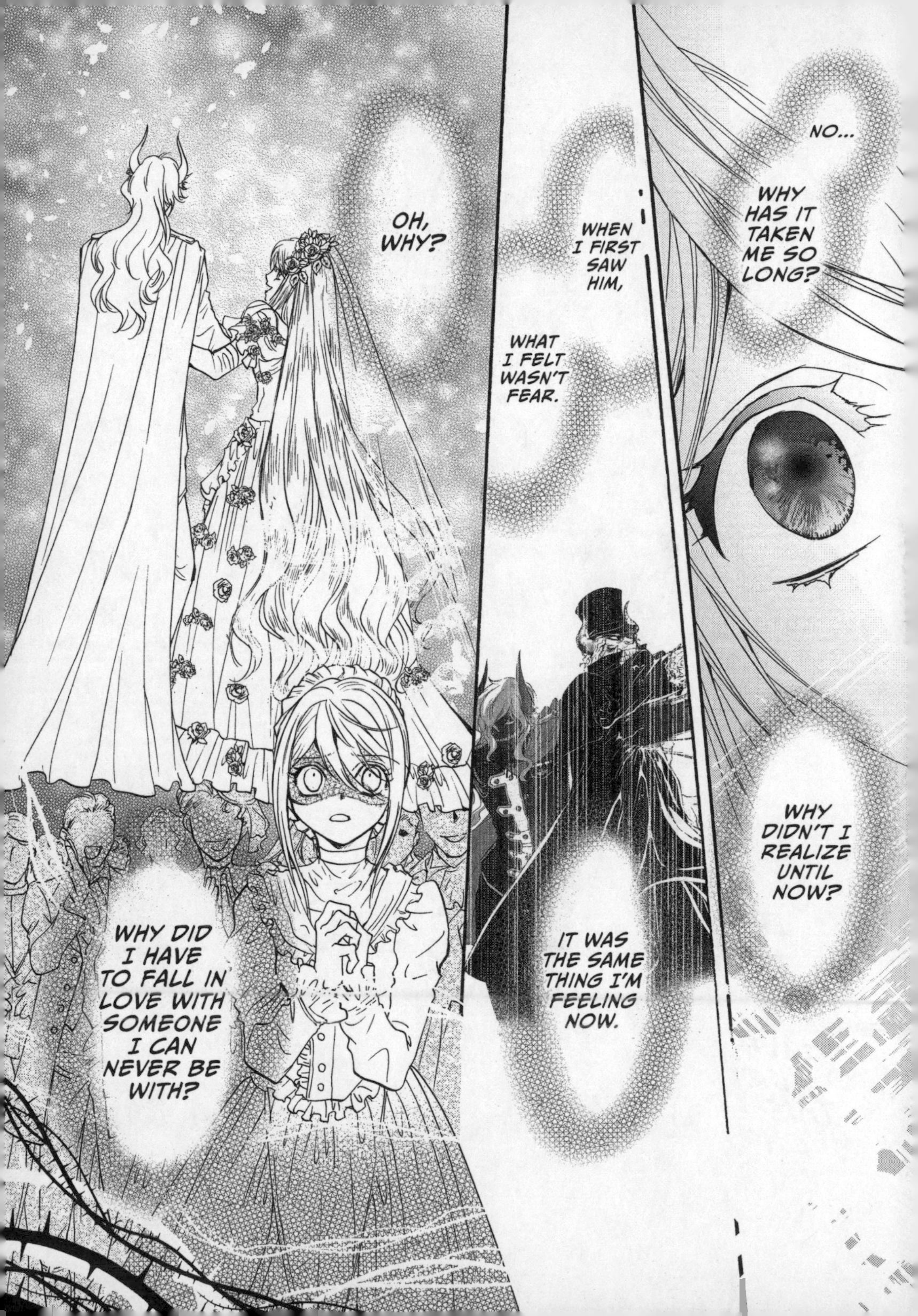
NO...
WHY HAS IT TAKEN ME SO LONG?
WHY DIDN'T I REALIZE UNTIL NOW?
WHEN I FIRST SAW HIM,
WHAT I FELT WASN'T FEAR.
IT WAS THE SAME THING I'M FEELING NOW.
OH, WHY?
WHY DID I HAVE TO FALL IN LOVE WITH SOMEONE I CAN NEVER BE WITH?

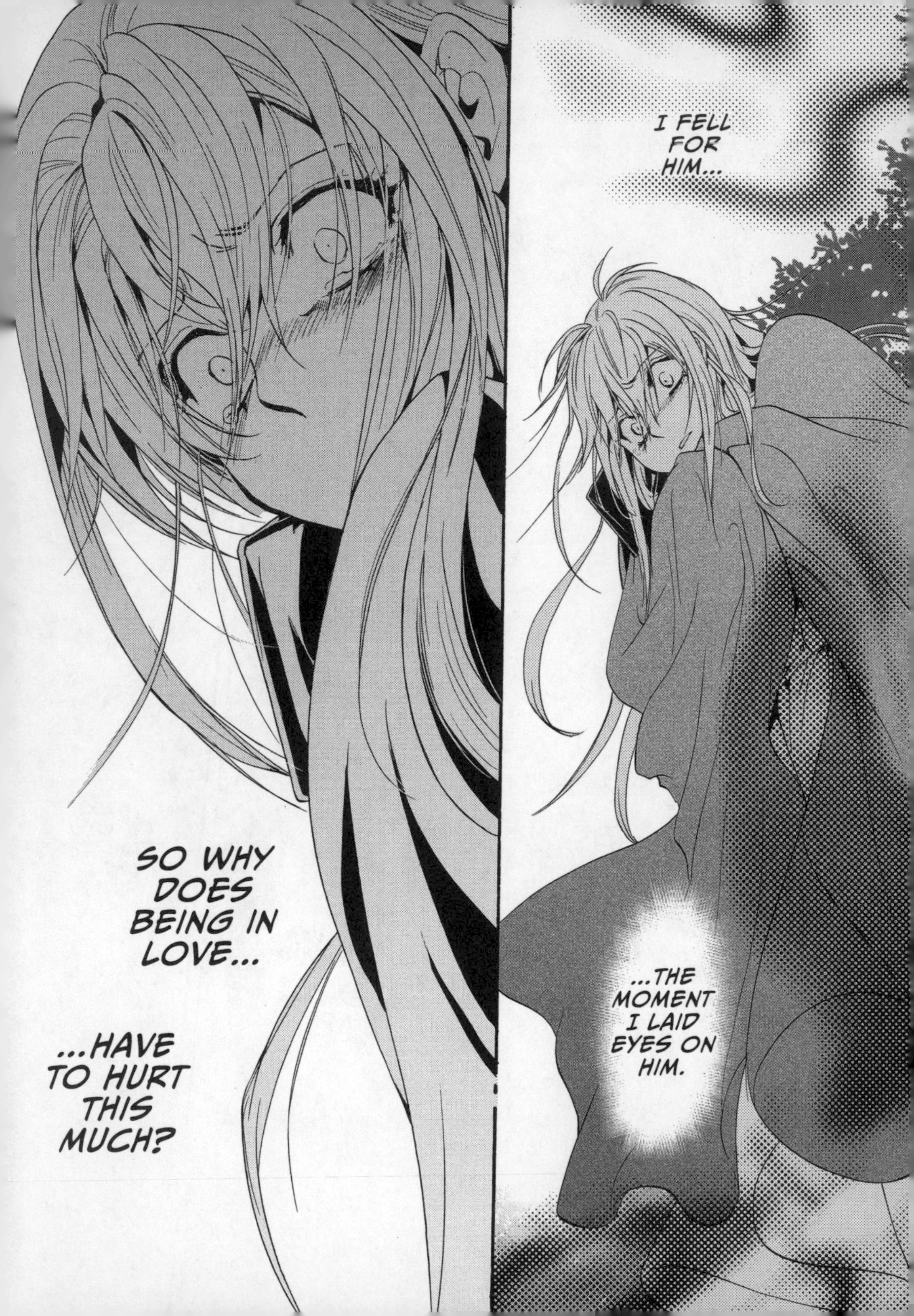
I FELL FOR HIM...
...THE MOMENT I LAID EYES ON HIM.
SO WHY DOES BEING IN LOVE...
...HAVE TO HURT THIS MUCH?

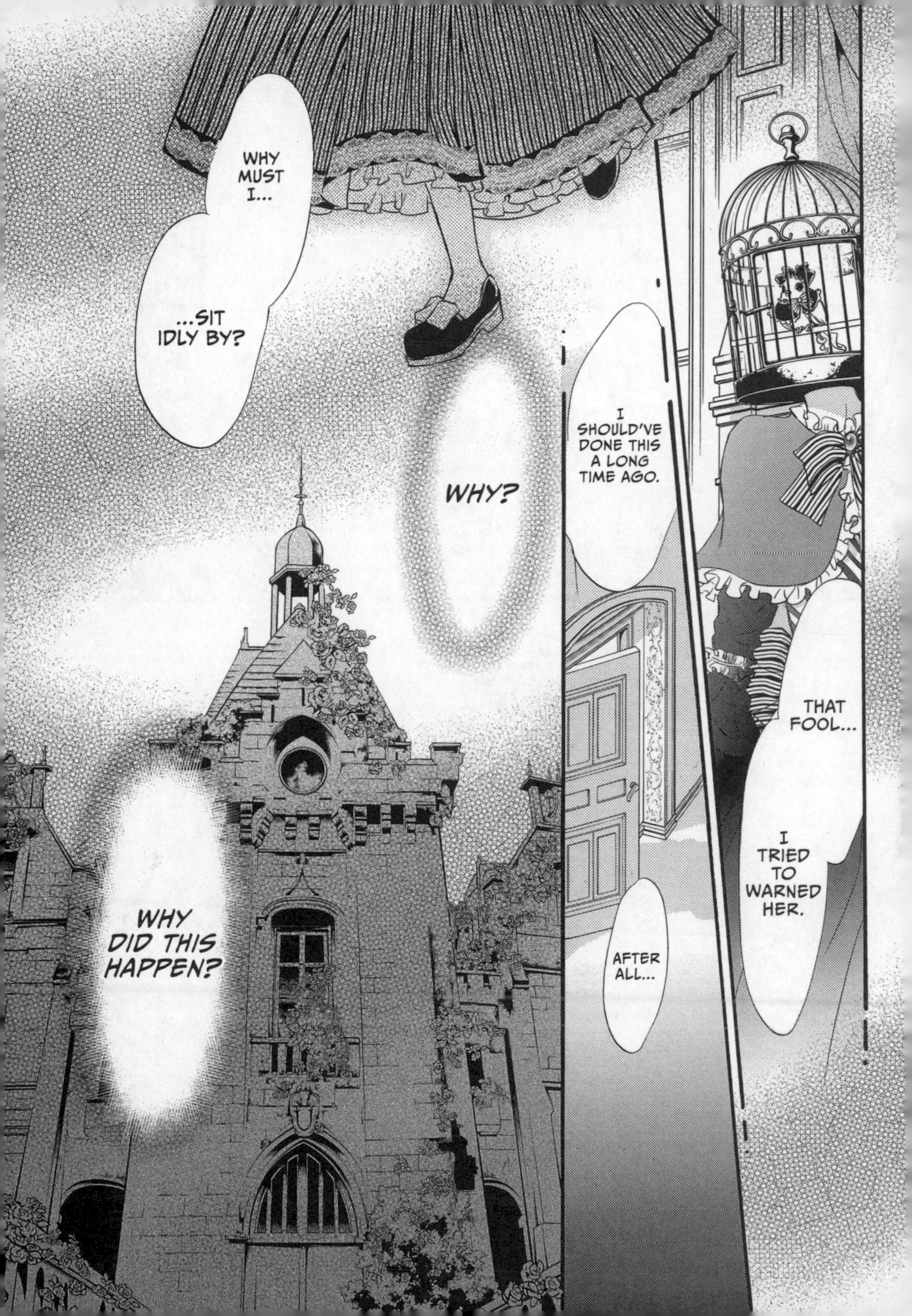
THAT FOOL...
I TRIED TO WARNED HER.
AFTER ALL...
I SHOULD'VE DONE THIS A LONG TIME AGO.
WHY MUST I...
...SIT IDLY BY?
WHY?
WHY DID THIS HAPPEN?

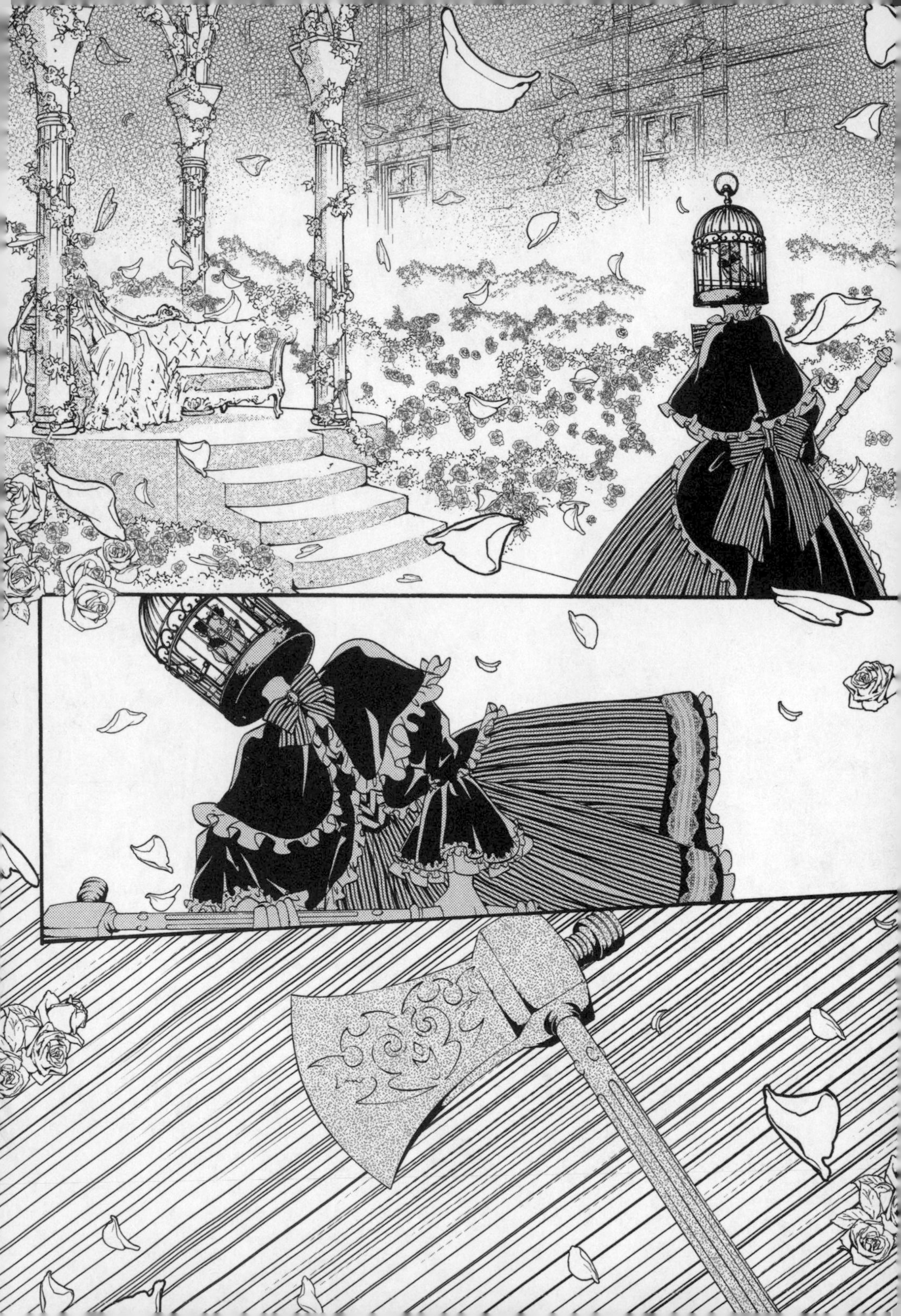

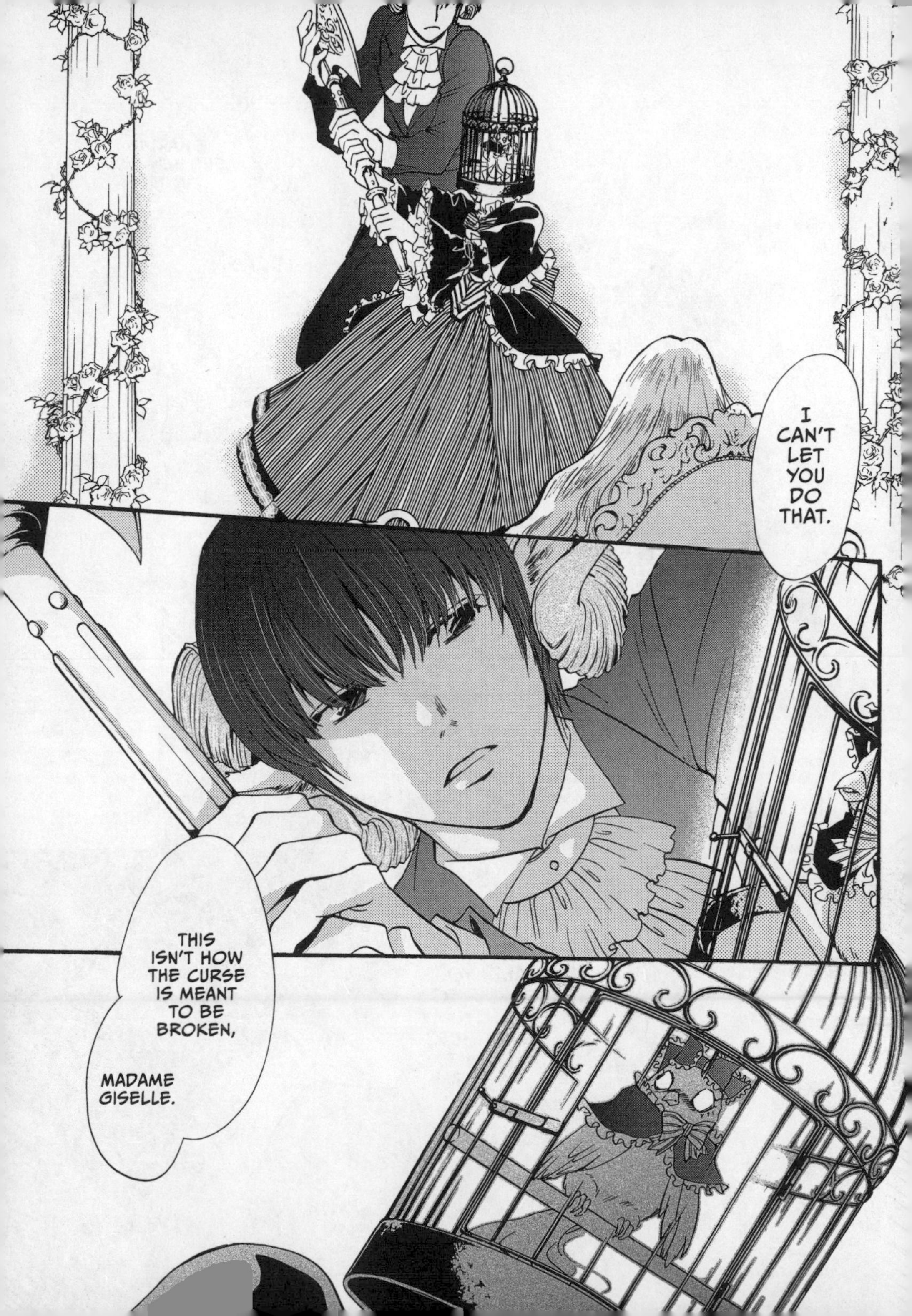
I CAN'T LET YOU DO THAT.
THIS ISN'T HOW THE CURSE IS MEANT TO BE BROKEN,
MADAME GISELLE.

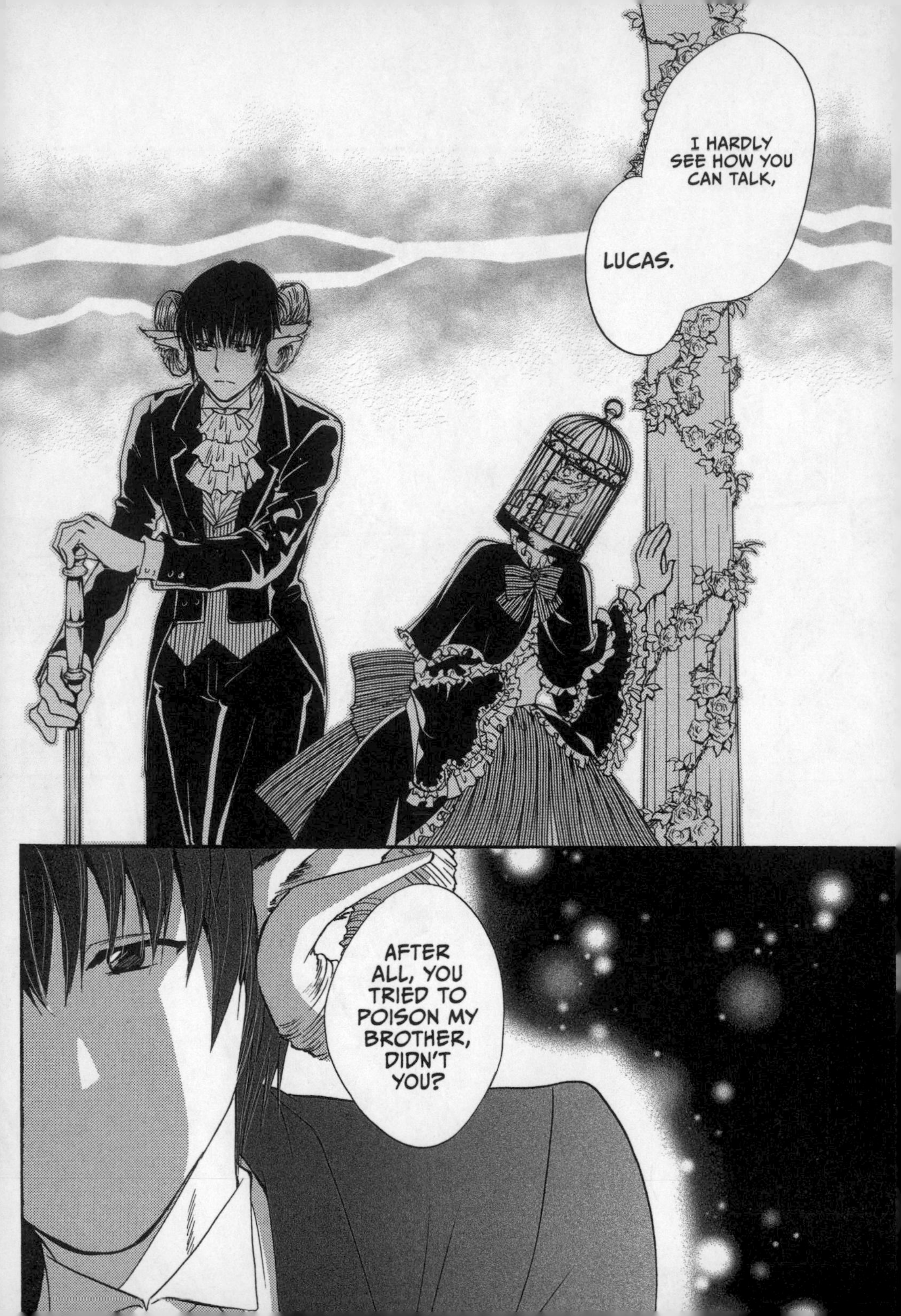
I HARDLY SEE HOW YOU CAN TALK,
LUCAS.
AFTER ALL, YOU TRIED TO POISON MY BROTHER, DIDN'T YOU?

LA BELLE ET LA BÊTE

DU PARADIS PERDU

CONTE
07

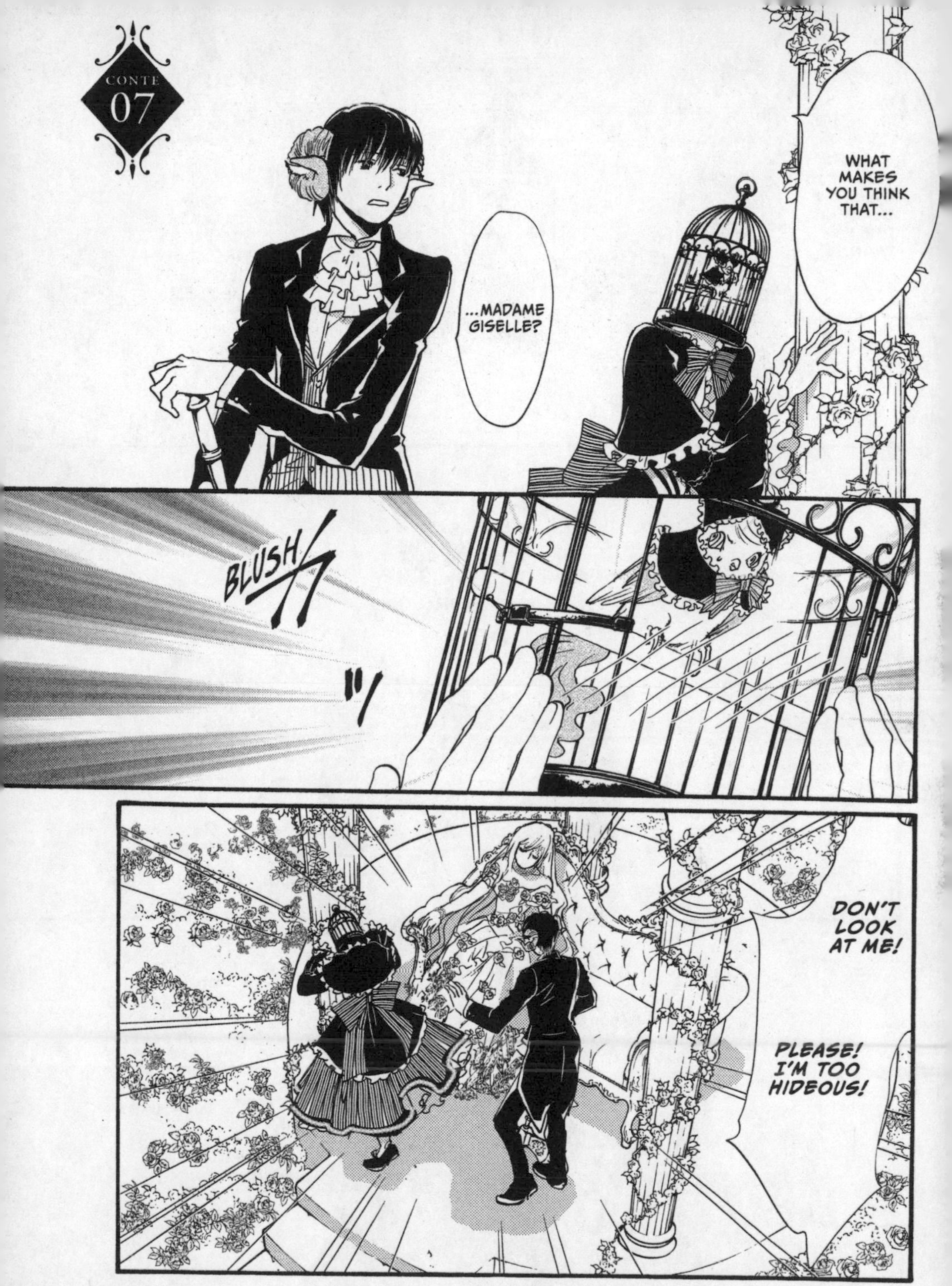
WHAT MAKES YOU THINK THAT...
...MADAME GISELLE?
BLUSH
DON'T LOOK AT ME!
PLEASE! I'M TOO HIDEOUS!

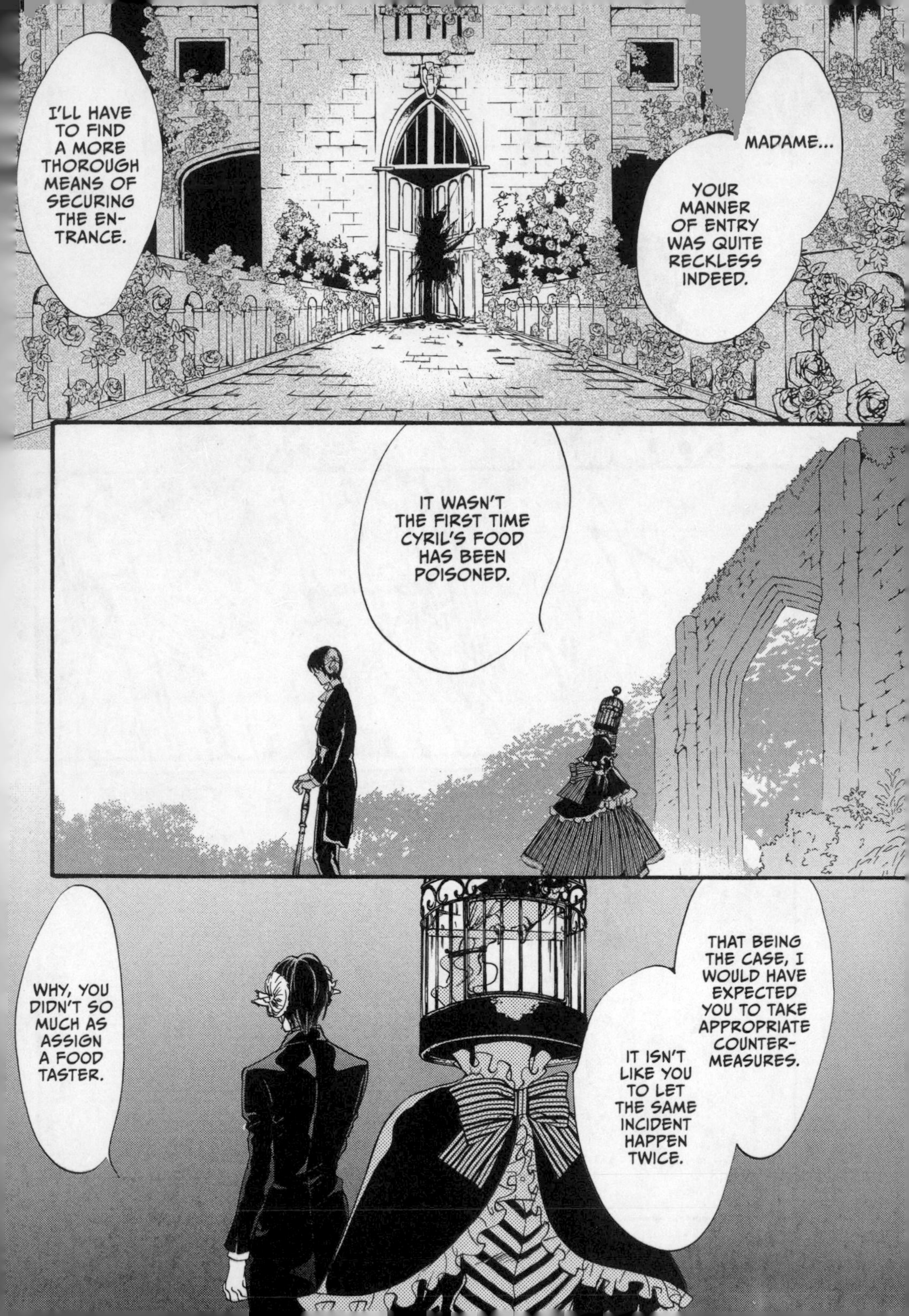
MADAME...
YOUR MANNER OF ENTRY WAS QUITE RECKLESS INDEED.
I'LL HAVE TO FIND A MORE THOROUGH MEANS OF SECURING THE EN-TRANCE.
IT WASN'T THE FIRST TIME CYRIL'S FOOD HAS BEEN POISONED.
THAT BEING THE CASE, I WOULD HAVE EXPECTED YOU TO TAKE APPROPRIATE COUNTER-MEASURES.
IT ISN'T LIKE YOU TO LET THE SAME INCIDENT HAPPEN TWICE.
WHY, YOU DIDN'T SO MUCH AS ASSIGN A FOOD TASTER.

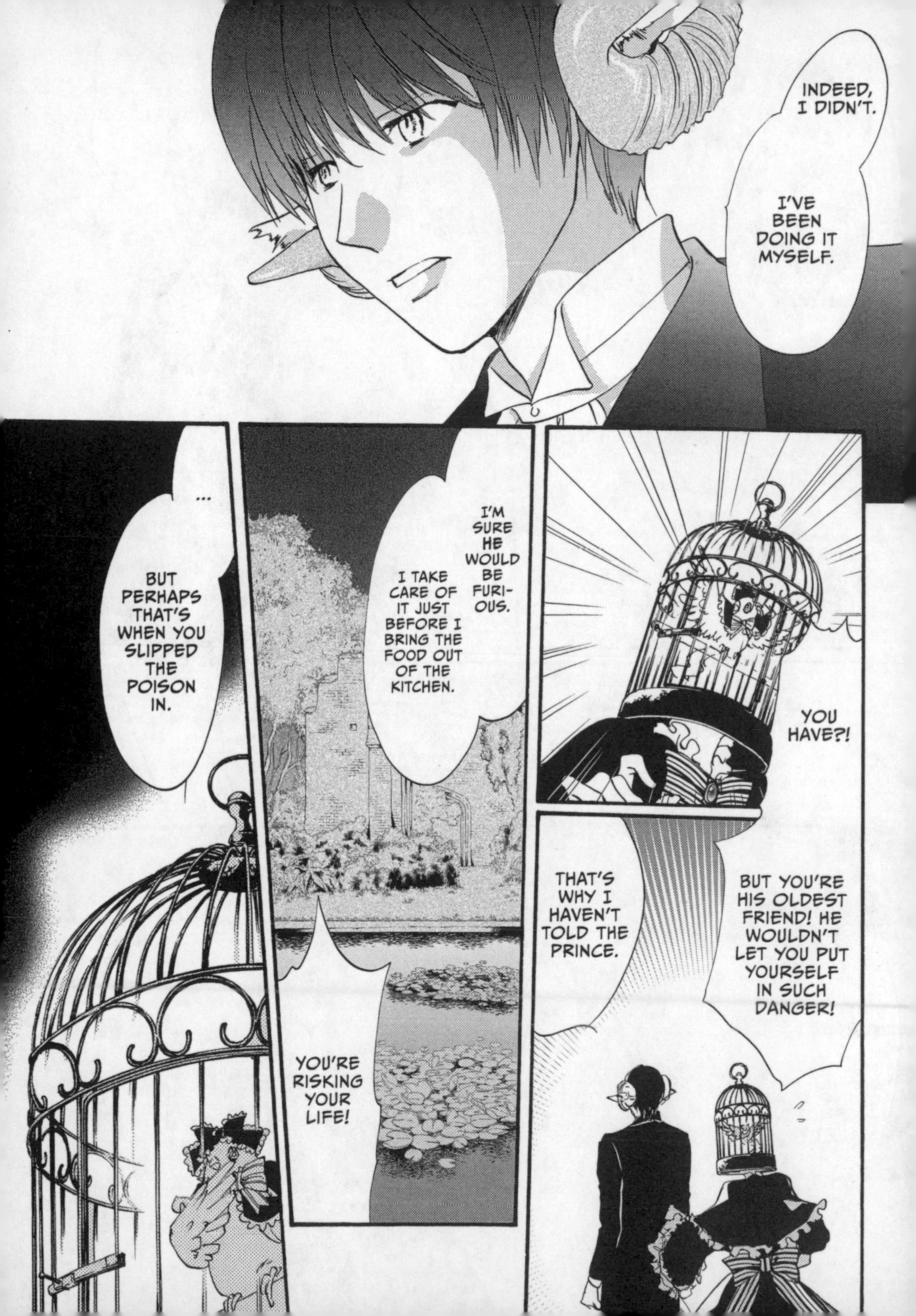
INDEED, I DIDN'T.
I'VE BEEN DOING IT MYSELF.
YOU HAVE?!
BUT YOU'RE HIS OLDEST FRIEND! HE WOULDN'T LET YOU PUT YOURSELF IN SUCH DANGER!
THAT'S WHY I HAVEN'T TOLD THE PRINCE.
I'M SURE HE WOULD BE FURI-OUS.
I TAKE CARE OF IT JUST BEFORE I BRING THE FOOD OUT OF THE KITCHEN.
YOU'RE RISKING YOUR LIFE!
...
BUT PERHAPS THAT'S WHEN YOU SLIPPED THE POISON IN.

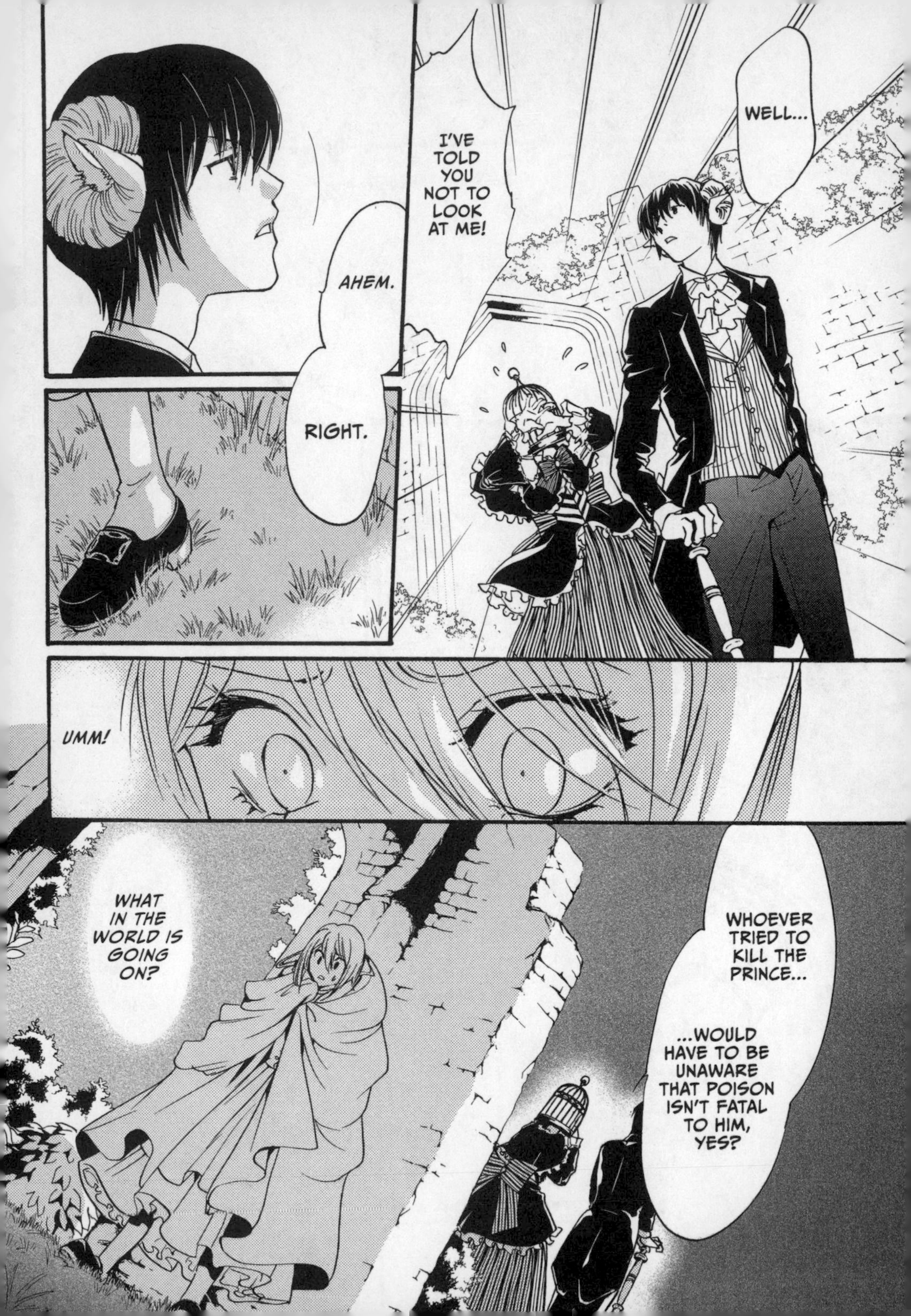
WELL...
I'VE TOLD YOU NOT TO LOOK AT ME!
AHEM.
RIGHT.
UMM!
WHOEVER TRIED TO KILL THE PRINCE...
...WOULD HAVE TO BE UNAWARE THAT POISON ISN'T FATAL TO HIM, YES?
WHAT IN THE WORLD IS GOING ON?

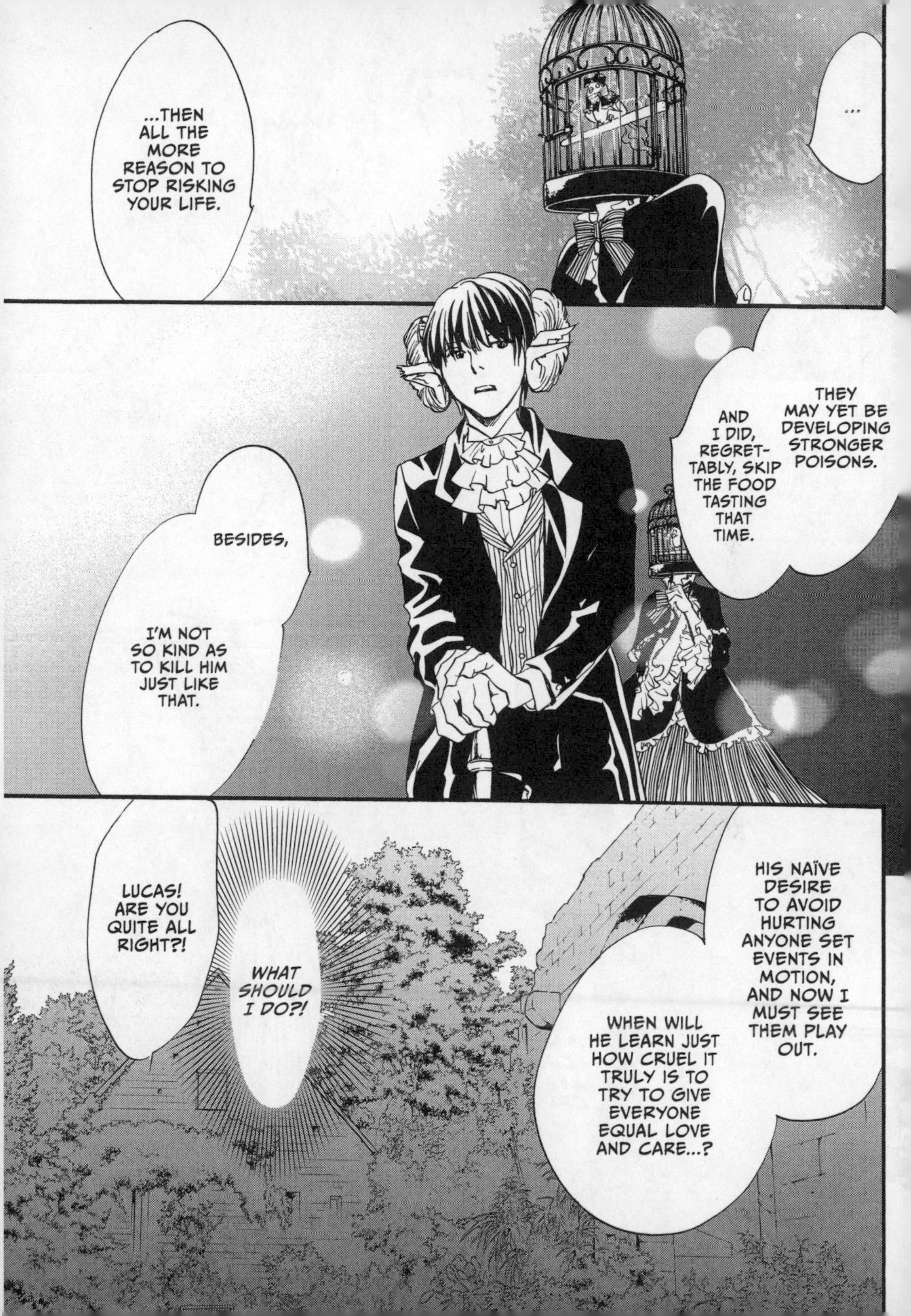
...
...THEN ALL THE MORE REASON TO STOP RISKING YOUR LIFE.
THEY MAY YET BE DEVELOPING STRONGER POISONS.
AND I DID, REGRET-TABLY, SKIP THE FOOD TASTING THAT TIME.
BESIDES,
I'M NOT SO KIND AS TO KILL HIM JUST LIKE THAT.
HIS NAÏVE DESIRE TO AVOID HURTING ANYONE SET EVENTS IN MOTION, AND NOW I MUST SEE THEM PLAY OUT.
WHEN WILL HE LEARN JUST HOW CRUEL IT TRULY IS TO TRY TO GIVE EVERYONE EQUAL LOVE AND CARE...?
LUCAS! ARE YOU QUITE ALL RIGHT?!
WHAT SHOULD I DO?!

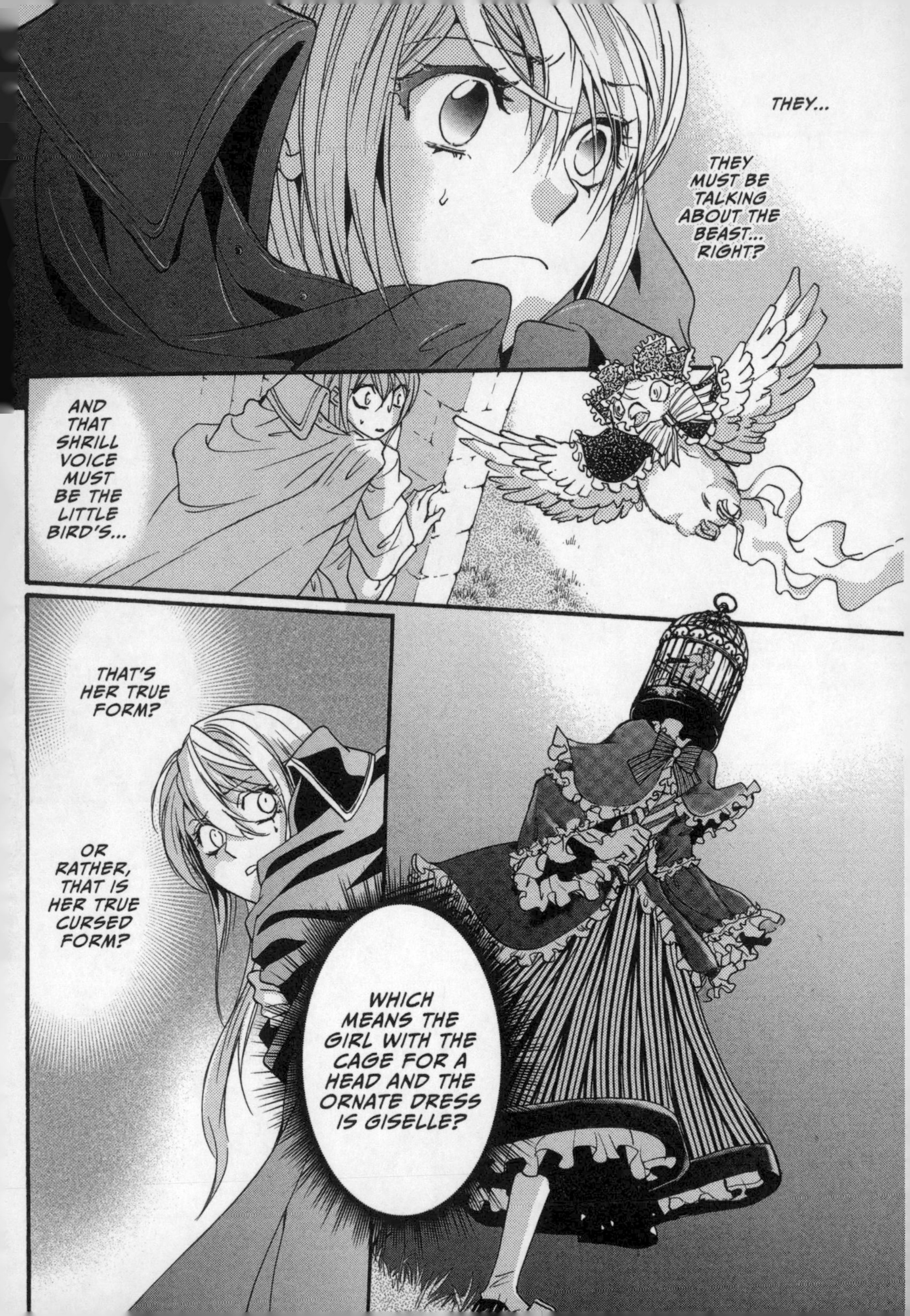
THEY...
THEY MUST BE TALKING ABOUT THE BEAST... RIGHT?
AND THAT SHRILL VOICE MUST BE THE LITTLE BIRD'S...
THAT'S HER TRUE FORM?
OR RATHER, THAT IS HER TRUE CURSED FORM?
WHICH MEANS THE GIRL WITH THE CAGE FOR A HEAD AND THE ORNATE DRESS IS GISELLE?

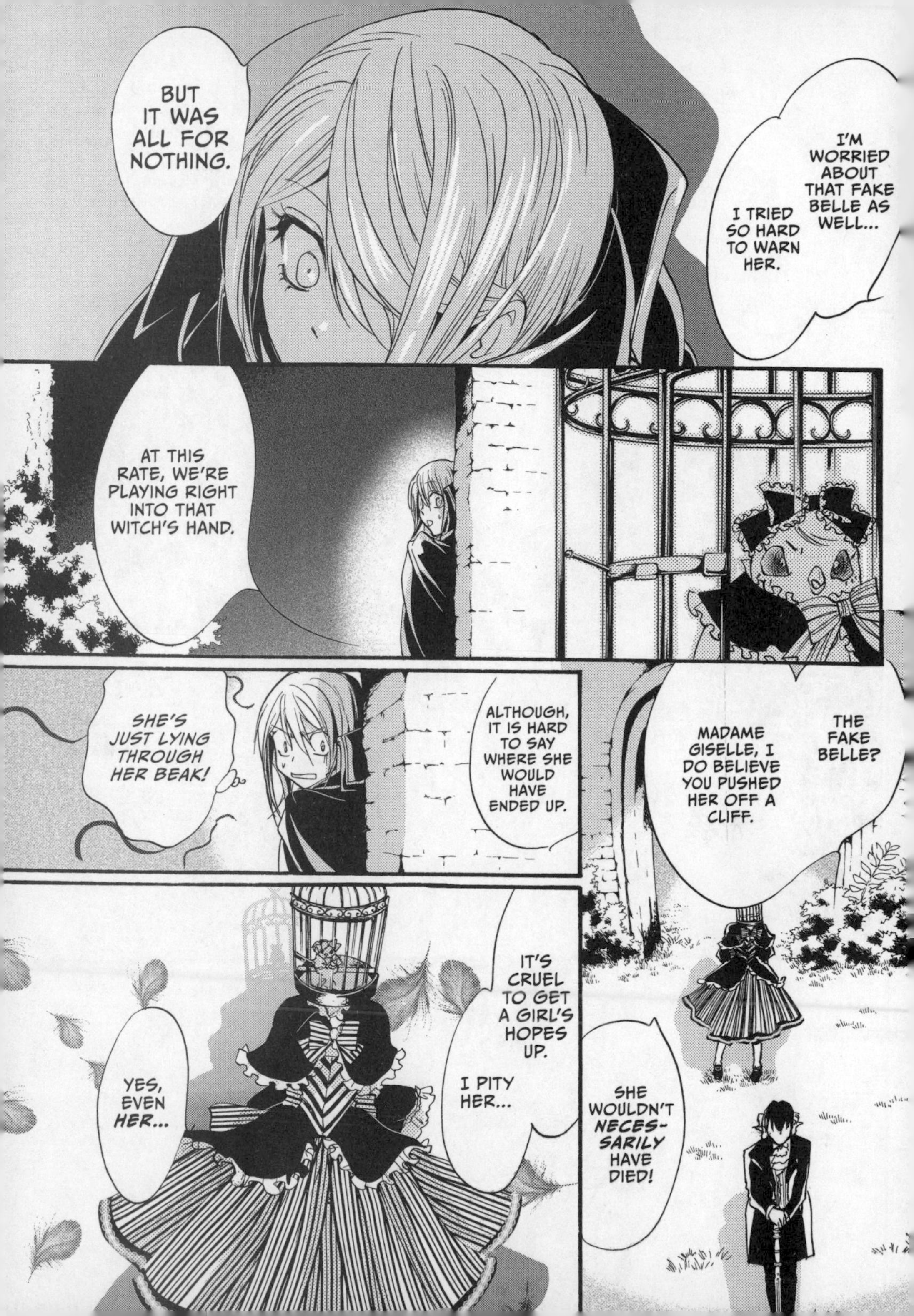
I'M WORRIED ABOUT THAT FAKE BELLE AS WELL...
I TRIED SO HARD TO WARN HER.
BUT IT WAS ALL FOR NOTHING.
AT THIS RATE, WE'RE PLAYING RIGHT INTO THAT WITCH'S HAND.
THE FAKE BELLE?
MADAME GISELLE, I DO BELIEVE YOU PUSHED HER OFF A CLIFF.
SHE WOULDN'T *NECES-SARILY* HAVE DIED!
ALTHOUGH, IT IS HARD TO SAY WHERE SHE WOULD HAVE ENDED UP.
SHE'S JUST LYING THROUGH HER BEAK!
IT'S CRUEL TO GET A GIRL'S HOPES UP.
I PITY HER...
YES, EVEN *HER*...

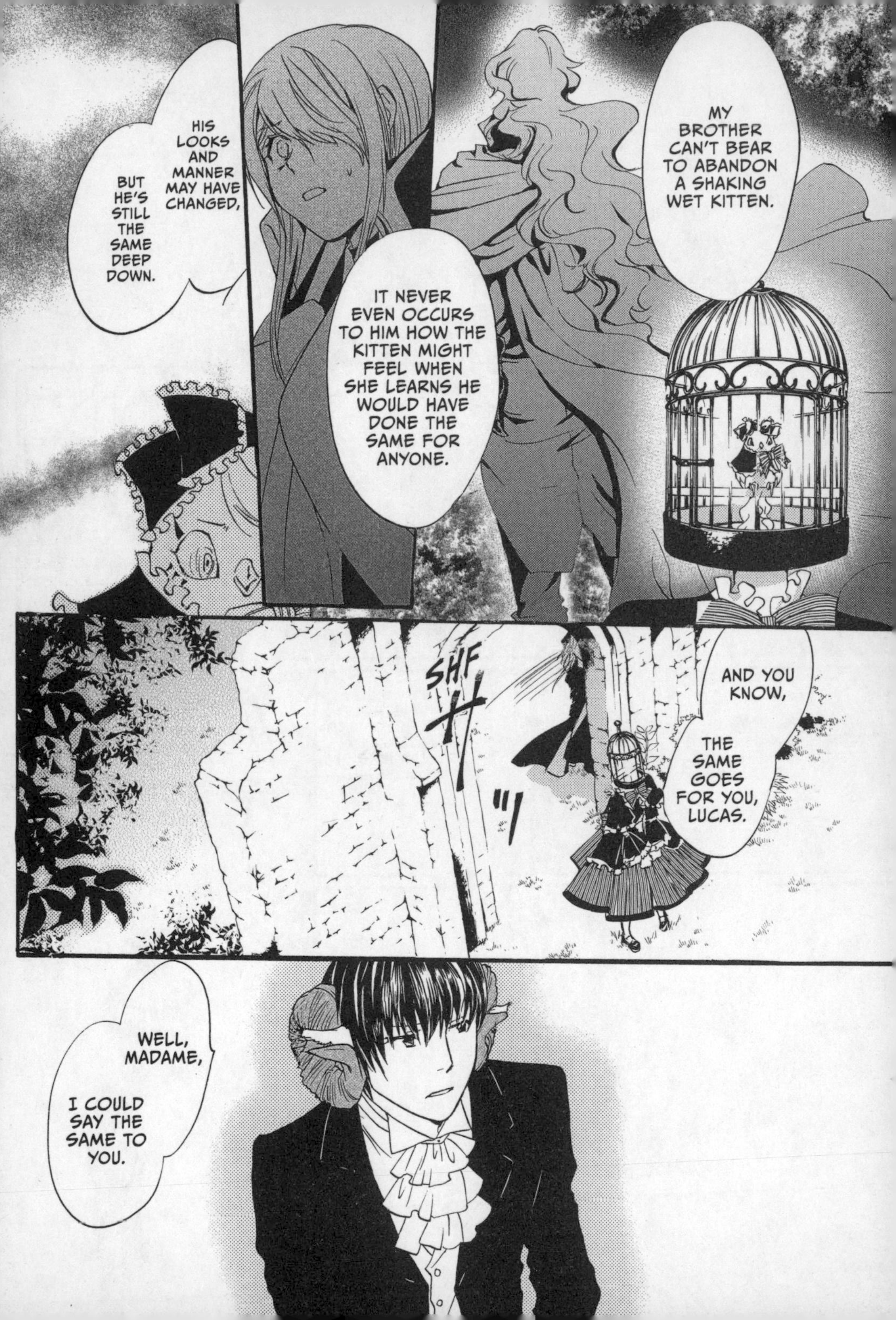
MY BROTHER CAN'T BEAR TO ABANDON A SHAKING WET KITTEN.
IT NEVER EVEN OCCURS TO HIM HOW THE KITTEN MIGHT FEEL WHEN SHE LEARNS HE WOULD HAVE DONE THE SAME FOR ANYONE.
HIS LOOKS AND MANNER MAY HAVE CHANGED,
BUT HE'S STILL THE SAME DEEP DOWN.
AND YOU KNOW,
THE SAME GOES FOR YOU, LUCAS.
SHF
WELL, MADAME,
I COULD SAY THE SAME TO YOU.

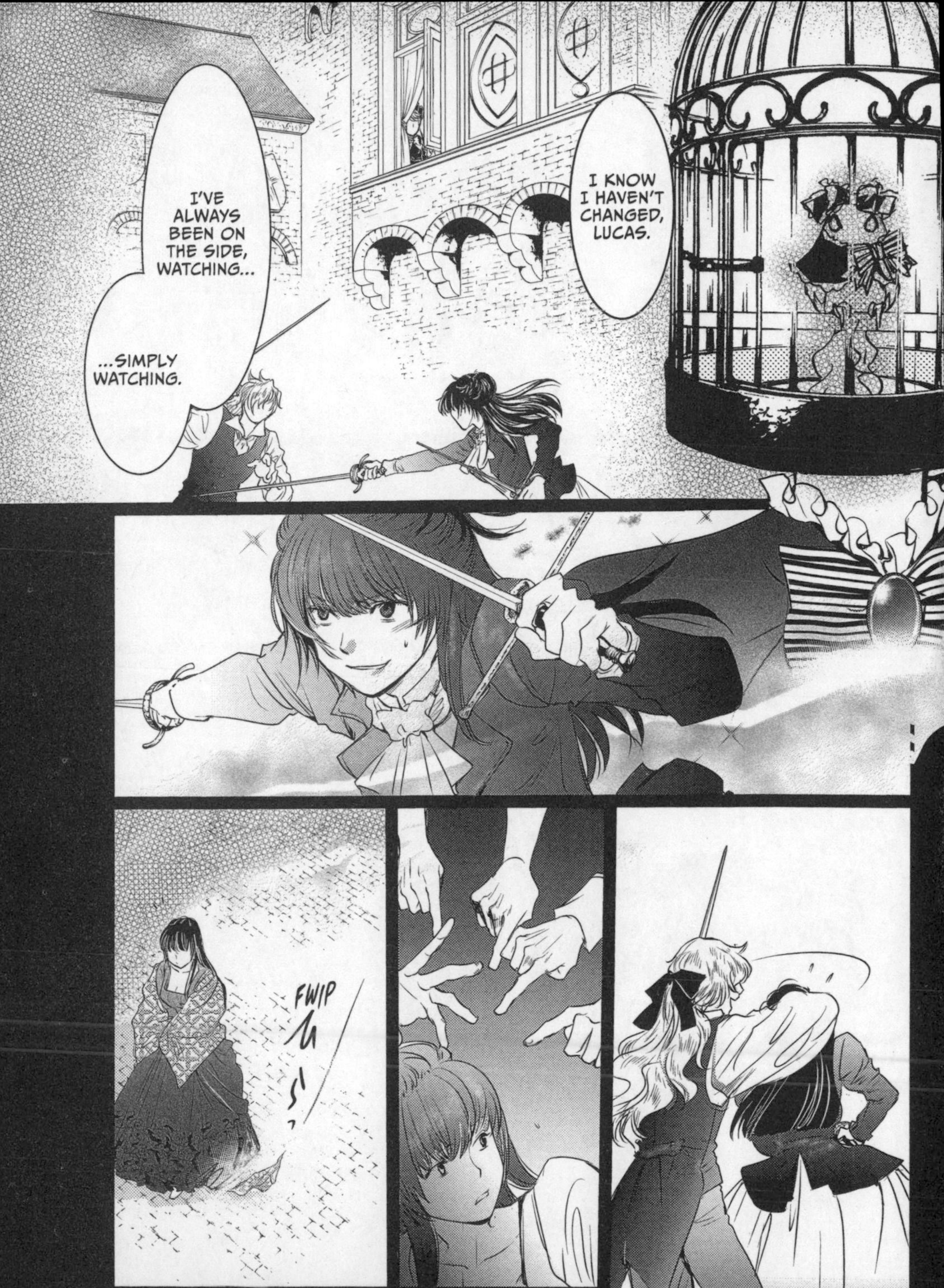
I KNOW I HAVEN'T CHANGED, LUCAS.
I'VE ALWAYS BEEN ON THE SIDE, WATCHING...
...SIMPLY WATCHING.
FWIP

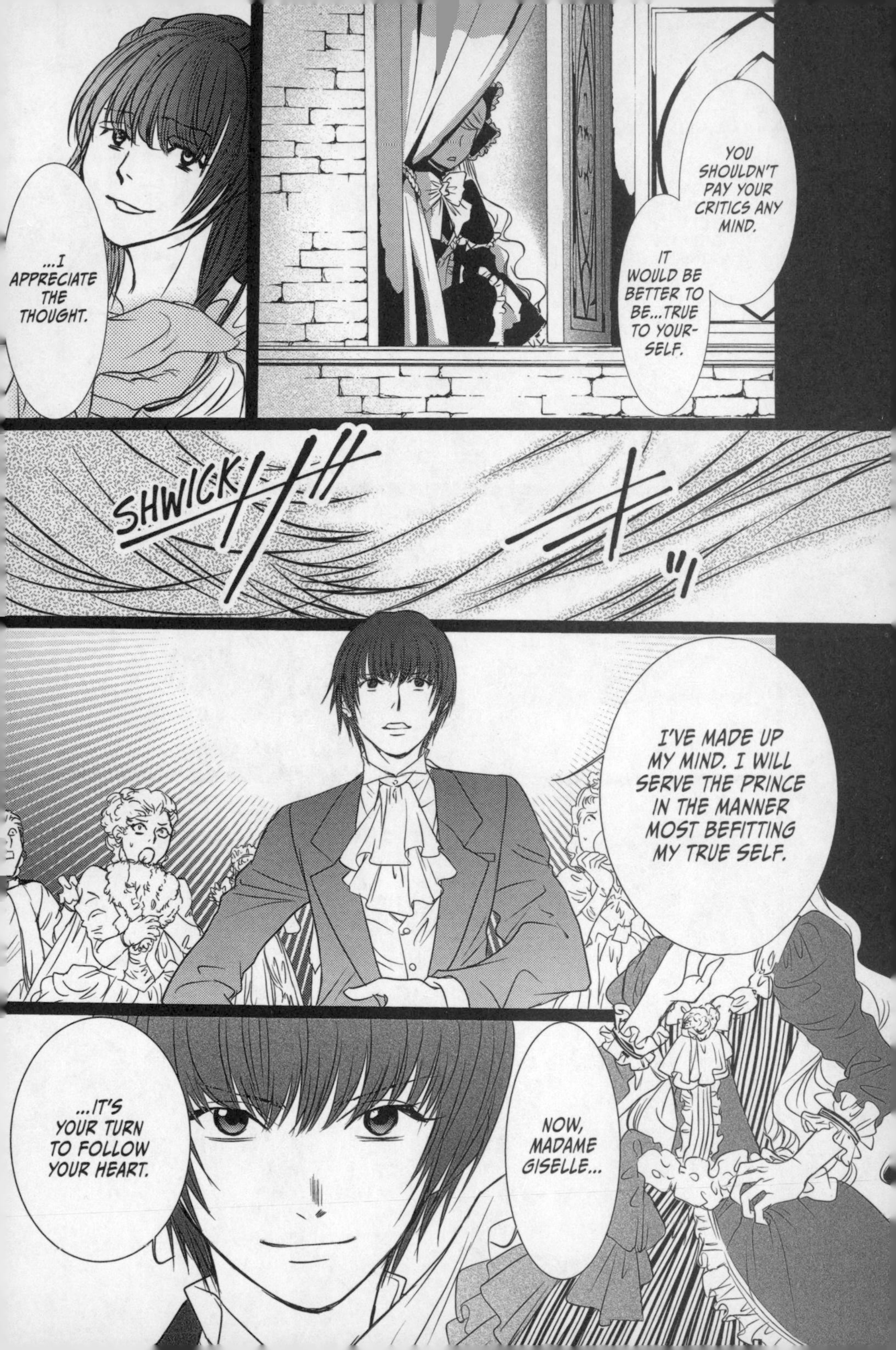
YOU SHOULDN'T PAY YOUR CRITICS ANY MIND.
IT WOULD BE BETTER TO BE...TRUE TO YOURSELF.
...I APPRECIATE THE THOUGHT.
SHWICK
I'VE MADE UP MY MIND. I WILL SERVE THE PRINCE IN THE MANNER MOST BEFITTING MY TRUE SELF.
NOW, MADAME GISELLE...
...IT'S YOUR TURN TO FOLLOW YOUR HEART.

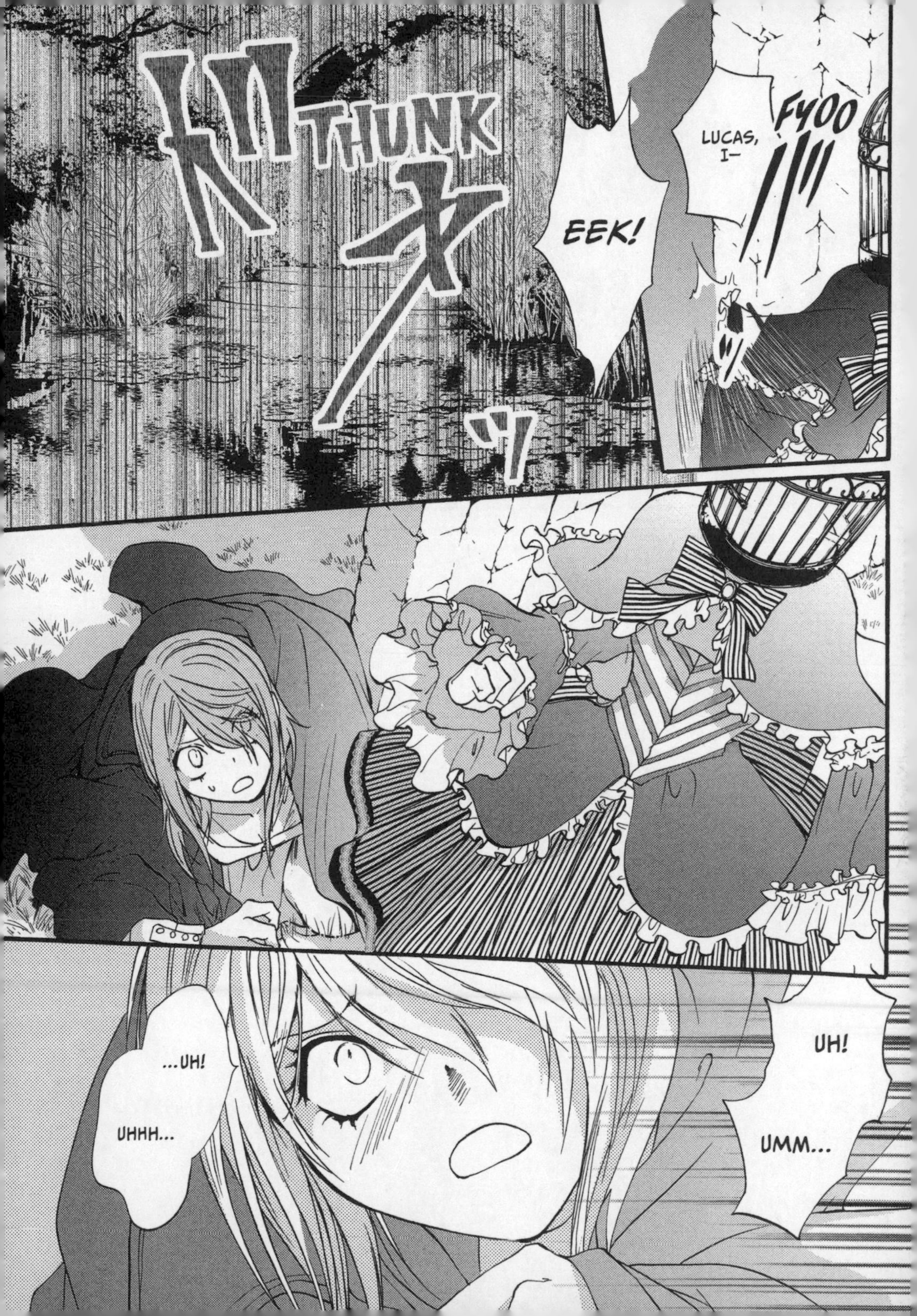

FYOO
LUCAS, I—
EEK!
THUNK
UH!
UMM...
...UH!
UHHH...

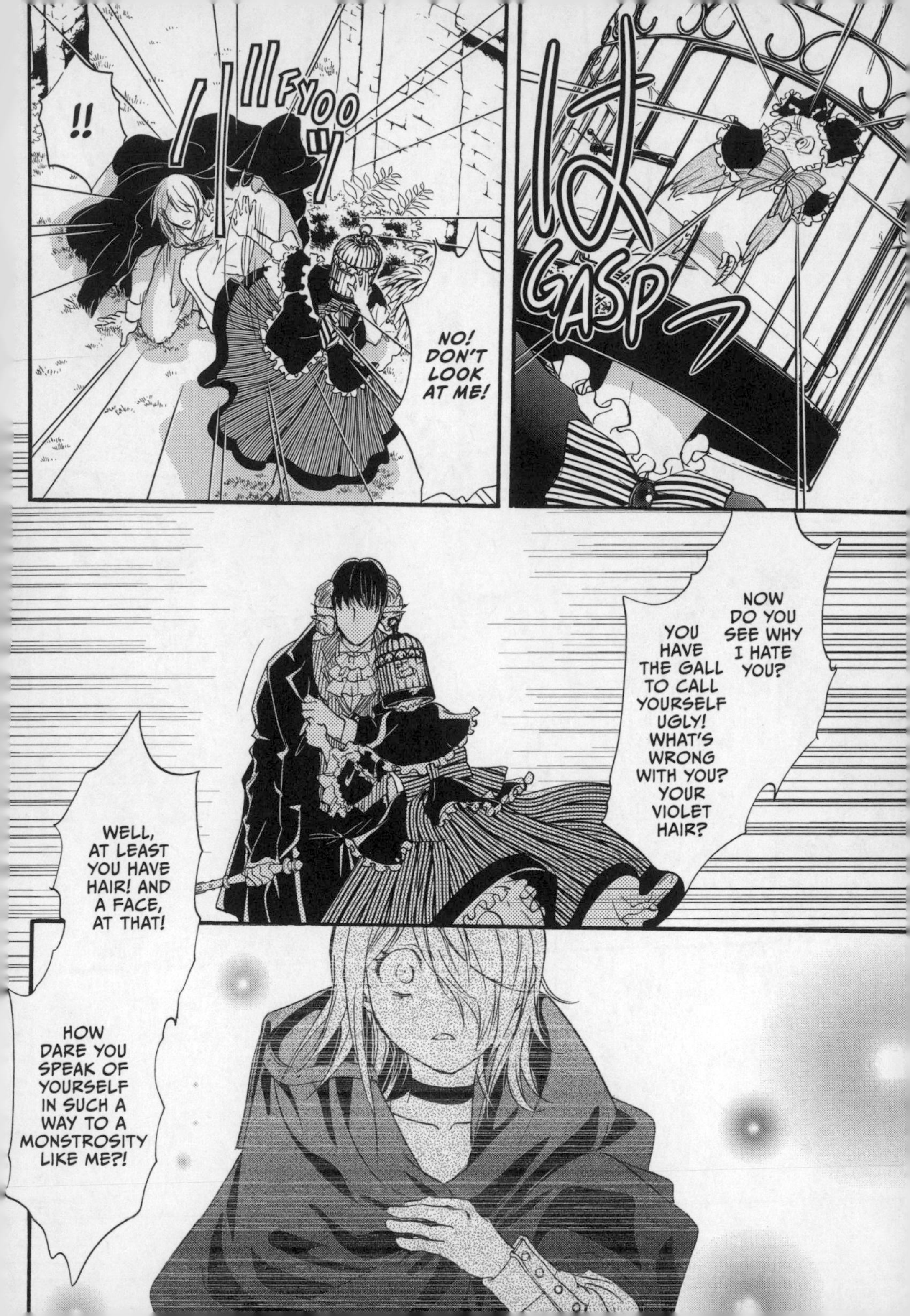
GASP
FYOO
!!
NO! DON'T LOOK AT ME!
NOW DO YOU SEE WHY I HATE YOU?
YOU HAVE THE GALL TO CALL YOURSELF UGLY! WHAT'S WRONG WITH YOU? YOUR VIOLET HAIR?
WELL, AT LEAST YOU HAVE HAIR! AND A FACE, AT THAT!
HOW DARE YOU SPEAK OF YOURSELF IN SUCH A WAY TO A MONSTROSITY LIKE ME?!

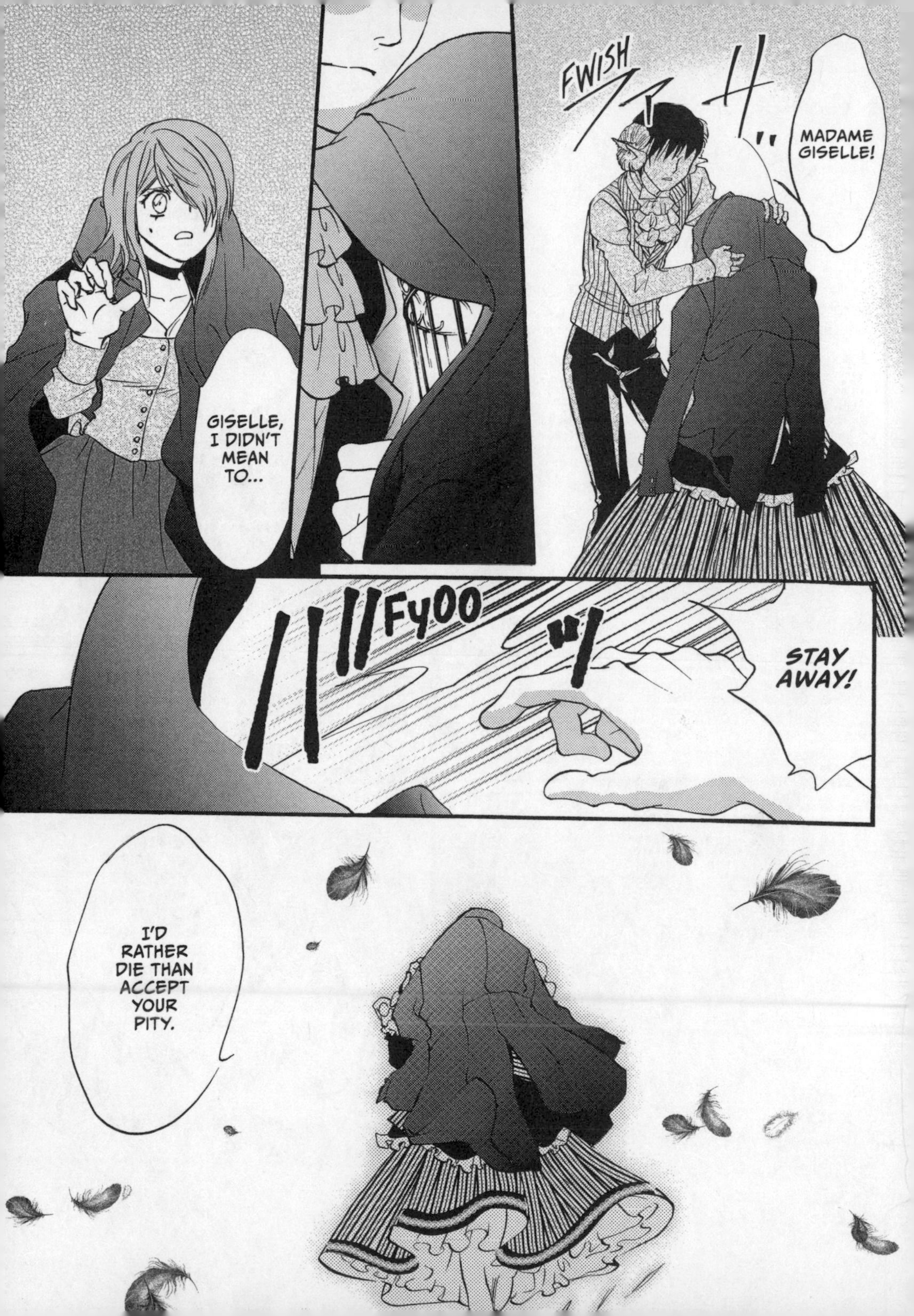
MADAME GISELLE!
FWISH
GISELLE, I DIDN'T MEAN TO...
STAY AWAY!
Fyoo
I'D RATHER DIE THAN ACCEPT YOUR PITY.

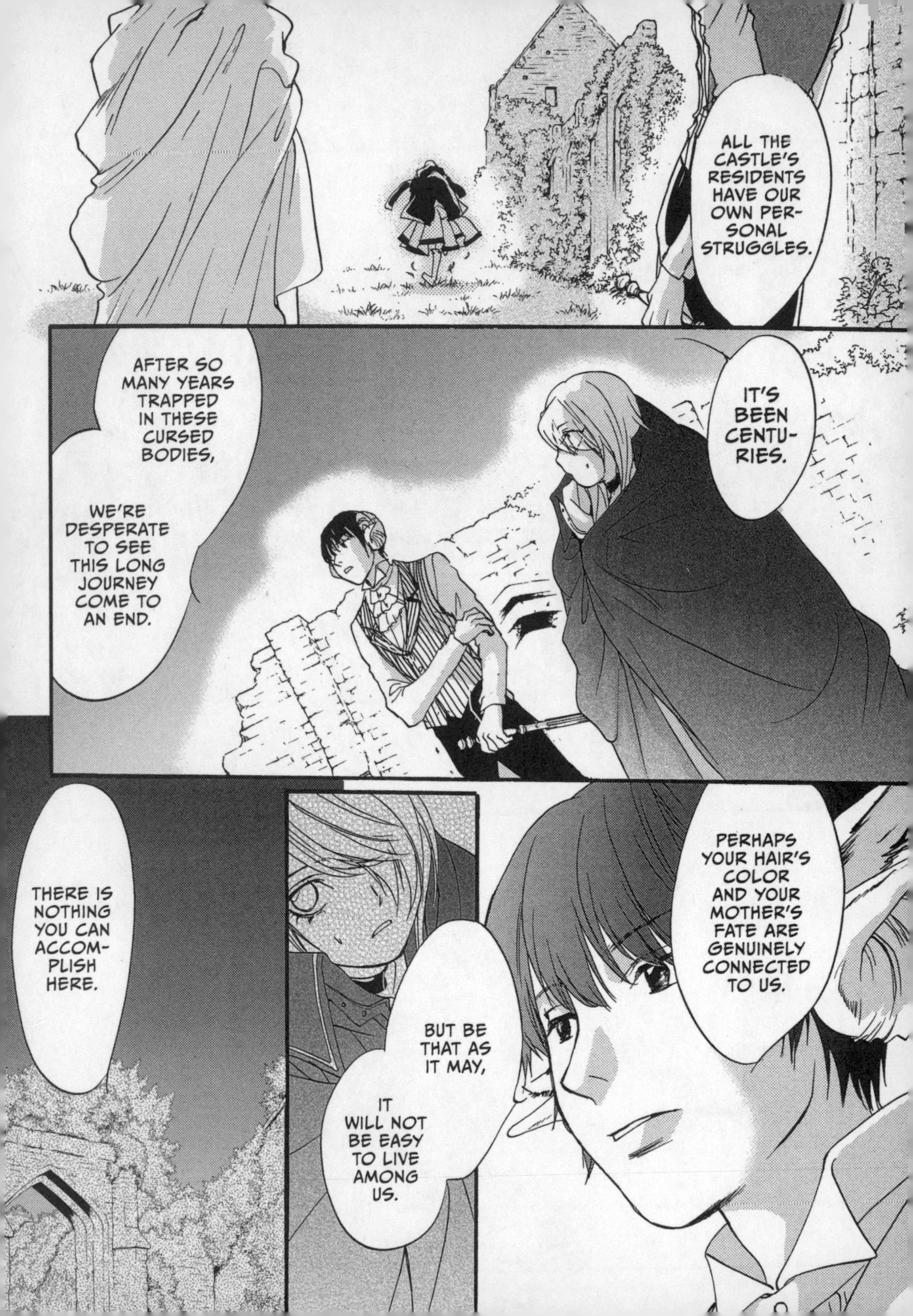
ALL THE CASTLE'S RESIDENTS HAVE OUR OWN PERSONAL STRUGGLES.
IT'S BEEN CENTURIES.
AFTER SO MANY YEARS TRAPPED IN THESE CURSED BODIES,
WE'RE DESPERATE TO SEE THIS LONG JOURNEY COME TO AN END.
PERHAPS YOUR HAIR'S COLOR AND YOUR MOTHER'S FATE ARE GENUINELY CONNECTED TO US.
BUT BE THAT AS IT MAY,
IT WILL NOT BE EASY TO LIVE AMONG US.
THERE IS NOTHING YOU CAN ACCOMPLISH HERE.

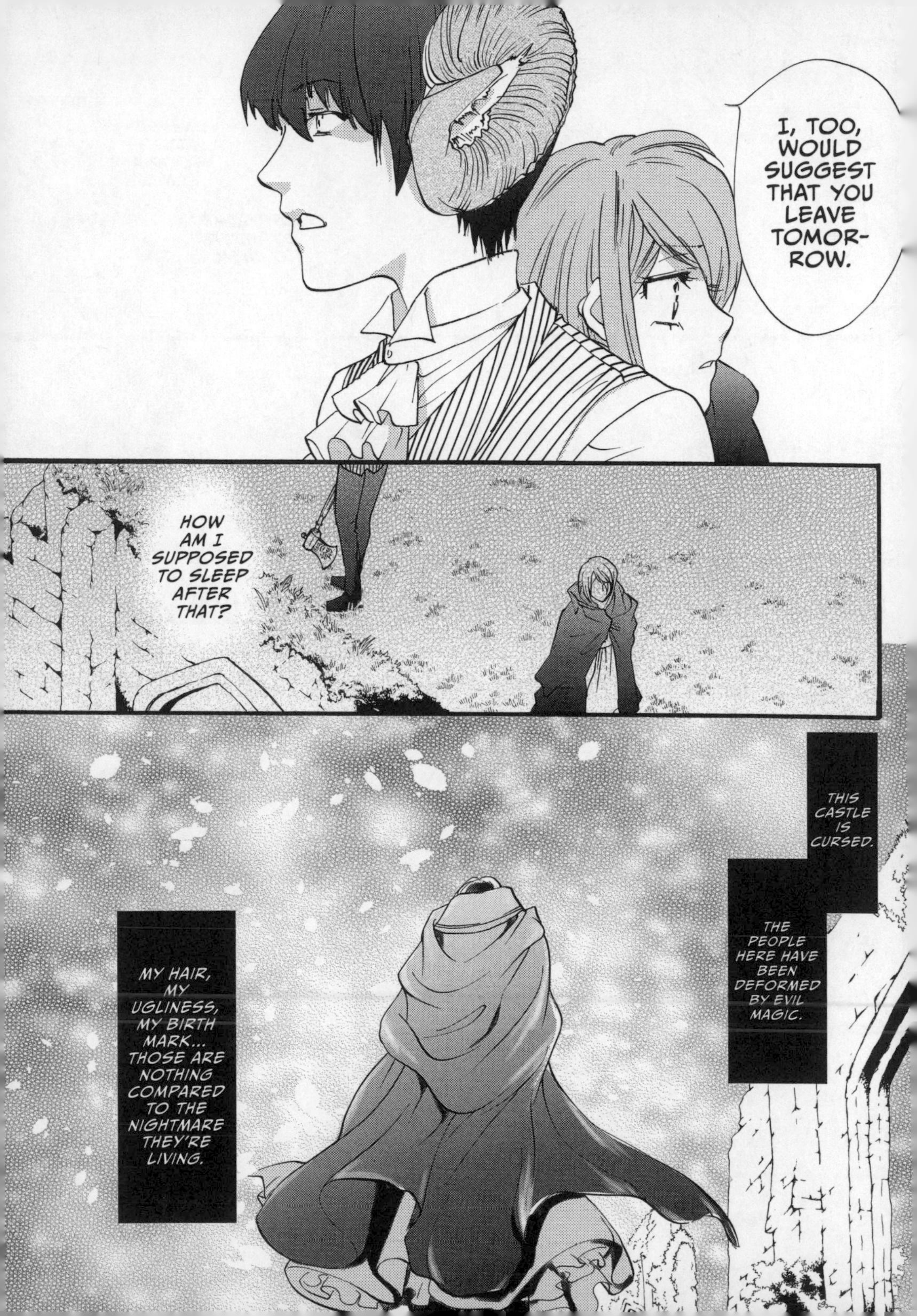
I, TOO, WOULD SUGGEST THAT YOU LEAVE TOMOR-ROW.
HOW AM I SUPPOSED TO SLEEP AFTER THAT?
THIS CASTLE IS CURSED.
THE PEOPLE HERE HAVE BEEN DEFORMED BY EVIL MAGIC.
MY HAIR, MY UGLINESS, MY BIRTH MARK... THOSE ARE NOTHING COMPARED TO THE NIGHTMARE THEY'RE LIVING.

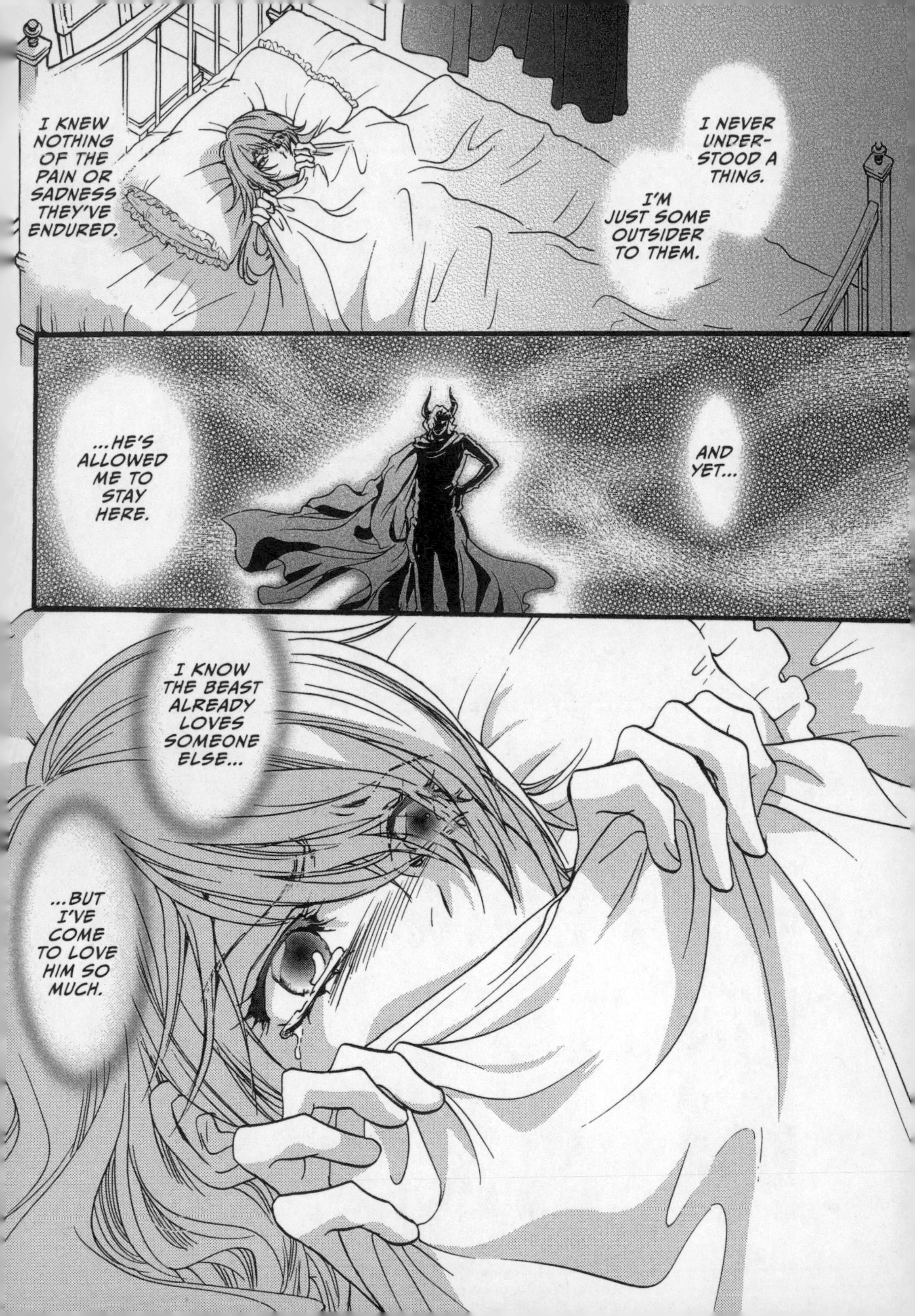
I NEVER UNDER-STOOD A THING.
I'M JUST SOME OUTSIDER TO THEM.
I KNEW NOTHING OF THE PAIN OR SADNESS THEY'VE ENDURED.
AND YET...
...HE'S ALLOWED ME TO STAY HERE.
I KNOW THE BEAST ALREADY LOVES SOMEONE ELSE...
...BUT I'VE COME TO LOVE HIM SO MUCH.

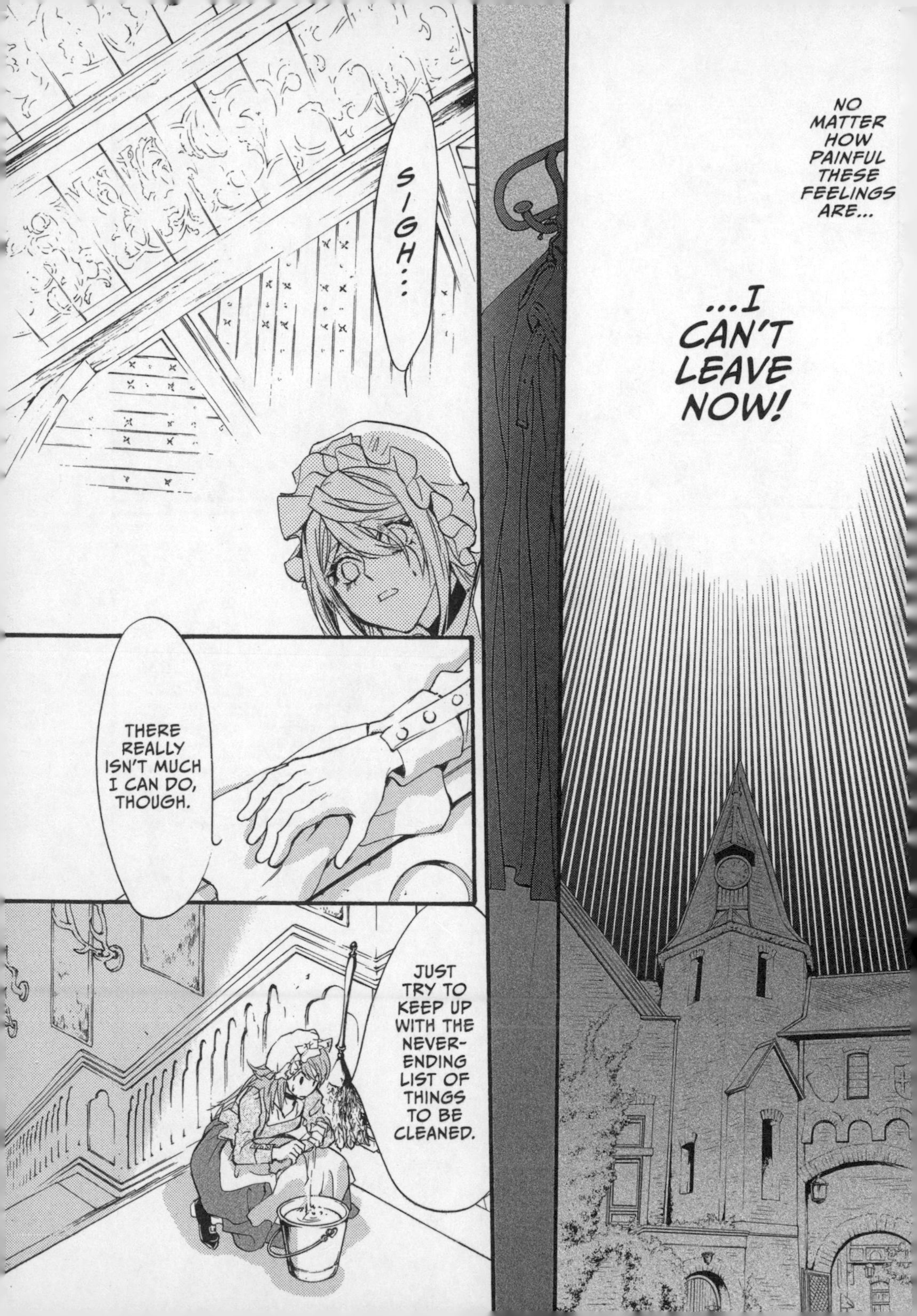
NO MATTER HOW PAINFUL THESE FEELINGS ARE...
...I CAN'T LEAVE NOW!
SIGH...
THERE REALLY ISN'T MUCH I CAN DO, THOUGH.
JUST TRY TO KEEP UP WITH THE NEVER-ENDING LIST OF THINGS TO BE CLEANED.

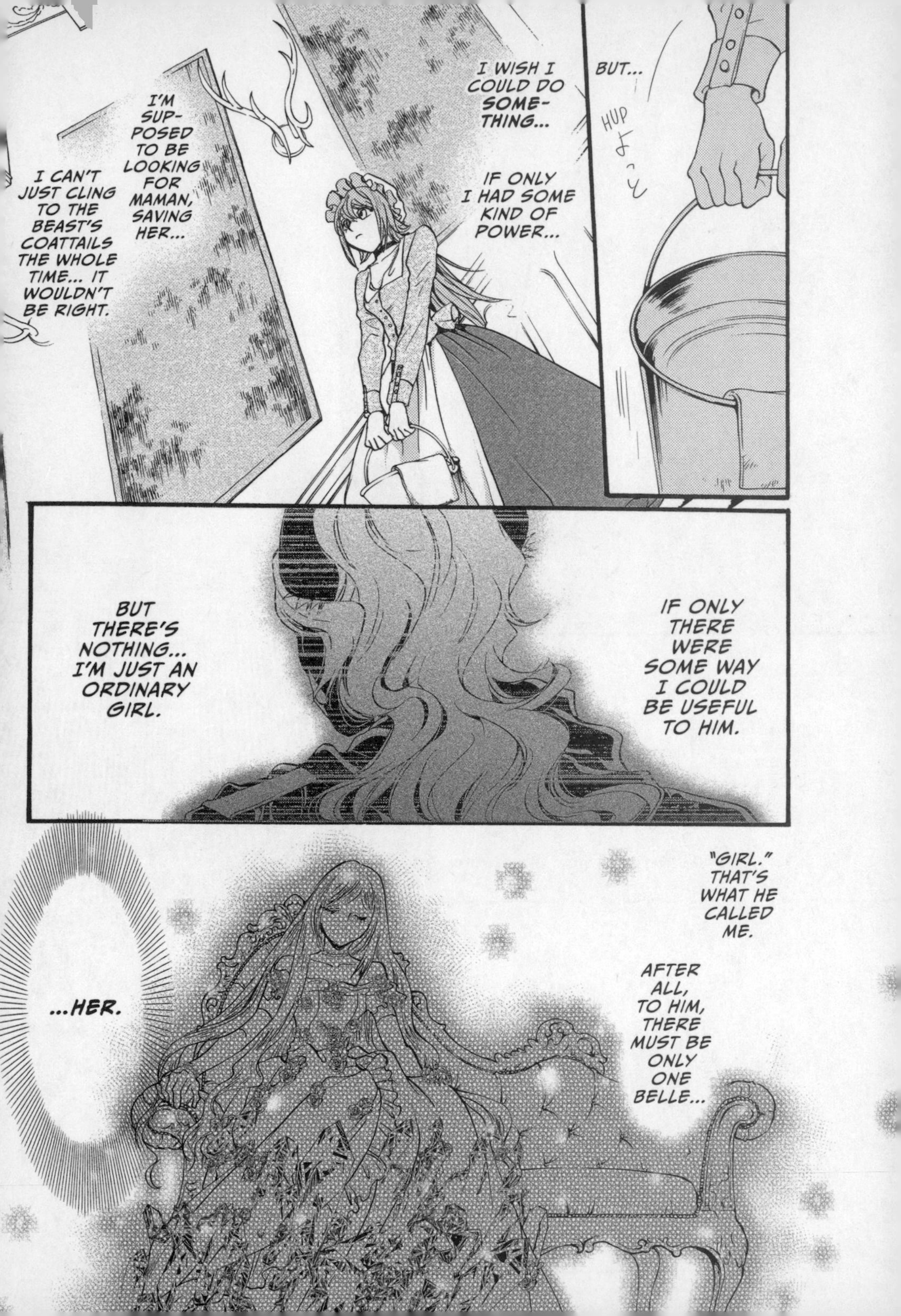
BUT...
HUP
I WISH I COULD DO SOME-THING...
IF ONLY I HAD SOME KIND OF POWER...
I'M SUP-POSED TO BE LOOKING FOR MAMAN, SAVING HER...
I CAN'T JUST CLING TO THE BEAST'S COATTAILS THE WHOLE TIME... IT WOULDN'T BE RIGHT.
IF ONLY THERE WERE SOME WAY I COULD BE USEFUL TO HIM.
BUT THERE'S NOTHING... I'M JUST AN ORDINARY GIRL.
"GIRL." THAT'S WHAT HE CALLED ME.
AFTER ALL, TO HIM, THERE MUST BE ONLY ONE BELLE...
...HER.

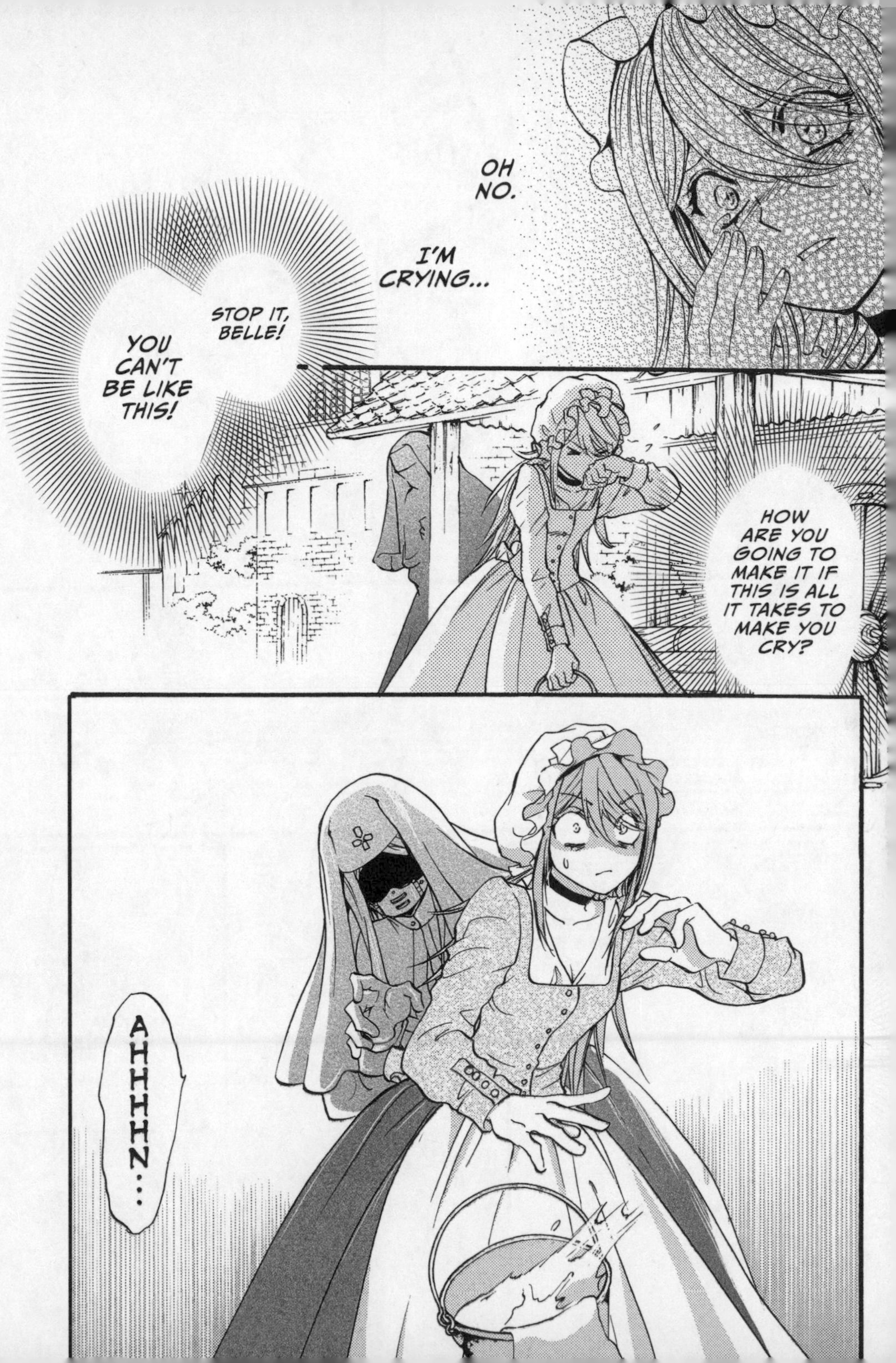
OH NO.
I'M CRYING...
HOW ARE YOU GOING TO MAKE IT IF THIS IS ALL IT TAKES TO MAKE YOU CRY?
STOP IT, BELLE!
YOU CAN'T BE LIKE THIS!
AHHHHN...

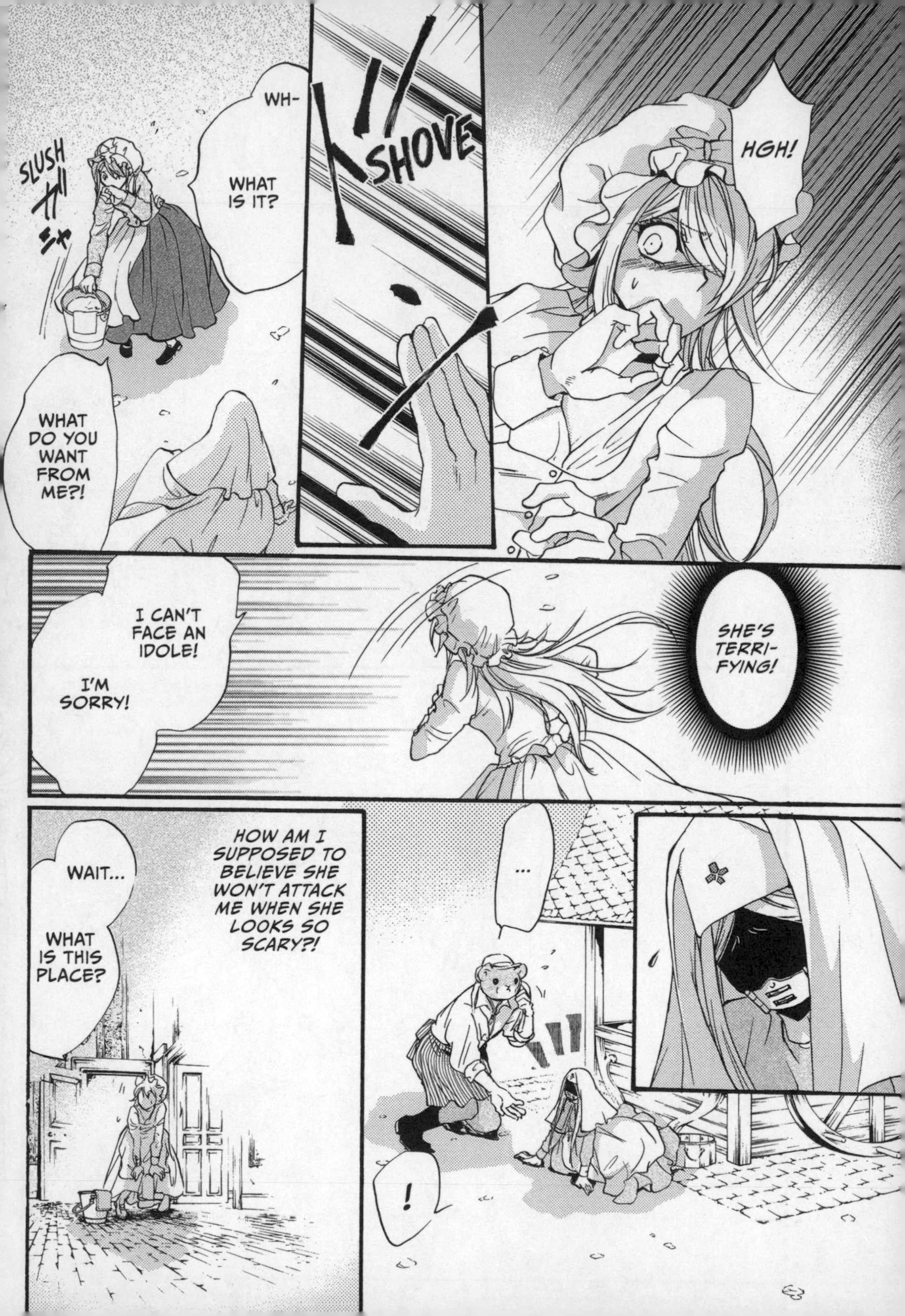
HGH!
SHOVE
WH-
WHAT IS IT?
SLUSH
WHAT DO YOU WANT FROM ME?!
SHE'S TERRI-FYING!
I CAN'T FACE AN IDOLE!
I'M SORRY!
...
!
HOW AM I SUPPOSED TO BELIEVE SHE WON'T ATTACK ME WHEN SHE LOOKS SO SCARY?!
WAIT...
WHAT IS THIS PLACE?

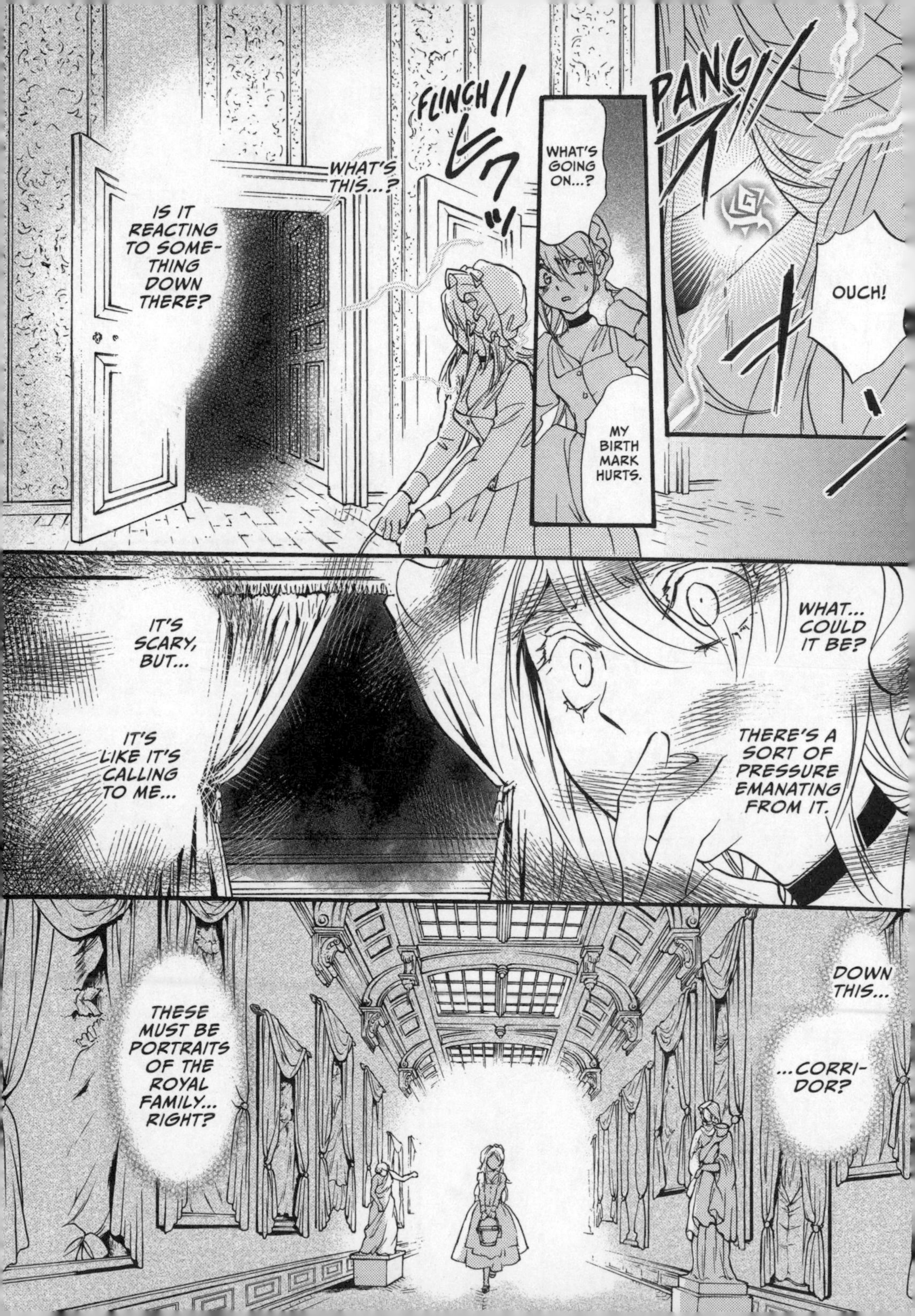
PANG!!
OUCH!
WHAT'S GOING ON...?
MY BIRTH MARK HURTS.
FLINCH!!
WHAT'S THIS...?
IS IT REACTING TO SOME-THING DOWN THERE?
WHAT... COULD IT BE?
THERE'S A SORT OF PRESSURE EMANATING FROM IT.
IT'S SCARY, BUT...
IT'S LIKE IT'S CALLING TO ME...
DOWN THIS...
...CORRI-DOR?
THESE MUST BE PORTRAITS OF THE ROYAL FAMILY... RIGHT?

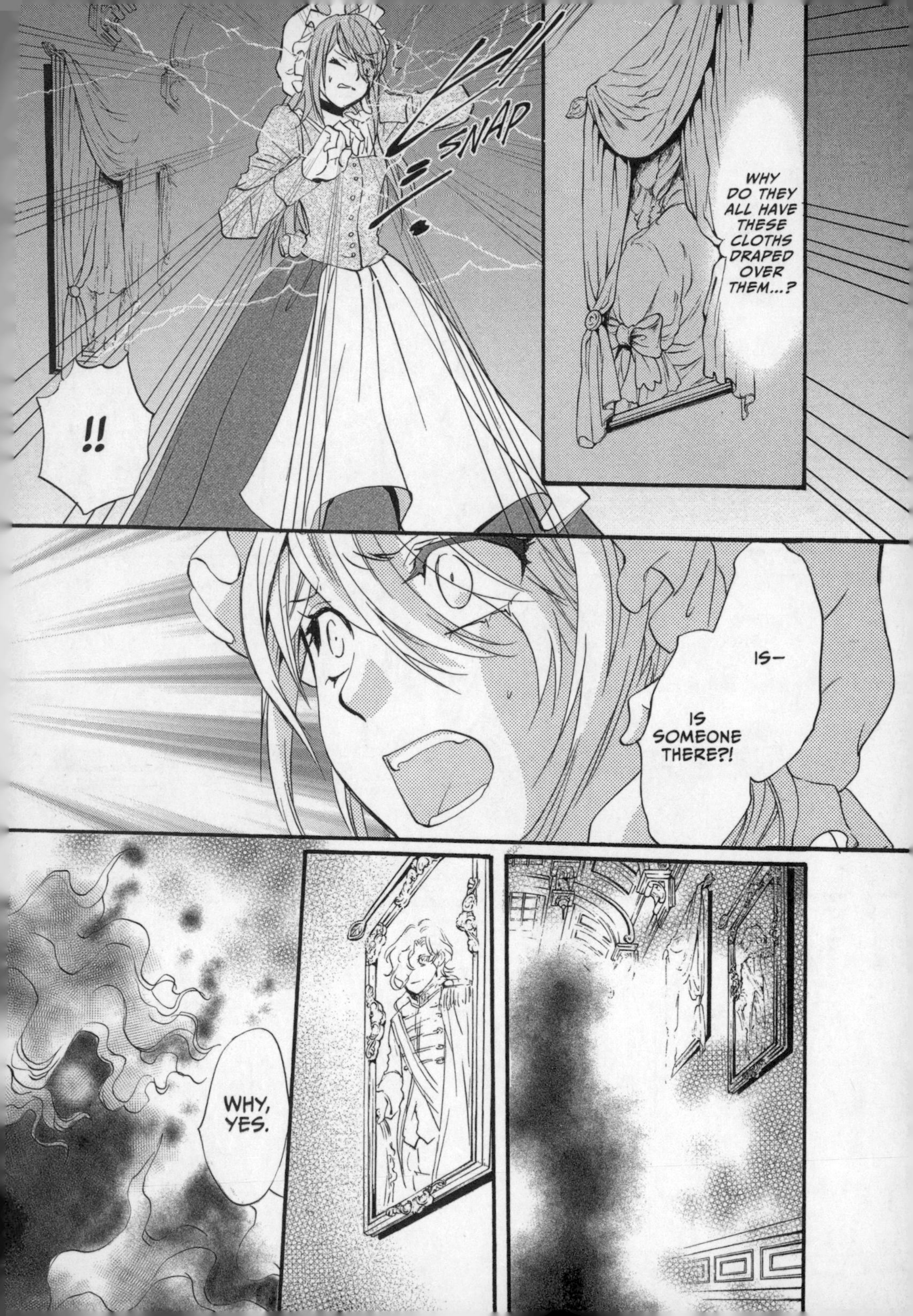
WHY DO THEY ALL HAVE THESE CLOTHS DRAPED OVER THEM...?
SNAP
!!
IS—
IS SOMEONE THERE?!
WHY, YES.

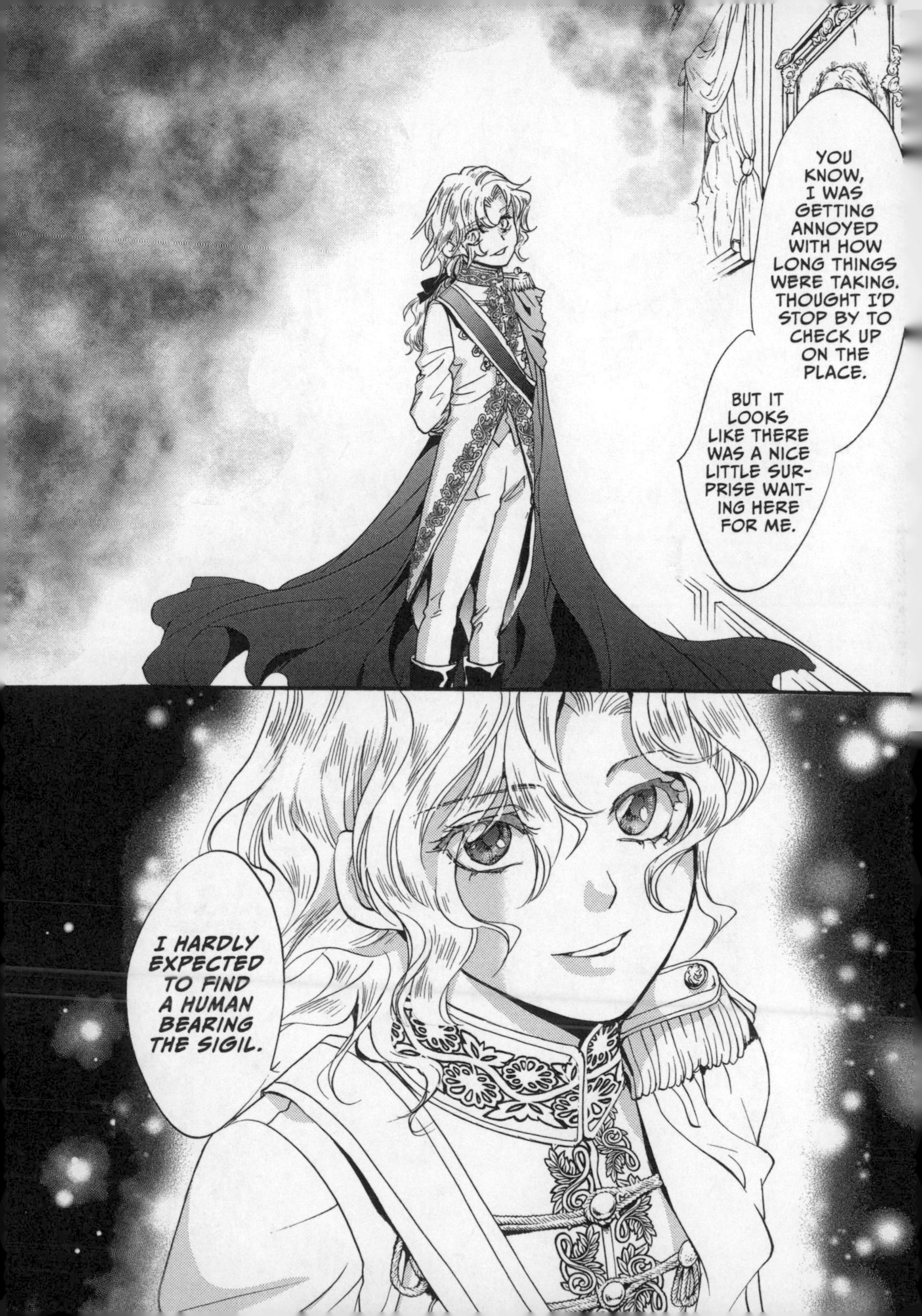
YOU KNOW, I WAS GETTING ANNOYED WITH HOW LONG THINGS WERE TAKING. THOUGHT I'D STOP BY TO CHECK UP ON THE PLACE.
BUT IT LOOKS LIKE THERE WAS A NICE LITTLE SUR-PRISE WAIT-ING HERE FOR ME.
I HARDLY EXPECTED TO FIND A HUMAN BEARING THE SIGIL.

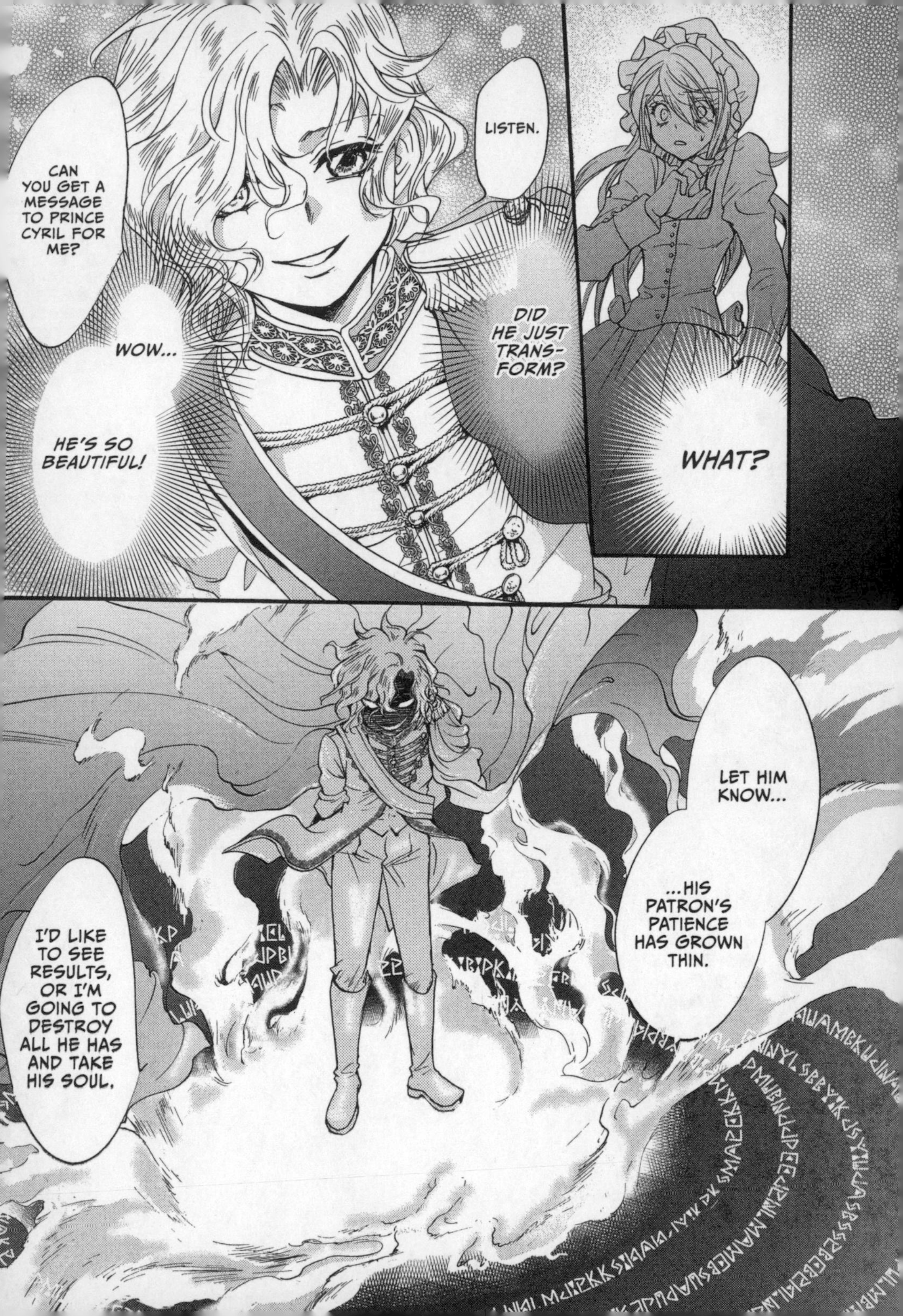
WHAT?
LISTEN.
CAN YOU GET A MESSAGE TO PRINCE CYRIL FOR ME?
DID HE JUST TRANS-FORM?
WOW...
HE'S SO BEAUTIFUL!
LET HIM KNOW...
...HIS PATRON'S PATIENCE HAS GROWN THIN.
I'D LIKE TO SEE RESULTS, OR I'M GOING TO DESTROY ALL HE HAS AND TAKE HIS SOUL.

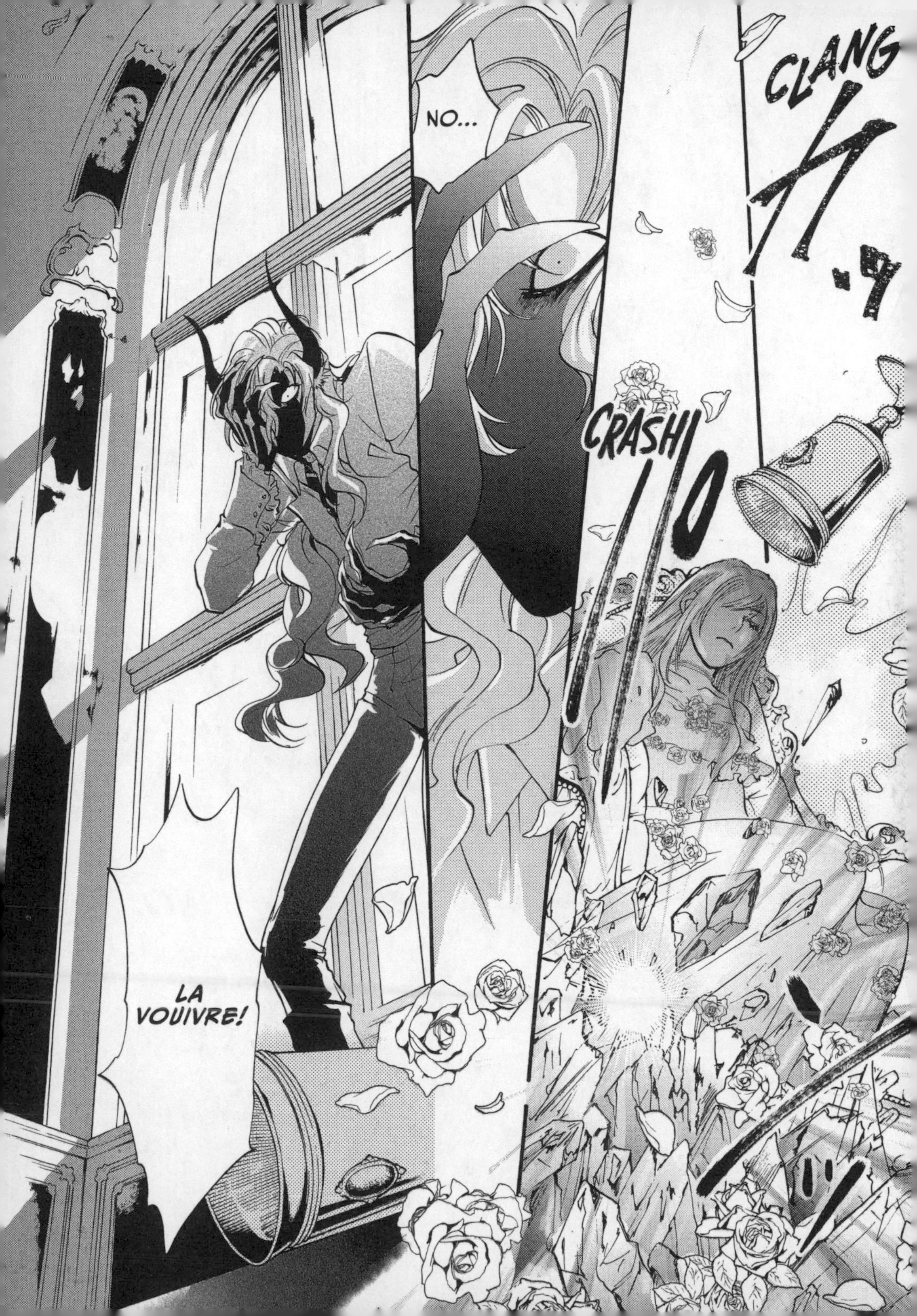
CLANG
CRASH!
NO...
LA VOUIVRE!

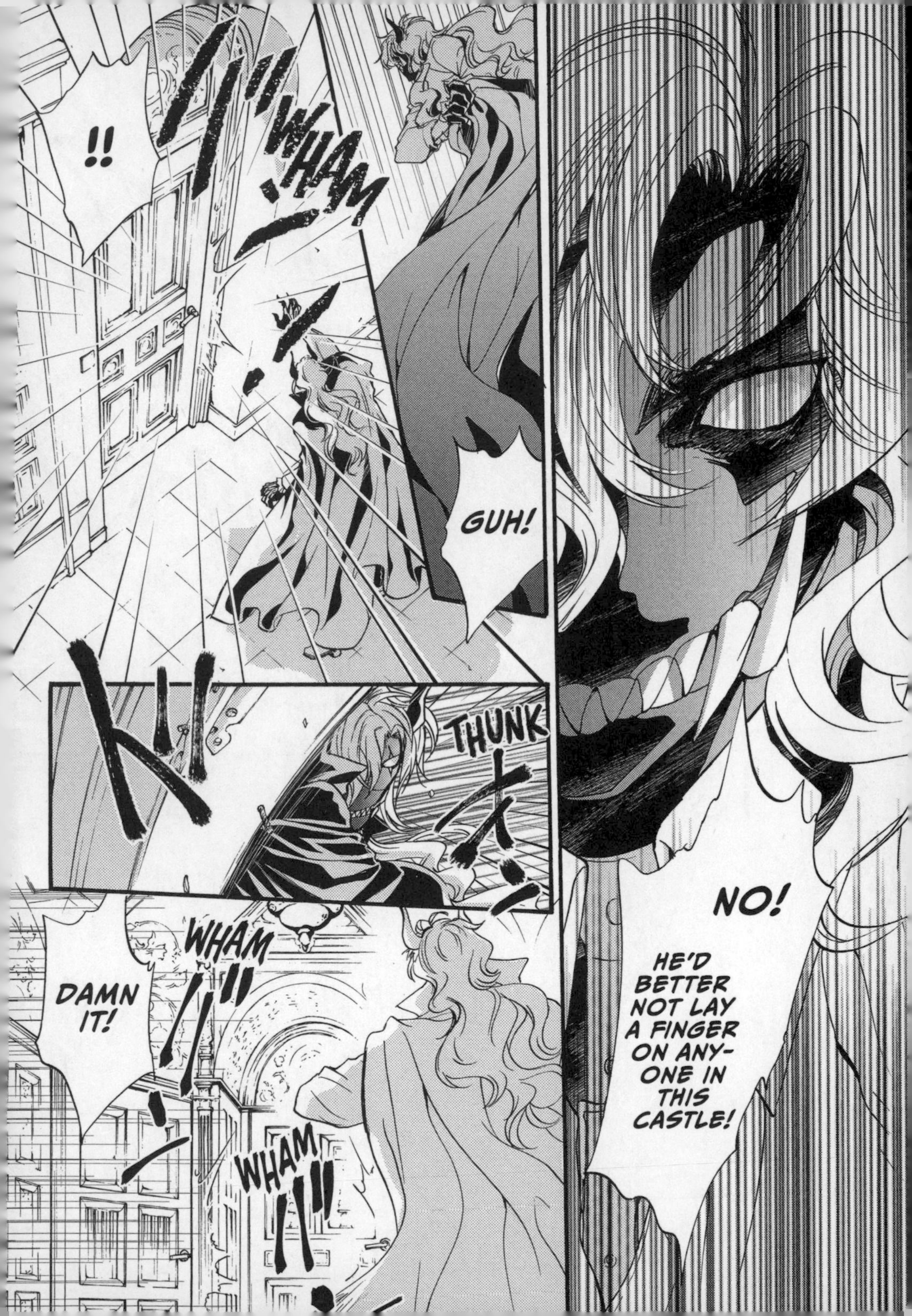
NO!
HE'D BETTER NOT LAY A FINGER ON ANYONE IN THIS CASTLE!
WHAM
!!
GUH!
THUNK
WHAM
DAMN IT!
WHAM

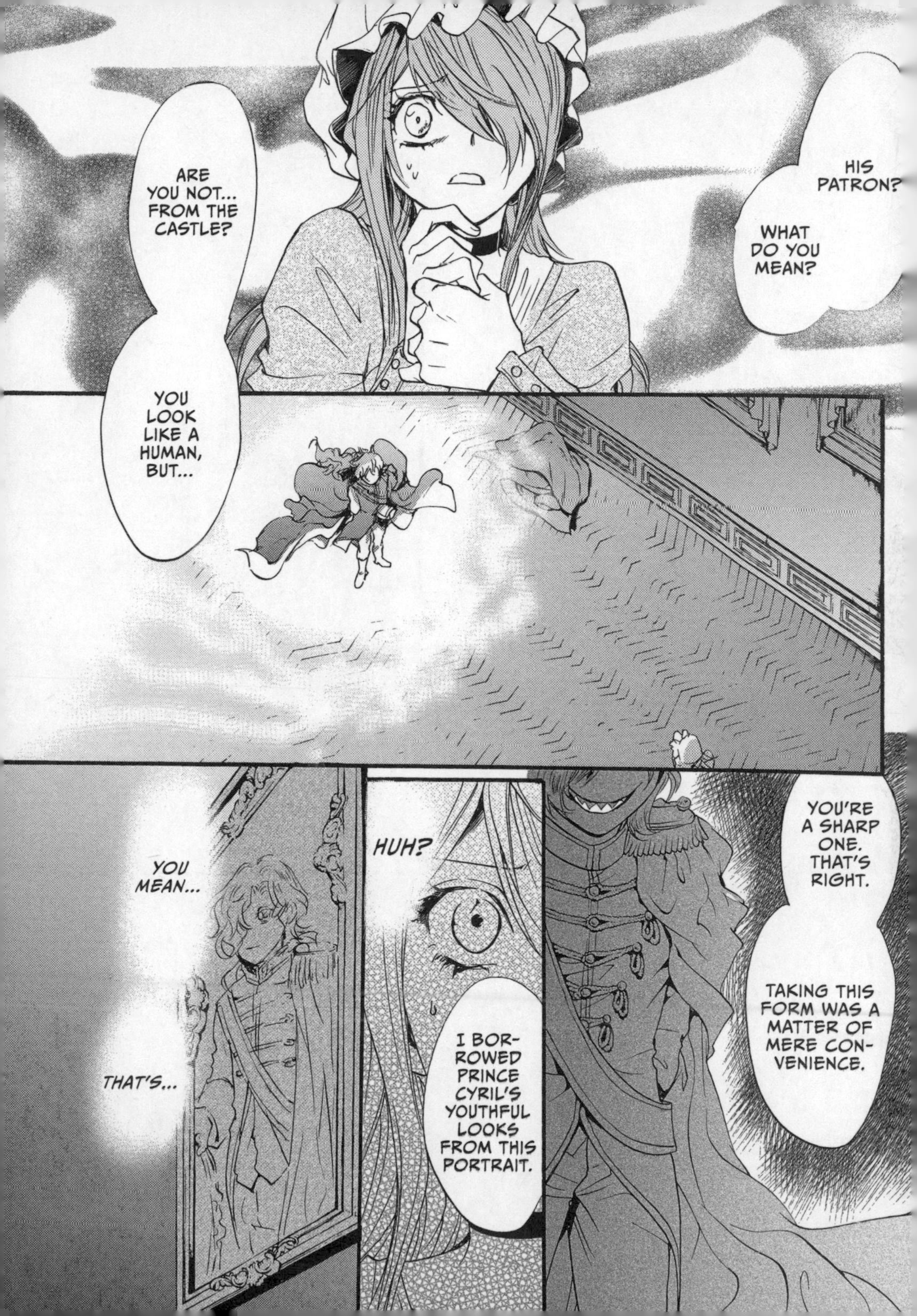
HIS PATRON?
WHAT DO YOU MEAN?
ARE YOU NOT... FROM THE CASTLE?
YOU LOOK LIKE A HUMAN, BUT...
YOU'RE A SHARP ONE. THAT'S RIGHT.
TAKING THIS FORM WAS A MATTER OF MERE CON-VENIENCE.
HUH?
I BOR-ROWED PRINCE CYRIL'S YOUTHFUL LOOKS FROM THIS PORTRAIT.
YOU MEAN...
THAT'S...

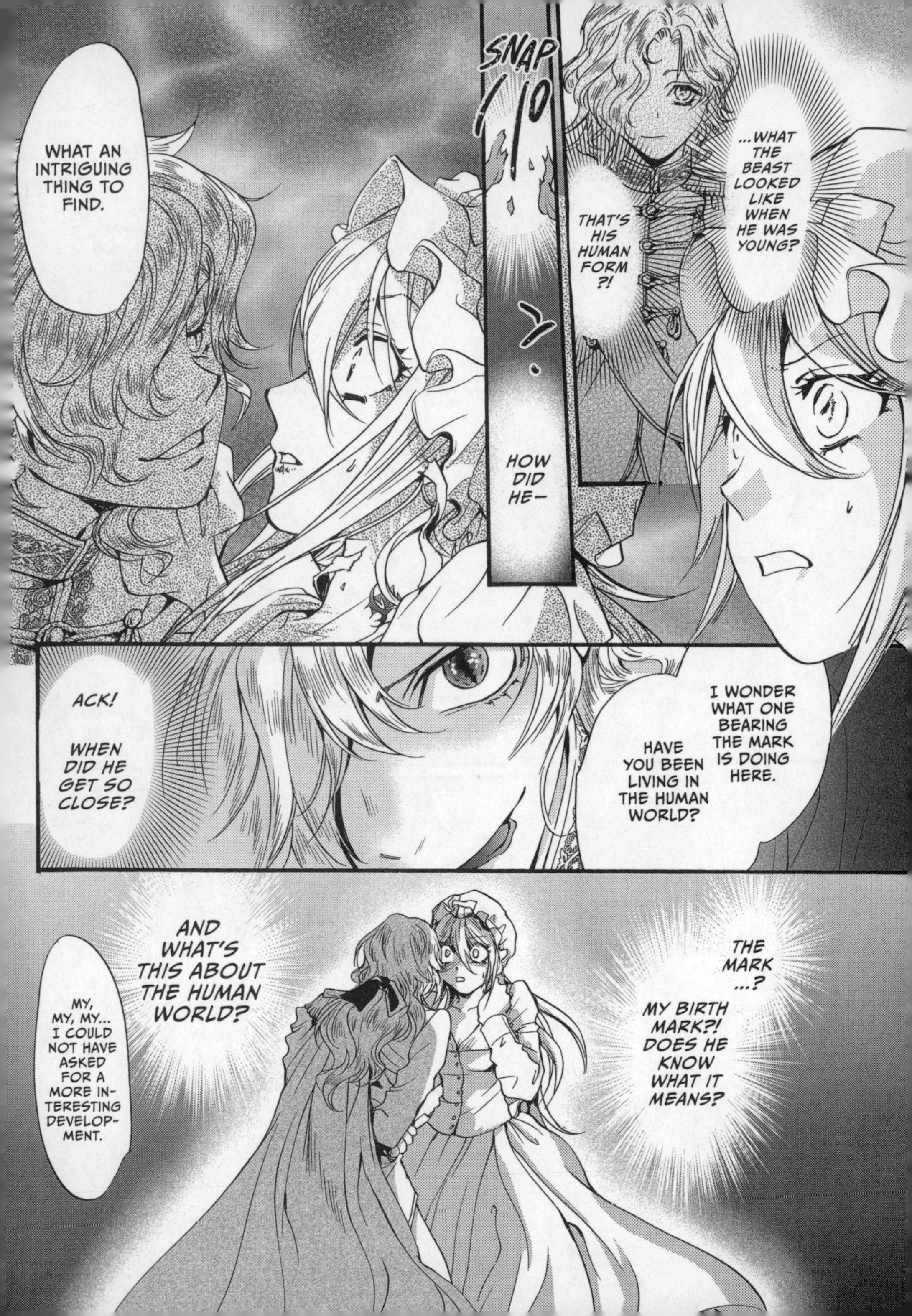
SNAP
...WHAT THE BEAST LOOKED LIKE WHEN HE WAS YOUNG?
THAT'S HIS HUMAN FORM?!
HOW DID HE—
WHAT AN INTRIGUING THING TO FIND.
I WONDER WHAT ONE BEARING THE MARK IS DOING HERE.
HAVE YOU BEEN LIVING IN THE HUMAN WORLD?
ACK!
WHEN DID HE GET SO CLOSE?
THE MARK ...?
MY BIRTH MARK?! DOES HE KNOW WHAT IT MEANS?
AND WHAT'S THIS ABOUT THE HUMAN WORLD?
MY, MY, MY... I COULD NOT HAVE ASKED FOR A MORE INTERESTING DEVELOPMENT.

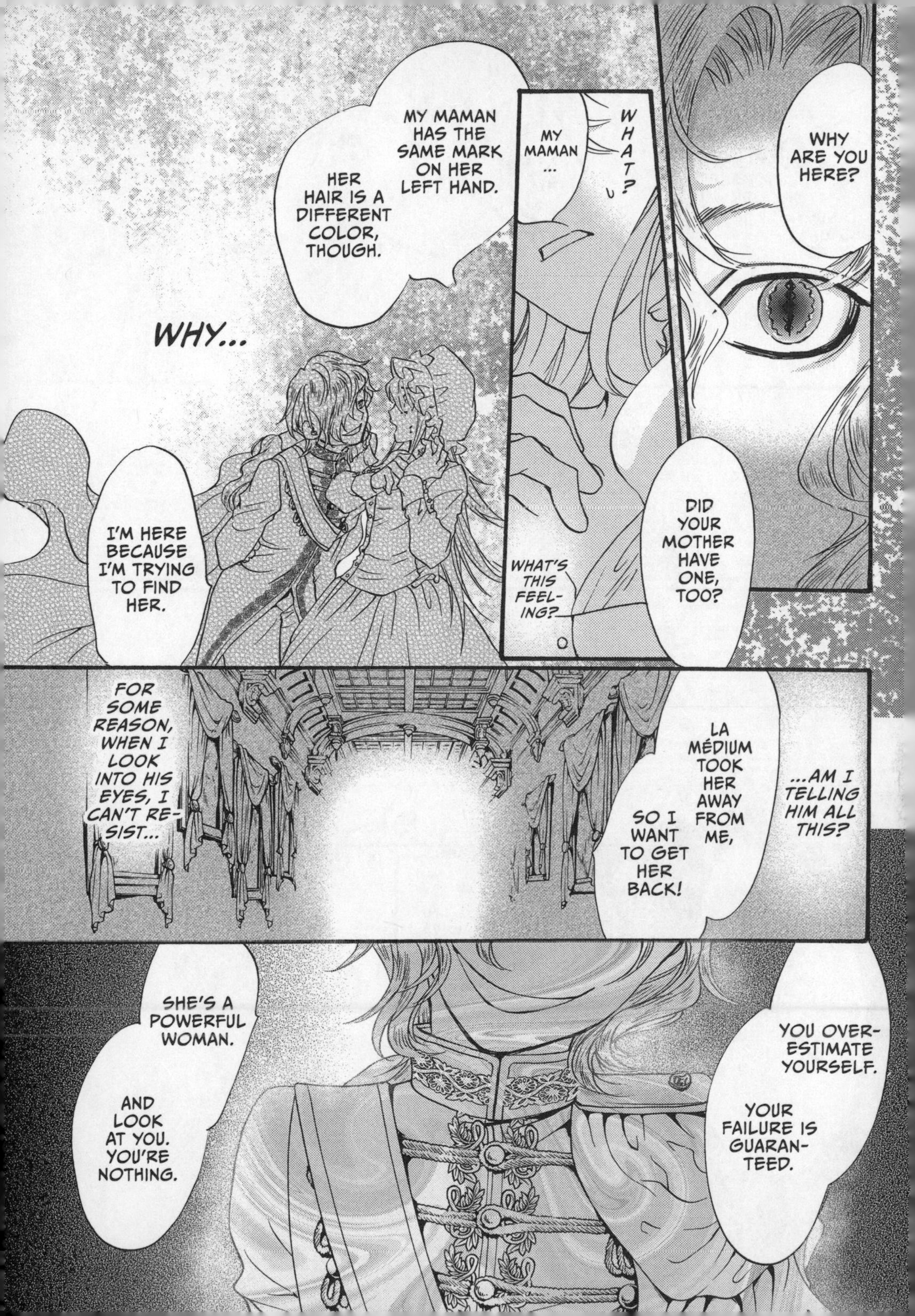
WHY ARE YOU HERE?
DID YOUR MOTHER HAVE ONE, TOO?
WHAT?
MY MAMAN...
WHAT'S THIS FEELING?
MY MAMAN HAS THE SAME MARK ON HER LEFT HAND.
HER HAIR IS A DIFFERENT COLOR, THOUGH.
WHY...
I'M HERE BECAUSE I'M TRYING TO FIND HER.
...AM I TELLING HIM ALL THIS?
LA MÉDIUM TOOK HER AWAY FROM ME,
SO I WANT TO GET HER BACK!
FOR SOME REASON, WHEN I LOOK INTO HIS EYES, I CAN'T RESIST...
YOU OVERESTIMATE YOURSELF.
YOUR FAILURE IS GUARANTEED.
SHE'S A POWERFUL WOMAN.
AND LOOK AT YOU. YOU'RE NOTHING.

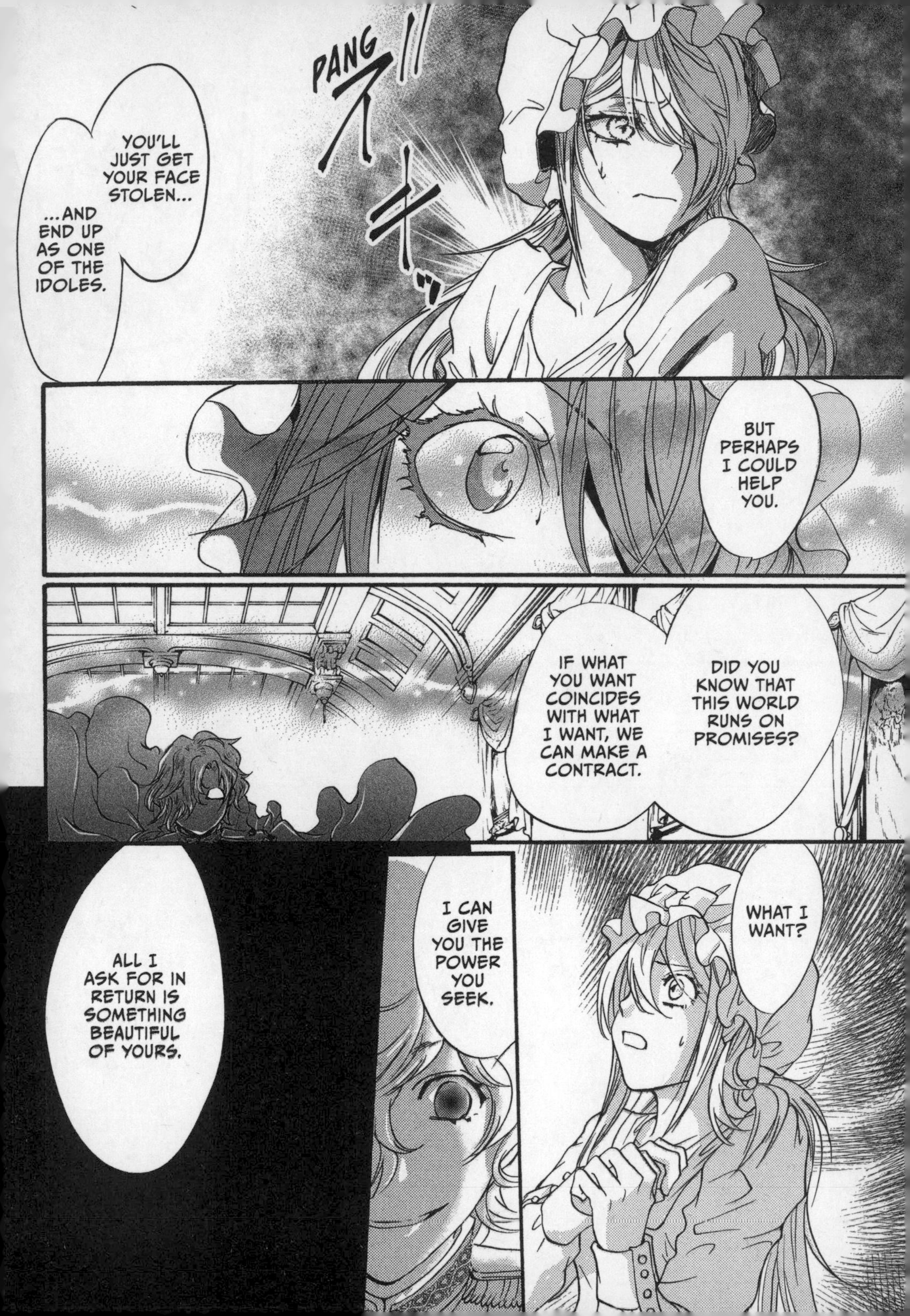
PANG
YOU'LL JUST GET YOUR FACE STOLEN...
...AND END UP AS ONE OF THE IDOLES.
BUT PERHAPS I COULD HELP YOU.
DID YOU KNOW THAT THIS WORLD RUNS ON PROMISES?
IF WHAT YOU WANT COINCIDES WITH WHAT I WANT, WE CAN MAKE A CONTRACT.
WHAT I WANT?
I CAN GIVE YOU THE POWER YOU SEEK.
ALL I ASK FOR IN RETURN IS SOMETHING BEAUTIFUL OF YOURS.

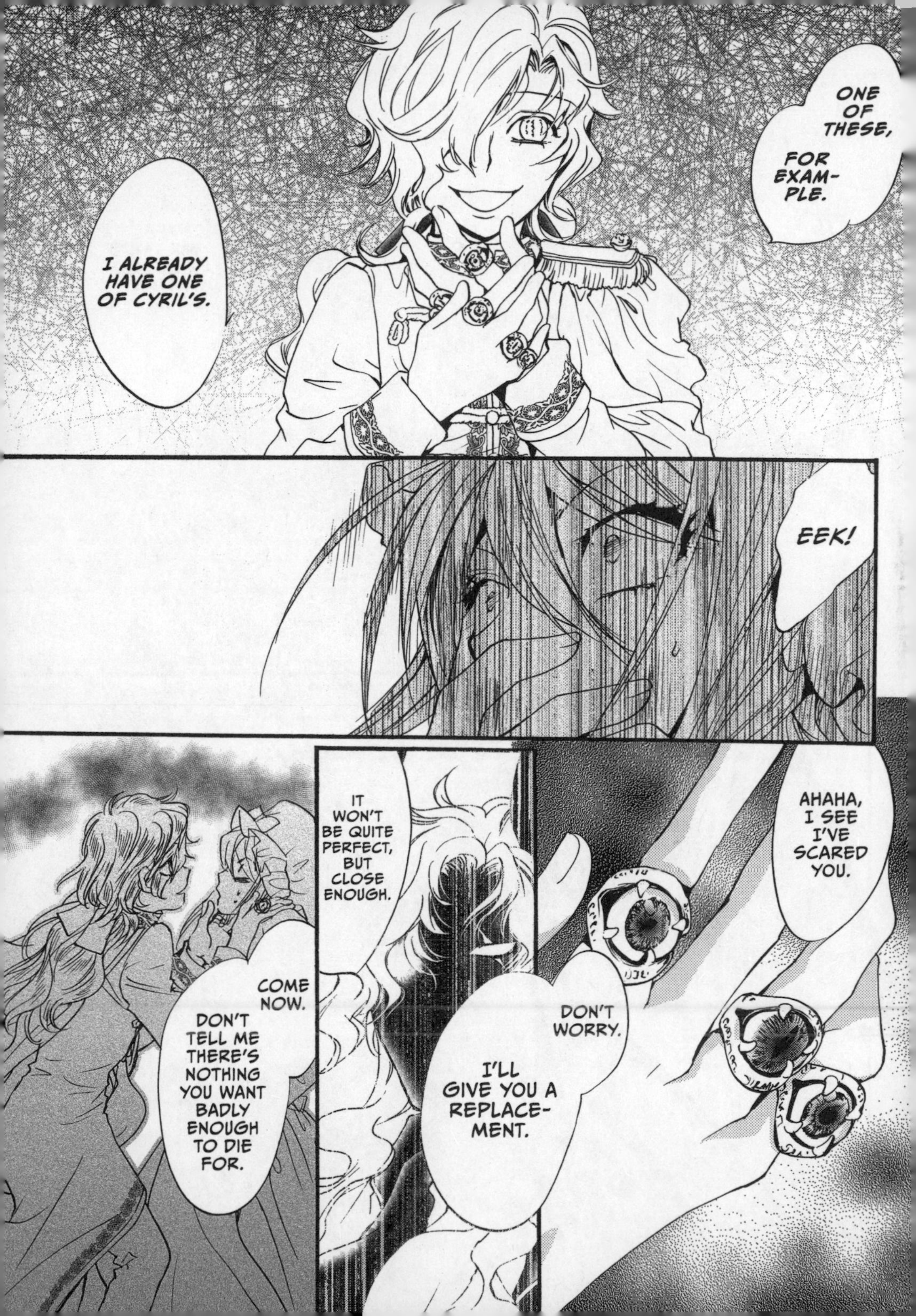
ONE OF THESE, FOR EXAMPLE.
I ALREADY HAVE ONE OF CYRIL'S.
EEK!
AHAHA, I SEE I'VE SCARED YOU.
DON'T WORRY.
I'LL GIVE YOU A REPLACEMENT.
IT WON'T BE QUITE PERFECT, BUT CLOSE ENOUGH.
COME NOW.
DON'T TELL ME THERE'S NOTHING YOU WANT BADLY ENOUGH TO DIE FOR.

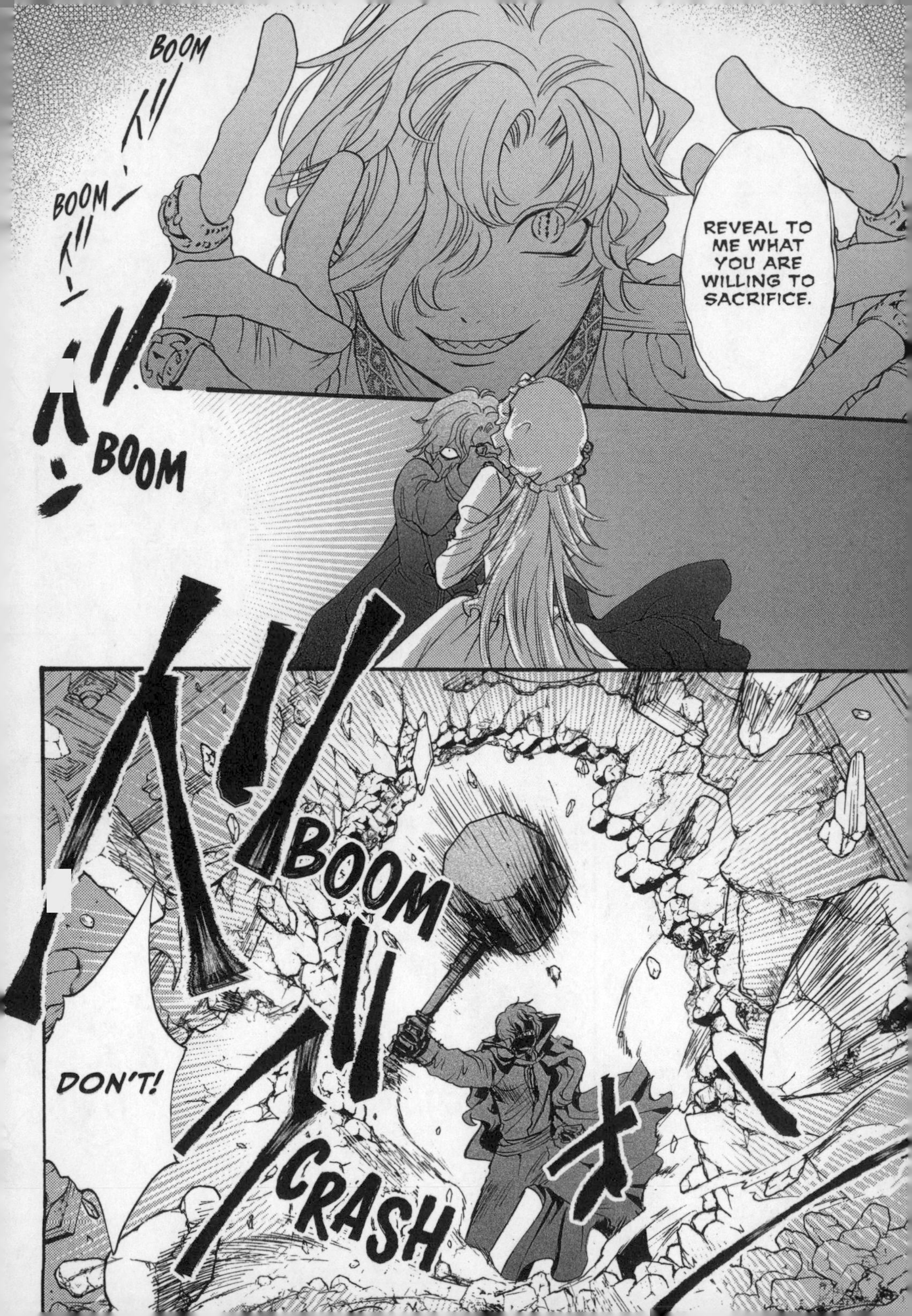
REVEAL TO ME WHAT YOU ARE WILLING TO SACRIFICE.
BOOM
BOOM
BOOM
BOOM
DON'T!
CRASH

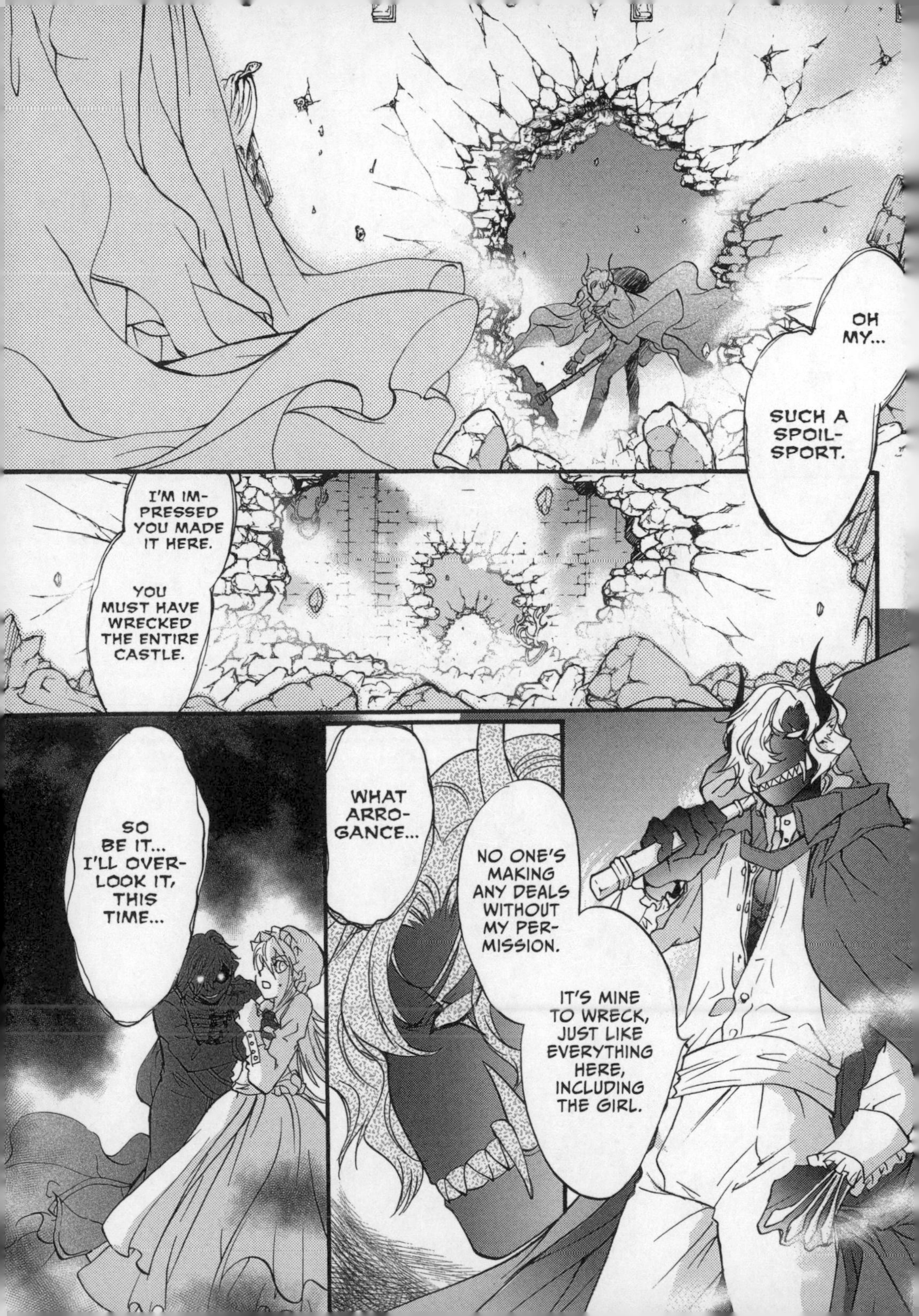
OH MY...
SUCH A SPOIL-SPORT.
I'M IMPRESSED YOU MADE IT HERE.
YOU MUST HAVE WRECKED THE ENTIRE CASTLE.
WHAT ARROGANCE...
NO ONE'S MAKING ANY DEALS WITHOUT MY PERMISSION.
IT'S MINE TO WRECK, JUST LIKE EVERYTHING HERE, INCLUDING THE GIRL.
SO BE IT... I'LL OVERLOOK IT, THIS TIME...

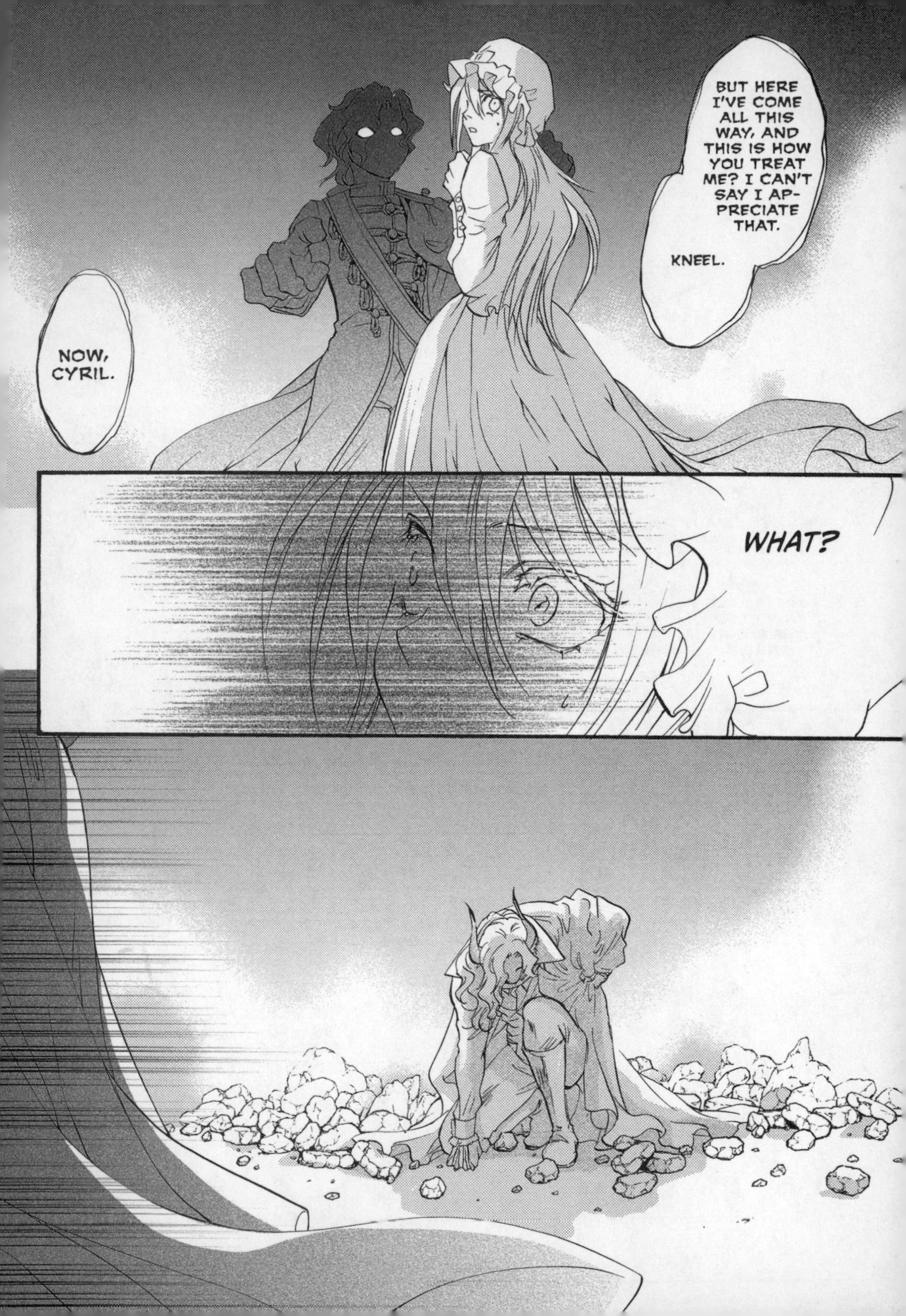
BUT HERE I'VE COME ALL THIS WAY, AND THIS IS HOW YOU TREAT ME? I CAN'T SAY I AP-PRECIATE THAT.
KNEEL.
NOW, CYRIL.
WHAT?

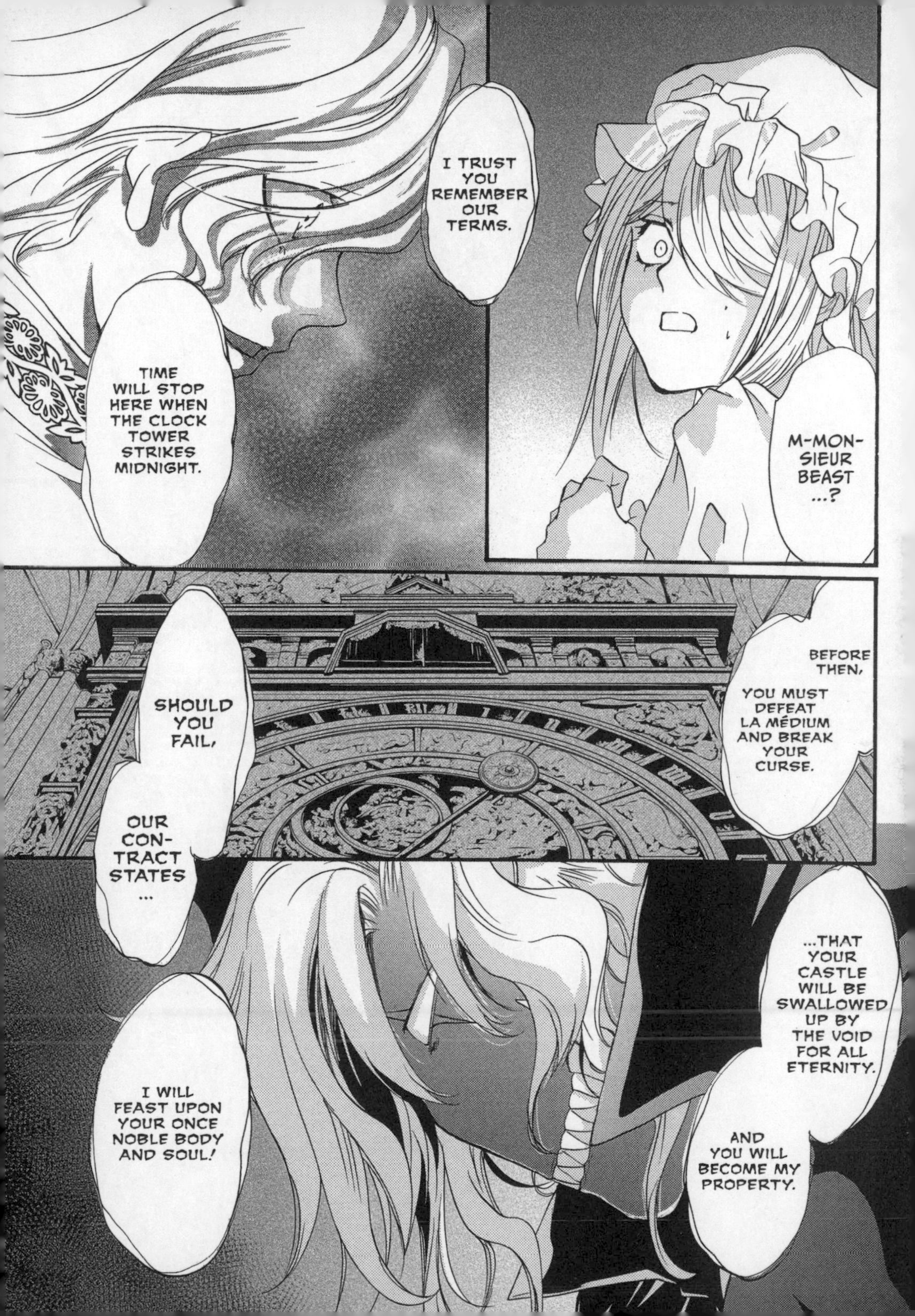
M-MONSIEUR BEAST ...?
I TRUST YOU REMEMBER OUR TERMS.
TIME WILL STOP HERE WHEN THE CLOCK TOWER STRIKES MIDNIGHT.
BEFORE THEN, YOU MUST DEFEAT LA MÉDIUM AND BREAK YOUR CURSE.
SHOULD YOU FAIL,
OUR CONTRACT STATES ...
...THAT YOUR CASTLE WILL BE SWALLOWED UP BY THE VOID FOR ALL ETERNITY.
AND YOU WILL BECOME MY PROPERTY.
I WILL FEAST UPON YOUR ONCE NOBLE BODY AND SOUL!

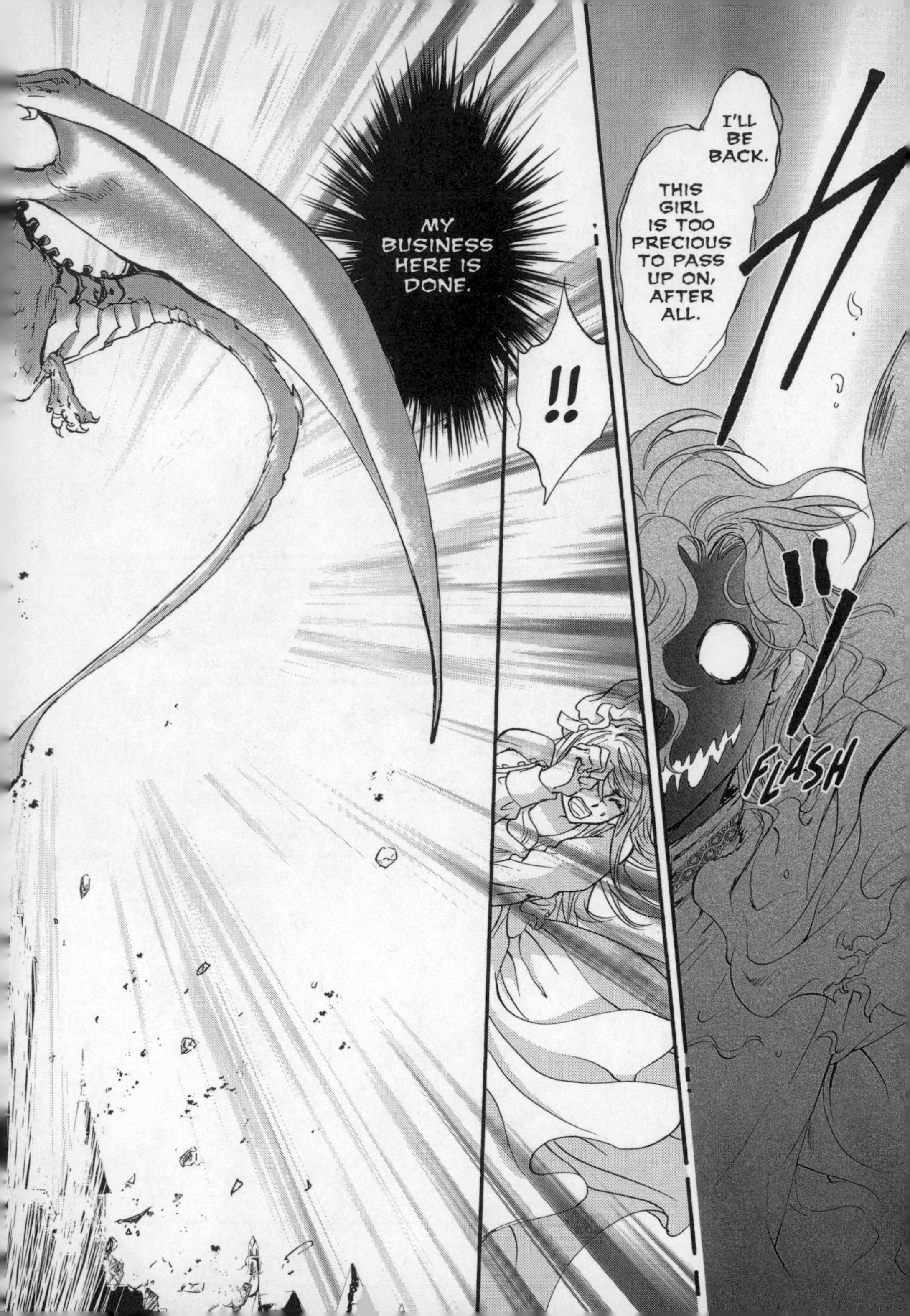
I'LL BE BACK.
THIS GIRL IS TOO PRECIOUS TO PASS UP ON, AFTER ALL.
FLASH
!!
MY BUSINESS HERE IS DONE.

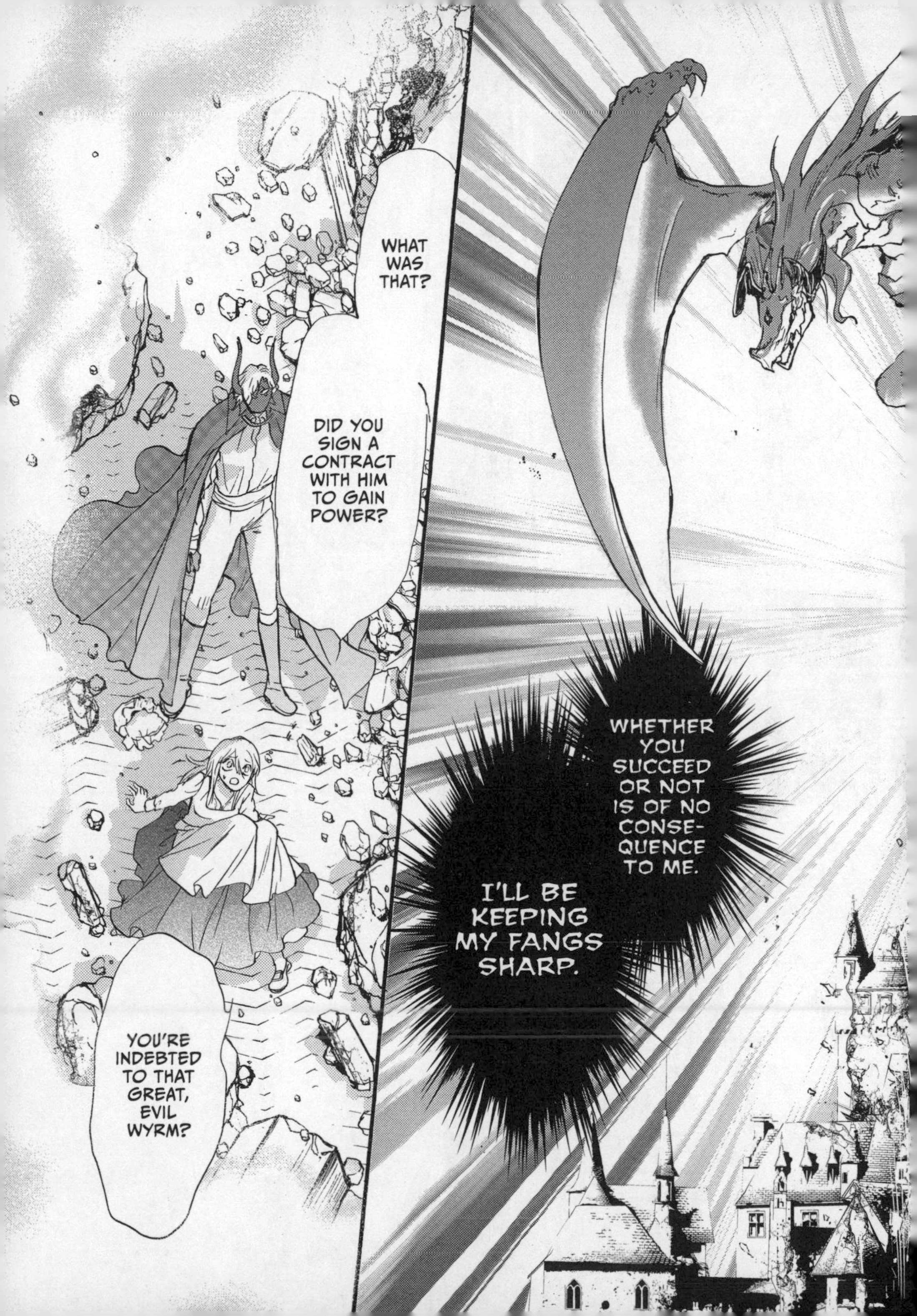
WHETHER YOU SUCCEED OR NOT IS OF NO CONSE-QUENCE TO ME.
I'LL BE KEEPING MY FANGS SHARP.
WHAT WAS THAT?
DID YOU SIGN A CONTRACT WITH HIM TO GAIN POWER?
YOU'RE INDEBTED TO THAT GREAT, EVIL WYRM?

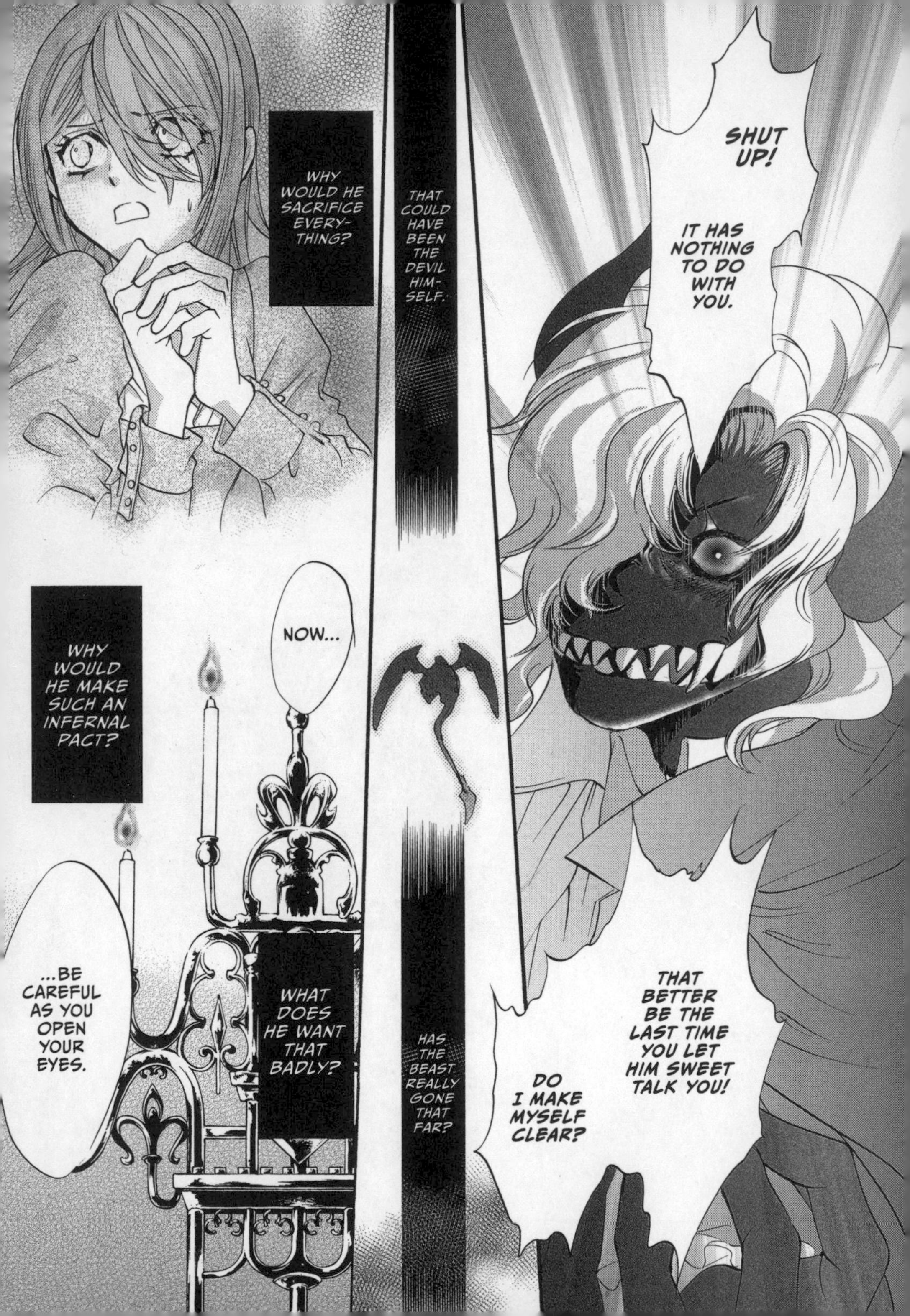
SHUT UP!
IT HAS NOTHING TO DO WITH YOU.
THAT BETTER BE THE LAST TIME YOU LET HIM SWEET TALK YOU!
DO I MAKE MYSELF CLEAR?
THAT COULD HAVE BEEN THE DEVIL HIM-SELF.
HAS THE BEAST REALLY GONE THAT FAR?
WHY WOULD HE SACRIFICE EVERY-THING?
NOW...
WHY WOULD HE MAKE SUCH AN INFERNAL PACT?
WHAT DOES HE WANT THAT BADLY?
...BE CAREFUL AS YOU OPEN YOUR EYES.

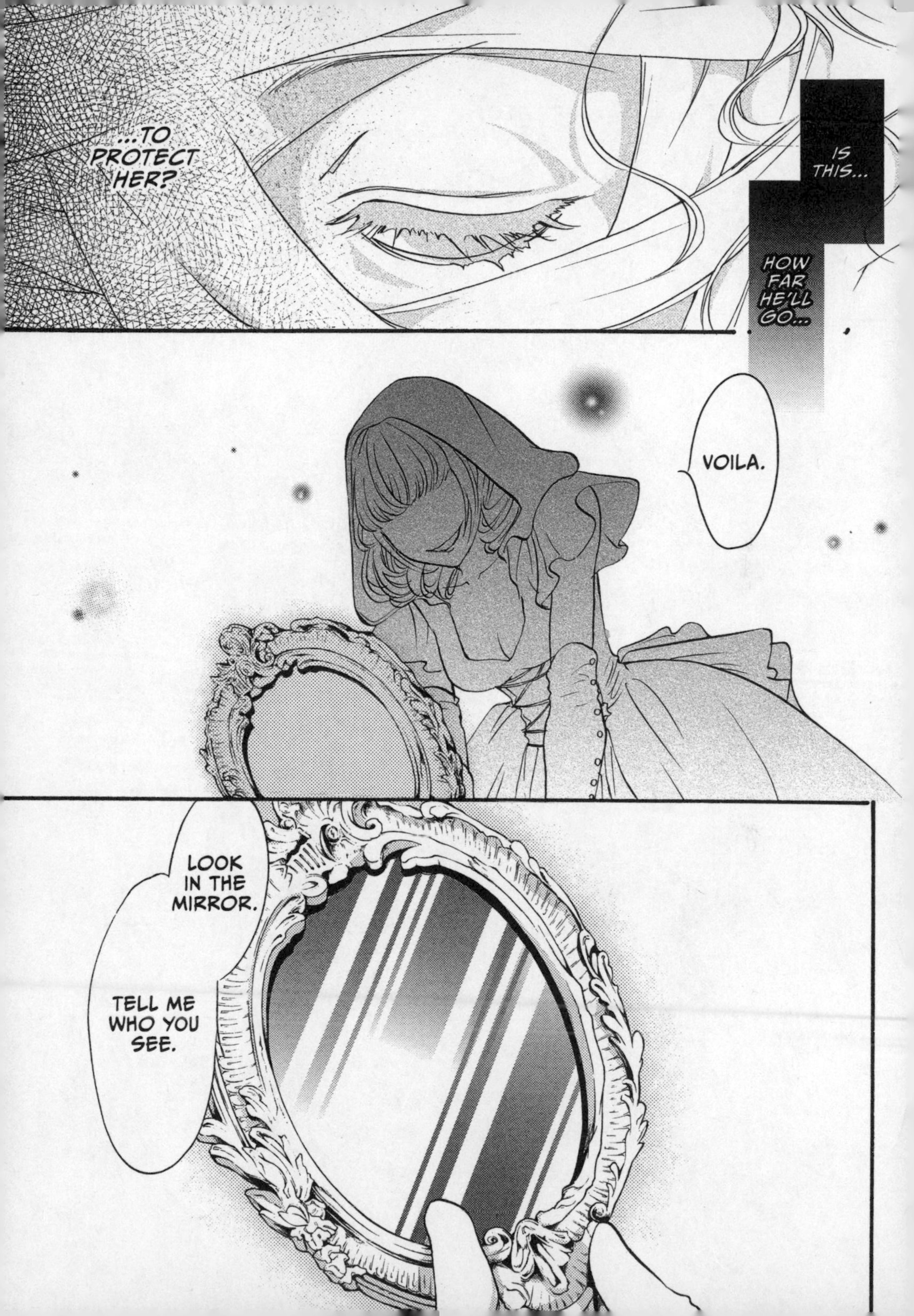
IS THIS...
HOW FAR HE'LL GO...
...TO PROTECT HER?
VOILA.
LOOK IN THE MIRROR.
TELL ME WHO YOU SEE.

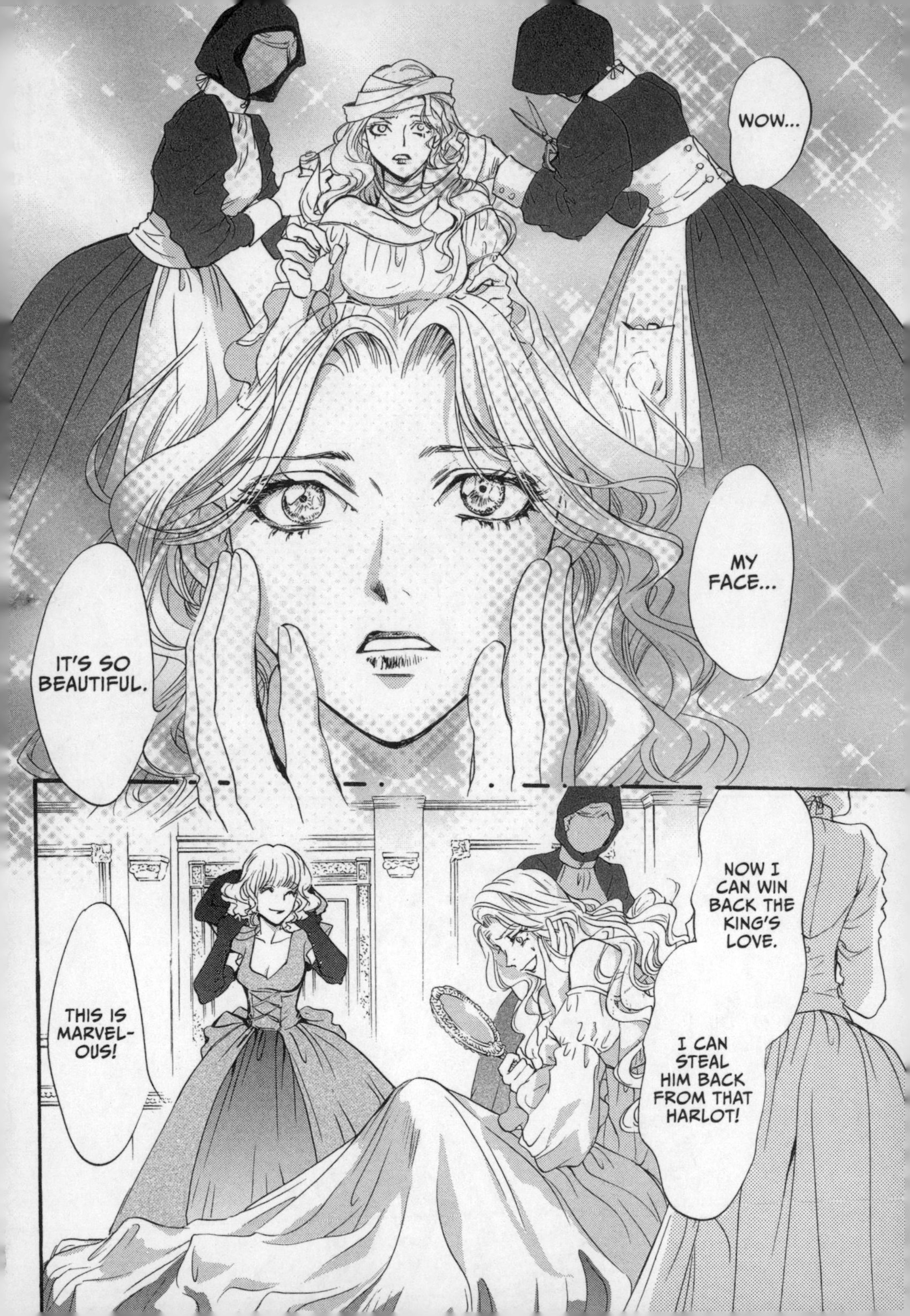
WOW...
MY FACE...
IT'S SO BEAUTIFUL.
NOW I CAN WIN BACK THE KING'S LOVE.
I CAN STEAL HIM BACK FROM THAT HARLOT!
THIS IS MARVEL-OUS!

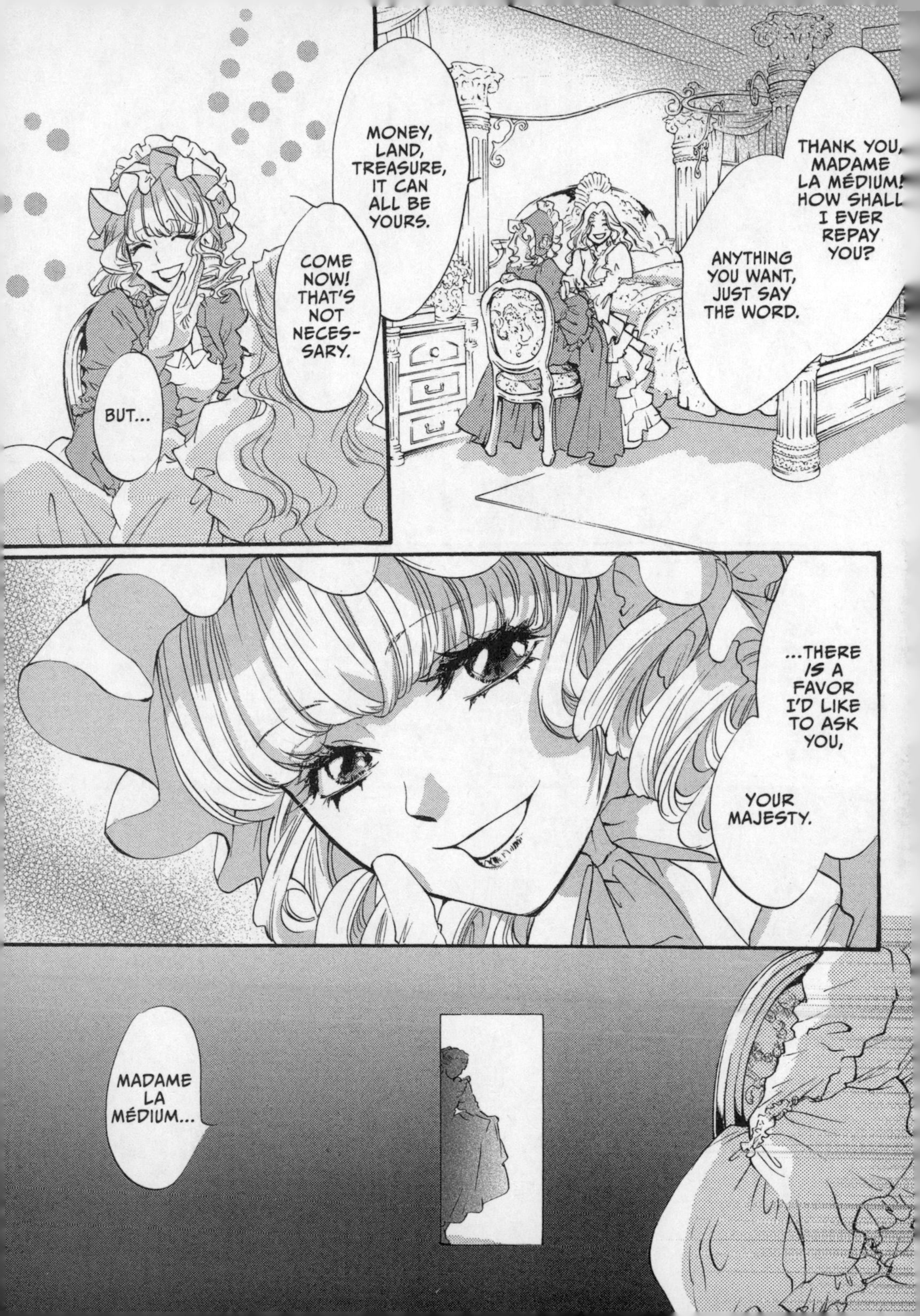
THANK YOU, MADAME LA MÉDIUM! HOW SHALL I EVER REPAY YOU?
ANYTHING YOU WANT, JUST SAY THE WORD.
MONEY, LAND, TREASURE, IT CAN ALL BE YOURS.
COME NOW! THAT'S NOT NECES-SARY.
BUT...
...THERE *IS* A FAVOR I'D LIKE TO ASK YOU,
YOUR MAJESTY.
MADAME LA MÉDIUM...

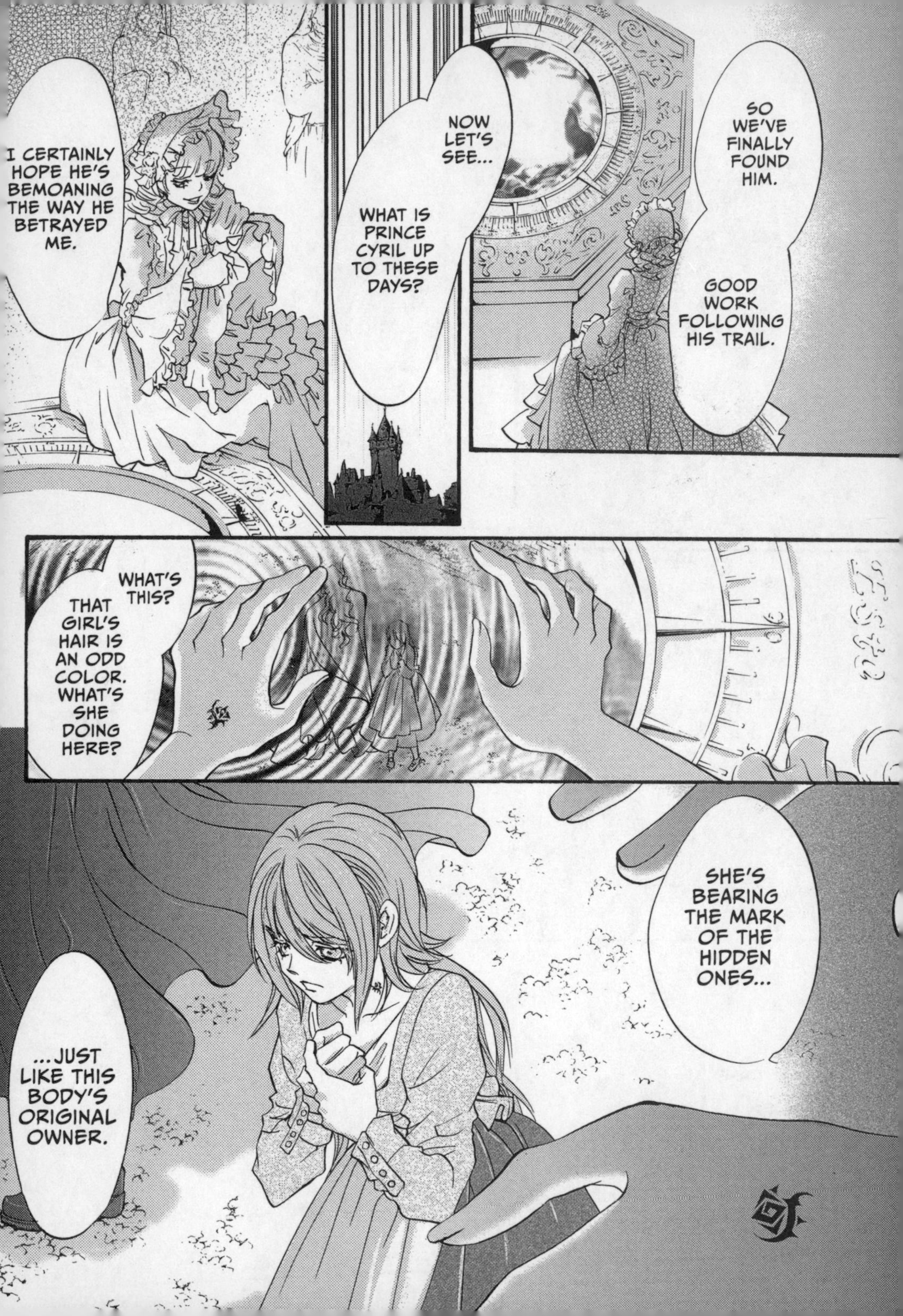

SO WE'VE FINALLY FOUND HIM.
GOOD WORK FOLLOWING HIS TRAIL.
NOW LET'S SEE...
WHAT IS PRINCE CYRIL UP TO THESE DAYS?
I CERTAINLY HOPE HE'S BEMOANING THE WAY HE BETRAYED ME.
WHAT'S THIS?
THAT GIRL'S HAIR IS AN ODD COLOR. WHAT'S SHE DOING HERE?
SHE'S BEARING THE MARK OF THE HIDDEN ONES...
...JUST LIKE THIS BODY'S ORIGINAL OWNER.

LA BELLE ET LA BÊTE

DU PARADIS PERDU

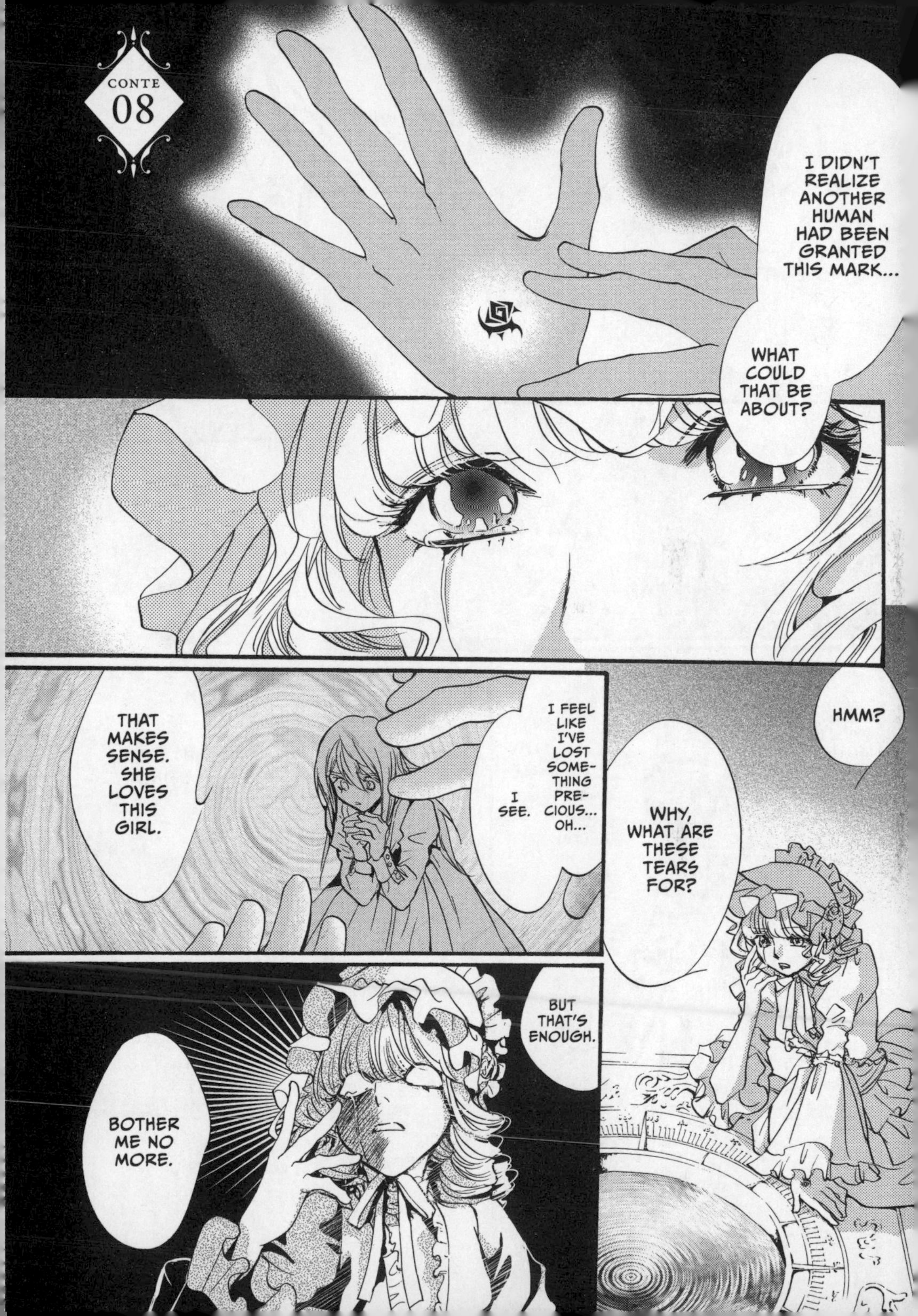
CONTE
08
I DIDN'T REALIZE ANOTHER HUMAN HAD BEEN GRANTED THIS MARK...
WHAT COULD THAT BE ABOUT?
HMM?
WHY, WHAT ARE THESE TEARS FOR?
I FEEL LIKE I'VE LOST SOME-THING PRE-CIOUS... OH...
I SEE.
THAT MAKES SENSE. SHE LOVES THIS GIRL.
BUT THAT'S ENOUGH.
BOTHER ME NO MORE.

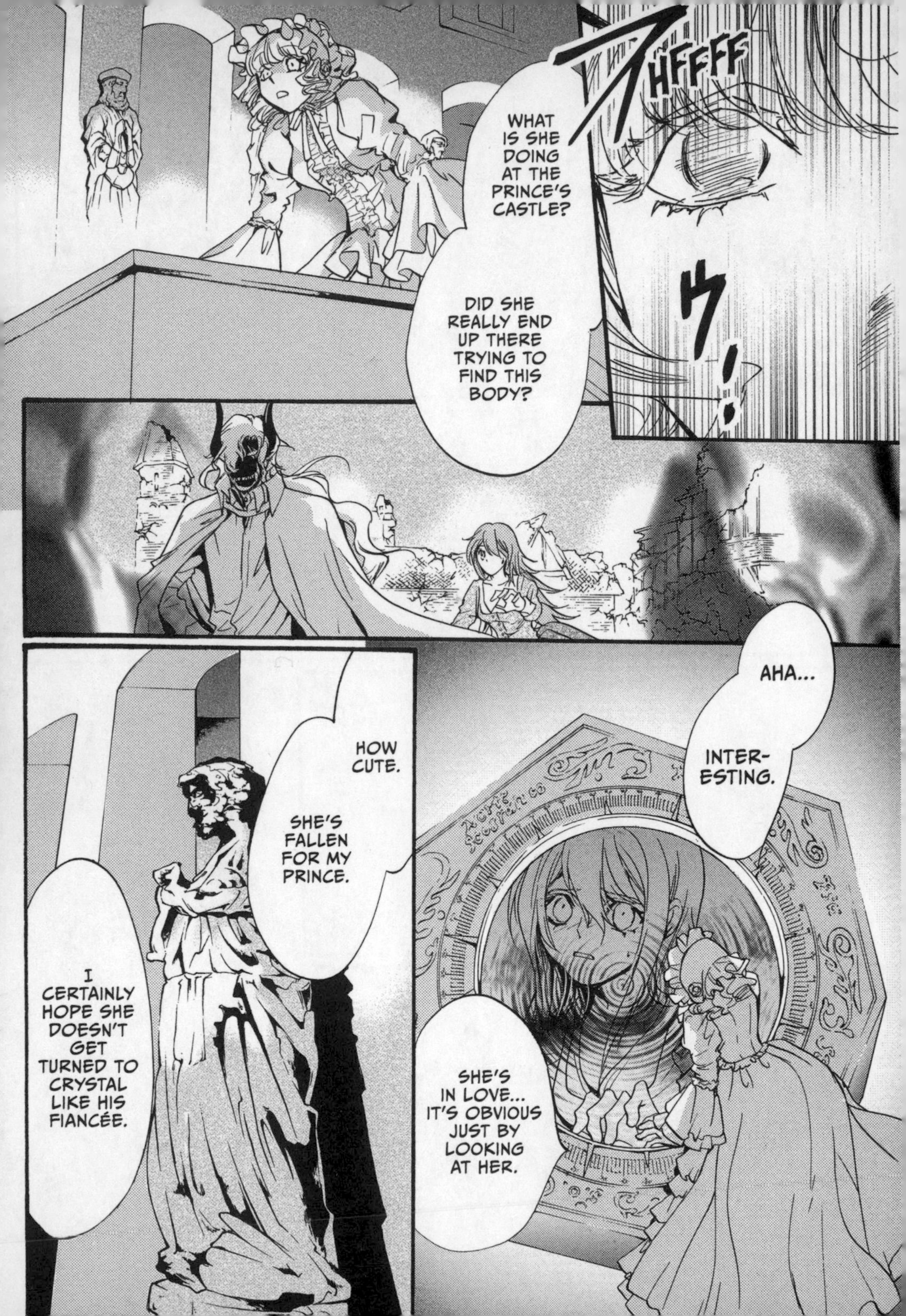
HFFFF
ウ
WHAT IS SHE DOING AT THE PRINCE'S CASTLE?
DID SHE REALLY END UP THERE TRYING TO FIND THIS BODY?
AHA...
INTERESTING.
SHE'S IN LOVE... IT'S OBVIOUS JUST BY LOOKING AT HER.
HOW CUTE.
SHE'S FALLEN FOR MY PRINCE.
I CERTAINLY HOPE SHE DOESN'T GET TURNED TO CRYSTAL LIKE HIS FIANCÉE.

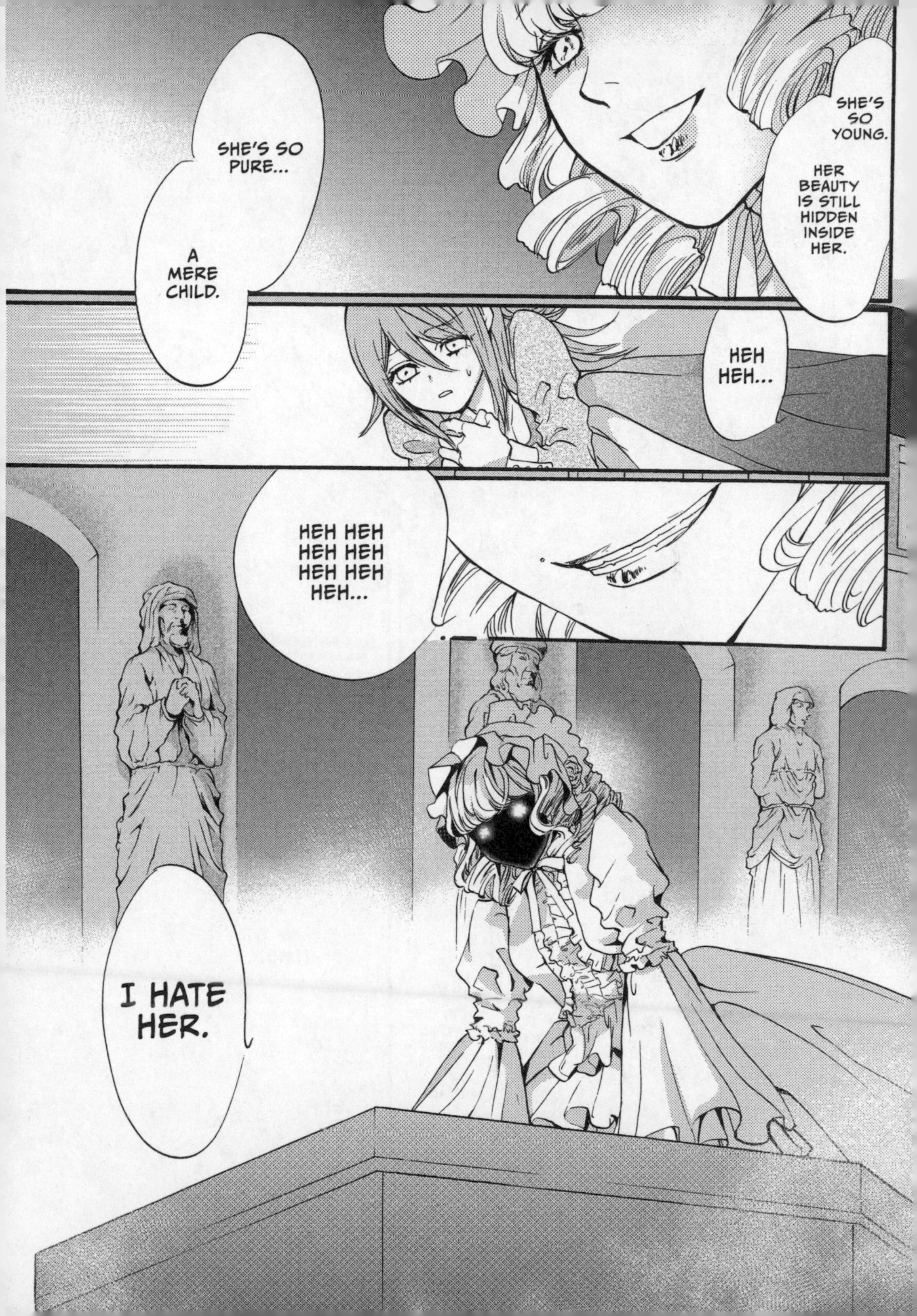
SHE'S SO YOUNG.
HER BEAUTY IS STILL HIDDEN INSIDE HER.
SHE'S SO PURE...
A MERE CHILD.
HEH HEH...
HEH HEH HEH HEH HEH HEH HEH...
I HATE HER.

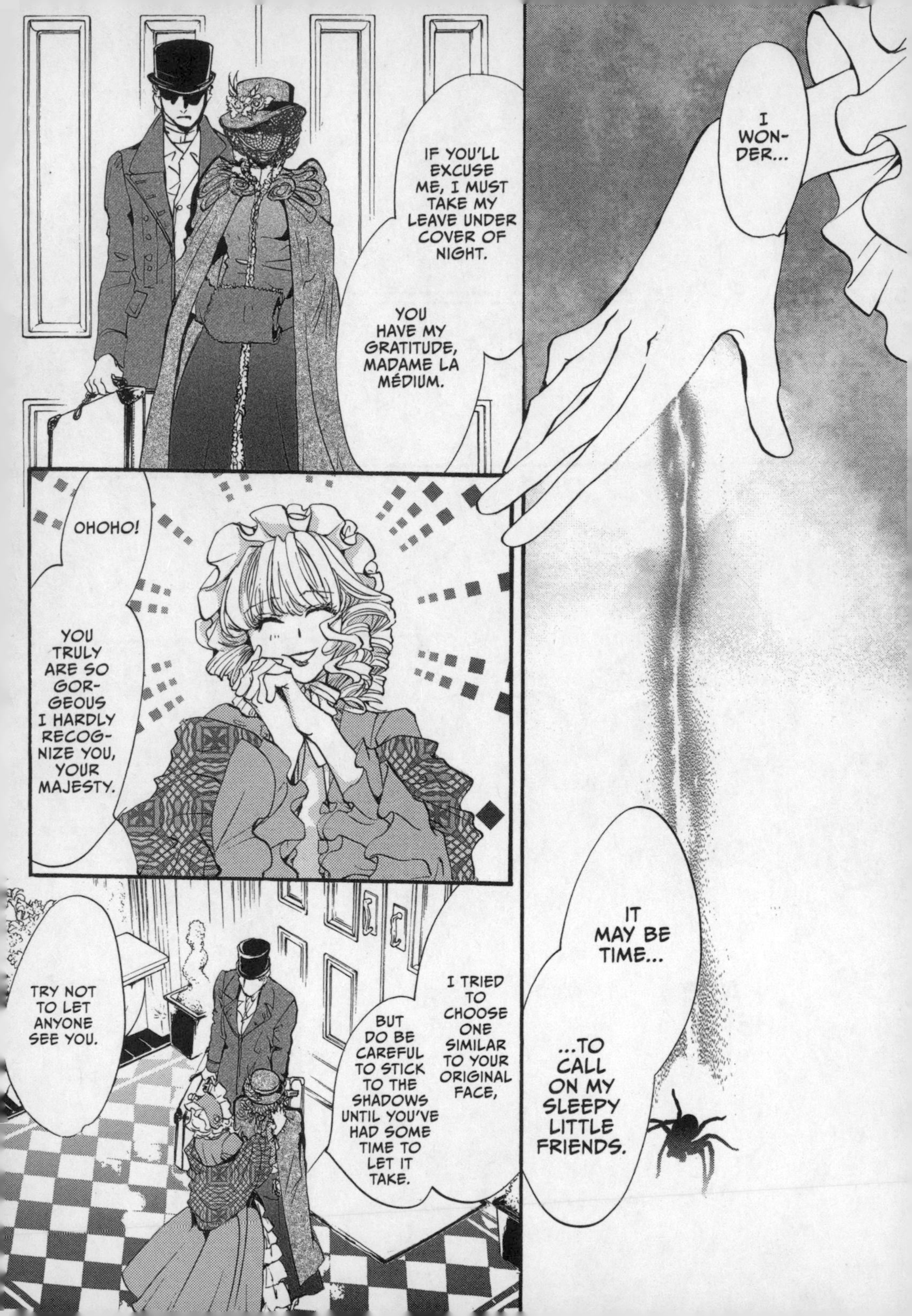
I WONDER...
IT MAY BE TIME...
...TO CALL ON MY SLEEPY LITTLE FRIENDS.
IF YOU'LL EXCUSE ME, I MUST TAKE MY LEAVE UNDER COVER OF NIGHT.
YOU HAVE MY GRATITUDE, MADAME LA MÉDIUM.
OHOHO!
YOU TRULY ARE SO GORGEOUS I HARDLY RECOGNIZE YOU, YOUR MAJESTY.
I TRIED TO CHOOSE ONE SIMILAR TO YOUR ORIGINAL FACE,
BUT DO BE CAREFUL TO STICK TO THE SHADOWS UNTIL YOU'VE HAD SOME TIME TO LET IT TAKE.
TRY NOT TO LET ANYONE SEE YOU.

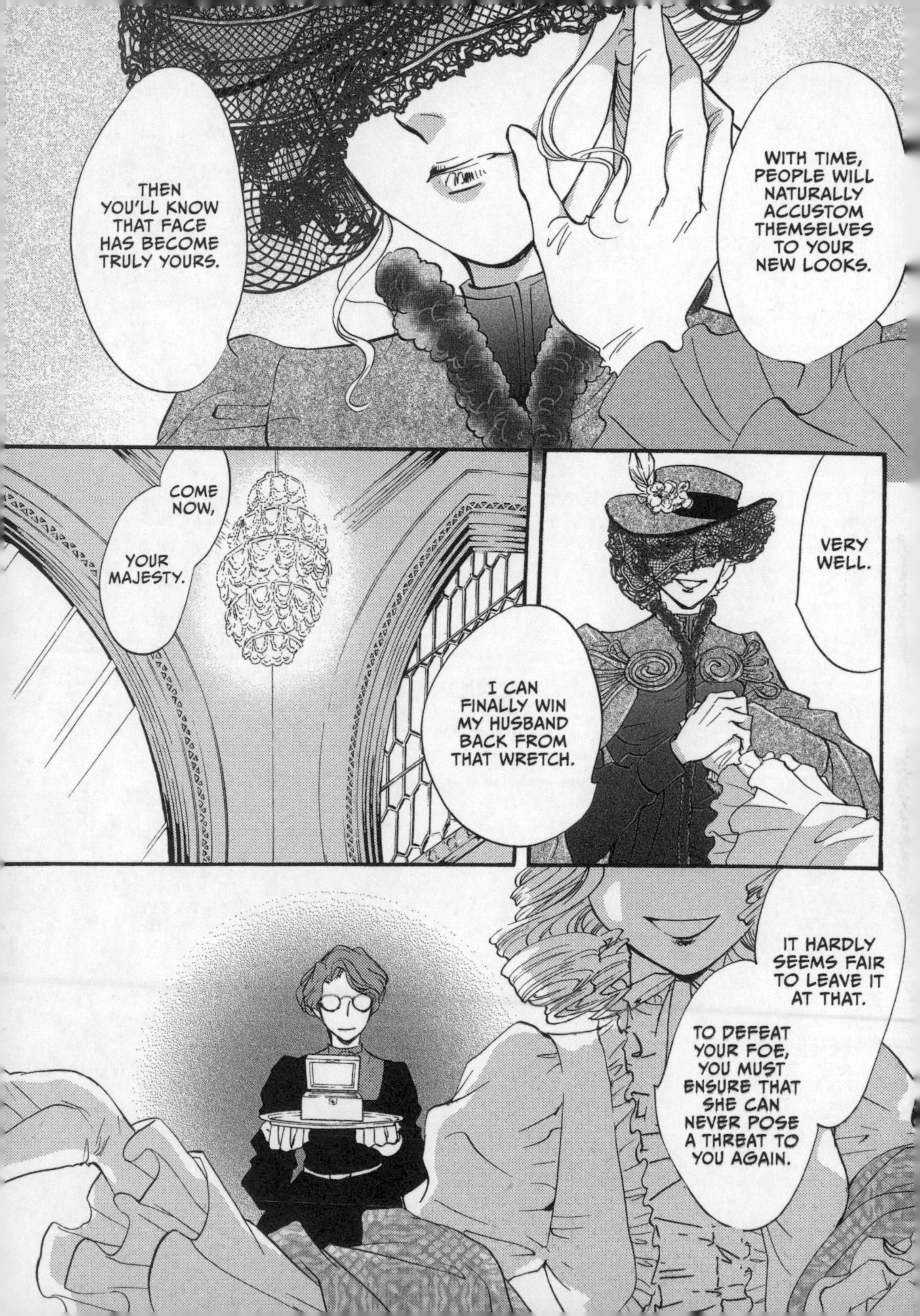
WITH TIME, PEOPLE WILL NATURALLY ACCUSTOM THEMSELVES TO YOUR NEW LOOKS.
THEN YOU'LL KNOW THAT FACE HAS BECOME TRULY YOURS.
VERY WELL.
I CAN FINALLY WIN MY HUSBAND BACK FROM THAT WRETCH.
COME NOW,
YOUR MAJESTY.
IT HARDLY SEEMS FAIR TO LEAVE IT AT THAT.
TO DEFEAT YOUR FOE, YOU MUST ENSURE THAT SHE CAN NEVER POSE A THREAT TO YOU AGAIN.

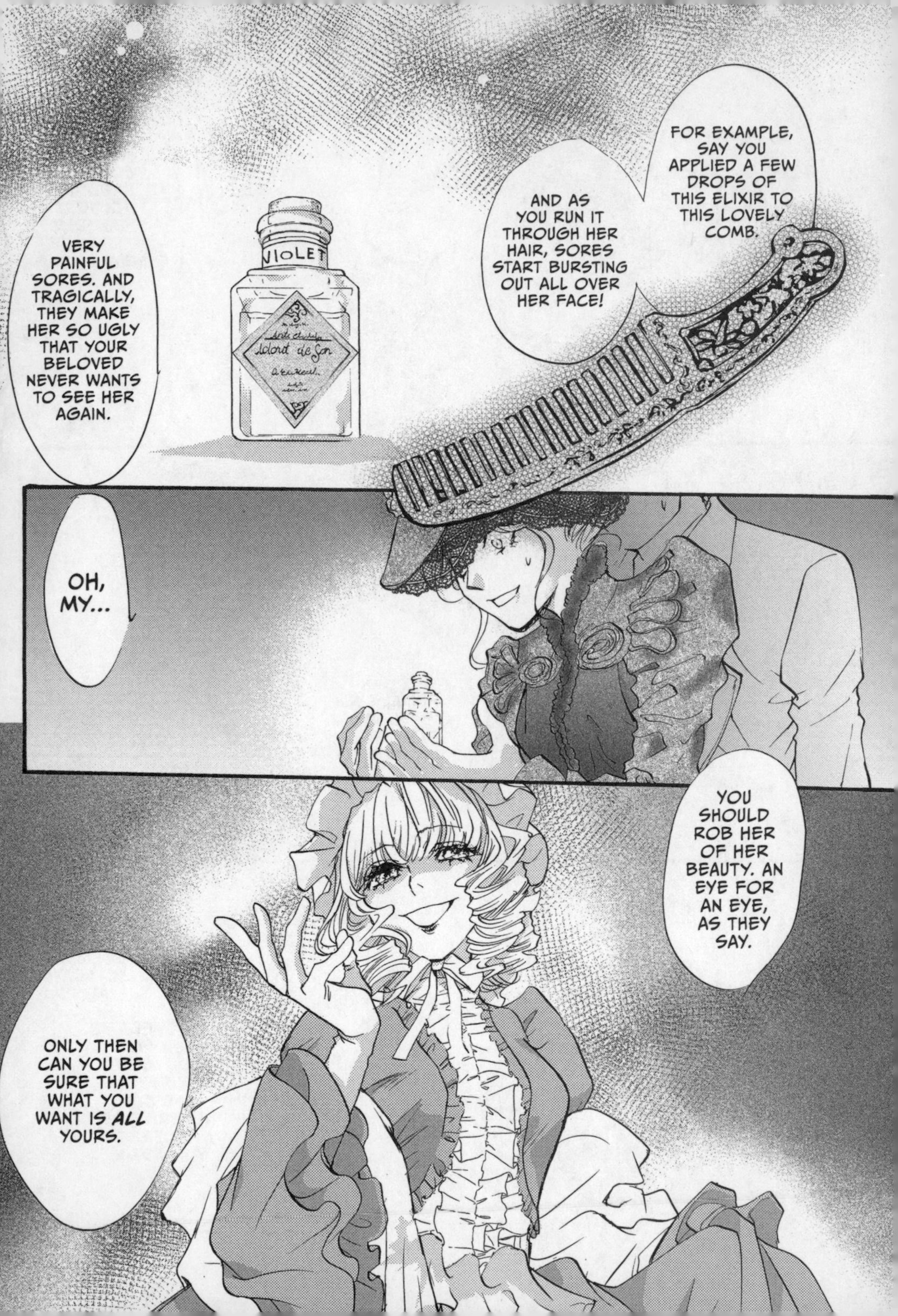
FOR EXAMPLE, SAY YOU APPLIED A FEW DROPS OF THIS ELIXIR TO THIS LOVELY COMB.
AND AS YOU RUN IT THROUGH HER HAIR, SORES START BURSTING OUT ALL OVER HER FACE!
VIOLET
VERY PAINFUL SORES. AND TRAGICALLY, THEY MAKE HER SO UGLY THAT YOUR BELOVED NEVER WANTS TO SEE HER AGAIN.
OH, MY...
YOU SHOULD ROB HER OF HER BEAUTY. AN EYE FOR AN EYE, AS THEY SAY.
ONLY THEN CAN YOU BE SURE THAT WHAT YOU WANT IS ***ALL*** YOURS.

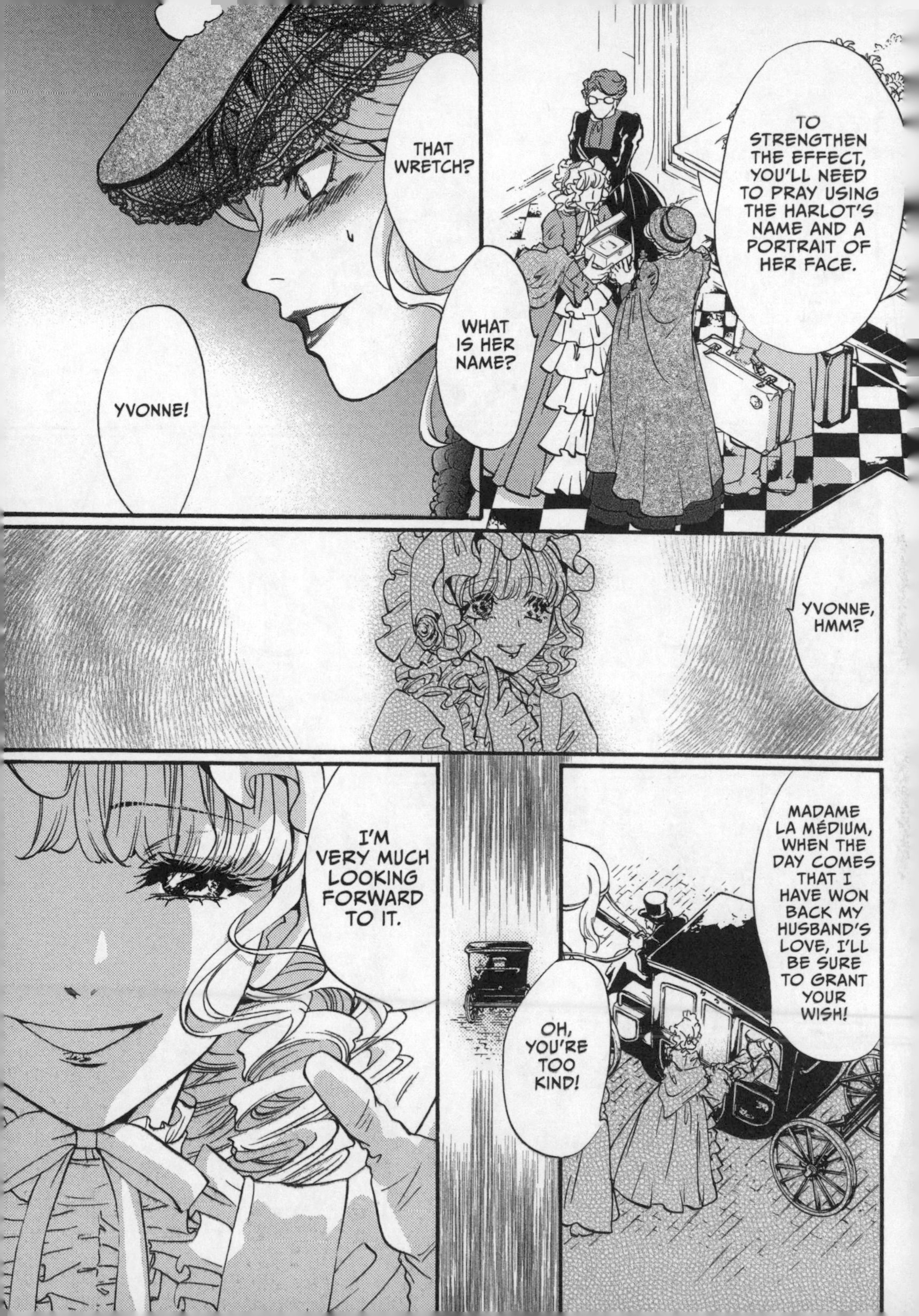
TO STRENGTHEN THE EFFECT, YOU'LL NEED TO PRAY USING THE HARLOT'S NAME AND A PORTRAIT OF HER FACE.
WHAT IS HER NAME?
THAT WRETCH?
YVONNE!
YVONNE, HMM?
MADAME LA MÉDIUM, WHEN THE DAY COMES THAT I HAVE WON BACK MY HUSBAND'S LOVE, I'LL BE SURE TO GRANT YOUR WISH!
OH, YOU'RE TOO KIND!
I'M VERY MUCH LOOKING FORWARD TO IT.

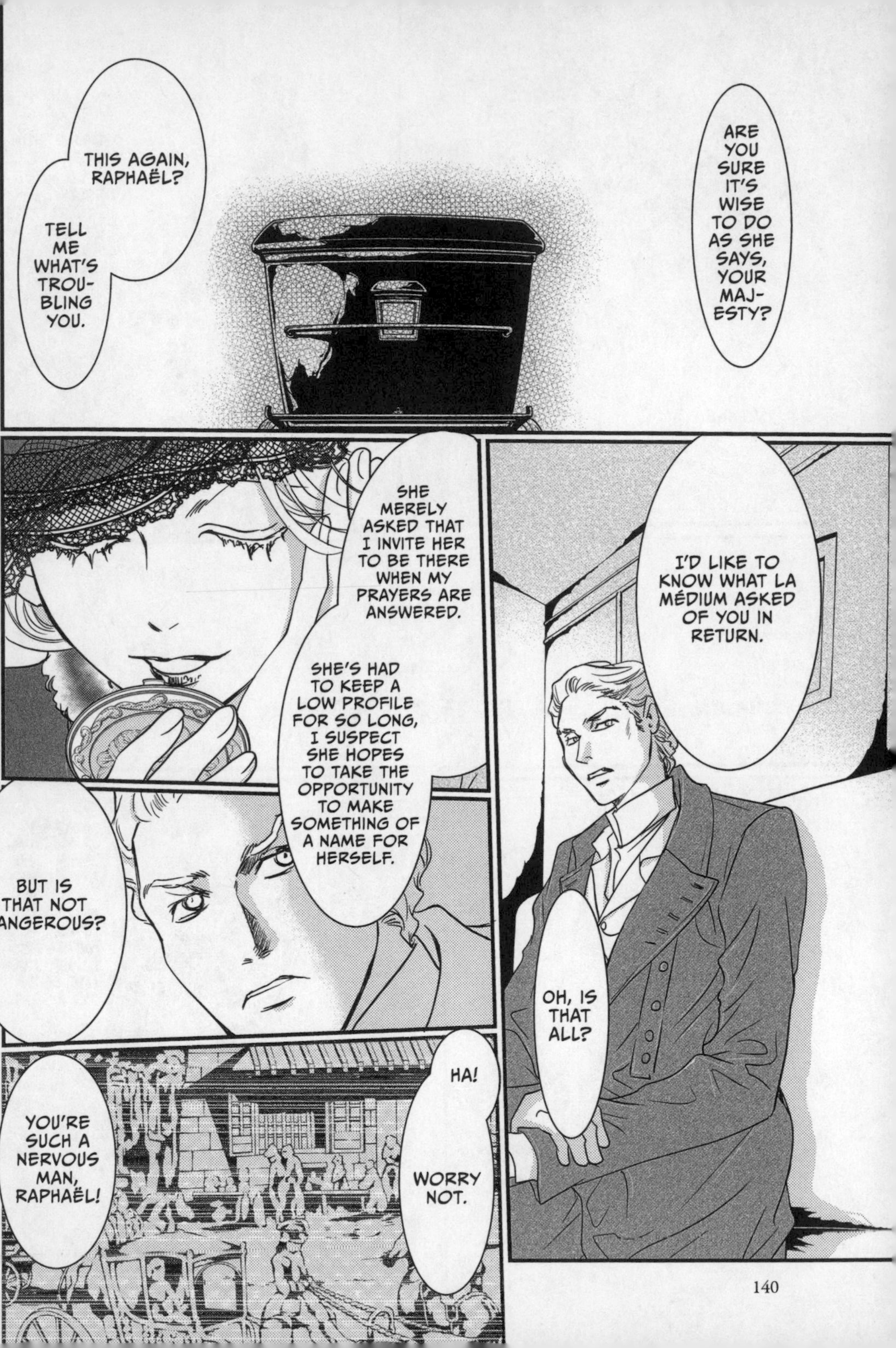
ARE YOU SURE IT'S WISE TO DO AS SHE SAYS, YOUR MAJ-ESTY?
THIS AGAIN, RAPHAËL?
TELL ME WHAT'S TROU-BLING YOU.
I'D LIKE TO KNOW WHAT LA MÉDIUM ASKED OF YOU IN RETURN.
SHE MERELY ASKED THAT I INVITE HER TO BE THERE WHEN MY PRAYERS ARE ANSWERED.
OH, IS THAT ALL?
SHE'S HAD TO KEEP A LOW PROFILE FOR SO LONG, I SUSPECT SHE HOPES TO TAKE THE OPPORTUNITY TO MAKE SOMETHING OF A NAME FOR HERSELF.
BUT IS THAT NOT DANGEROUS?
HA!
WORRY NOT.
YOU'RE SUCH A NERVOUS MAN, RAPHAËL!

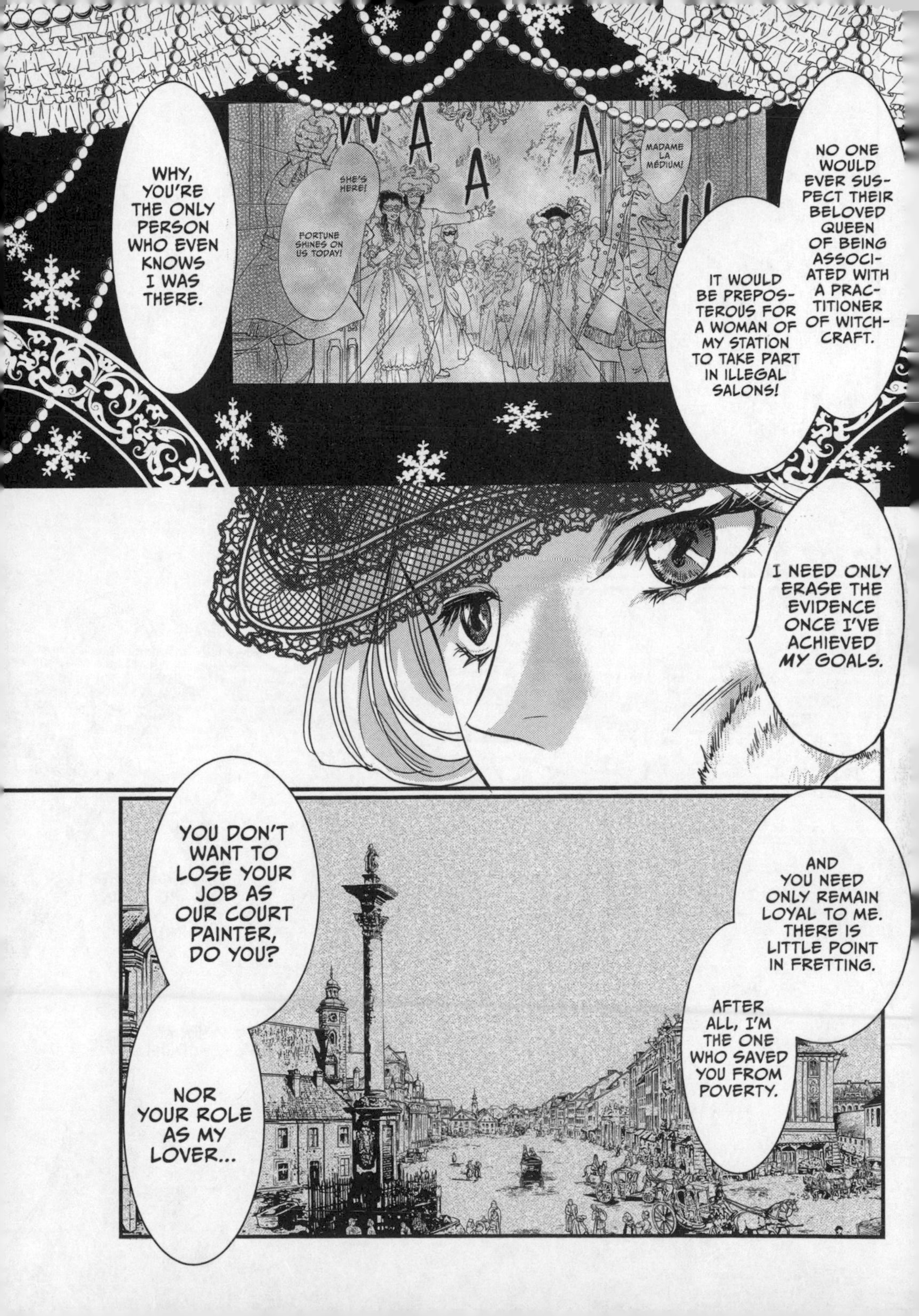
NO ONE WOULD EVER SUSPECT THEIR BELOVED QUEEN OF BEING ASSOCIATED WITH A PRACTITIONER OF WITCHCRAFT.
IT WOULD BE PREPOSTEROUS FOR A WOMAN OF MY STATION TO TAKE PART IN ILLEGAL SALONS!
MADAME LA MÉDIUM!
WAAA!!
SHE'S HERE!
FORTUNE SHINES ON US TODAY!
WHY, YOU'RE THE ONLY PERSON WHO EVEN KNOWS I WAS THERE.
I NEED ONLY ERASE THE EVIDENCE ONCE I'VE ACHIEVED MY GOALS.
AND YOU NEED ONLY REMAIN LOYAL TO ME. THERE IS LITTLE POINT IN FRETTING.
AFTER ALL, I'M THE ONE WHO SAVED YOU FROM POVERTY.
YOU DON'T WANT TO LOSE YOUR JOB AS OUR COURT PAINTER, DO YOU?
NOR YOUR ROLE AS MY LOVER...

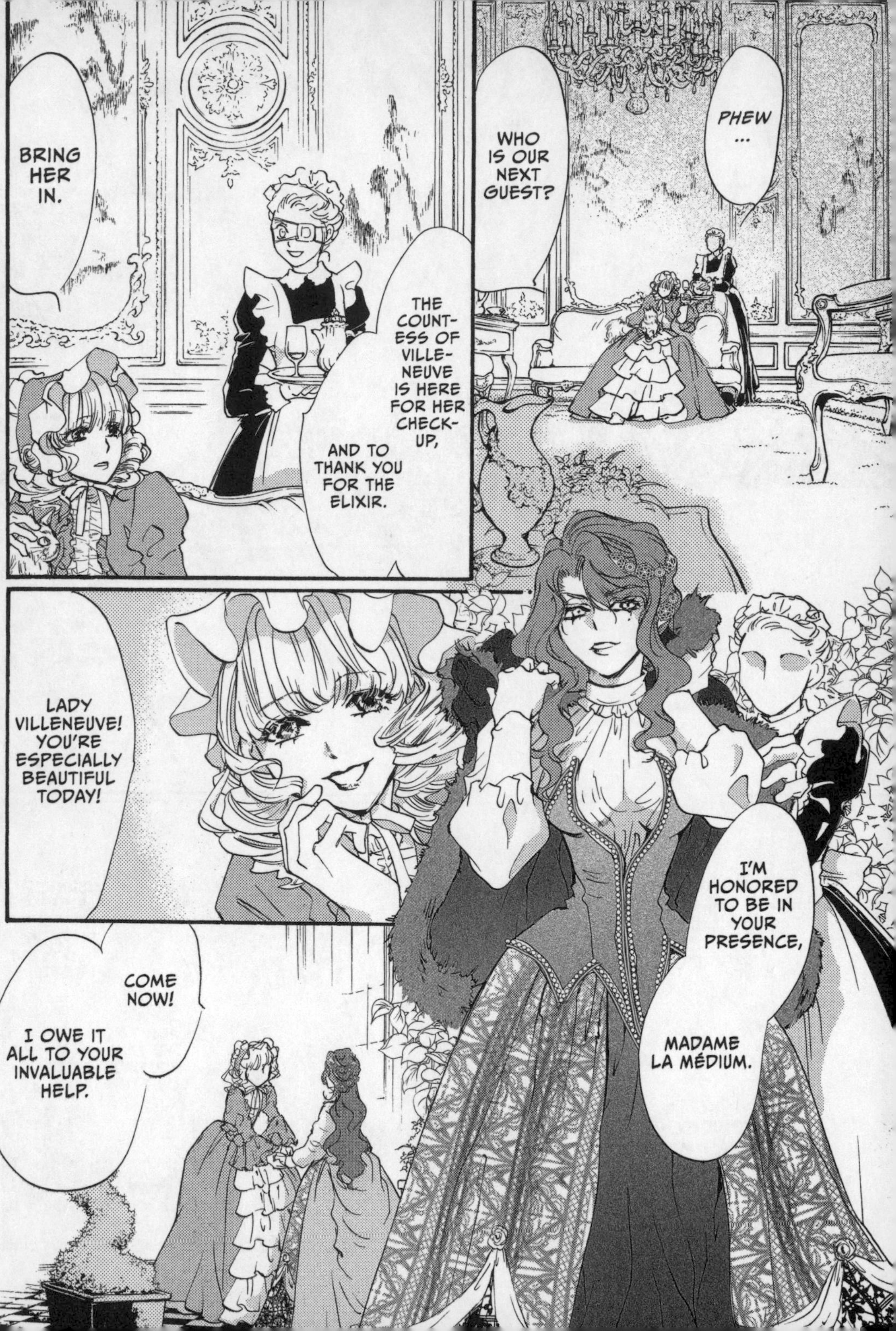
PHEW ...
WHO IS OUR NEXT GUEST?
THE COUNT-ESS OF VILLE-NEUVE IS HERE FOR HER CHECK-UP,
AND TO THANK YOU FOR THE ELIXIR.
BRING HER IN.
I'M HONORED TO BE IN YOUR PRESENCE,
MADAME LA MÉDIUM.
LADY VILLENEUVE! YOU'RE ESPECIALLY BEAUTIFUL TODAY!
COME NOW!
I OWE IT ALL TO YOUR INVALUABLE HELP.

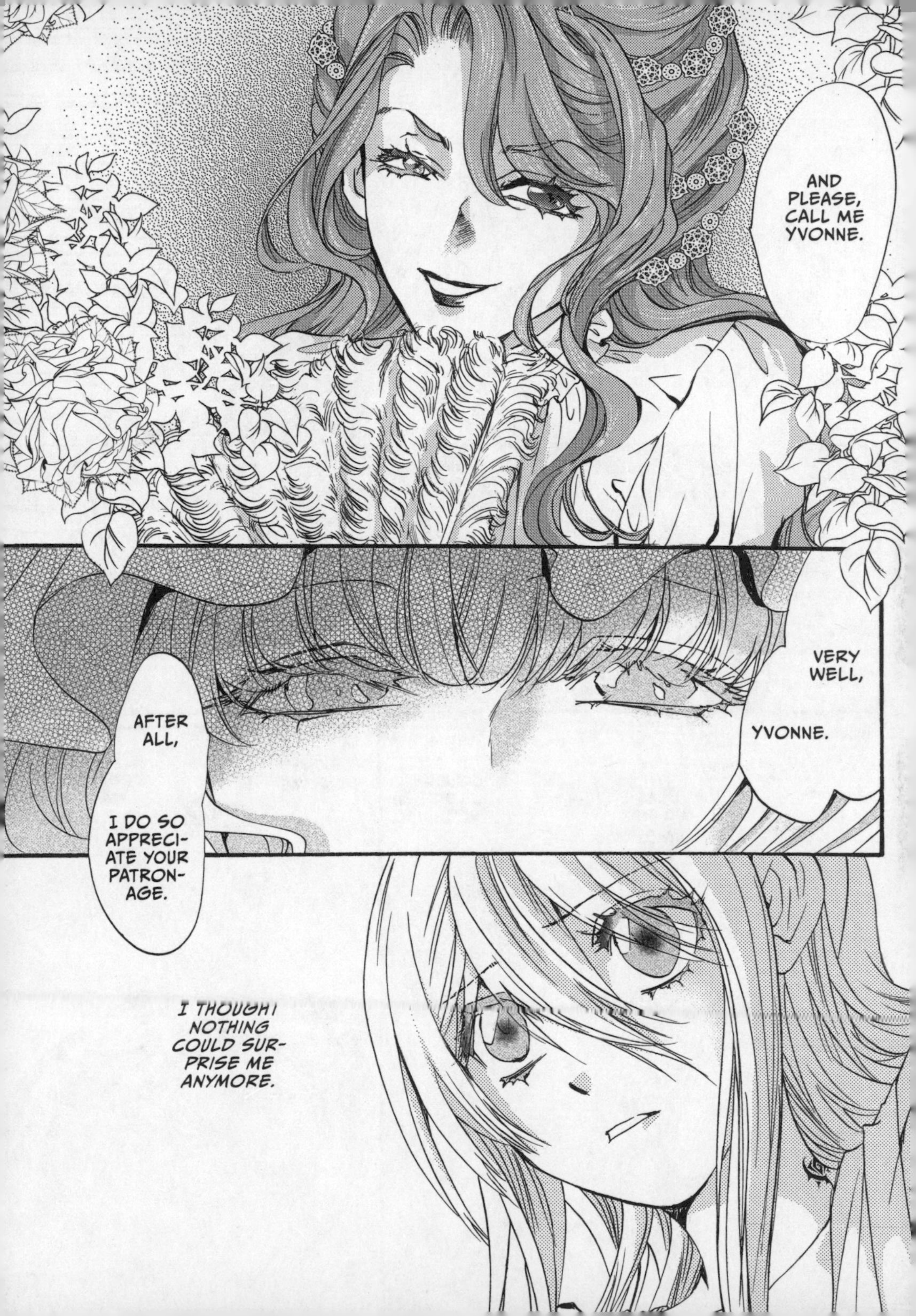
AND PLEASE, CALL ME YVONNE.
VERY WELL,
YVONNE.
AFTER ALL,
I DO SO APPRECIATE YOUR PATRONAGE.
I THOUGHT NOTHING COULD SURPRISE ME ANYMORE.

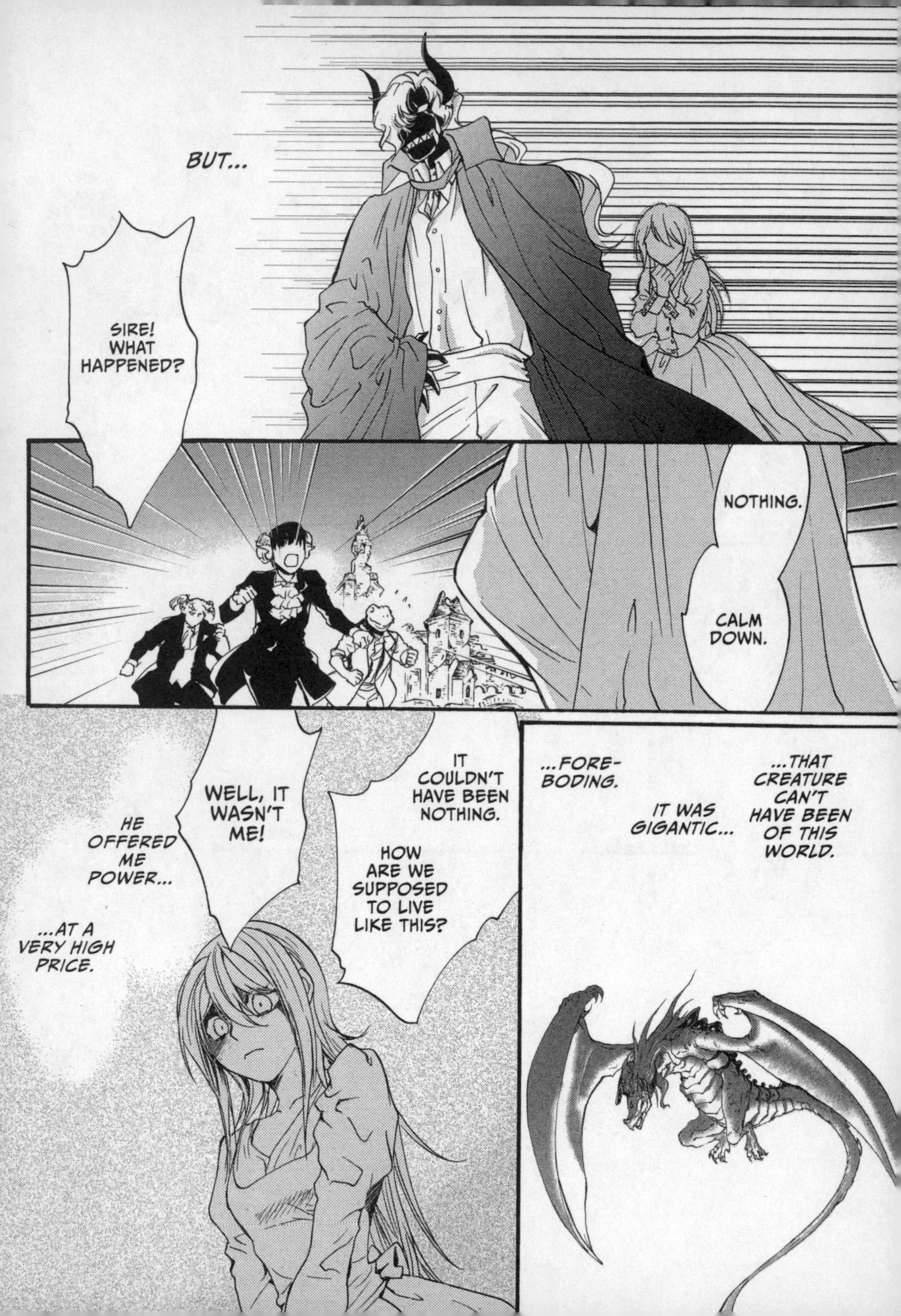
BUT...
SIRE! WHAT HAPPENED?
NOTHING.
CALM DOWN.
...THAT CREATURE CAN'T HAVE BEEN OF THIS WORLD.
IT WAS GIGANTIC...
...FORE-BODING.
IT COULDN'T HAVE BEEN NOTHING.
HOW ARE WE SUPPOSED TO LIVE LIKE THIS?
WELL, IT WASN'T ME!
HE OFFERED ME POWER...
...AT A VERY HIGH PRICE.

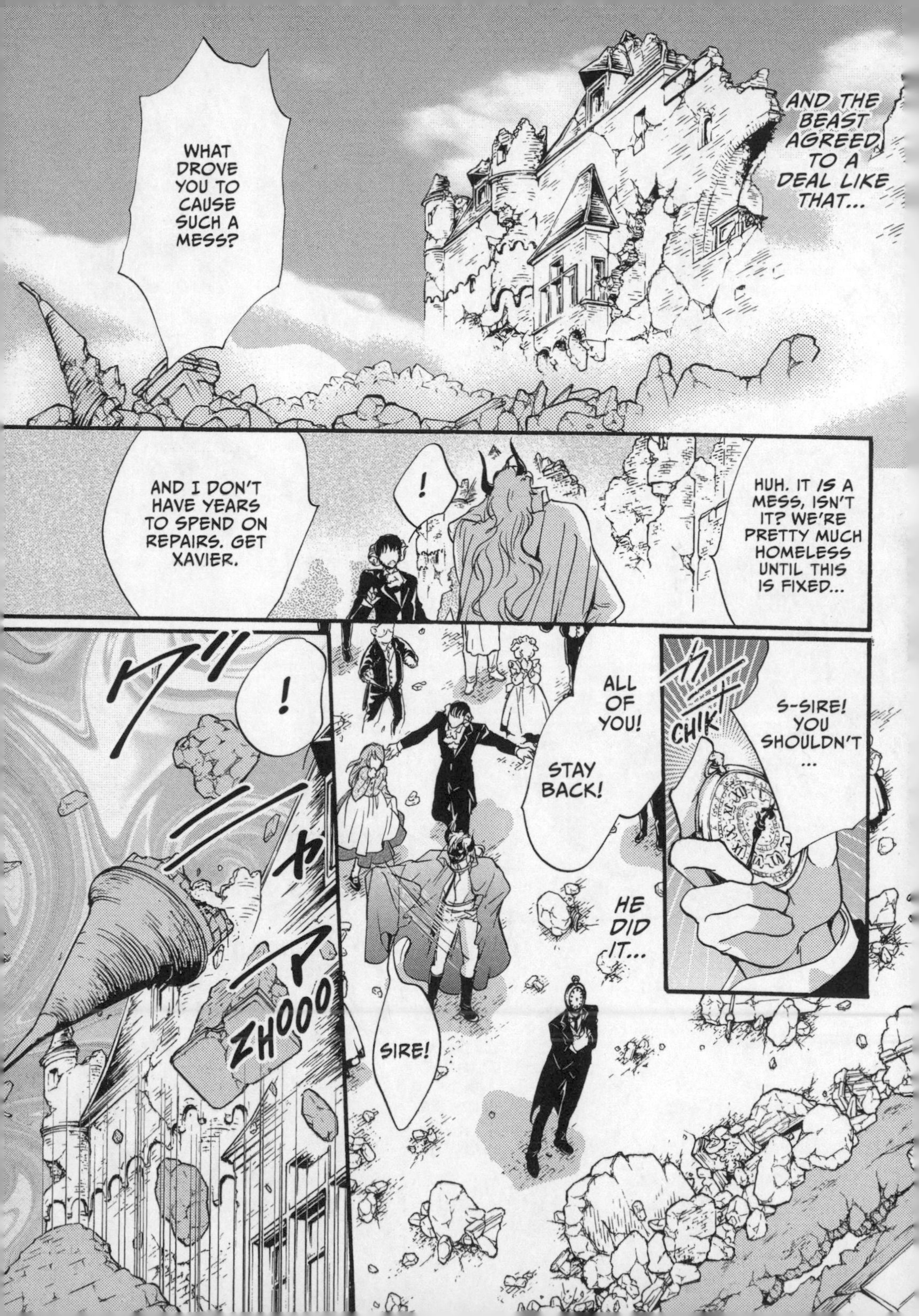
AND THE BEAST AGREED TO A DEAL LIKE THAT...
WHAT DROVE YOU TO CAUSE SUCH A MESS?
HUH. IT *IS* A MESS, ISN'T IT? WE'RE PRETTY MUCH HOMELESS UNTIL THIS IS FIXED...
!
AND I DON'T HAVE YEARS TO SPEND ON REPAIRS. GET XAVIER.
CHIK
S-SIRE! YOU SHOULDN'T ...
ALL OF YOU!
STAY BACK!
HE DID IT...
SIRE!
!
ZHOOO

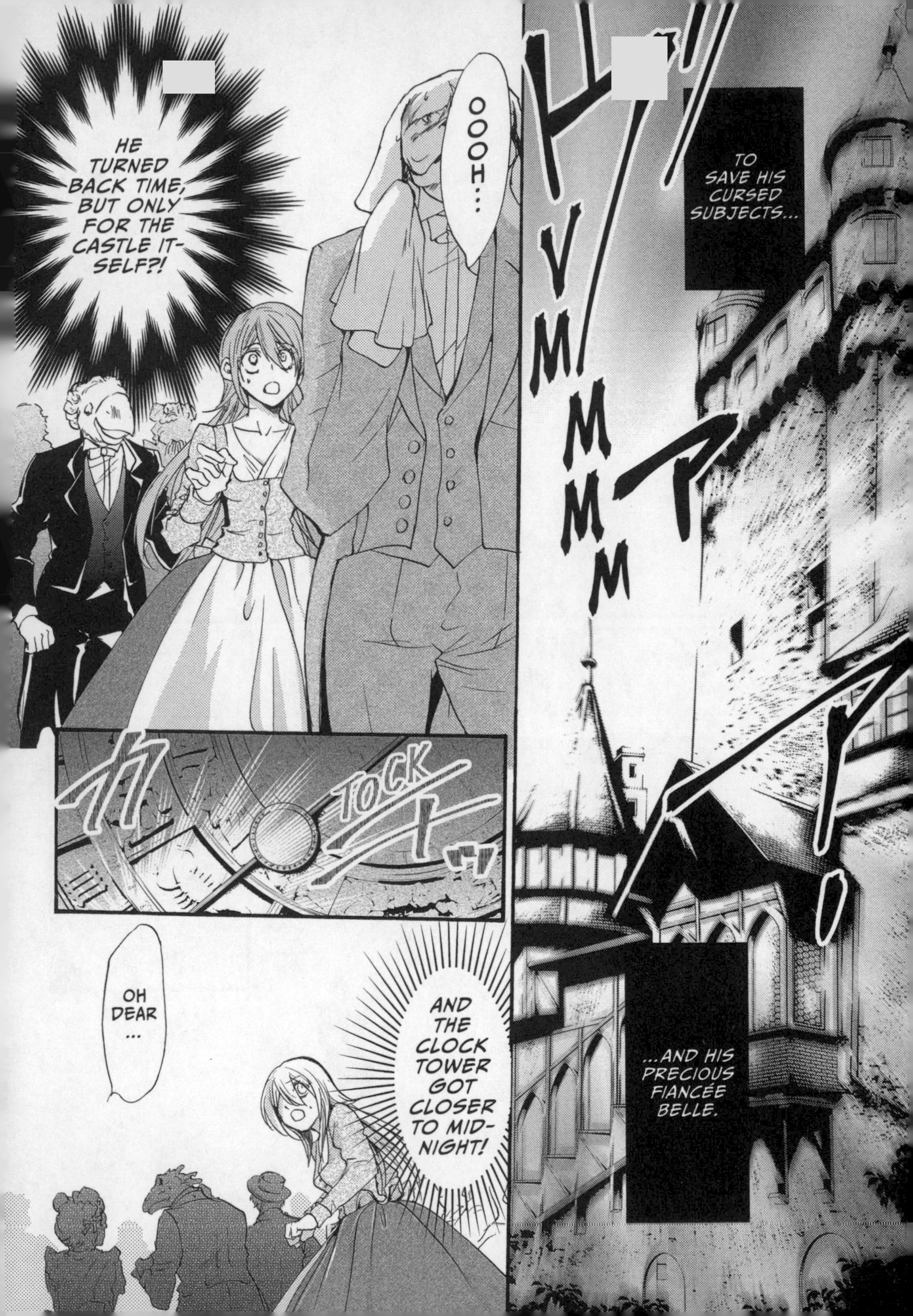
TO SAVE HIS CURSED SUBJECTS...
VVMMMMM
...AND HIS PRECIOUS FIANCÉE BELLE.
OOOH...
HE TURNED BACK TIME, BUT ONLY FOR THE CASTLE IT-SELF?!
TOCK
AND THE CLOCK TOWER GOT CLOSER TO MID-NIGHT!
OH DEAR...

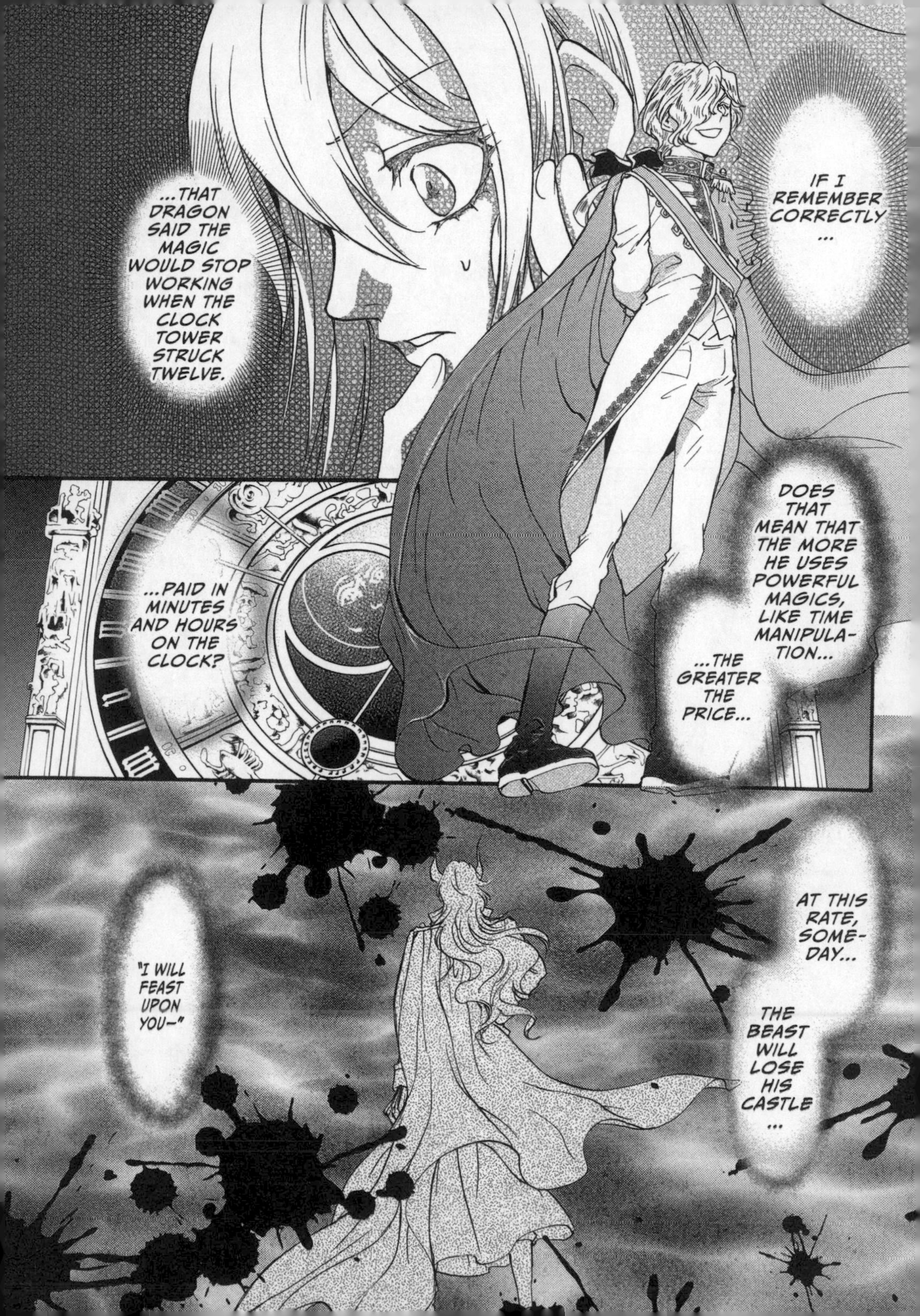
IF I REMEMBER CORRECTLY ...
...THAT DRAGON SAID THE MAGIC WOULD STOP WORKING WHEN THE CLOCK TOWER STRUCK TWELVE.
DOES THAT MEAN THAT THE MORE HE USES POWERFUL MAGICS, LIKE TIME MANIPULA-TION...
...THE GREATER THE PRICE...
...PAID IN MINUTES AND HOURS ON THE CLOCK?
AT THIS RATE, SOME-DAY...
THE BEAST WILL LOSE HIS CASTLE ...
"I WILL FEAST UPON YOU—"

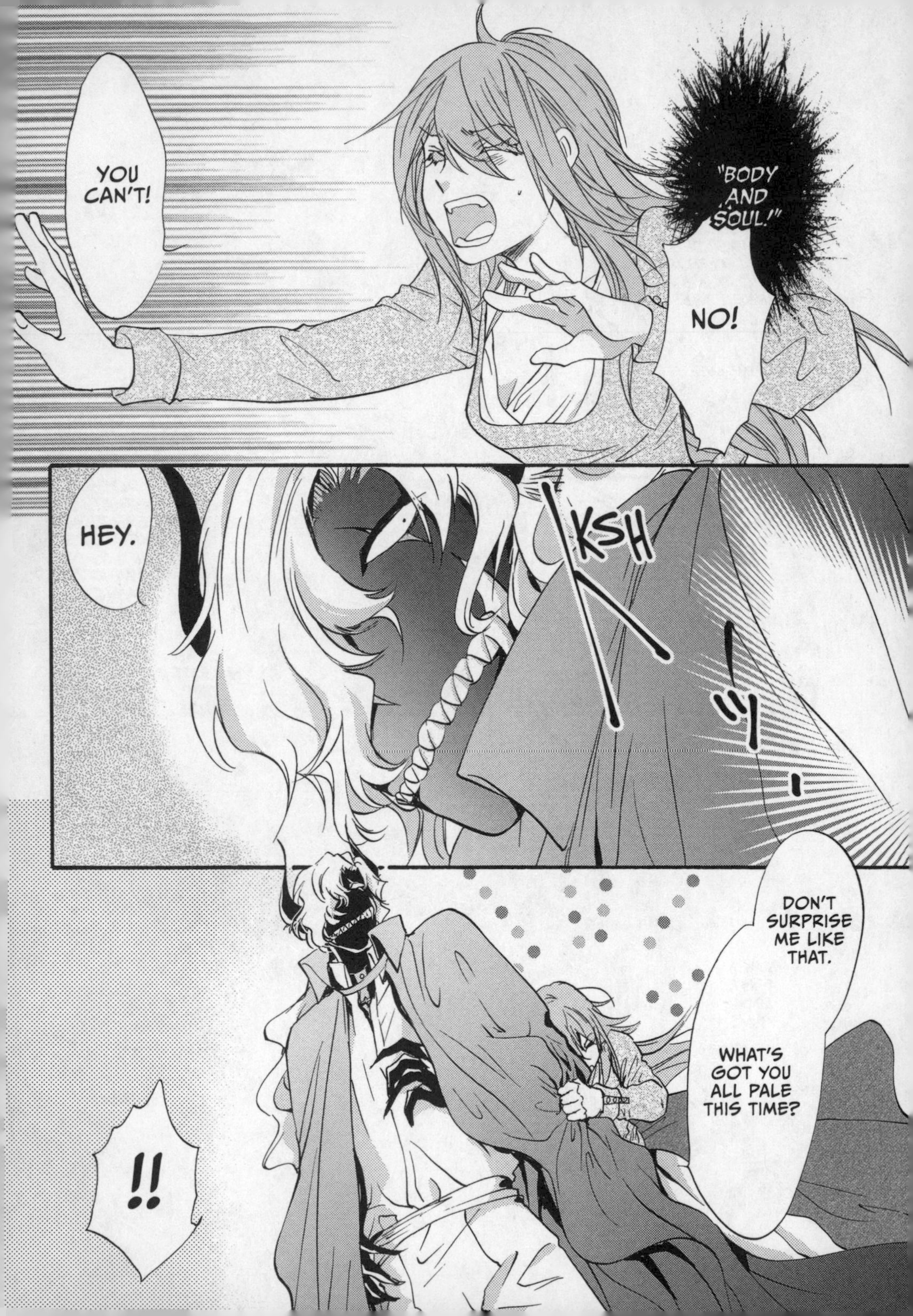
"BODY AND SOUL!"
NO!
YOU CAN'T!
KSH
HEY.
DON'T SURPRISE ME LIKE THAT.
WHAT'S GOT YOU ALL PALE THIS TIME?
!!

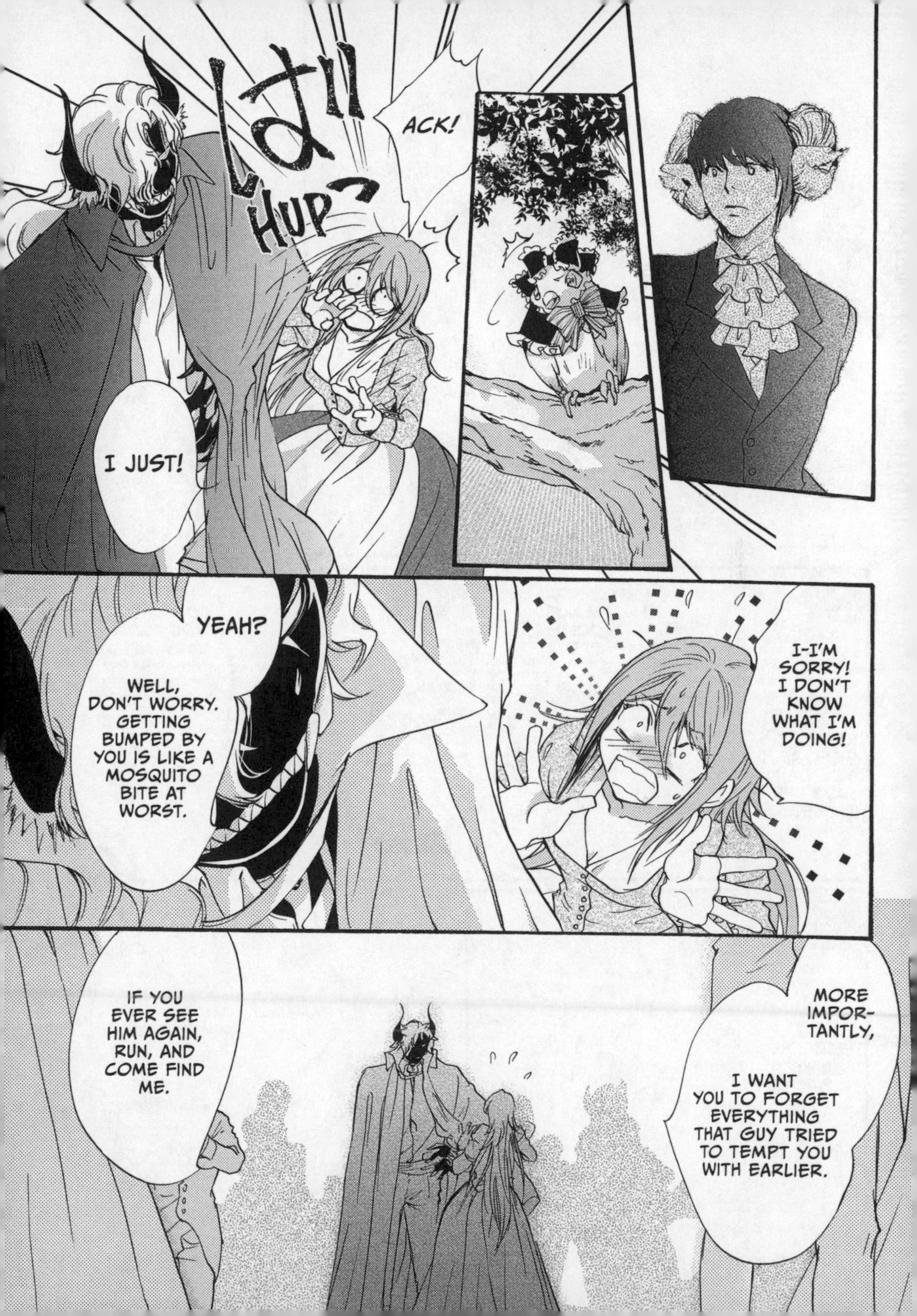
ACK!
HUP
I JUST!
I-I'M SORRY! I DON'T KNOW WHAT I'M DOING!
YEAH?
WELL, DON'T WORRY. GETTING BUMPED BY YOU IS LIKE A MOSQUITO BITE AT WORST.
MORE IMPORTANTLY,
I WANT YOU TO FORGET EVERYTHING THAT GUY TRIED TO TEMPT YOU WITH EARLIER.
IF YOU EVER SEE HIM AGAIN, RUN, AND COME FIND ME.

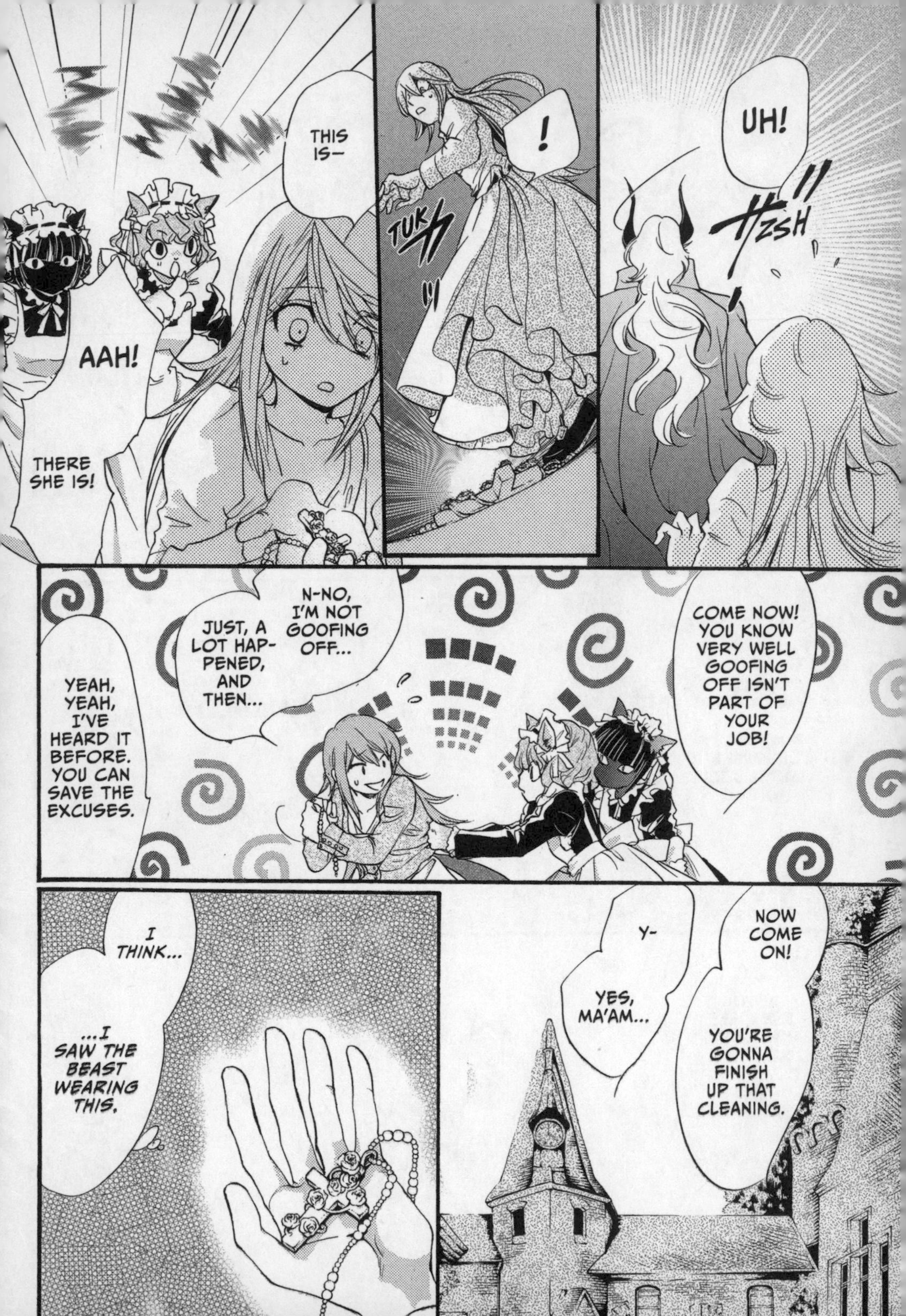
UH!
ZSH
!
TUK
THIS IS—
AAH!
THERE SHE IS!
COME NOW! YOU KNOW VERY WELL GOOFING OFF ISN'T PART OF YOUR JOB!
N-NO, I'M NOT GOOFING OFF...
JUST, A LOT HAP-PENED, AND THEN...
YEAH, YEAH, I'VE HEARD IT BEFORE. YOU CAN SAVE THE EXCUSES.
NOW COME ON!
YOU'RE GONNA FINISH UP THAT CLEANING.
Y-
YES, MA'AM...
I THINK...
...I SAW THE BEAST WEARING THIS.

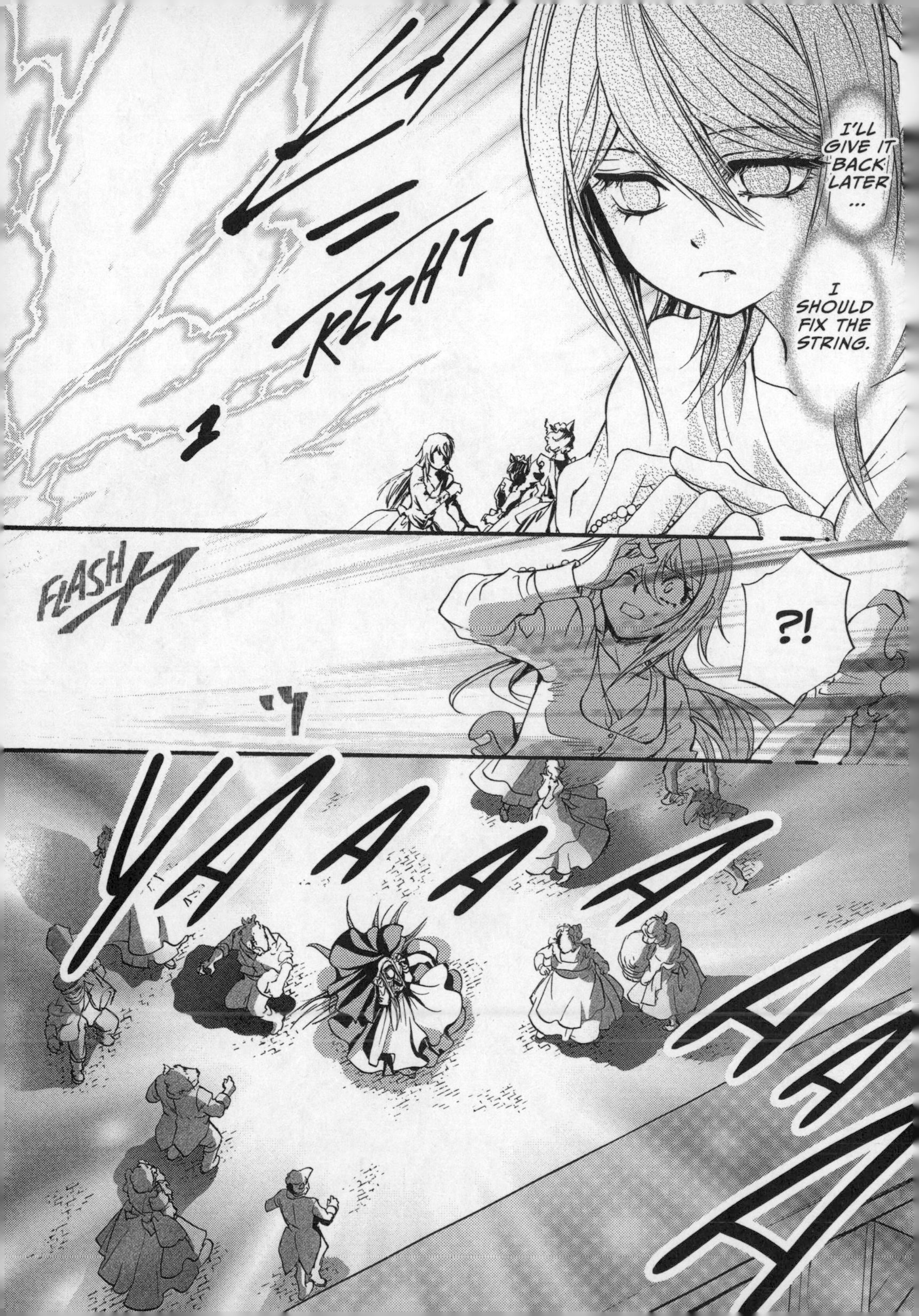
I'LL GIVE IT BACK LATER...
I SHOULD FIX THE STRING.
KZZZHT
?!
FLASH
YAAAAAAAAAAA

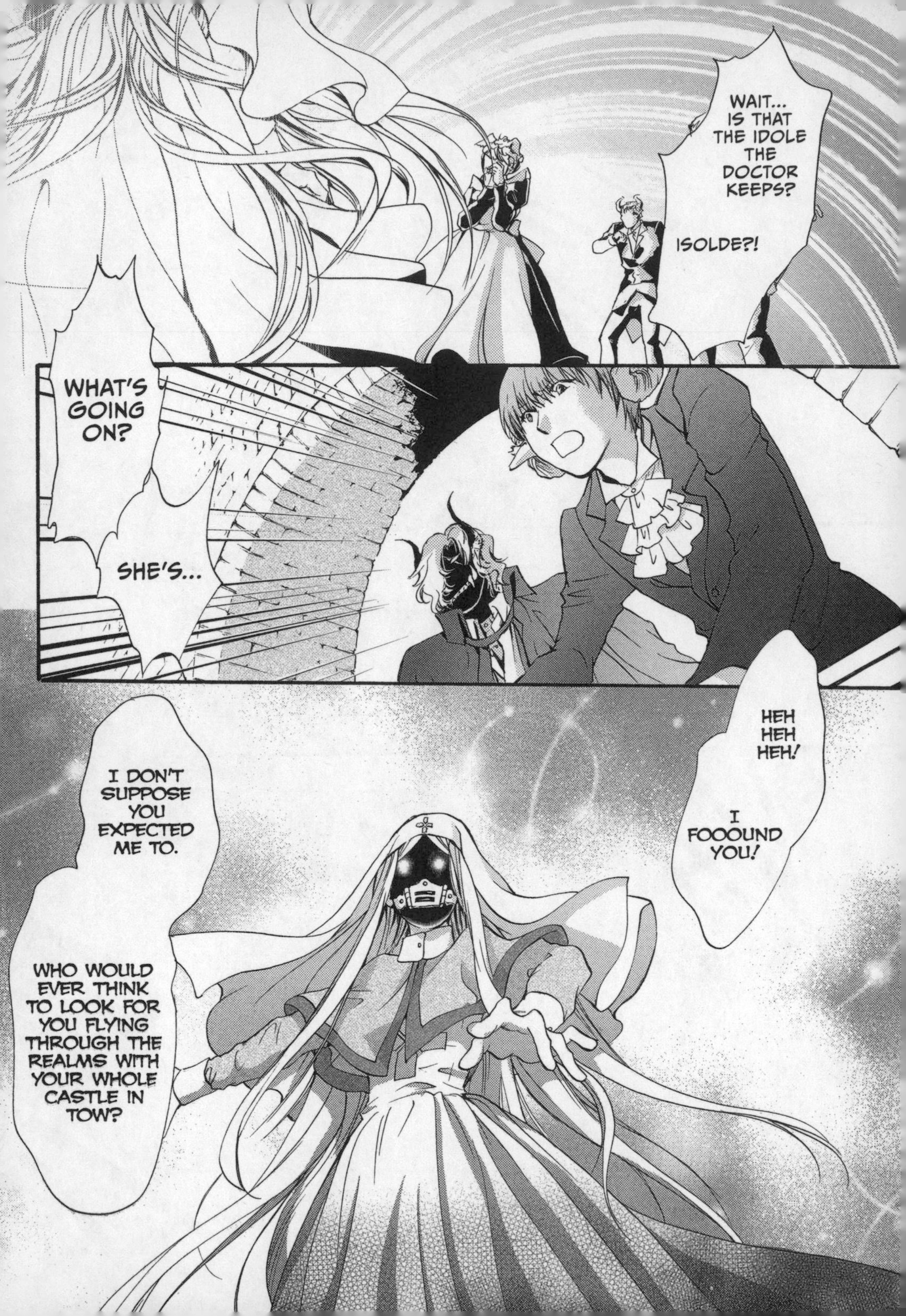
WAIT... IS THAT THE IDOLE THE DOCTOR KEEPS?
ISOLDE?!
WHAT'S GOING ON?
SHE'S...
HEH HEH HEH!
I FOOOUND YOU!
I DON'T SUPPOSE YOU EXPECTED ME TO.
WHO WOULD EVER THINK TO LOOK FOR YOU FLYING THROUGH THE REALMS WITH YOUR WHOLE CASTLE IN TOW?

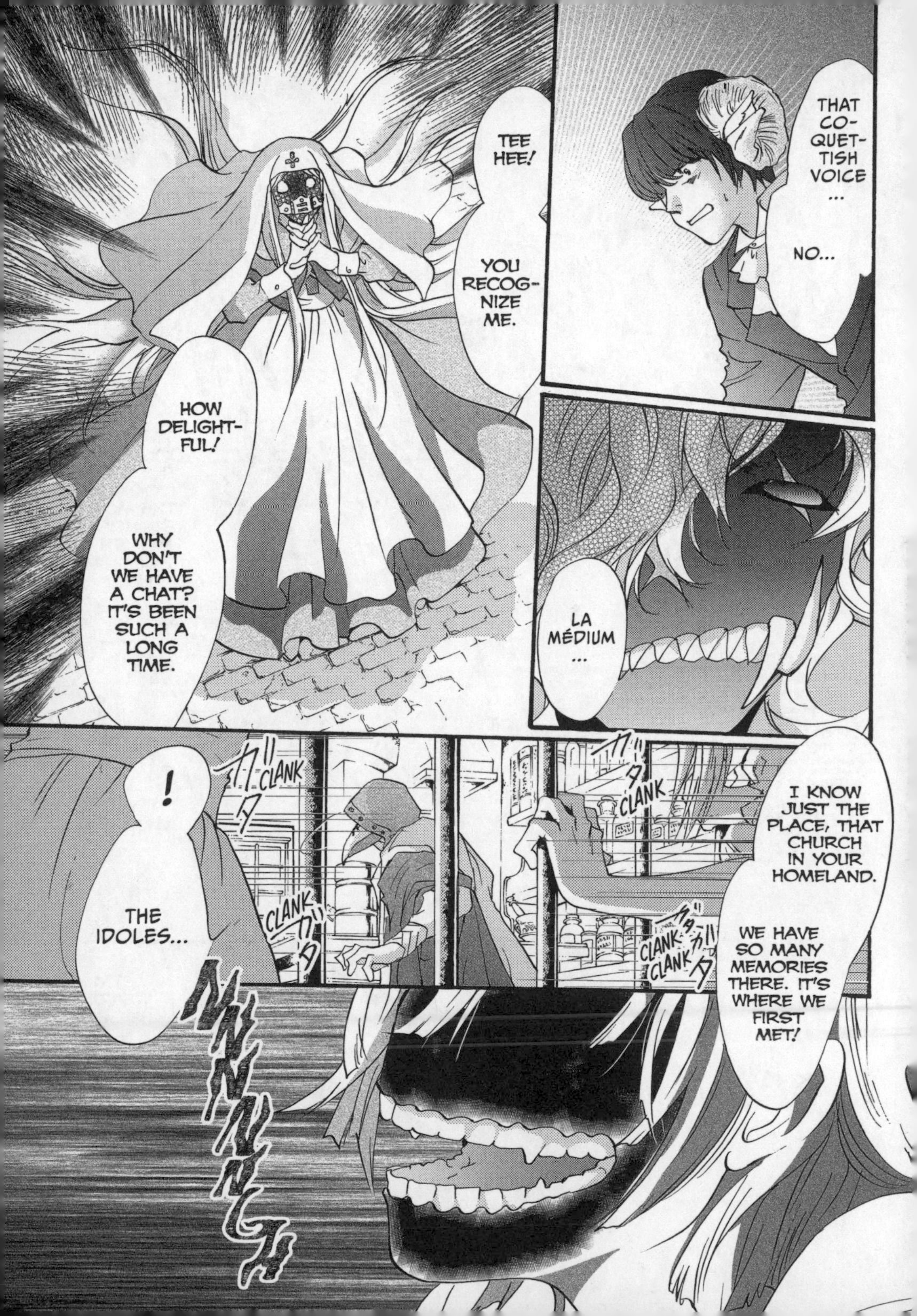
THAT CO-QUET-TISH VOICE ...
NO...
LA MÉDIUM ...
TEE HEE!
YOU RECOG-NIZE ME.
HOW DELIGHT-FUL!
WHY DON'T WE HAVE A CHAT? IT'S BEEN SUCH A LONG TIME.
I KNOW JUST THE PLACE, THAT CHURCH IN YOUR HOMELAND.
WE HAVE SO MANY MEMORIES THERE. IT'S WHERE WE FIRST MET!
CLANK
CLANK CLANK
CLANK
CLANK
CLANK
!
THE IDOLES...
MNNNNCH

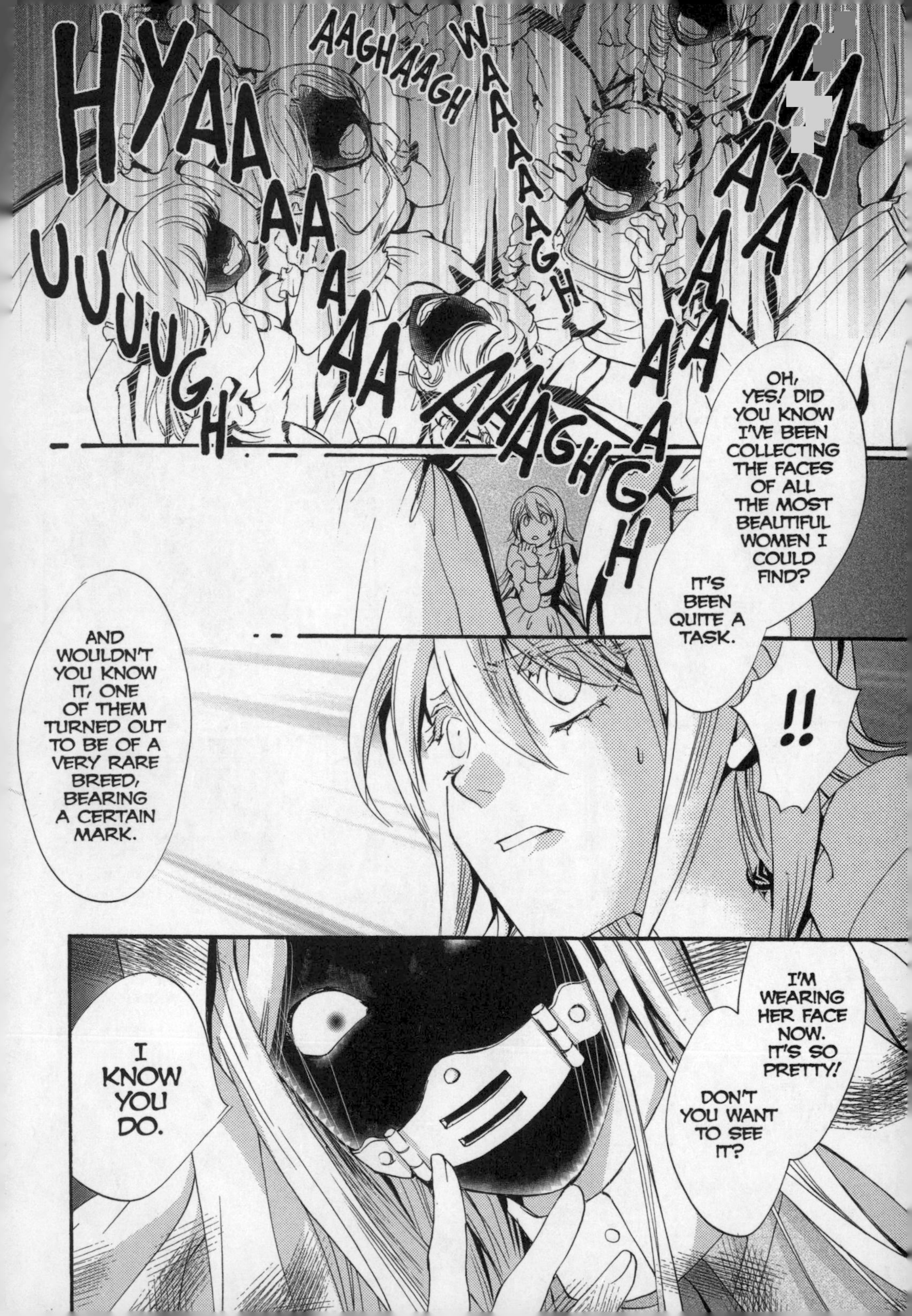
WAAAAAAAAAAGH
AAGHAAGH
WAAAAAAAGH
HYAAAAAAAAAAAGH
UUUUUGH
OH, YES! DID YOU KNOW I'VE BEEN COLLECTING THE FACES OF ALL THE MOST BEAUTIFUL WOMEN I COULD FIND?
IT'S BEEN QUITE A TASK.
!!
AND WOULDN'T YOU KNOW IT, ONE OF THEM TURNED OUT TO BE OF A VERY RARE BREED, BEARING A CERTAIN MARK.
I'M WEARING HER FACE NOW. IT'S SO PRETTY!
DON'T YOU WANT TO SEE IT?
I KNOW YOU DO.

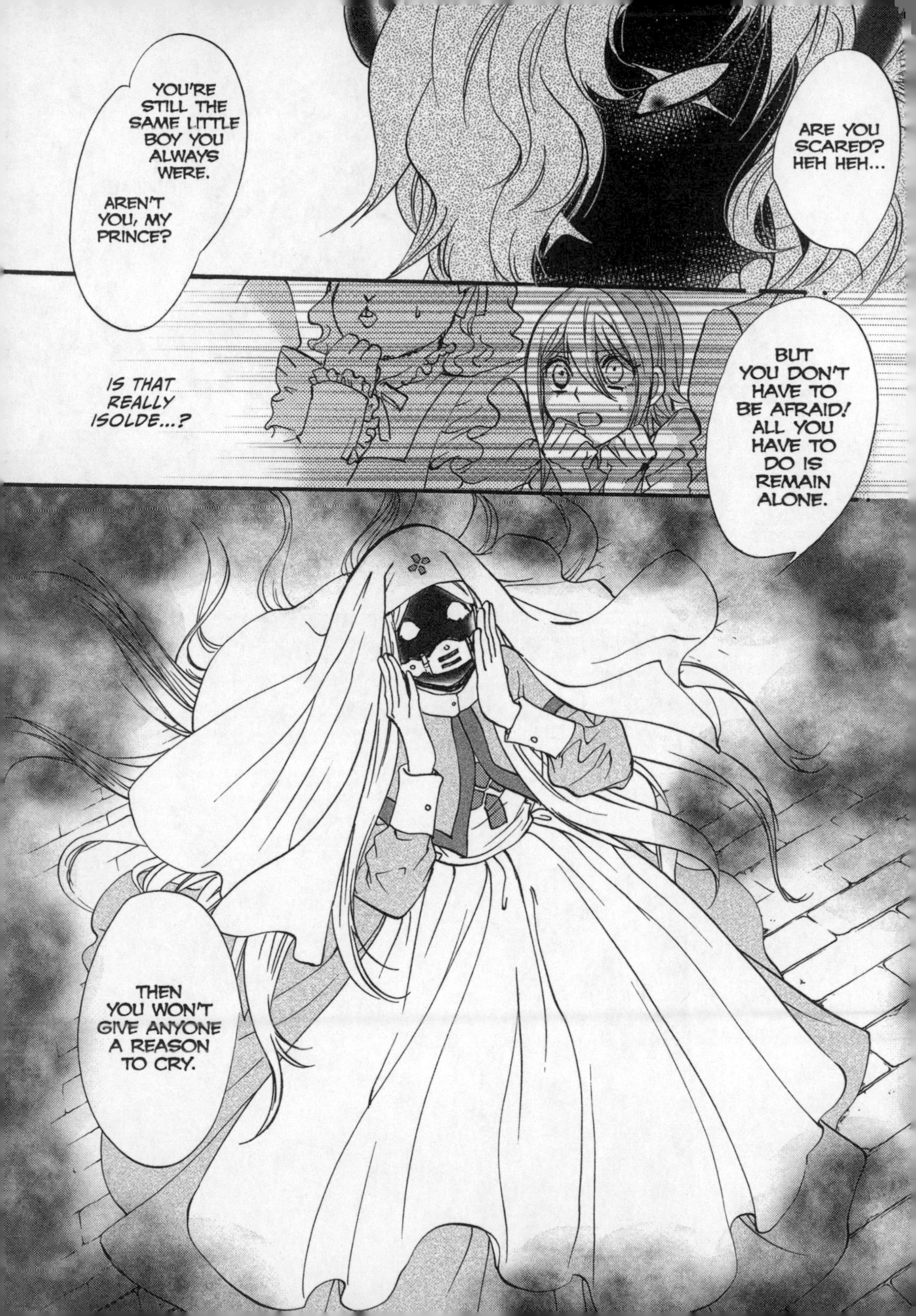
ARE YOU SCARED? HEH HEH...
YOU'RE STILL THE SAME LITTLE BOY YOU ALWAYS WERE.
AREN'T YOU, MY PRINCE?
BUT YOU DON'T HAVE TO BE AFRAID! ALL YOU HAVE TO DO IS REMAIN ALONE.
IS THAT REALLY ISOLDE...?
THEN YOU WON'T GIVE ANYONE A REASON TO CRY.

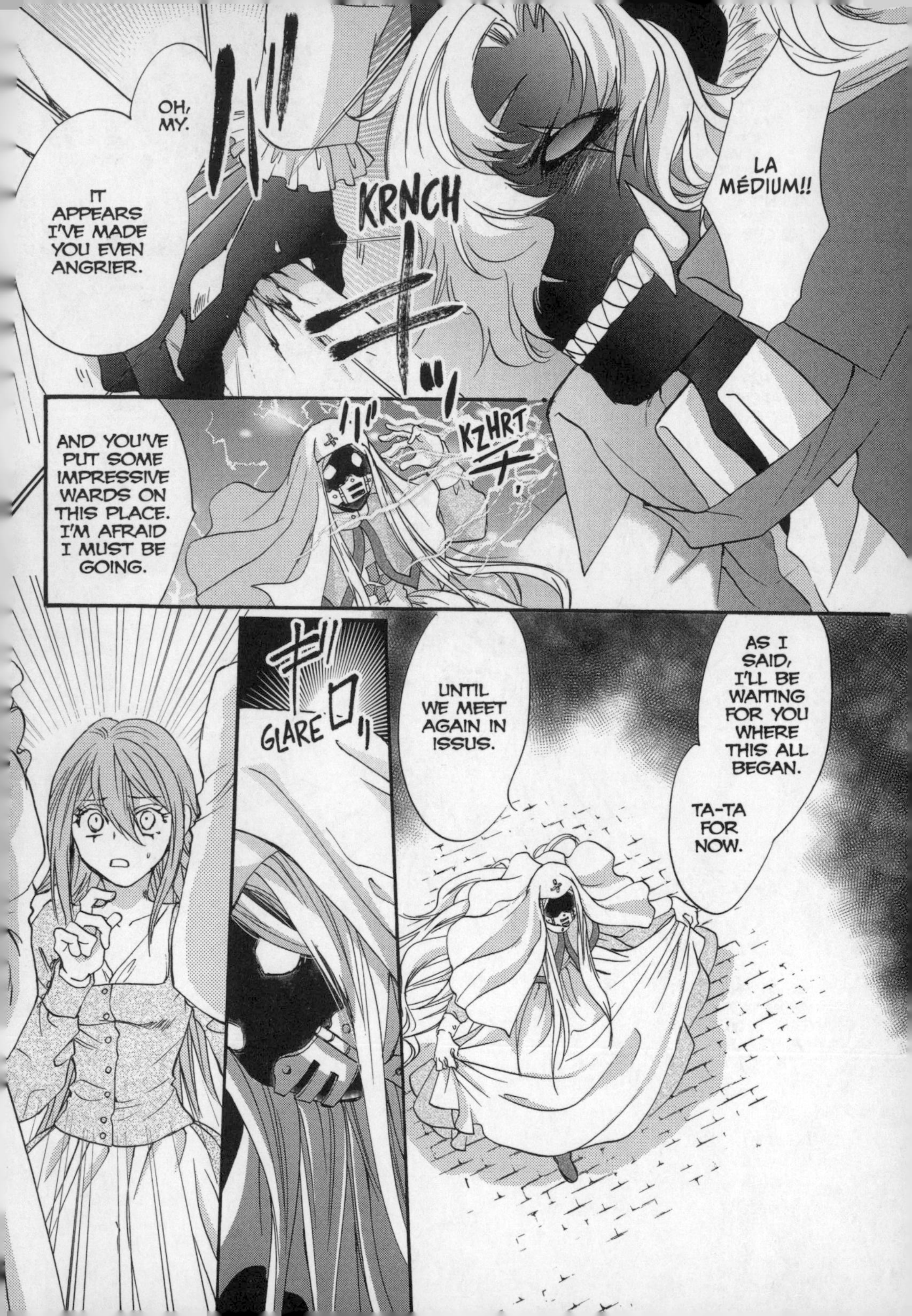
LA MÉDIUM!!
KRNCH
OH, MY.
IT APPEARS I'VE MADE YOU EVEN ANGRIER.
KZHRT
AND YOU'VE PUT SOME IMPRESSIVE WARDS ON THIS PLACE. I'M AFRAID I MUST BE GOING.
AS I SAID, I'LL BE WAITING FOR YOU WHERE THIS ALL BEGAN.
TA-TA FOR NOW.
UNTIL WE MEET AGAIN IN ISSUS.
GLARE

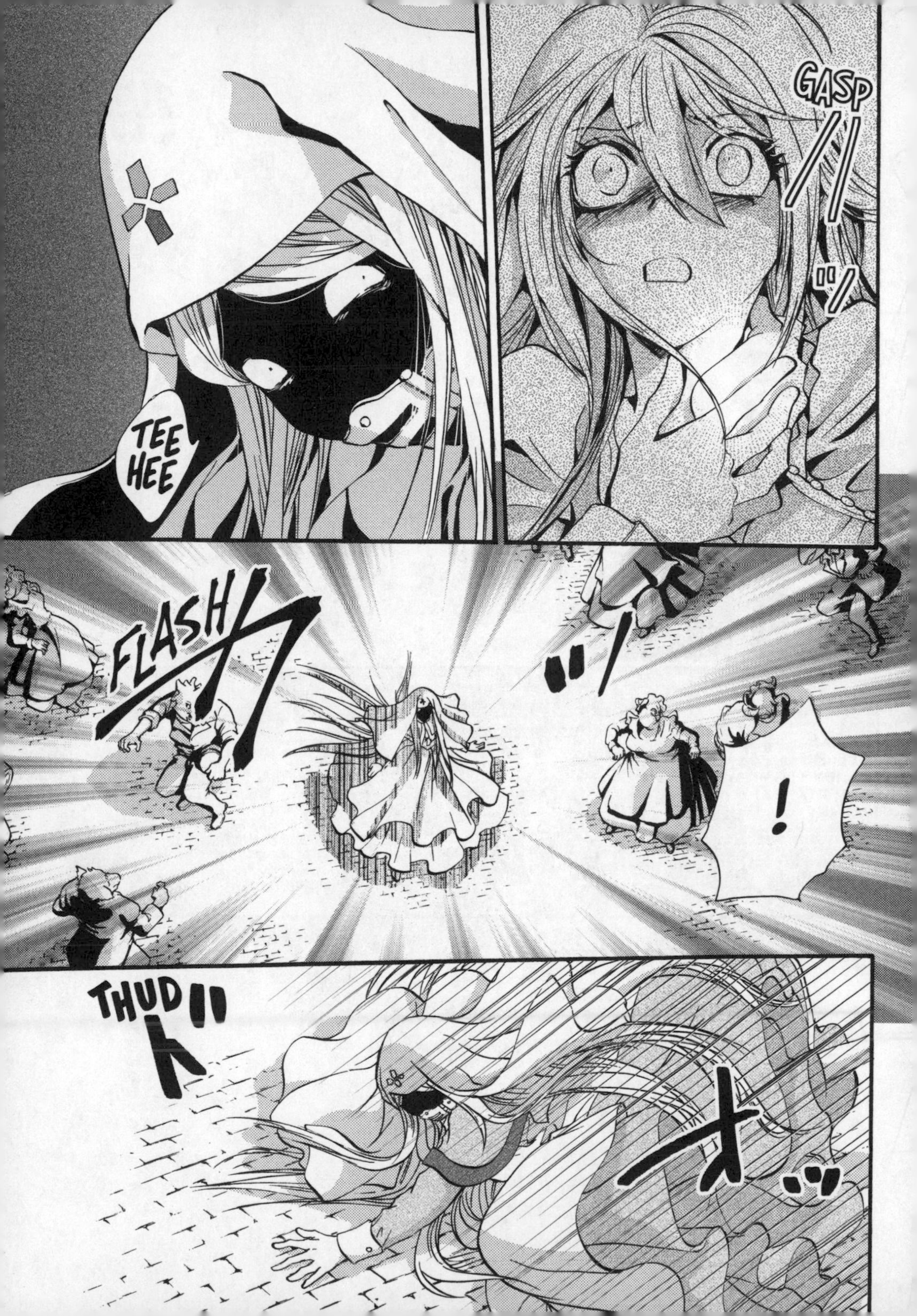
GASP
TEE HEE
!
FLASH
THUD

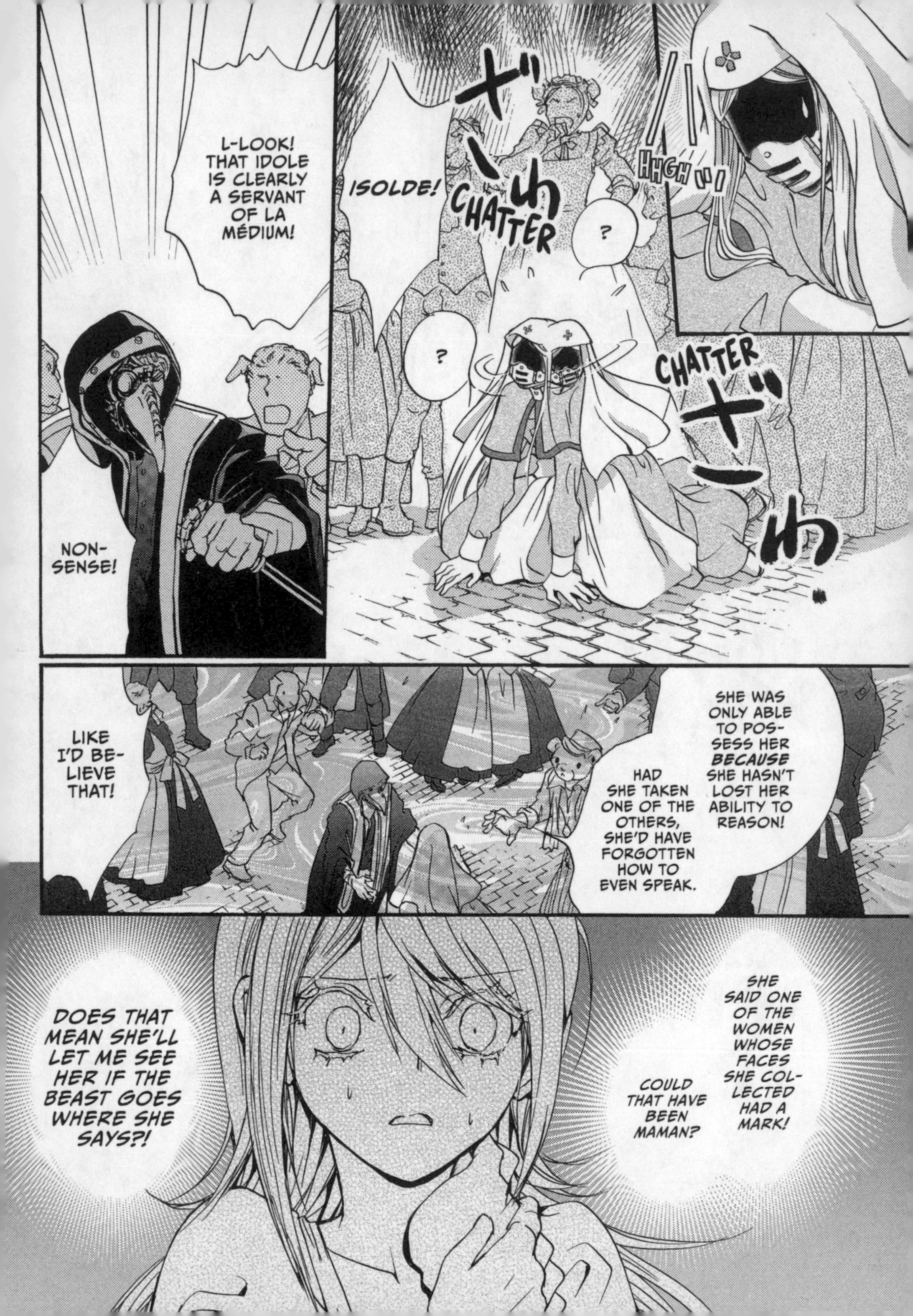
HHGH
ISOLDE!
CHATTER
?
?
CHATTER
L-LOOK! THAT IDOLE IS CLEARLY A SERVANT OF LA MÉDIUM!
NON-SENSE!
SHE WAS ONLY ABLE TO POS-SESS HER *BECAUSE* SHE HASN'T LOST HER ABILITY TO REASON!
HAD SHE TAKEN ONE OF THE OTHERS, SHE'D HAVE FORGOTTEN HOW TO EVEN SPEAK.
LIKE I'D BE-LIEVE THAT!
SHE SAID ONE OF THE WOMEN WHOSE FACES SHE COL-LECTED HAD A MARK!
COULD THAT HAVE BEEN MAMAN?
DOES THAT MEAN SHE'LL LET ME SEE HER IF THE BEAST GOES WHERE SHE SAYS?!

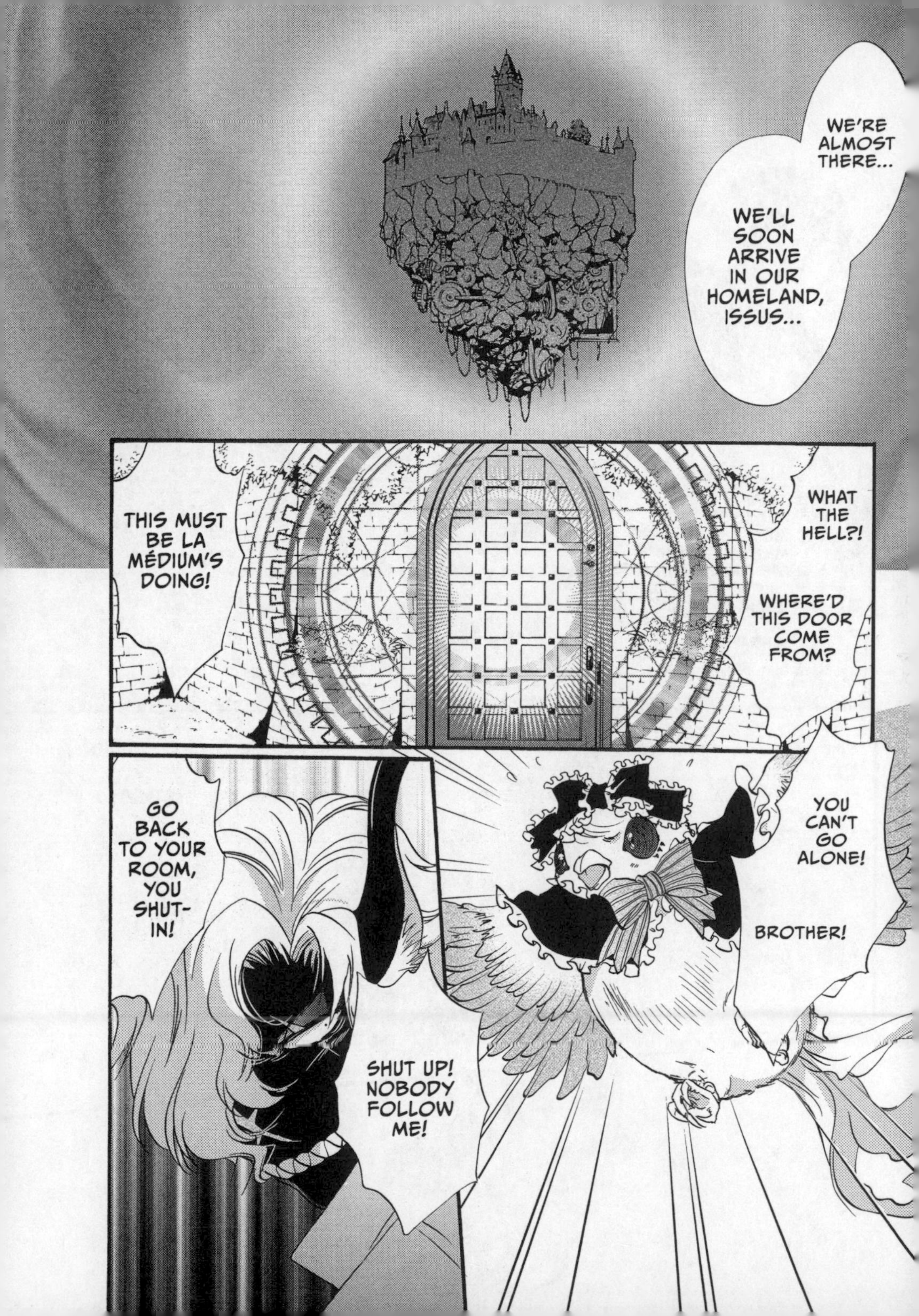
WE'RE ALMOST THERE...
WE'LL SOON ARRIVE IN OUR HOMELAND, ISSUS...
WHAT THE HELL?!
WHERE'D THIS DOOR COME FROM?
THIS MUST BE LA MÉDIUM'S DOING!
YOU CAN'T GO ALONE!
BROTHER!
GO BACK TO YOUR ROOM, YOU SHUT-IN!
SHUT UP! NOBODY FOLLOW ME!

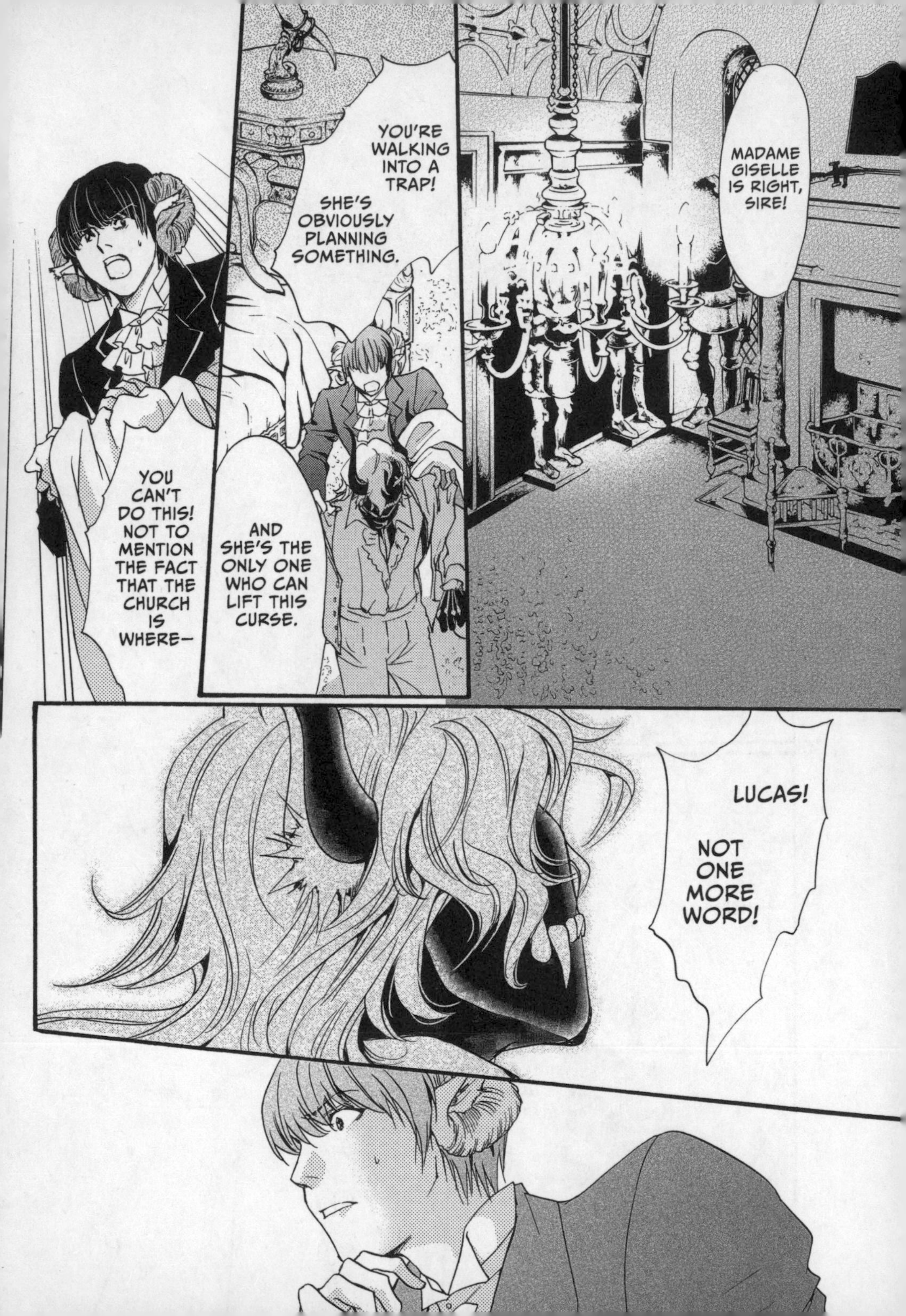
MADAME GISELLE IS RIGHT, SIRE!
YOU'RE WALKING INTO A TRAP!
SHE'S OBVIOUSLY PLANNING SOMETHING.
AND SHE'S THE ONLY ONE WHO CAN LIFT THIS CURSE.
YOU CAN'T DO THIS! NOT TO MENTION THE FACT THAT THE CHURCH IS WHERE—
LUCAS!
NOT ONE MORE WORD!

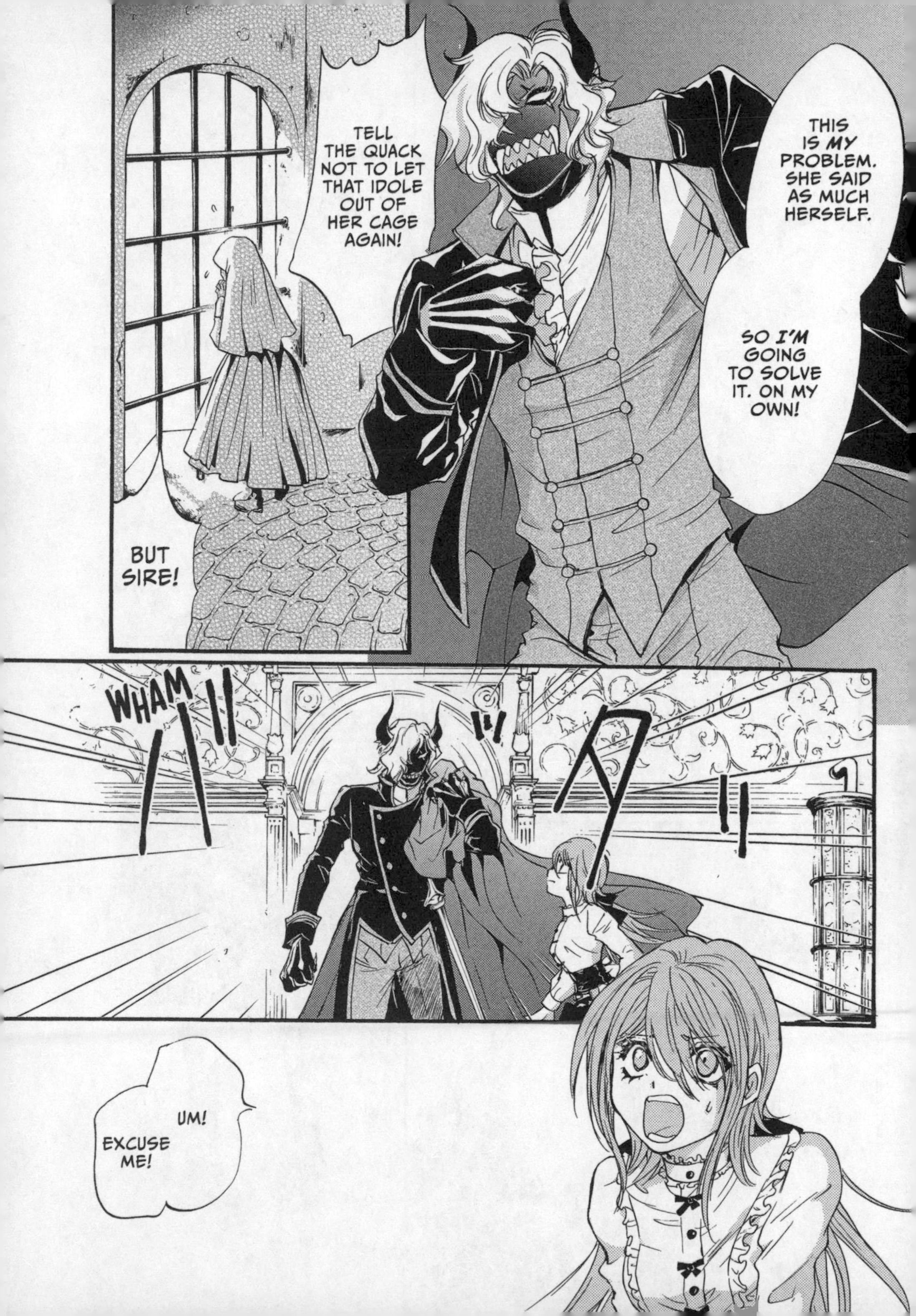
THIS IS MY PROBLEM. SHE SAID AS MUCH HERSELF.
SO I'M GOING TO SOLVE IT. ON MY OWN!
TELL THE QUACK NOT TO LET THAT IDOLE OUT OF HER CAGE AGAIN!
BUT SIRE!
WHAM
UM! EXCUSE ME!

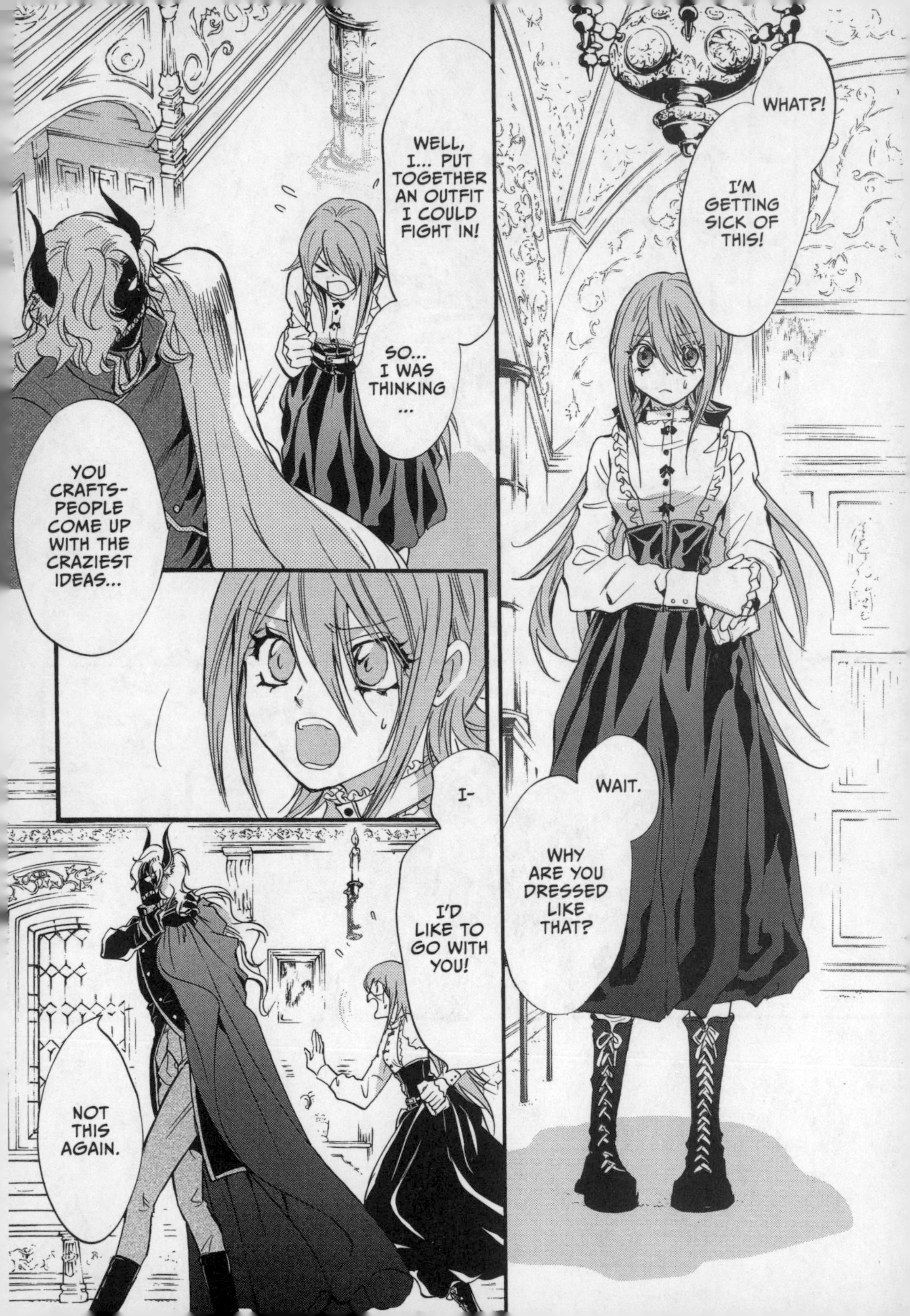
WHAT?!
I'M GETTING SICK OF THIS!
WAIT.
WHY ARE YOU DRESSED LIKE THAT?
WELL, I... PUT TOGETHER AN OUTFIT I COULD FIGHT IN!
SO... I WAS THINKING ...
YOU CRAFTS-PEOPLE COME UP WITH THE CRAZIEST IDEAS...
I-
I'D LIKE TO GO WITH YOU!
NOT THIS AGAIN.

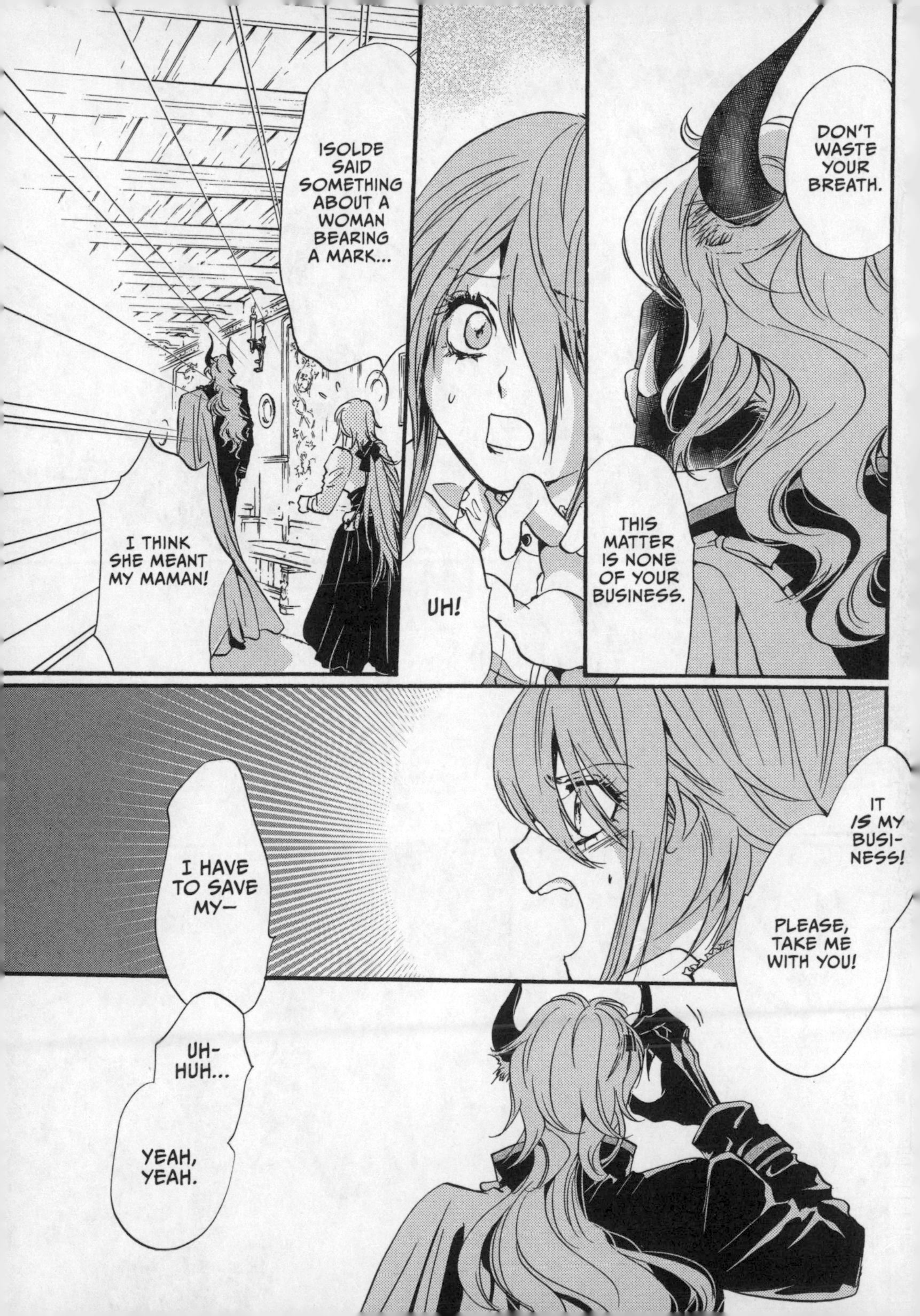
DON'T WASTE YOUR BREATH.
THIS MATTER IS NONE OF YOUR BUSINESS.
UH!
ISOLDE SAID SOMETHING ABOUT A WOMAN BEARING A MARK...
I THINK SHE MEANT MY MAMAN!
IT *IS* MY BUSINESS!
PLEASE, TAKE ME WITH YOU!
I HAVE TO SAVE MY—
UH-HUH...
YEAH, YEAH.

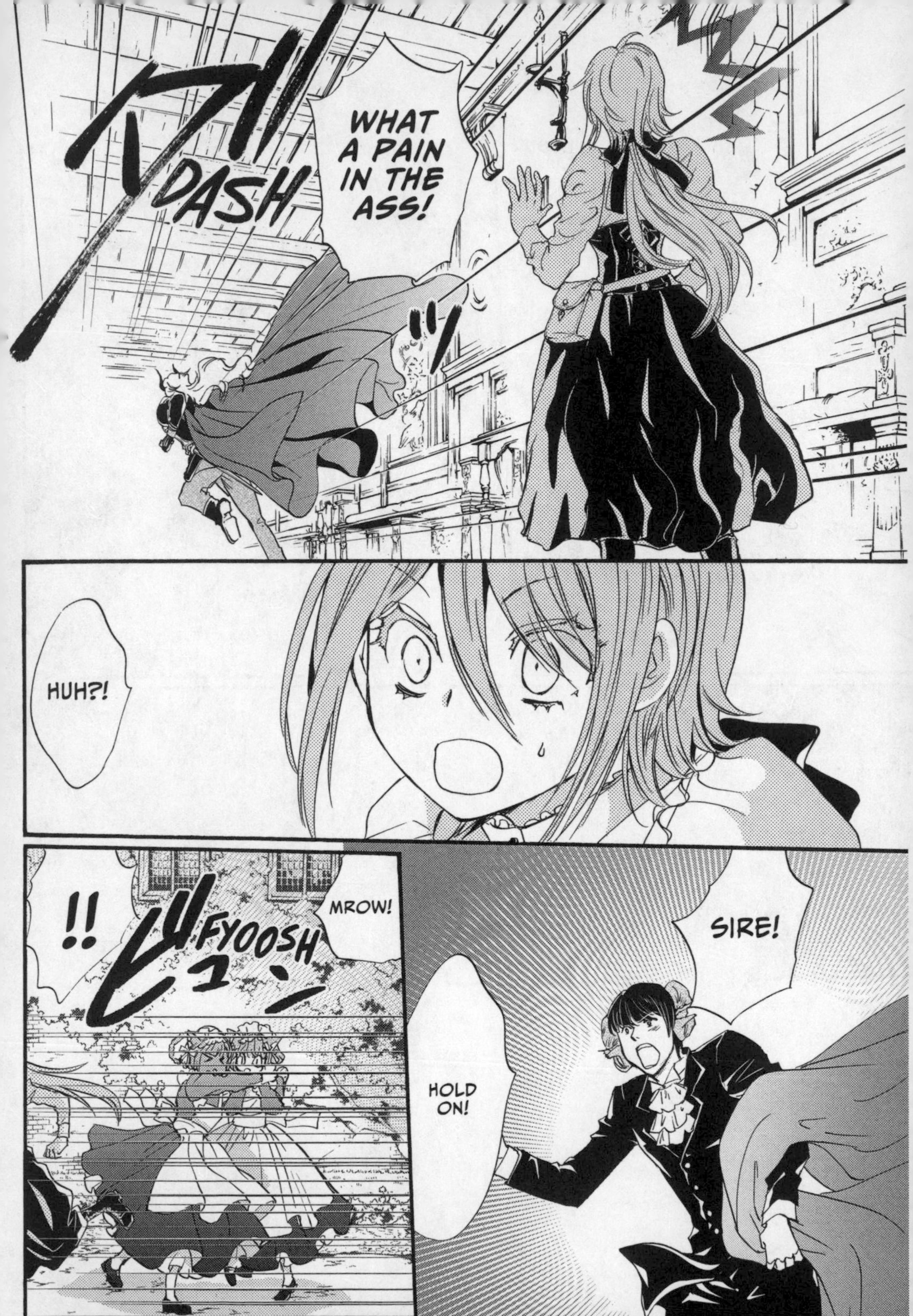
WHAT A PAIN IN THE ASS!
DASH
!!
HUH?!
SIRE!
HOLD ON!
MROW!
FYOOSH
!!

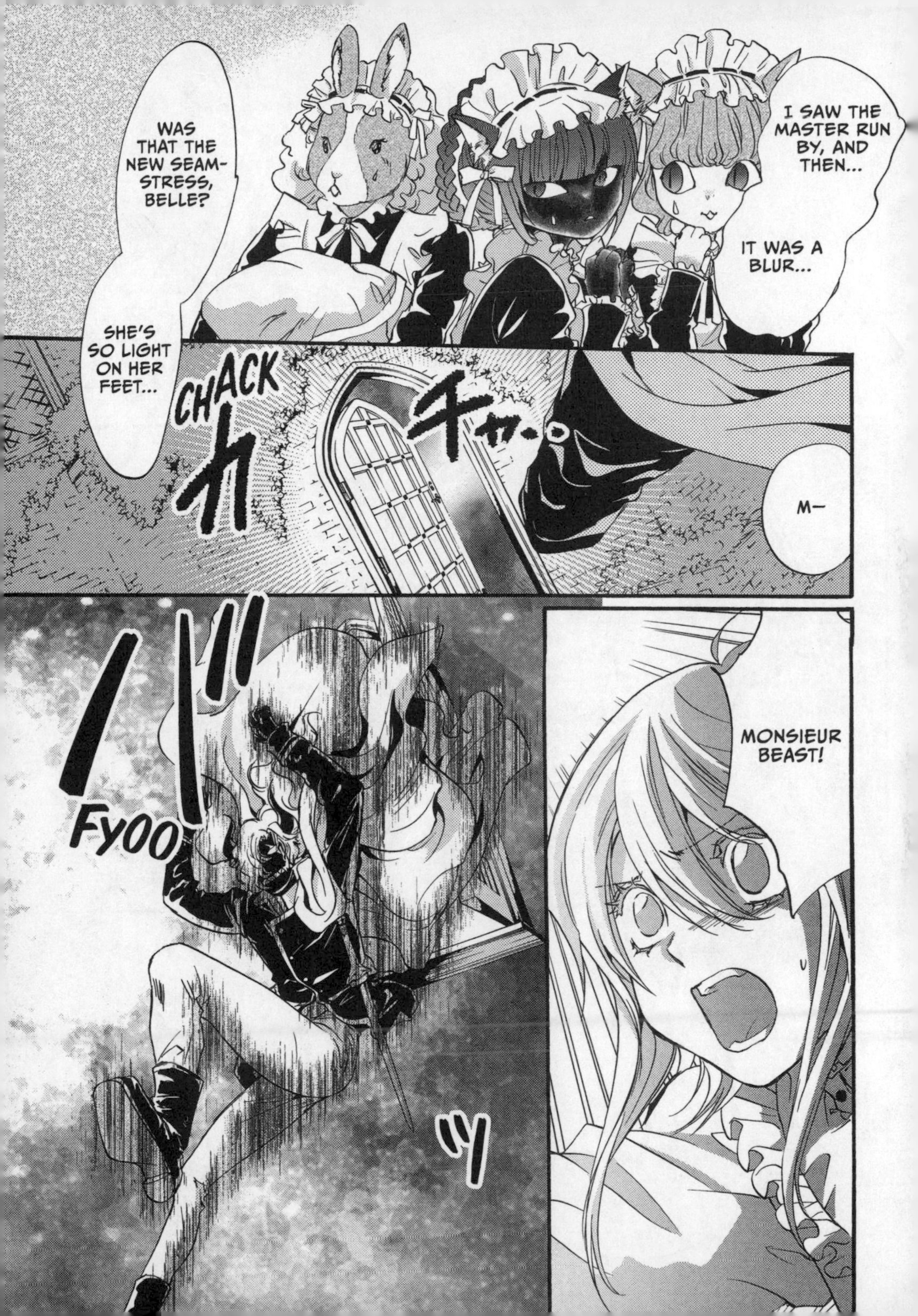
I SAW THE MASTER RUN BY, AND THEN...
IT WAS A BLUR...
WAS THAT THE NEW SEAM-STRESS, BELLE?
SHE'S SO LIGHT ON HER FEET...
M—
チャ
CHACK
カ
MONSIEUR BEAST!
Fyoo

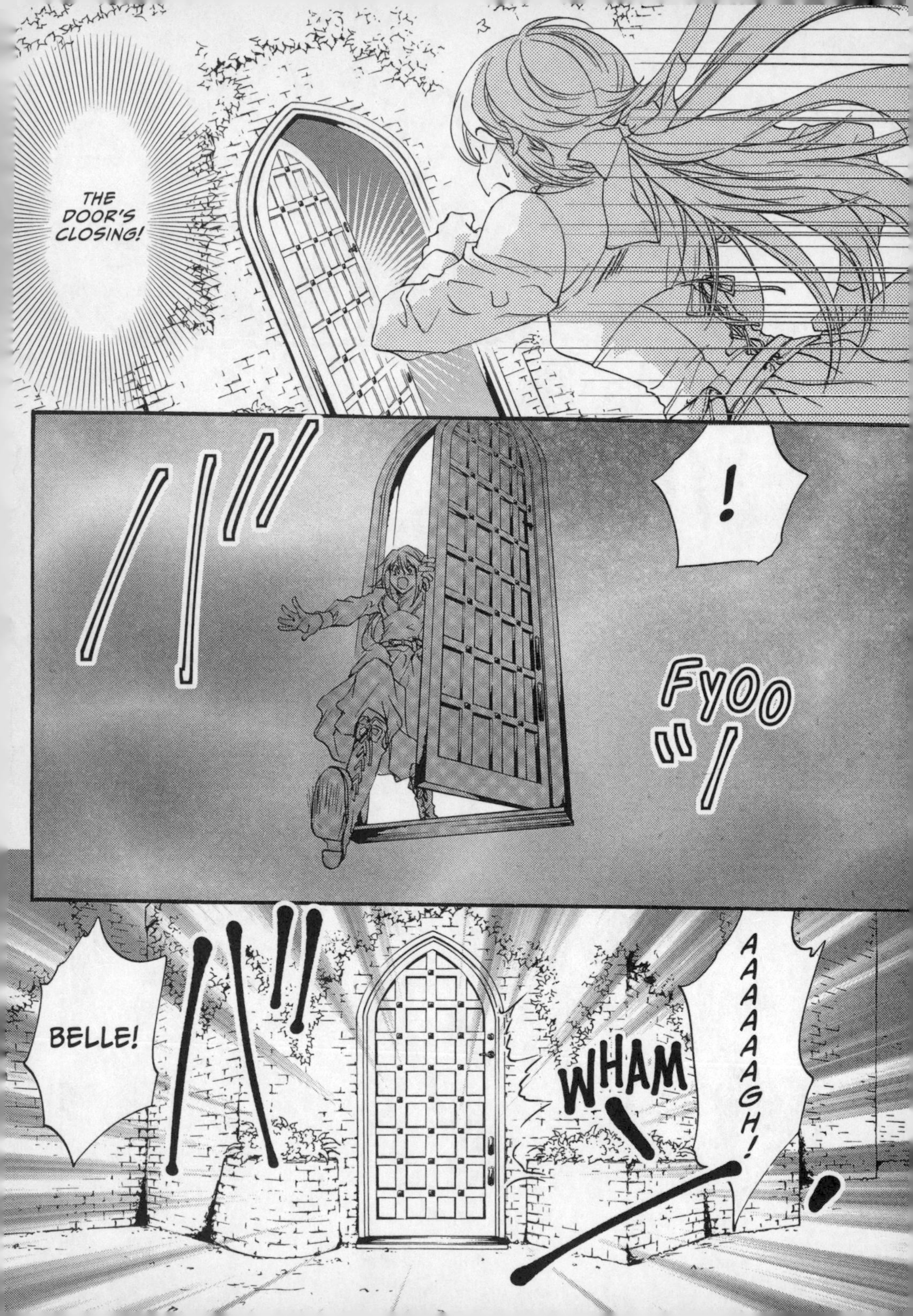
THE DOOR'S CLOSING!
!
FYOO
AAAAAAAGH!
WHAM
BELLE!

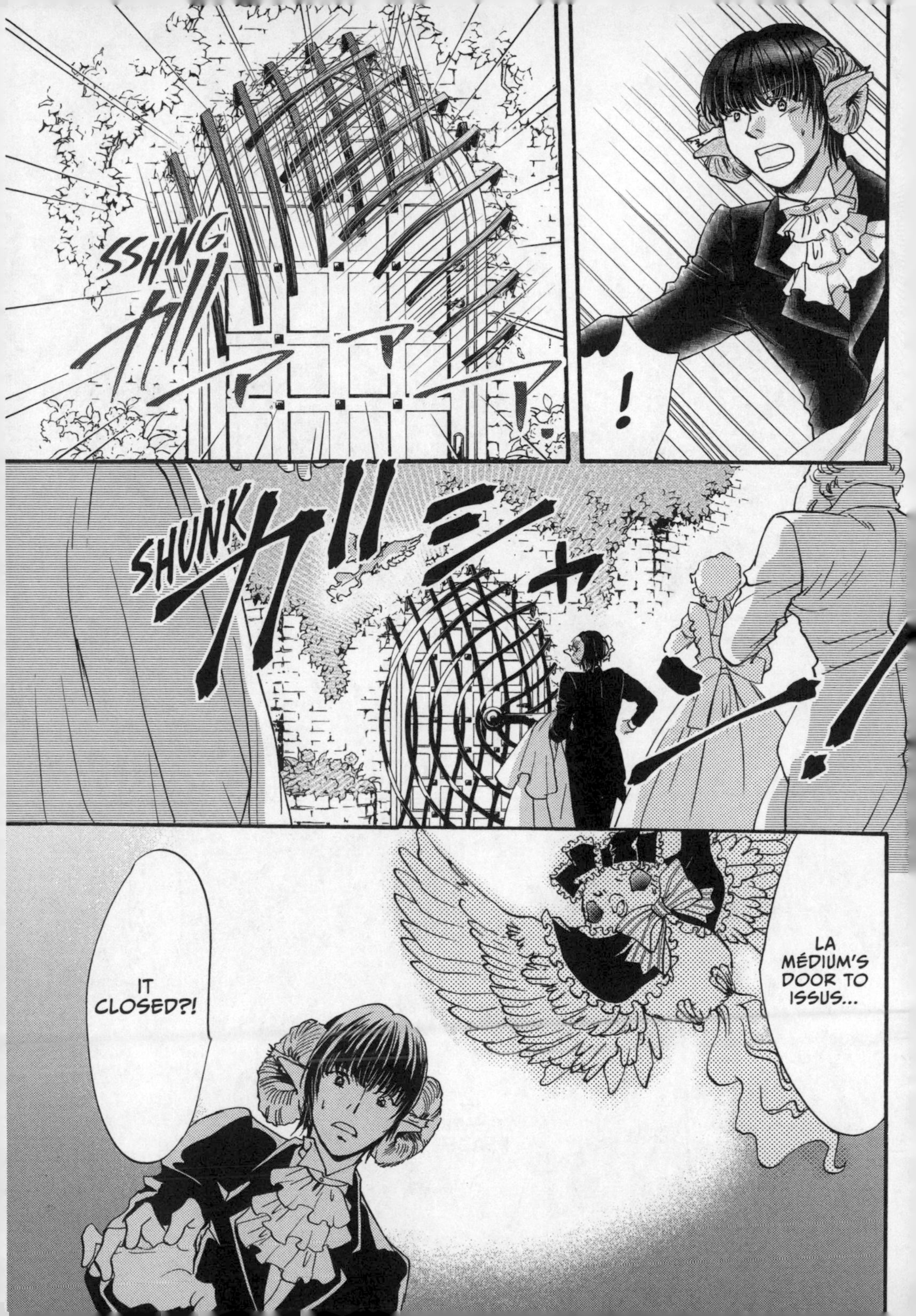
!
SSHNG
SHUNK
LA MÉDIUM'S DOOR TO ISSUS...
IT CLOSED?!

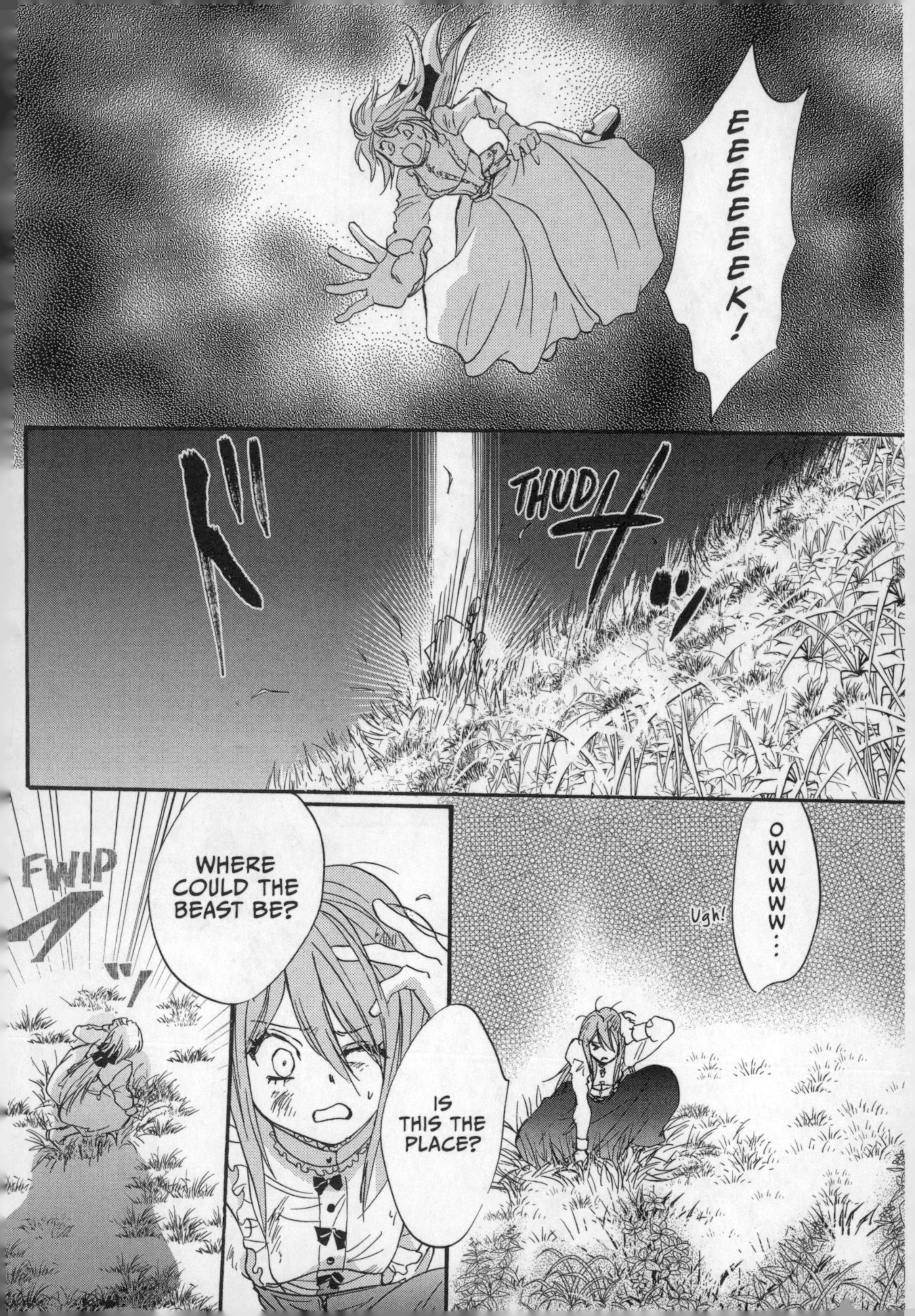
EEEEEEEK!
THUD
OWWWWW...
Ugh!
WHERE COULD THE BEAST BE?
IS THIS THE PLACE?
FWIP

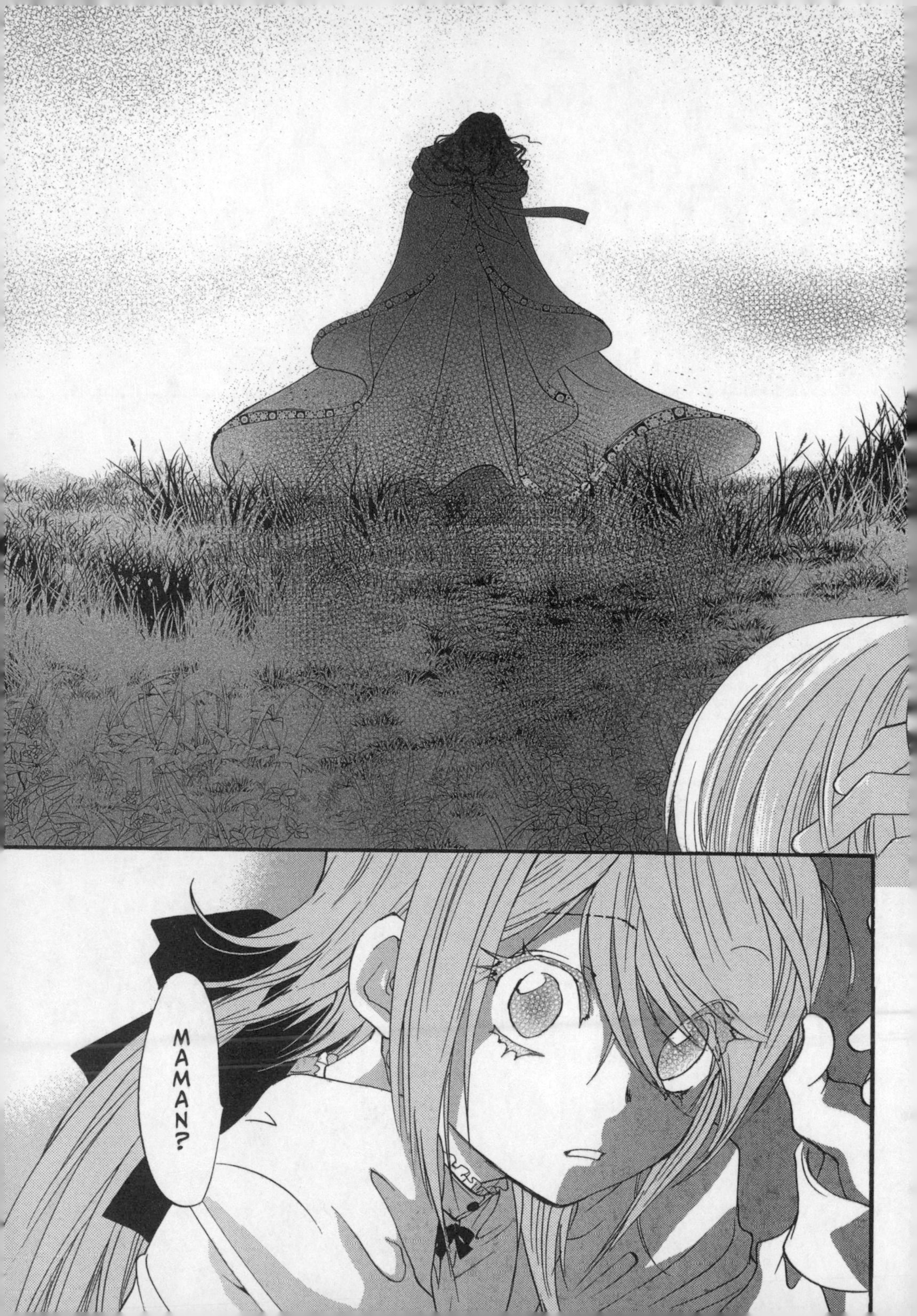
MAMAN?

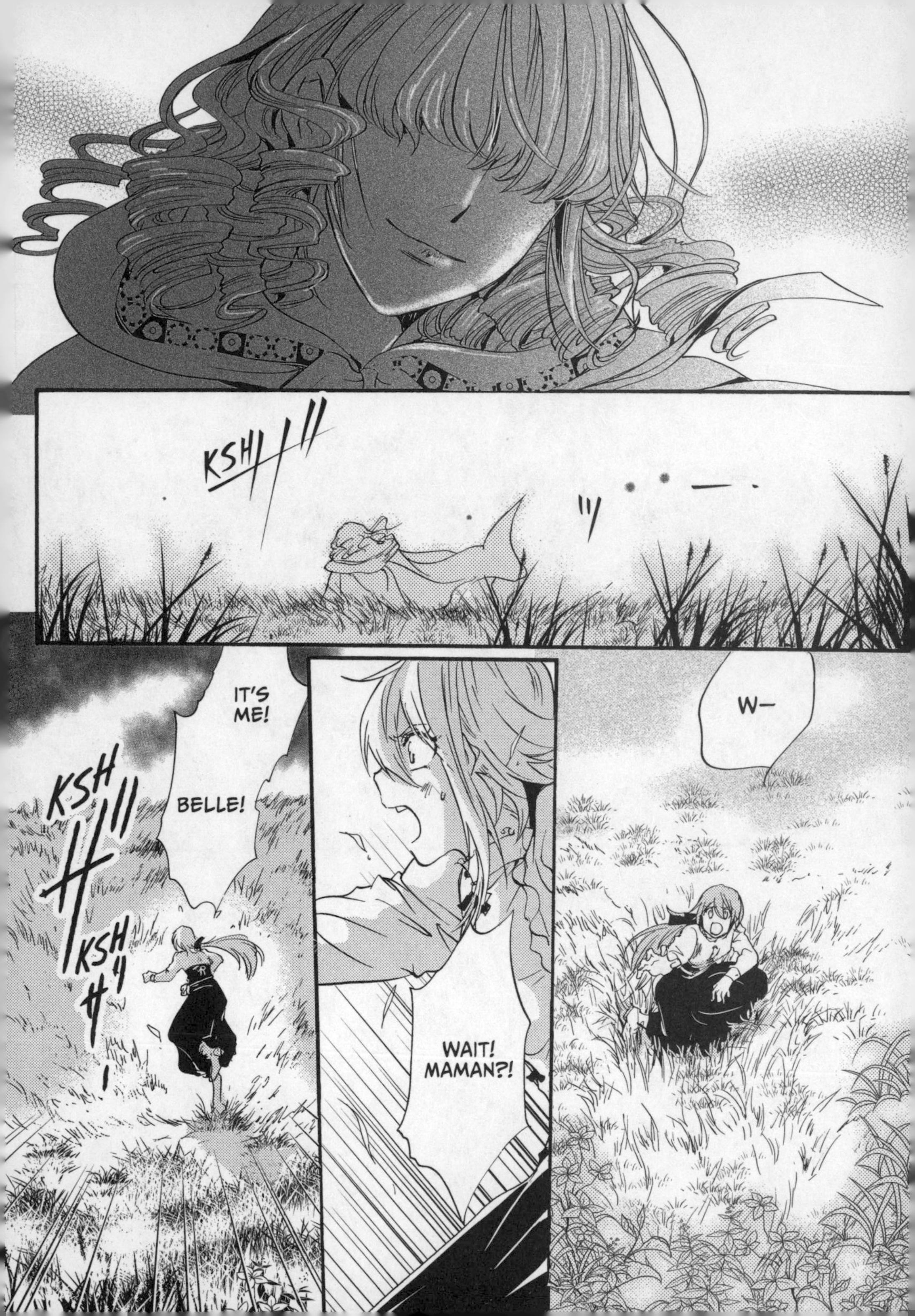
KSH
W–
WAIT! MAMAN?!
IT'S ME!
BELLE!
KSH
KSH

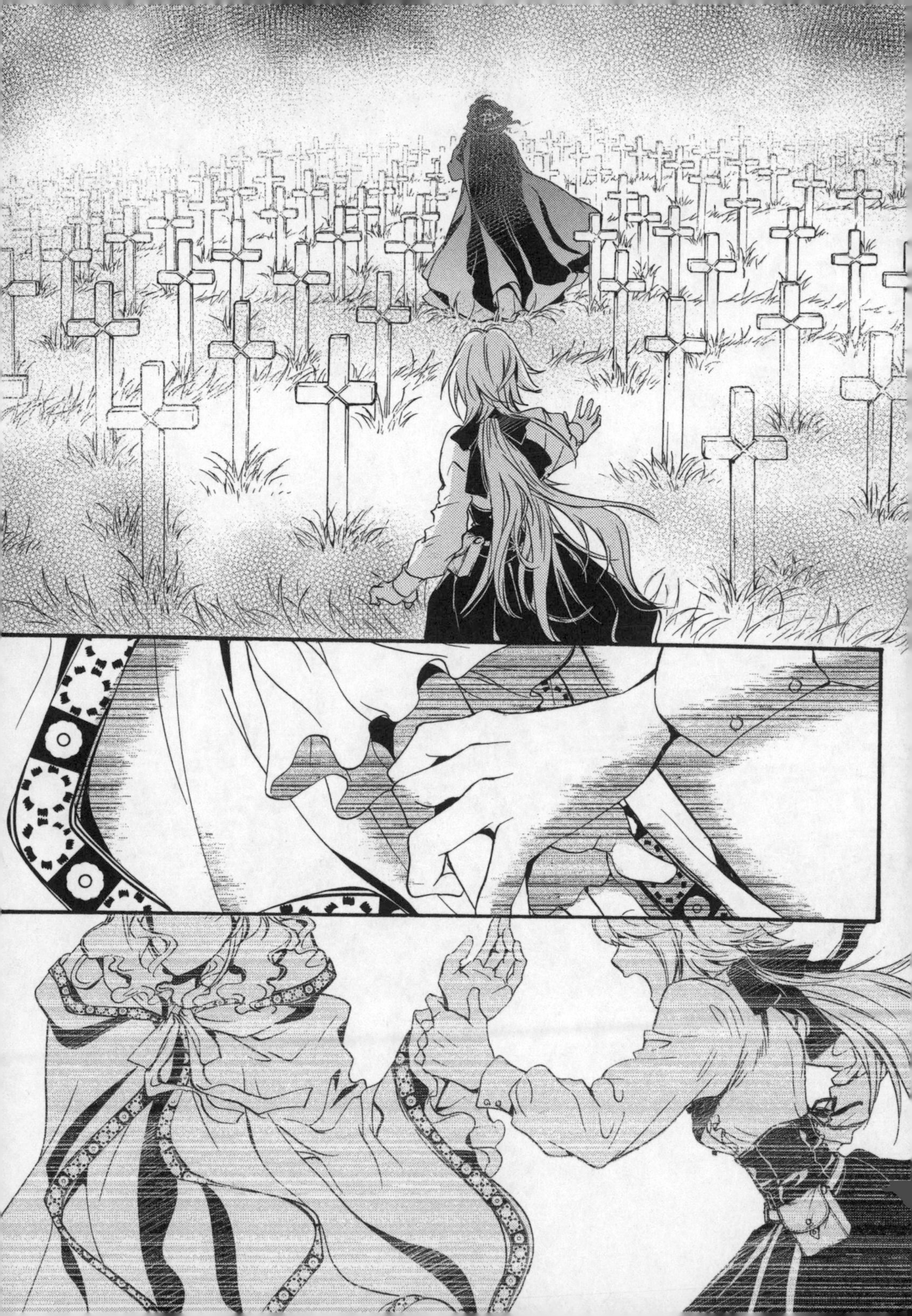

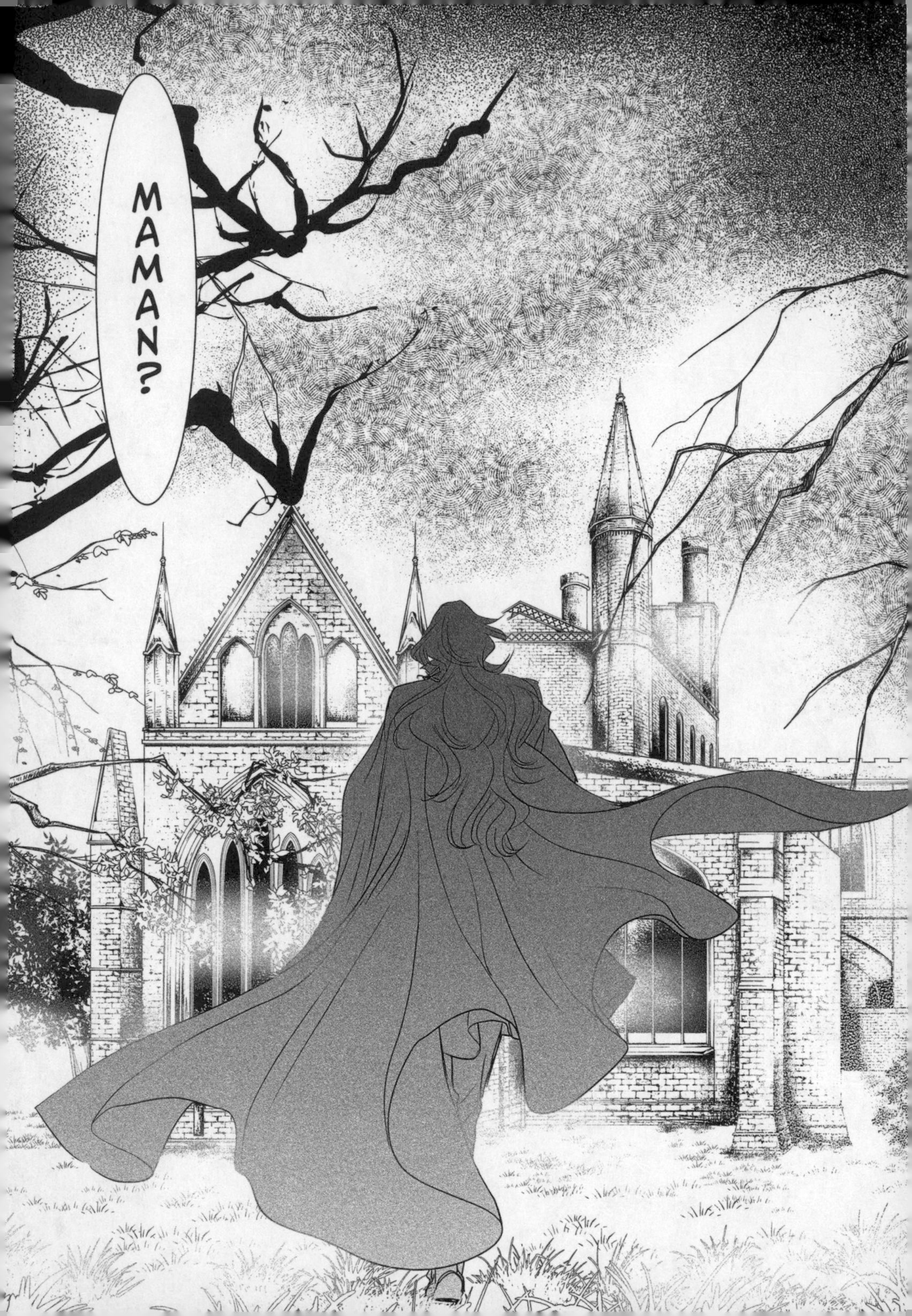
MAMAN?

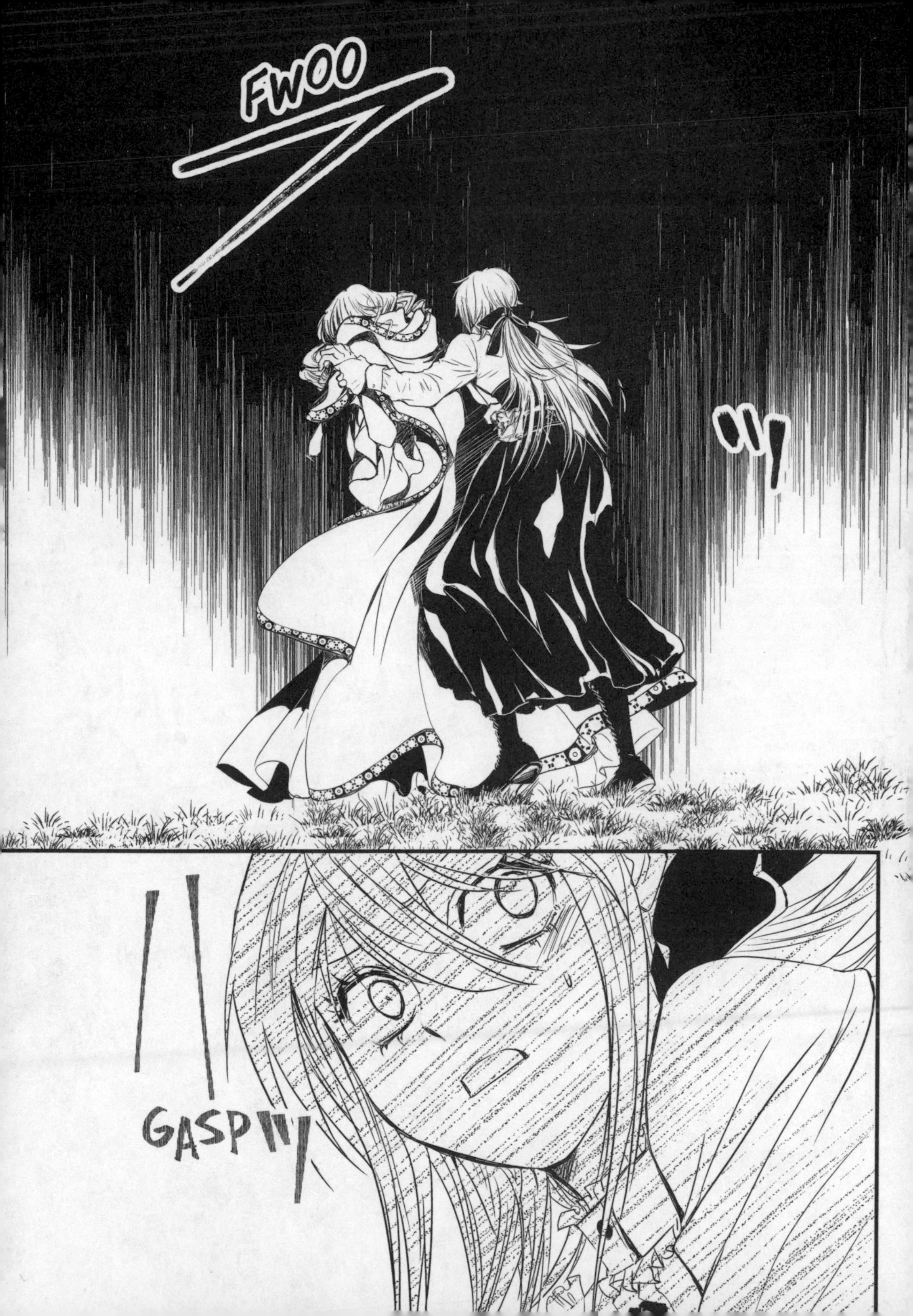
FWOO
GASP!!!

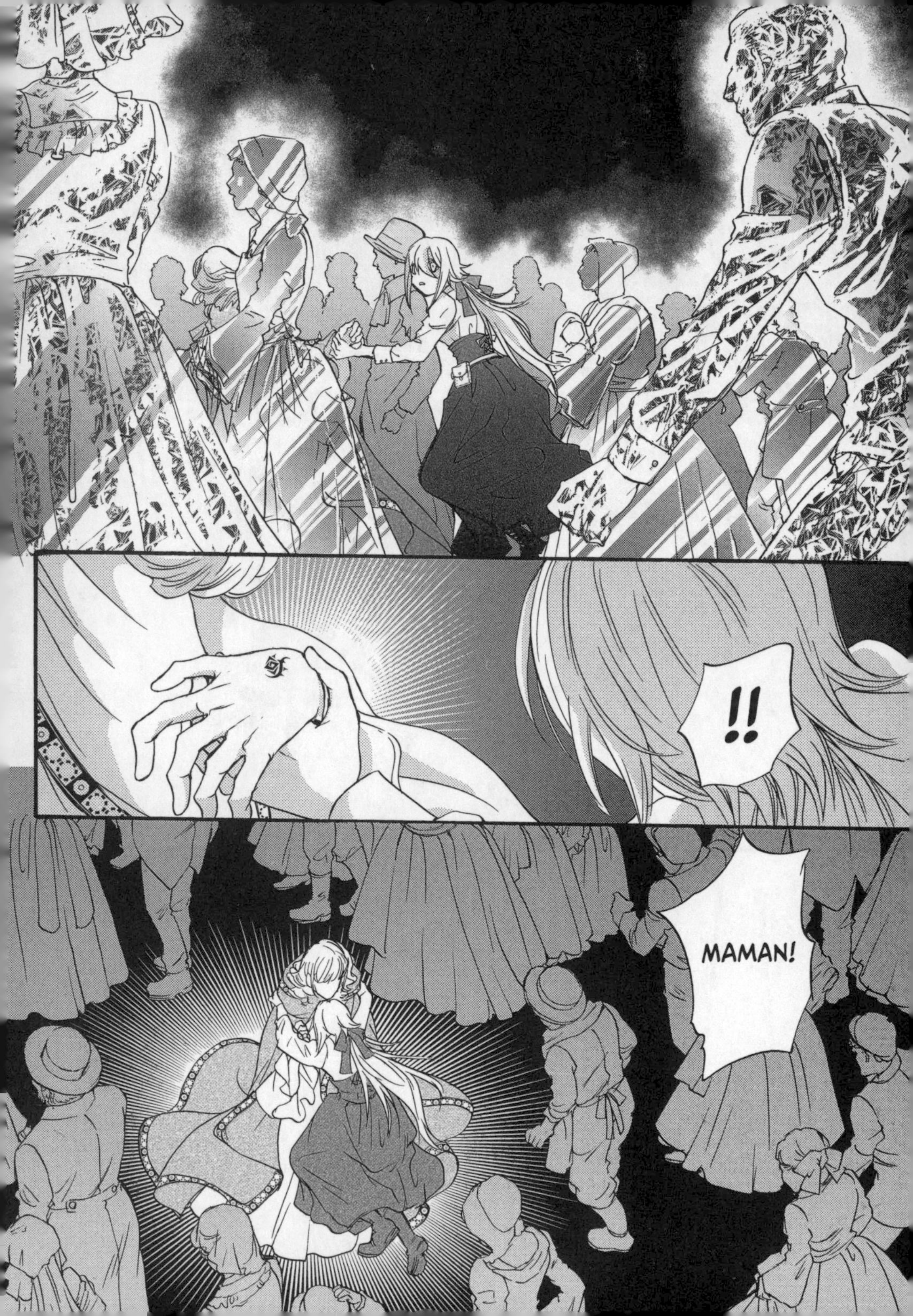
!!
MAMAN!

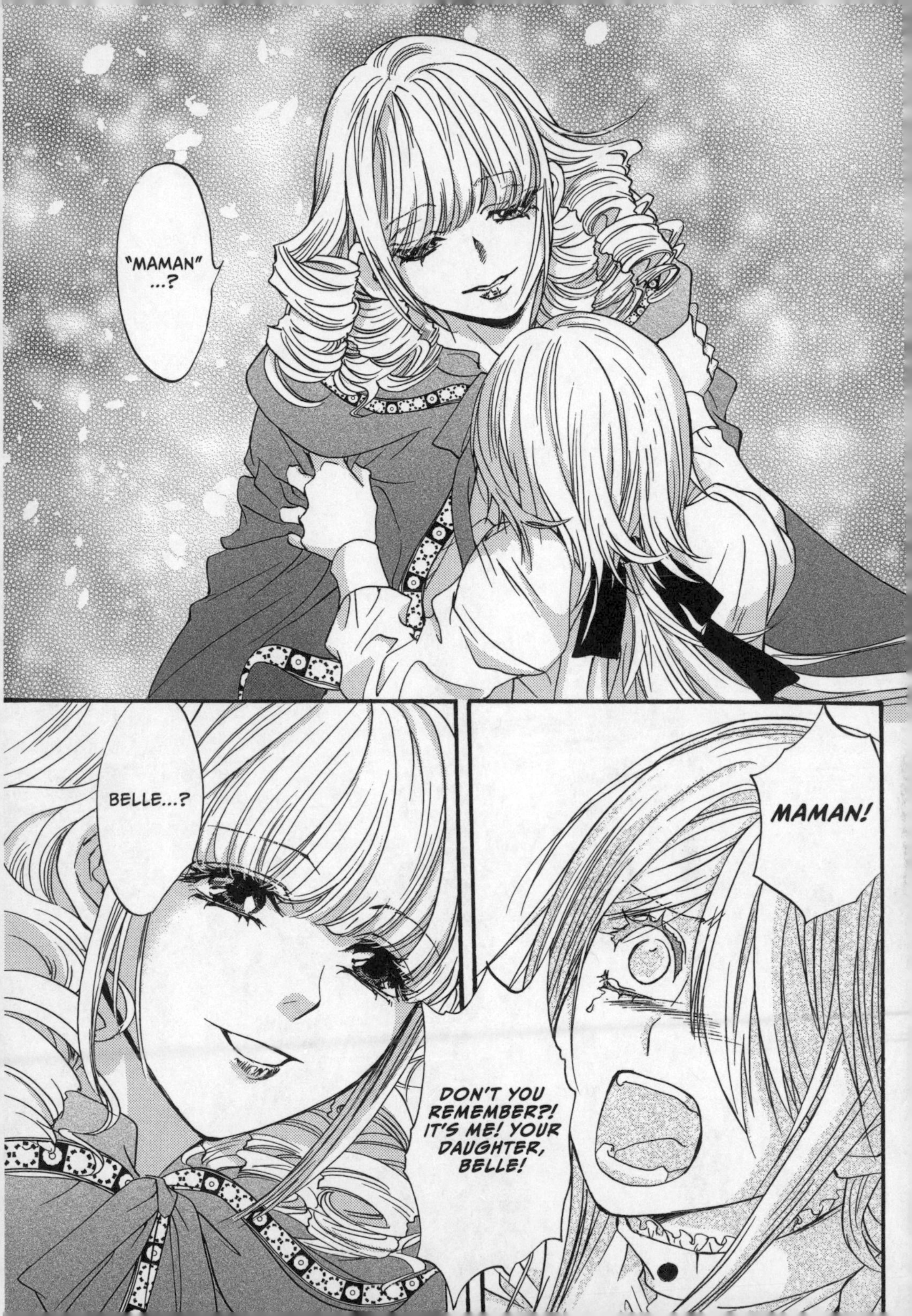
"MAMAN" ...?
MAMAN!
DON'T YOU REMEMBER?! IT'S ME! YOUR DAUGHTER, BELLE!
BELLE...?

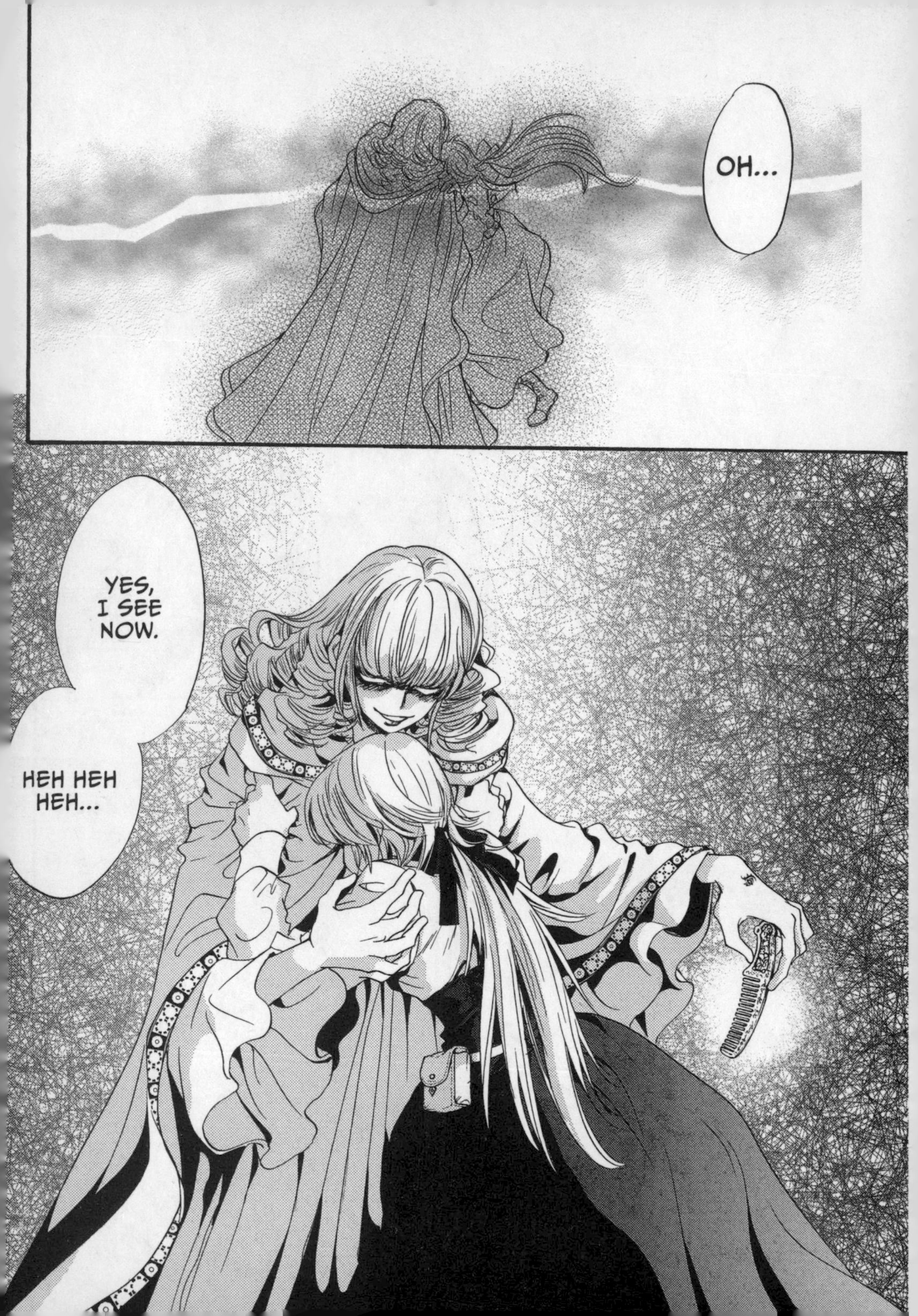
OH...
YES, I SEE NOW.
HEH HEH HEH...

TO BE CONTINUED...

LA BELLE ET LA BÊTE

DU PARADIS PERDU

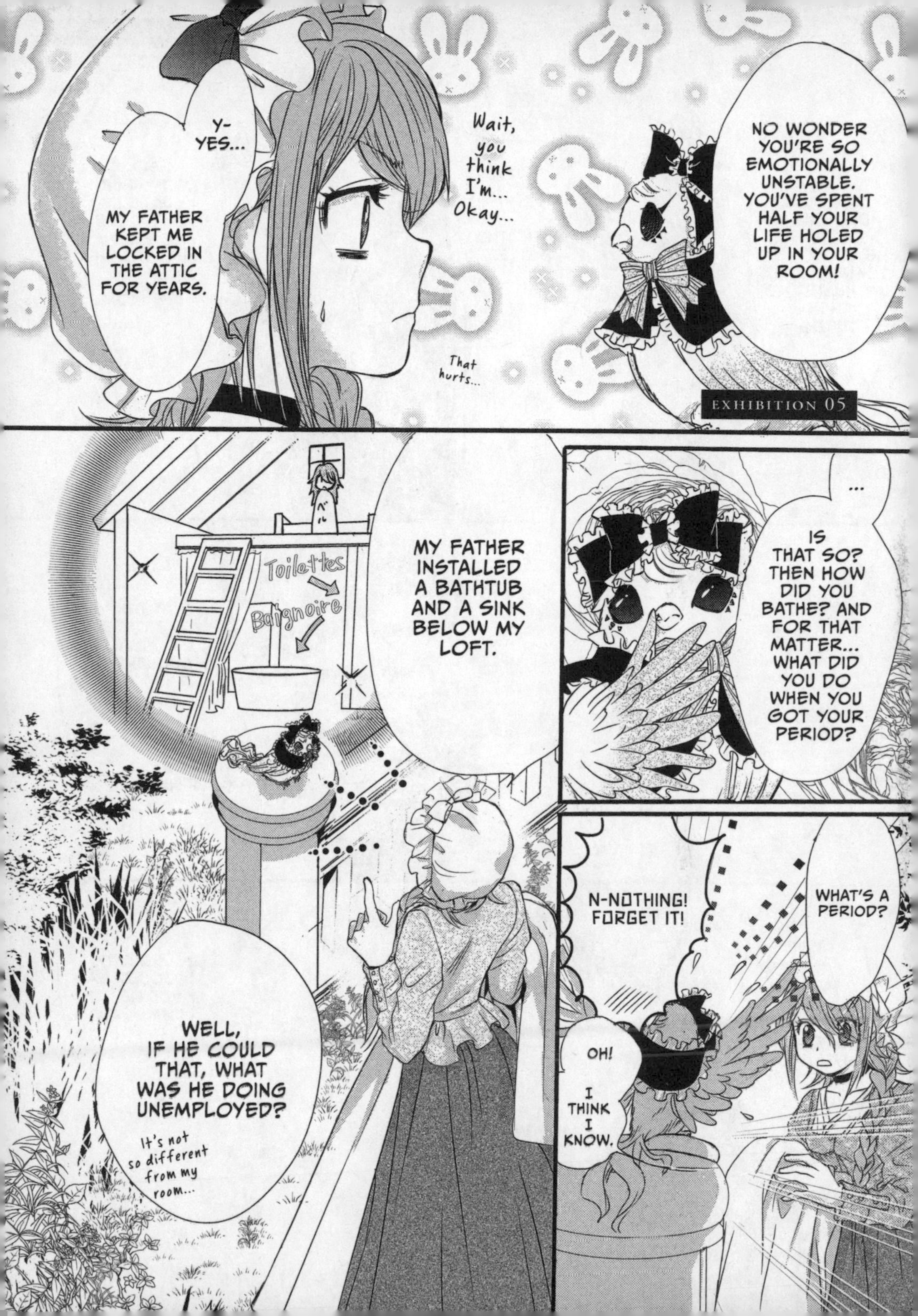

EXHIBITION 05
NO WONDER YOU'RE SO EMOTIONALLY UNSTABLE. YOU'VE SPENT HALF YOUR LIFE HOLED UP IN YOUR ROOM!
Wait, you think I'm... Okay...
Y-YES...
MY FATHER KEPT ME LOCKED IN THE ATTIC FOR YEARS.
That hurts...
...
IS THAT SO? THEN HOW DID YOU BATHE? AND FOR THAT MATTER... WHAT DID YOU DO WHEN YOU GOT YOUR PERIOD?
WHAT'S A PERIOD?
N-NOTHING! FORGET IT!
OH!
I THINK I KNOW.
MY FATHER INSTALLED A BATHTUB AND A SINK BELOW MY LOFT.
Toilettes
Baignoire
WELL, IF HE COULD THAT, WHAT WAS HE DOING UNEMPLOYED?
It's not so different from my room...

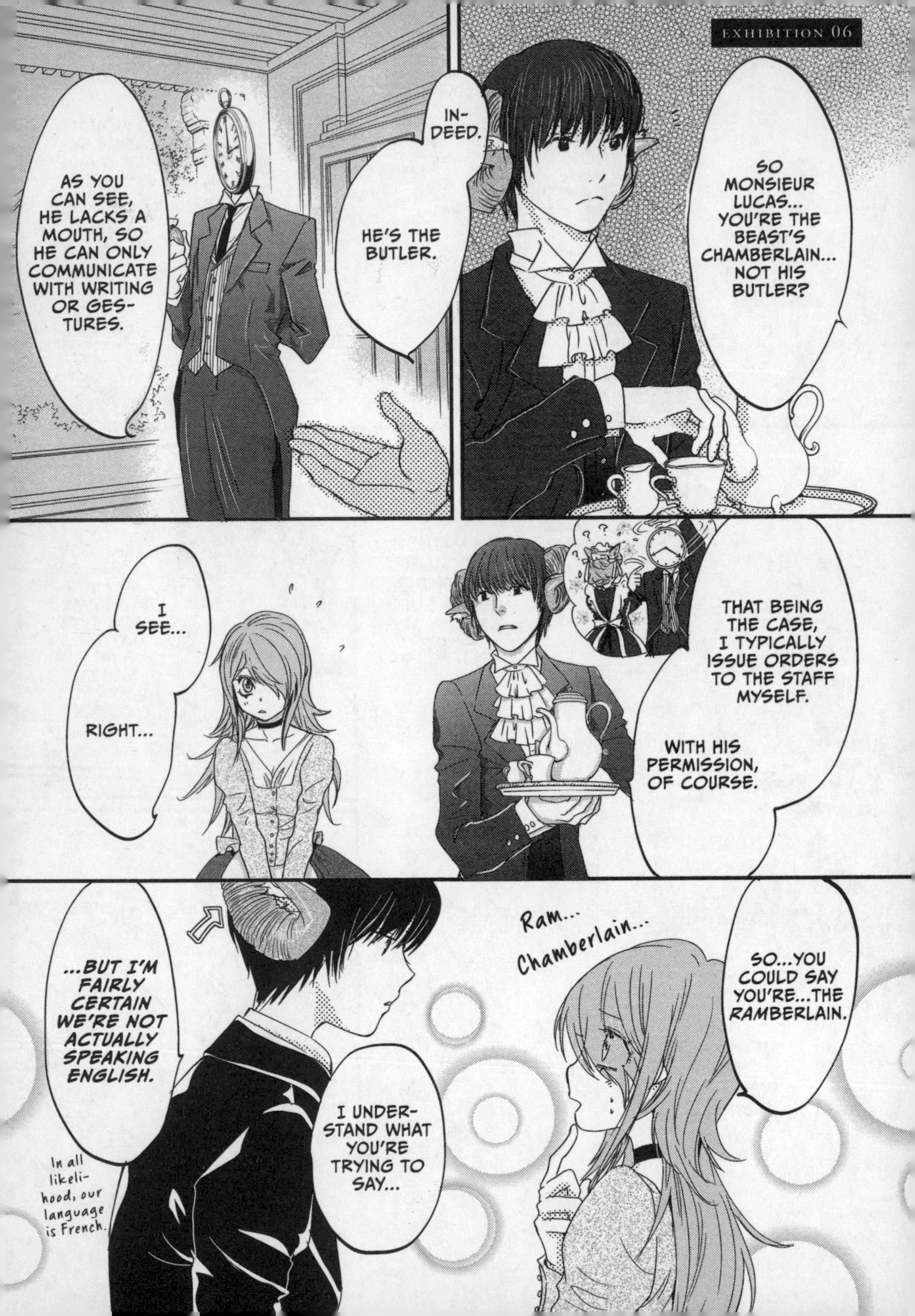
SO MONSIEUR LUCAS... YOU'RE THE BEAST'S CHAMBERLAIN... NOT HIS BUTLER?
IN-DEED.
HE'S THE BUTLER.
AS YOU CAN SEE, HE LACKS A MOUTH, SO HE CAN ONLY COMMUNICATE WITH WRITING OR GES-TURES.
THAT BEING THE CASE, I TYPICALLY ISSUE ORDERS TO THE STAFF MYSELF.
WITH HIS PERMISSION, OF COURSE.
I SEE...
RIGHT...
SO...YOU COULD SAY YOU'RE...THE *RAMBERLAIN.*
Ram...
Chamberlain...
I UNDER-STAND WHAT YOU'RE TRYING TO SAY...
...BUT I'M FAIRLY CERTAIN WE'RE NOT ACTUALLY SPEAKING ENGLISH.
In all likeli-hood, our language is French.

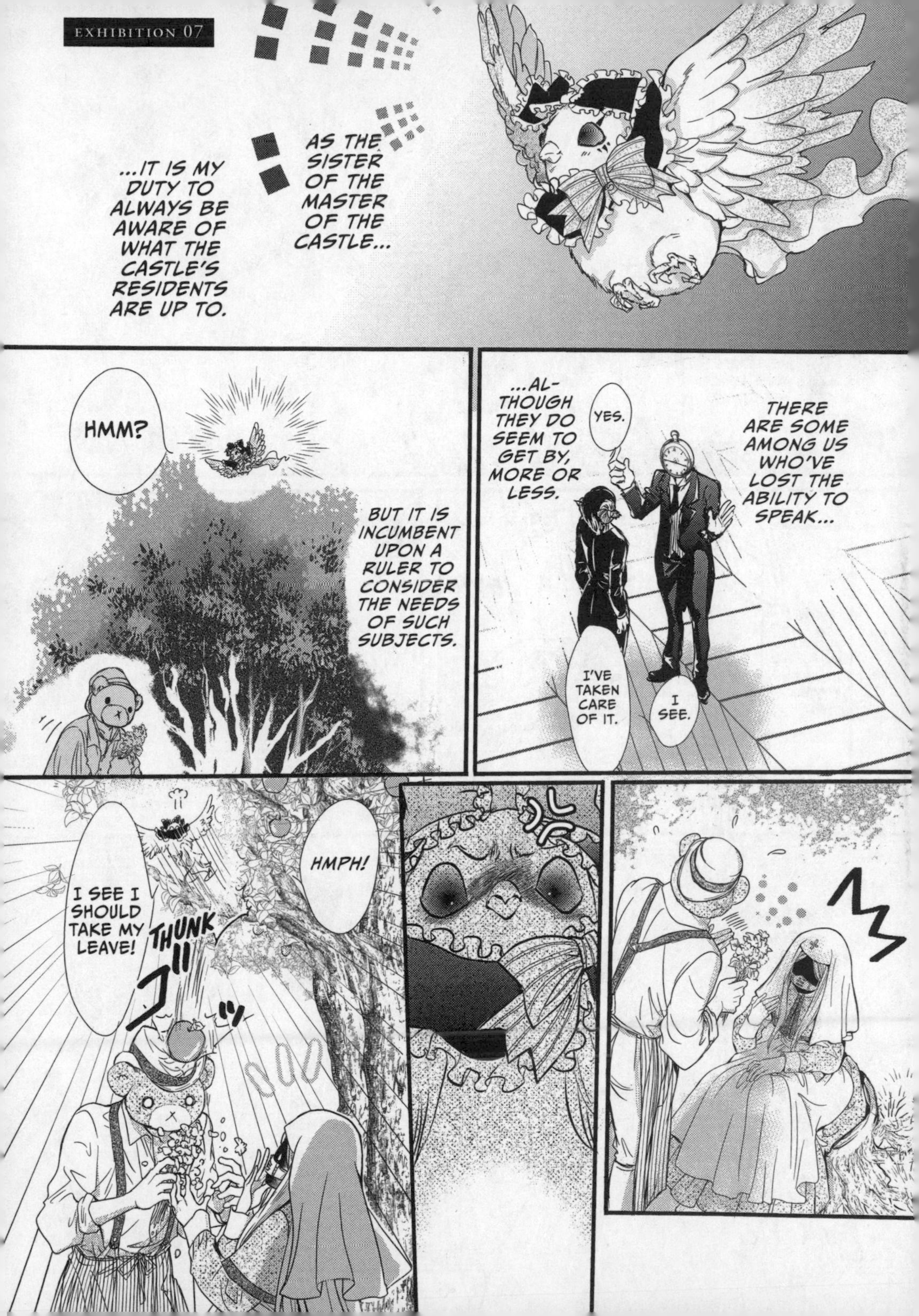
AS THE SISTER OF THE MASTER OF THE CASTLE...
...IT IS MY DUTY TO ALWAYS BE AWARE OF WHAT THE CASTLE'S RESIDENTS ARE UP TO.
THERE ARE SOME AMONG US WHO'VE LOST THE ABILITY TO SPEAK...
YES.
...AL-THOUGH THEY DO SEEM TO GET BY, MORE OR LESS.
I SEE.
I'VE TAKEN CARE OF IT.
BUT IT IS INCUMBENT UPON A RULER TO CONSIDER THE NEEDS OF SUCH SUBJECTS.
HMM?
HMPH!
I SEE I SHOULD TAKE MY LEAVE!
THUNK

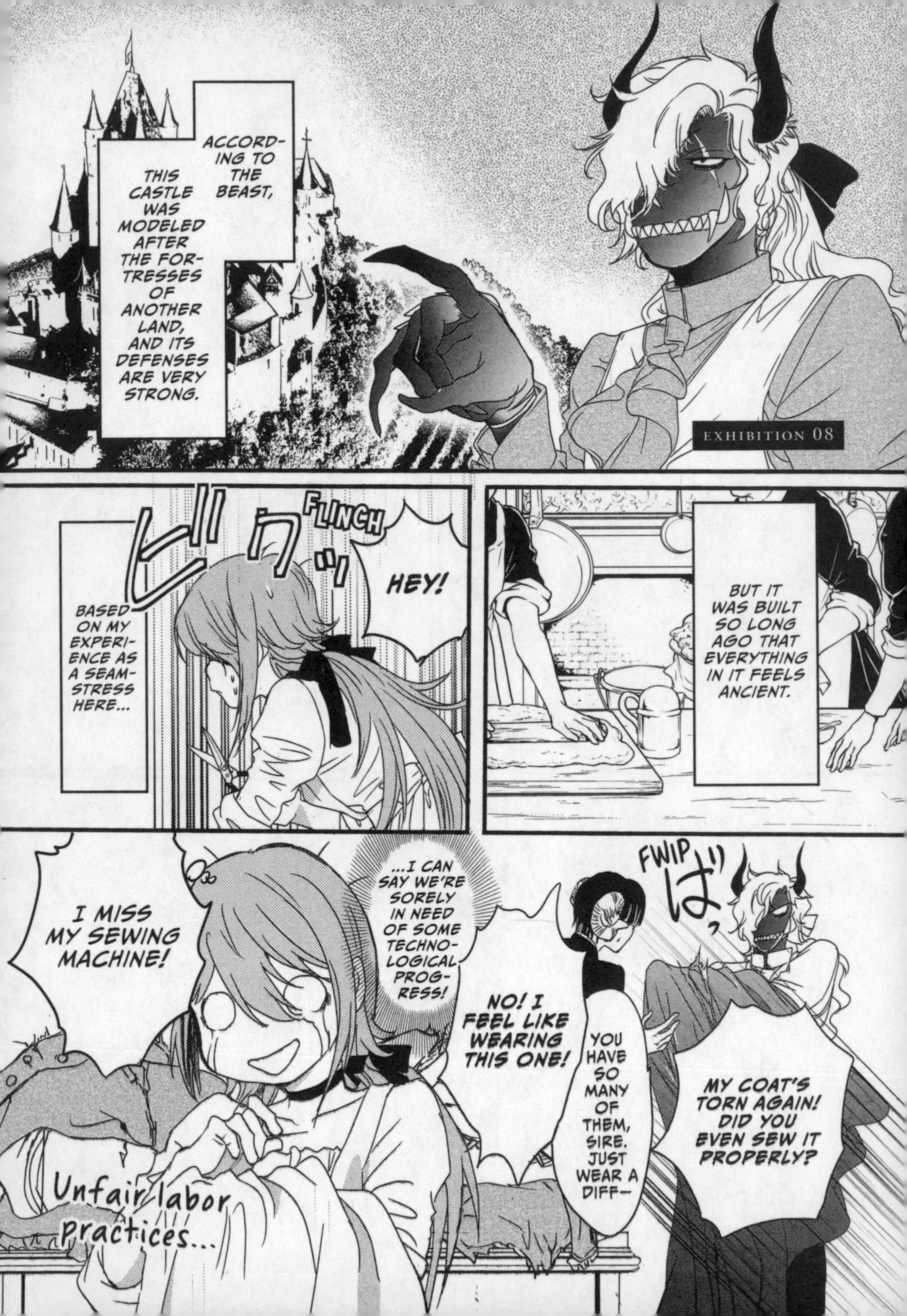
ACCORDING TO THE BEAST,
THIS CASTLE WAS MODELED AFTER THE FORTRESSES OF ANOTHER LAND, AND ITS DEFENSES ARE VERY STRONG.
EXHIBITION 08
BUT IT WAS BUILT SO LONG AGO THAT EVERYTHING IN IT FEELS ANCIENT.
HEY!
FLINCH
BASED ON MY EXPERIENCE AS A SEAMSTRESS HERE...
MY COAT'S TORN AGAIN! DID YOU EVEN SEW IT PROPERLY?
FWIP
YOU HAVE SO MANY OF THEM, SIRE. JUST WEAR A DIFF—
NO! I FEEL LIKE WEARING THIS ONE!
...I CAN SAY WE'RE SORELY IN NEED OF SOME TECHNOLOGICAL PROGRESS!
I MISS MY SEWING MACHINE!
Unfair labor practices...

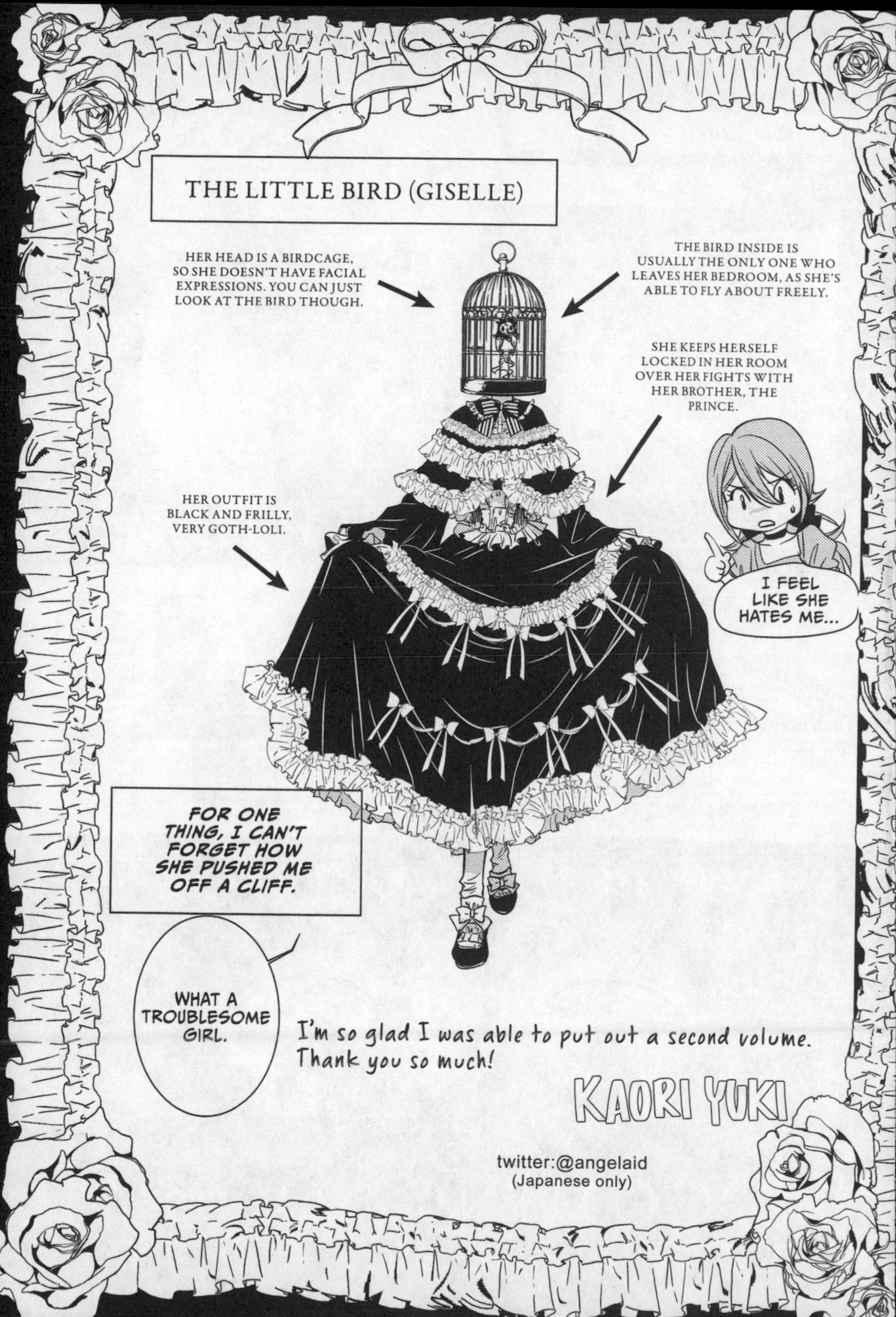
THE LITTLE BIRD (GISELLE)
THE BIRD INSIDE IS USUALLY THE ONLY ONE WHO LEAVES HER BEDROOM, AS SHE'S ABLE TO FLY ABOUT FREELY.
HER HEAD IS A BIRDCAGE, SO SHE DOESN'T HAVE FACIAL EXPRESSIONS. YOU CAN JUST LOOK AT THE BIRD THOUGH.
SHE KEEPS HERSELF LOCKED IN HER ROOM OVER HER FIGHTS WITH HER BROTHER, THE PRINCE.
HER OUTFIT IS BLACK AND FRILLY, VERY GOTH-LOLI.
I FEEL LIKE SHE HATES ME...
FOR ONE THING, I CAN'T FORGET HOW SHE PUSHED ME OFF A CLIFF.
WHAT A TROUBLESOME GIRL.
I'm so glad I was able to put out a second volume. Thank you so much!
KAORI YUKI
twitter:@angelaid
(Japanese only)

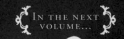

Belle and her mother...
...reunited.
Maman!
I knew you had to be alive!
Oh, this violet color...
It reminds me of times gone by.
But...
...is it truly her?!
The story...
When-ever I saw that smile,
my heart would ache...
Oh, Prince Cyril!
You've returned.
...as if it might burst.
...of Cyril and la Médium's past.
Just what happened between them?!

[redacted]OMING SO[redacted]N!

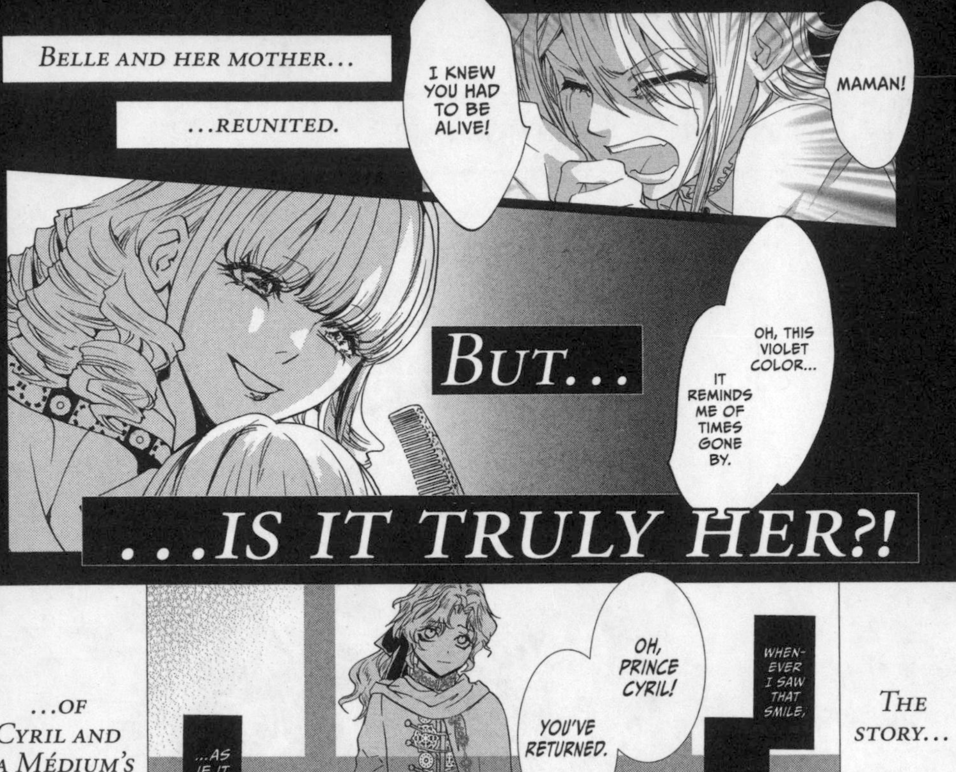

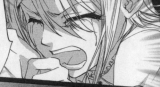

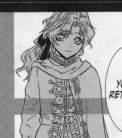

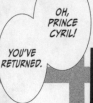

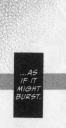

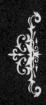

La Médium finally reveals…

Her true power !!!

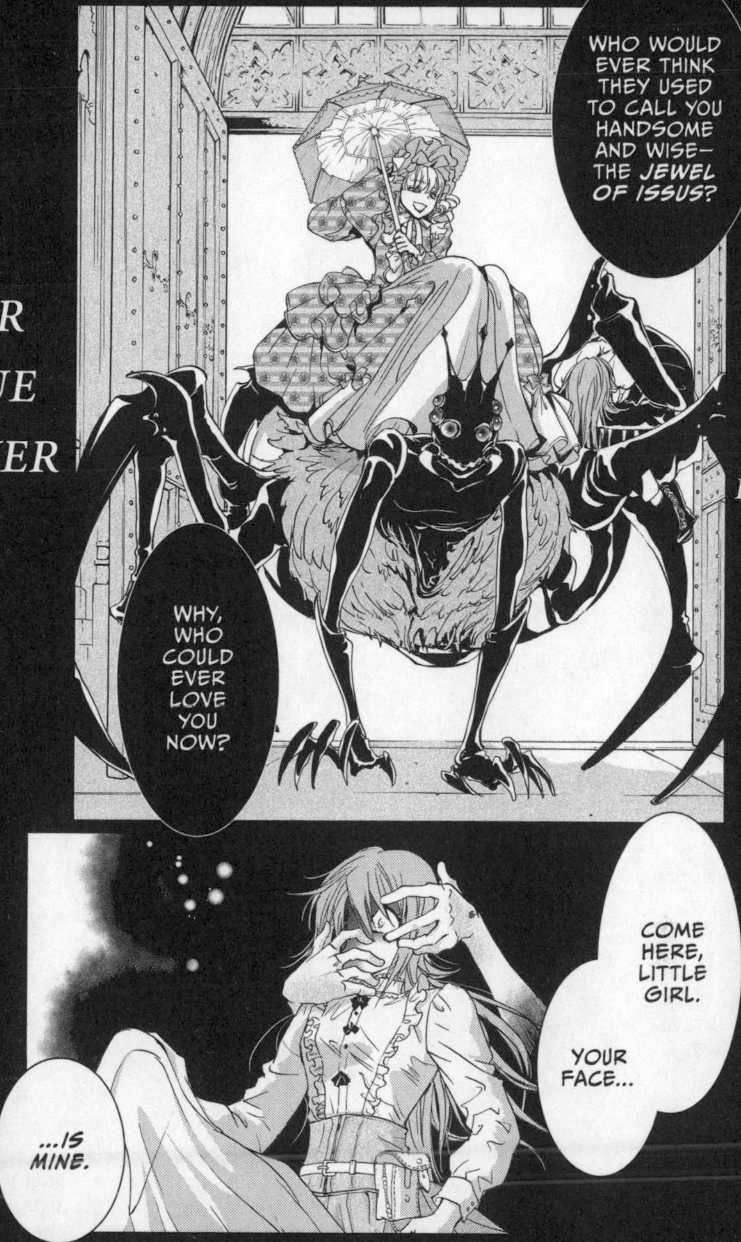
WHO WOULD EVER THINK THEY USED TO CALL YOU HANDSOME AND WISE—THE *JEWEL OF ISSUS*?
WHY, WHO COULD EVER LOVE YOU NOW?
COME HERE, LITTLE GIRL.
YOUR FACE...
...IS MINE.

Beauty and the Beast of Paradise Lost 3

PERFECT WORLD

Rie Aruga

A TOUCHING NEW SERIES ABOUT LOVE AND COPING WITH DISABILITY

An office party reunites Tsugumi with her high school crush Itsuki. He's realized his dream of becoming an architect, but along the way, he experienced a spinal injury that put him in a wheelchair. Now Tsugumi's rekindled feelings will butt up against prejudices she never considered — and Itsuki will have to decide if he's ready to let someone into his heart...

"Depicts with great delicacy and courage the difficulties some with disabilities experience getting involved in romantic relationships... Rie Aruga refuses to romanticize, pushing her heroine to face the reality of disability. She invites her readers to the same tasks of empathy, knowledge and recognition."
—Slate.fr

"An important entry [in manga romance]... The emotional core of both plot and characters indicates thoughtfulness... [Aruga's] research is readily apparent in the text and artwork, making this feel like a real story."
—Anime News Network

KC KODANSHA COMICS

Knight of the Ice ©Yayoi Ogawa/Kodansha Ltd.

SKATING THRILLS AND ICY CHILLS WITH THIS NEW TINGLY ROMANCE SERIES!

A rom-com on ice, perfect for fans of *Princess Jellyfish* and *Wotakoi*. Kokoro is the talk of the figure-skating world, winning trophies and hearts. But little do they know... he's actually a huge nerd! From the beloved creator of *You're My Pet* (*Tramps Like Us*).

Chitose is a serious young woman, working for the health magazine *SASSO*. Or at least, she would be, if she wasn't constantly getting distracted by her childhood friend, international figure skating star Kokoro Kijinami! In the public eye and on the ice, Kokoro is a gallant, flawless knight, but behind his glittery costumes and breathtaking spins lies a secret: He's actually a hopelessly romantic otaku, who can only land his quad jumps when Chitose is on hand to recite a spell from his favorite magical girl anime!

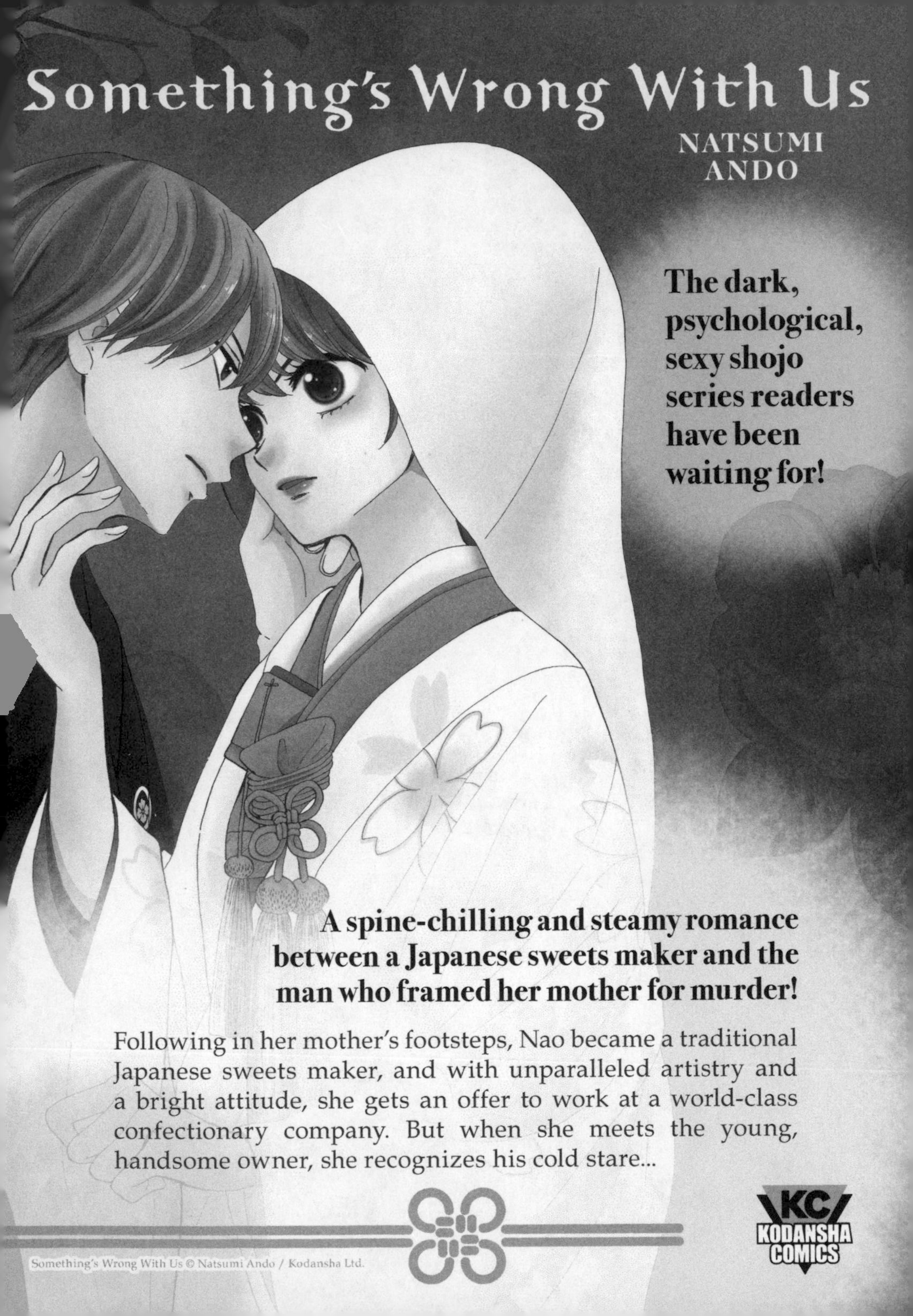
Something's Wrong With Us
NATSUMI ANDO
The dark, psychological, sexy shojo series readers have been waiting for!
A spine-chilling and steamy romance between a Japanese sweets maker and the man who framed her mother for murder!
Following in her mother's footsteps, Nao became a traditional Japanese sweets maker, and with unparalleled artistry and a bright attitude, she gets an offer to work at a world-class confectionary company. But when she meets the young, handsome owner, she recognizes his cold stare...
KC KODANSHA COMICS
Something's Wrong With Us © Natsumi Ando / Kodansha Ltd.

A SMART, NEW ROMANTIC COMEDY FOR FANS OF *SHORTCAKE CAKE* AND *TERRACE HOUSE!*

A romance manga starring high school girl Meeko, who learns to live on her own in a boarding house whose living room is home to the odd (but handsome) Matsunaga-san. She begins to adjust to her new life away from her parents, but Meeko soon learns that no matter how far away from home she is, she's still a young girl at heart — especially when she finds herself falling for Matsunaga-san.

The boys are back, in 400-page hardcovers that are as pretty and badass as they are!

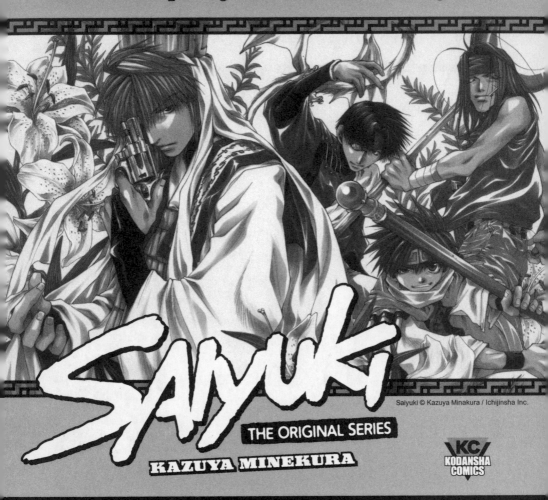

Saiyuki © Kazuya Minekura / Ichijinsha Inc.

SAIYUKI
THE ORIGINAL SERIES
KAZUYA MINEKURA

KC KODANSHA COMICS

"AN EDGY COMIC LOOK AT AN ANCIENT CHINESE TALE." —YALSA

Genjo Sanzo is a Buddhist priest in the city of Togenkyo, which is being ravaged by yokai spirits that have fallen out of balance with the natural order. His superiors send him on a journey far to the west to discover why this is happening and how to stop it. His companions are three yokai with human souls. But this is no day trip — the four will encounter many discoveries and horrors on the way.

FEATURES NEW TRANSLATION, COLOR PAGES, AND BEAUTIFUL WRAPAROUND COVER ART!

THE SWEET SCENT OF LOVE IS IN THE AIR! FOR FANS OF OFFBEAT ROMANCES LIKE *WOTAKOI*

Sweat and Soap © Kintetsu Yamada / Kodansha Ltd.

In an office romance, there's a fine line between sexy and awkward... and that line is where Asako — a woman who sweats copiously — meets Koutarou — a perfume developer who can't get enough of Asako's, er, scent. Don't miss a romcom manga like no other!

A Kodansha Comics Trade Paperback Original
Beauty and the Beast of Paradise Lost 2 copyright © 2020 Kaori Yuki
English translation copyright © 2021 Kaori Yuki

All rights reserved.

Published in the United States by Kodansha Comics, an imprint of Kodansha USA Publishing, LLC, New York.

Publication rights for this English edition arranged through Kodansha Ltd., Tokyo.

First published in Japan in 2020 by Kodansha Ltd., Tokyo as *Rakuen no bijo to yaju*, volume 2.

ISBN 978-1-64651-293-5

Printed in the United States of America.

www.kodansha.us

9 8 7 6 5 4 3 2 1
Translation: Rose Padgett
Lettering: Phil Christie
Editing: Vanessa Tenazas
Kodansha Comics edition cover design by Phil Balsman

Publisher: Kiichiro Sugawara

Director of publishing services: Ben Applegate
Associate director of operations: Stephen Pakula
Publishing services managing editors: Alanna Ruse, Madison Salters
Production managers: Emi Lotto, Angela Zurlo
Logo and character art ©Kodansha USA Publishing, LLC